V&R Academic

Novum Testamentum et Orbis Antiquus/
Studien zur Umwelt des Neuen Testaments

Volume 116

Vandenhoeck & Ruprecht

Samuel Byrskog/Raimo Hakola/Jutta Jokiranta (eds.)

Social Memory and Social Identity in the Study of Early Judaism and Early Christianity

Vandenhoeck & Ruprecht

Bibliographic information published by the Deutsche Nationalbibliothek
The Deutsche Nationalbibliothek lists this publication in the Deutsche Nationalbibliografie; detailed bibliographic data available online: http://dnb.d-nb.de.

ISSN 1420-4592
ISBN 978-3-525-59375-2

You can find alternative editions of this book and additional material on our Website: www.v-r.de

Typesetting by Konrad Triltsch GmbH, Ochsenfurt
Printed and bound by Hubert & Co GmbH & Co. KG, Robert-Bosch-Breite 6, D-37079 Göttingen

Printed on aging-resistant paper.

Contents

Raimo Hakola/Samuel Byrskog/Jutta Jokiranta

Introduction

During recent years, social memory and social identity perspectives have been increasingly used in the study of ancient Jewish and Christian sources. The use of these concepts is a part of a larger trend that has resulted in the application of various interdisciplinary methodologies to explain those diverse and complex sociological, psychological or cognitive processes that might explain early Judaism or Christianity as historical phenomena or certain aspects of them in the surviving ancient literary material. As such, it is not surprising that scholars have found the concepts of social or collective memory and social identity attractive. These concepts recapitulate something that has been on the agenda of Biblical and cognate studies for a long time. Such late Second Temple sources as the Dead Sea Scrolls or early Christian writings present various illustrations of how past events became part of mnemonic processes and were reinterpreted for contemporary purposes. In a similar way, scholars have studied social ramifications of these sources that give voice to different groups by expressing their collective convictions and shared view of the world. While scholars have become more and more cautious in reading ancient sources as direct reflections of sociohistorical situations of specific communities, it is still a legitimate and meaningful objective to examine in what ways these sources participate in the processes of collective recollection and commemoration and in this way contribute to the construction and maintenance of distinctive social identities.

The recent interest in social memory and social identity thus continues the long tradition of historical-critical Biblical studies in that the same methods that are prominent in the study of other historical sources or corresponding social and cultural phenomena are applied to Biblical and related material. The articles in this collection demonstrate the benefits of these kinds of interdisciplinary experiments but they also discuss potential pitfalls and problems that have emerged when modern theories are applied to ancient material.

The interest in social memory and social identity represent social-scientific criticism that has received an established and recognised position in the field of Biblical studies from 1970's onwards.[1] Social-scientific criticism originally

1 For example, see A.J. Blasi/J. Duhaime/P.-A. Turcotte (ed.), *Handbook of Early Christianity: Social Science Approaches* (Walnut Creek, California, AltaMira Press, 2002); W. Stegemann/R.E. De-

developed as a conscious reaction against mainstream Biblical scholarship that was seen to focus one-sidedly on theological beliefs and influential individual personalities. Roughly speaking, Biblical scholars interested in social topics have represented two types of methodological approaches: some scholars have focused on the description of ancient social history and social contexts of written source material, while others have applied more specific sociological and anthropological models and theories. An important discussion has emerged on the benefits of each of these approaches among scholars.[2] There can be no question that both approaches should be included in the study of social and collective memory and social identities in the ancient world. The ways in which various Jewish and Christian groups and individuals negotiated mnemonically and used collective memory to foster their social identities were always deeply bound on specific sociohistorical realities, which means that the study of memory and identity processes cannot succeed without accurate and comprehensive information of the surrounding social world. Then again, modern theories of corresponding social processes can clarify the study of ancient society and sources because these theories provide scholars analytical tools to understand and compare basic human processes reflected in their source material.[3] The application of theoretical concepts like social and collective memory or social identity does not mean that specific aspects of each particular culture and sociohistorical context are ignored, but these notions may help in recognising cross-cultural processes behind specific sociohistorical situations.[4]

Maris (ed.), *Alte Texte in neuen Kontexten: Wo Steht die sozialwissenschaftliche Bibelexegese?* (Stuttgart: Kohlhammer, 2015).

2 See P.F. Esler (ed.), *Modelling Early Christianity: Social-Scientific Studies of the New Testament in Its Context* (London: Routledge, 1995); idem, "Models in New Testament Interpretation: A Reply to David Horrell", *JSNT* 78 (2000) 107–13; D.G. Horrell, "Models and Methods in Social-Scientific Interpretation: A Response to Philip Esler", *JSNT* 78 (2000) 83–105; P. Luomanen/I. Pyysiäinen/R. Uro, "Introduction: Social and Cognitive Perspectives in the Study of Christian Origins and Early Judaism", in P. Luomanen/I. Pyysiäinen/R. Uro (ed.), *Explaining Christian Origins and Early Judaism: Contributions from Cognitive and Social Science* (BibInt Series 89; Leiden: Brill, 2007) 1–33, on pp. 18–20; P. Luomanen, "Social-Scientific Modeling in Biblical and Related Studies", *Perspectives on Science* 21 (2013) 202–220.

3 Cf. Luomanen et al., "Introduction", 20: "In the case of social identity approach, it seems clear that its usability is at least partly based on the fact that modern observations about basic human processes of social categorization find responsive data in the text because the writers of the texts were subject to same constraints of perception as we are."

4 Cf. N. Hopkins/S. Reicher, "Identity, Culture and Contestation: Social Identity as Cross-Cultural Theory", *Psychological Studies* 56 (2011) 36–43.

Social and Collective Memory

The modern study of memory as a social construction goes back to the 1920s. With the publication of *Les cadres sociaux de la mémoire* in 1925,[5] the French sociologist and philosopher Maurice Halbwachs initiated a line of thought that stressed the collective memory of societies and groups, insisting that all memory depends upon the social frameworks within which it is situated. As a product of social change, memory is always in process and produces ever-changing representations of the past. Halbwachs died in Buchenwald in 1945. Five years later his sister Jeanne Alexandre published *La mémoire collective* on the basis of manuscripts found among his papers.[6] The two studies constitute the classics for the study of social and collective memory. Halbwachs clarified in his second study that he distinguished between autobiographical memory, historical memory (the past to which we have no "organic" relation), and collective memory (the past forming our realities), and pointed out that individuals always remember as members of groups, opening up a long scholarly discussion of what is sometimes labelled as social and sometimes as collective memory.

Various theoretical perspectives have modified Halbwachs' emphasis on the importance of the social framework. Barry Schwartz, who is a sociologist and leading specialist on social memory, is one of the most influential critics of Halbwachs and expresses criticism against his "pejorative conception of collective memory".[7] While important in the field of collectivistic notions of memory, Halbwachs tended, according to Schwartz, to simplify both the temporal notion of memory in favour of its orientation to the present as well as the interaction between individual and collective memories, to the extent that individual recollections almost always operated within the framework of collective memory. Several of the contributions of the present volume discuss the temporality of memory and the possibility of identifying specific cognitive aspects of memory.

Halbwachs was careful to keep his concept of collective memory apart from the realm of traditions and transmissions across generations. Memory was communication and social interaction. Another recent influential avenue which takes into account the temporal notion of memory focuses on its cultural dimension. Without replacing the concept of collective memory, Jan Assmann, a German Egyptologist, divides it into communicative memory and cultural memory and distinguishes between collective memory and cultural

5 M. Halbwachs, *Les cadres sociaux de la mémoire* (Paris: Presses Universitaires de France, new ed. 1952).

6 M. Halbwachs, *La mémoire collective* (Paris: Presses Universitaires de France, 1950).

7 B. Schwartz, "Christian Origins: Historical Truth and Social Memory", in A. Kirk/T. Thatcher (ed.), *Memory, Tradition, and Text: Uses of the Past in Early Christianity* (SBLSS 52; Atlanta: SBL, 2005) 43–56, on p. 49.

memory as two different *modi memorandi*.[8] The key difference between Halbwachs' and Assmann's theories lies in the function attributed to past events when no one is alive to tell the tale from her/his own experience. Assmann argues that when all eyewitnesses have vanished, the socially conditioned collective memory will change and the communicative memory transforms itself into cultural memory.

Today there is a bewildering array of different theories of social or collective memory. They represent, it has been said, a nonparadigmatic, transdisciplinary, and centreless enterprise.[9] There is no single theory, and handbooks present different avenues.[10] In her book *Theories of Social Remembering*, the sociologist Barbara Misztal includes a chapter entitled "The dynamics of memory approach: memory as a process of negotiation" and discusses the active mediation of temporal meanings of the past, locating memory in the space between an imposed ideology of the present and the possibility of an alternative way of understanding the past.[11] This approach, in short, "stresses the presence of the past in the present through psychological, social, linguistic and political processes".[12] This might be said to represent the central core features of today's discussion of social and collective memory.

The vital component in any such theory is the mnemonic community. Such a community maintains traditions and teaches new generations what to remember and forget through socialization, the monitoring of mnemonically important persons in a group, and through controlling what and how to remember. Language – oral and written – makes possible certain linguistic locations of memory and allows memory to pass from one person to another, providing a mnemonic transitivity in terms of transmitted traditions. In this way, the mnemonic community integrates different personal pasts into a single common past that all members eventually might come to remember collectively. Such mnemonic synchronization, to use an expression from the cognitive sociologist Eviathar Zerubavel,[13] takes place in joint acts of remembrance. Remembering is thus a kind of control system regulated by social rules of remembrance. Being socialized into a community means to be

8 J. Assmann, *Das kulturelle Gedächtnis: Schrift, Erinnerung und politische Identität in frühen Hochkulturen* (München: C. H. Beck, 1992).

9 J.K. Olick/J. Robbins, "Social Memory Studies: From 'Collective Memory' to the Historical Sociology of Mnemonic Practices", *Annual Review of Sociology* 24 (1998) 105–40. For new avenues in Cognitive Science of Religion, see Petri Luomanen, "How Religions Remember: Memory Theories in Biblical Studies and in the Cognitive Study of Religion", in I. Czachesz/R. Uro (ed.), *Mind, Morality, and Magic: Cognitive Science Approaches in Biblical Studies* (Durham: Acumen, 2013) 24–42.

10 Cf. James Fentress and Chris Wickham, *Social Memory* (Oxford: Blackwell, 1992).

11 B.A. Misztal, *Theories of Social Remembering* (Philadelphia: Open University Press, 2003) 67–74.

12 Misztal, *Theories*, 70.

13 E. Zerubavel, *Time Maps: Collective Memory and the Social Shape of the Past* (Chicago: Chicago University Press, 2003).

taught socially what to remember and what to forget and to be given the plot structures according to which the past is narrated.

During the last decade, the notion of social and collective memory has become a prominent conceptual framework for understanding the development of the Jesus tradition. The editors of the multi-authored volume *Memory, Tradition, and Text* from 2005 recognize that "social memory theory presents a number of far-reaching implications for the study of the Gospel traditions, the composition history of the Gospels, and the quest for the historical Jesus".[14] To this could be added the vast concept of how the early Christians thought of themselves, their social identity. From the perspective of social memory, it becomes essential to look closely into the dynamics involved as they struggled to find their identity in relation to the past history that they cherished and performed. Social memory is intrinsically linked to questions of identity and challenges scholars to seek for a clearer conception as to how each Gospel narrative reflects the interaction with the social construction of the past.

Social Identity Approach

The social identity theory was first developed by social psychologist Henri Tajfel and his colleagues in Great Britain in the late 1960s and early 1970s and it was later developed into a more general explanation of the processes connected to group formation in the so-called self-categorization theory. These two theories have become known as the social identity approach, which continues to be developed and applied to new phenomena in the field of social psychology.[15] The theory was originally developed to explain intergroup discrimination and it addressed such questions as "Why do people in groups discriminate against each other?" One of the key ideas behind the social identity theory was formulated by Tajfel as the "minimal group paradigm".[16] In a series of laboratory experiments Tajfel and his colleagues found out that, even in minimal groups whose members do not know each other, people tend to favor ingroup members over outgroup members. These findings challenged

14 A. Kirk/T. Thatcher, "Jesus Tradition as Social Memory", in Kirk/Thatcher (ed.), *Memory, Tradition, and Text: Uses of the Past in Early Christianity* (SBLSS 52; Atlanta: SBL, 2005) 25–42, on p. 39.

15 For general introductions to social identity approach, see S. Reicher/R. Spears/ S.A. Haslam, "The Social Identity Approach in Social Psychology", in M. Wetherell/ C.T. Mohanty (ed.), *The Sage Handbook of Identities* (London: Sage Publications, 2010), 45–62; R. Jenkins, *Social Identity* (4th Edition; London and New York: Routledge, 2014).

16 For minimal groups, see H. Tajfel, *Human Groups and Social Categories: Studies in Social Psychology* (Cambridge: Cambridge University Press, 1981) 33–238 and 268–76; H. Tajfel/J.C. Turner, "An Integrative Theory of Intergroup Conflict", in W.G. Austin/S. Worchel (ed.), *The Social Psychology of Intergroup Relations* (Monterey, California: Brooks/Cole Publishing Company, 1979) 33–47, on pp. 38–40.

earlier social psychological theories that had claimed that ingroup favoritism and intergroup conflicts arise only if groups are in competition with each other for limited and desired resources.[17] Another basic observation of the social identity theory is that human social behavior varies along the "interpersonal and intergroup continuum".[18] At the interpersonal extreme, social encounters are determined by personal relationships between individuals while at the intergroup extreme, membership in different social groups determines human behavior. The point of this observation is that various cognitive, emotional and motivational processes connected to intergroup relations cannot be seen as an extension of interpersonal relations and cannot be explained simply in terms of personal psychology. Tajfel summarized his theoretical findings in the formulation of the concept of social identity. Social identity is understood as "that part of an individual's self-concept which derives from his [sic] knowledge of his membership of a social group (or groups) together with the value and emotional significance attached to that membership."[19]

The distinction between personal and social identity was further clarified by the self-categorization theory developed in particular by John Turner and his colleagues.[20] The self-categorization theory is based on the observation that social categorization is a fundamental aspect of group behavior. According to this theory, "the central hypothesis for group behavior is that, as shared social identity becomes salient, individual self-perception tends to become depersonalized."[21] As a result, people experience themselves and other members in the group not as differentiated individuals but as approximating common characteristics of their group. According to the social identity approach, the sense of sameness among fellow group members and social cohesion are not a precondition for a shared social identity but rather its outcome which enables a disparate collective of people to agree on their shared values and objectives and to function as a cohesive social force.

Many basic concepts in the social identity approach are based on various laboratory experiments which naturally raises the question whether and to what extent these concepts are applicable to different real-life groups in varying cultural, historical and social contexts. However, many social identity theorists have concluded that it is not enough to theorise about general social psychological processes in the abstract without examining how these

17 This was the basic claim in the so-called realistic conflict theory, see M. Sherif, *Group Conflict and Cooperation: Their Social Psychology* (London: Routledge, 1966).

18 Cf. Tajfel, *Human Groups*, 228–53.

19 Tajfel, *Human Groups*, 255

20 J. Turner, *Rediscovering the Social Group: A Self-Categorization Theory* (Oxford: Blackwell, 1987); idem, "Some Current Issues in Research on Social Identity and Self-Categorization Theories," in N. Ellemers/R. Spears/B. Doosje (ed.), *Social Identity: Context, Commitment, Content* (Oxford: Blackwell, 1999) 6–34.

21 Turner, "Some Current Issues", 12.

processes manifest themselves within specific contexts. In recent years, the social identity approach has increasingly been applied to real historical and actual intergroup situations in the study of nationalism, leadership, or various ethnic conflicts.[22] The relevance of the social identity approach for explaining historical intergroup processes has also been demonstrated in various applications of this approach to early Jewish and Christian sources.[23] It is interesting for the study of Biblical and related literature that many social psychological studies have recently stressed the importance of history for actual social identities and seen how various claims for historical continuity are tightly connected to the construction of collective identities.[24] This suggests that the applications of social or collective memory and social identity to early Jewish and Christian sources have some shared interests as also the articles in this collection demonstrate.

The Articles of the Book

Samuel Byrskog takes Paul Ricoeur's discussion of personal versus collective memory as a point of departure in his "Philosophical Aspects on Memory: Aristotle, Augustine and Bultmann". Byrskog uses the ancient philosophical reflections by Aristotle and Augustine as an avenue to bridge the gap between studies of cognitive memory and studies of social or collective memory and to ponder the hermeneutical dimension of history and time visible in Rudolf Bultmann's work. In order to grasp the hermeneutical dimensions of memory through ancient philosophy, Byrskog focuses on how Aristotle and Augustine,

22 Cf. S. Reicher/N. Hopkins, *Self and Nation: Categorization, Contestation and Moblization* (London: Sage Publications, 2001); B. Doosje/ N.R. Branscombe, N.R. Branscombe, "Attributions for the Negative Historical Actions of a Group", *European Journal of Social Psychology* 33 (2003) 235–48; M.J.A. Wohl/N.R. Branscombe, "Remembering Historical Victimization: Collective Guilt for Current Ingroup Transgressions", *Journal of Personality and Social Psychology* 94 (2008) 988–1006; S.A. Haslam/S.D. Reicher/M.J. Platlow, *The New Psychology of Leadership: Identity, Influence and Power* (Hove and New York: Psychology Press, 2011).

23 P.F. Esler, *Galatians* (London and New York: Routledge, 1998), 40–57; idem, *Conflict and Identity in Romans: The Social Setting of Paul's Letter* (Minneapolis: Fortress Press, 2003), 19–39; P. Luomanen, "The Sociology of Knowledge, the Social Identity Approach and the Cognitive Science of Religion", in P. Luomanen/I. Pyysiäinen/R. Uro (ed.), *Explaining Christian Origins and Early Judaism: Contributions from Cognitive and Social Science* (BibInt Series 89; Leiden: Brill, 2007), 199–229; J. Jokiranta, *Social Identity and Sectarianism in the Qumran* Movement (STDJ 105; Leiden: Brill, 2013); J.B. Tucker/C.A. Baker (ed.), *T&T Clark Handbook to Social Identity in the New Testament* (London: Bloomsbury, 2014); R. Hakola, *Reconsidering Johannine Christianity: A Social Identity Approach* (New York and London: Routledge, 2015).

24 Cf. Cf. S. Reicher/N. Hopkins, *Self and Nation*, 131–51; S. Reicher, "Making a Past Fit for the Future: The Political Dimensions of Historical Continuity", in F. Sani (ed.), *Self Continuity: Individual and Collective Perspectives* (New York: Psychology Press, 2008) 145–58; Haslam/Reicher/Platlow, *The New Psychology*, 147–55.

each in their own specific way, comment on the individuality of memory, its relation to time and narrative, its place in the present and evasive "now", and on its dependence on mental images.

To the ancients, Byrskog argues, memory was philosophically part of the individual and her/his experiences and thoughts. Memory also implied an understanding of time and narrative. It was intrinsically temporal and as such linked to a structure of temporal existence that reached language in narrativity, be that by the linking of events (Aristotle) or by basing memory on autobiography (Augustine). Time and narrative are, furthermore, synchronized in the evasive "now", which is the essence of temporal existence and the crucial moment when the past can be narratively ordered or felt to be part of a narrative flow. This narrative configuration of the past in the present, finally, designs the past according to mnemonic pictures and images and thus reconfigures the past through cognitive processes that interact with the process of recall and the individual's capacity to capture the past in images. In all this, Byrskog detects significant hermeneutical implications similar to Bultmann's interest in history and time and his idea that the absent past becomes existentially present through the invention of historical myths, urging today's scholars of the historical Jesus to take seriously the existential notions that were intrinsic to memory and intruded into the transmission process.

In his "The Formation of the Synoptic Tradition: Cognitive and Cultural Memory Approaches to an Old Problem", Alan Kirk criticizes in a similar vein the form-critical way of separating the "individual" and the "psychological" from the "social" and "cultural" and the distinction between individual "reminiscences" and the sociological forces of the *Sitz im Leben.* Focusing on memory as a neurobiological phenomenon, Kirk seeks to find a link between cognitive and social sciences in the field of memory and to clarify theoretically how the synoptic tradition emerges at the interface of the two.

Culture penetrates, according to Kirk, to the neural encoding of memories. These memories are filtered through cognitive schemas that make them intelligible and, when similar to each other, form the generic memory. It is this cognitive and cultural interface of schematic encoding that is implicated in the formation of tradition and leads to the variability as well as the stability of memories. When communicated socially, such memories are conformed to formulaic and narrative patterns drawn from the genres of the ambient culture. Commemorative remembering relates to specific group strategies employed to subsume individual contributions of memory into shared representations interacting with wider cultural patterns. Tradition artifacts thus become functions of cultural symbols. Through cognitive-cultural coupling, tradition emerges as meaning-laden externalisation of cognitive memory processes and cycles back into cognition with the result of enduring modifications to one's cognitive apparatus, to the extent that tradition can be labelled cybernetic memory. The cognitive-cultural coupling gives an explanation to the absence of individual eyewitness memories in the synoptic tradition while at the same time confirming that memory was a principal factor in the origin of tradition. As an autonomous cognitive system, loosened from originating historical contexts and extended by means of oral and written media and culturally relevant genres, the synoptic tradition cannot be reduced to homeostatic functions of sociological processes but is a paradigm of the cognitive-cultural interface.

Sandra Huebenthal argues in her "Reading the Gospel of Mark as Collective Memory" that memory studies have sometimes been used in the study of the New Testament to support the historical reliability of the New Testament Gospels as eyewitness testimonies. However, these interpretations do not pay due attention to various studies that have emphasised the constructive nature of collective memory. Already according to Maurice Halbwachs, memory is not a storehouse that preserves the past as such because individuals locate their memories in a social framework that directs the interpretation and communication of their memories.

In addition to Halbwachs' pivotal insights, Huebenthal uses, for example, Jan and Aleida Assman's notion of cultural memory in order to investigate how various recollections of Jesus are incorporated into Mark's narrative that can be regarded as a textual externalisation of collective memory. Huebenthal demonstrates that while the Markan narrator uses direct narrative commentary quite sparingly, the way Mark's story is structured indicates how the reader is supposed to respond to the events and the characters. The Gospel of Mark not only records what happened in the past but also imbues past events with specific meanings and interpretations. In this way, the Gospel contributes to the construction of a common identity for those who are willing to accept its message. Huebenthal shows how collective memory is closely related to the construction of identity which suggests that there are promising points in common between approaches applying the concepts of social memory and social identity.

Kari Syreeni examines in "Eyewitness Testimony, First-Person Narration and Authorial Presence as Means of Legitimation in Early Gospel Literature" how covert hints of eyewitness testimonies or explicit references to eyewitnesses in early Christian sources should be assessed. Syreeni remarks that scholars who have maintained that the canonical Gospels are somehow based on eyewitness memories quite rarely discuss the evidence found in non-canonical sources. Syreeni argues that this evidence should not be overlooked because a broader look at the development of early Christian literature reveals tendencies that already begin with the canonical documents and become clearer in various second century or later sources.

Syreeni concludes that both Mark and Matthew – most likely the earliest of the canonical Gospels – show little interest in eyewitness testimony. Syreeni claims that the allusions to eyewitnesses in the Gospels of Luke (1:1–4) and John (21:24–25) should not be isolated from similar mentions appearing in such sources as the Gospel of Thomas, the Gospel of Peter, the Gospel of Mary, the Jewish Christian Gospel fragments and the infancy Gospels. The study of this material shows that references to eyewitnesses, authorial fiction and first person narration become more and more common in various Christian sources. Syreeni suggests that the need to legitimate diverse understandings of Jesus traditions among distinct early Christian groups could explain this development.

Dan Nässelqvist examines in his "Dual Conventions: The Oral Delivery of New Testament Writings in Light of First-Century Delivery Practices" different models for understanding the oral delivery of New Testament writings. He finds evidence in favour of the existence in antiquity of both oral performance from memory and public reading directly from a manuscript. These types of oral delivery not only involved different delivery practices, but were also used in dissimilar settings for distinct text genres. Nässelqvist finds, for instance, that in antiquity oral performance was largely confined to the delivery of oratory and drama, whereas public reading was used for all literary genres, including oratory and drama.

As to the early Christian practice, Nässelqvist gives a corrective to the notion of oral performance and argues that the sources describe the oral delivery of New Testament writings in terms of public reading from a manuscript. He distinguishes this carefully from oral performance, which is a notion forwarded by scholars engaged in performance criticism. Nässelqvist finally points to the practical details of the two types of delivery and compares them in relation to the stance of the performer, the skills required, and the use of gestures, movement, facial expressions, vocal expression, manuscripts, and furniture.

The articles in the second part of the book make use of the social identity approach. Several articles study the Qumran movement or texts found among the Qumran texts from this perspective. Cecilia Wassén argues in her "The Importance of Marriage in the Construction of Sectarian Identity in the Dead Sea Scrolls" that marriage, not celibacy, was a prominent feature in the identity formation of the Qumran movement. Outsiders were criticized for their behaviour related to marital relations. Proper marital relations were necessary for keeping the holiness of the people. Wassén analyses the sectarian text, 4QMMT, for its views on illicit marriages; marriages with non-Jews were forbidden and seen as defiling the holy seed of Israel. In social identity terms, 4QMMT can be interpreted both as an attempt to appeal to the shared values between the implied author and the addressee and as an instruction to the ingroup members to distinguish themselves from close and similar priestly groups who refused to follow their path.

According to Wassén, the claim that wrongful marriage and sexual practices had led the people astray is even stronger in the *Damascus Document*. Furthermore, polygyny, uncle-niece marriages, and sexual intercourse during menstruation were seen as traps by Belial, and outsiders were thus demonized for following these practices, which would have discouraged interaction with them. Such marital laws could have been a new way of creating positive distinctiveness in a situation where some other comparative features were no longer favourable for the ingroup.

Jutta Jokiranta studies other social identity phenomena within the Qumran movement in "Black Sheep, Outsiders, and the Qumran Movement: Social-Psychological Perspectives on Norm-Deviant Behaviour". Typically, the outgroup is viewed as being more homogeneous than the ingroup. Whereas the social identity approach generally predicts that ingroup members are viewed more positively than the corresponding outgroup members, the ingroup deviants present a challenge to this tendency. Research on the so-called "black sheep effect" has grown during recent years to explain when the ingroup deviants are excused and when they are punished. Jokiranta studies the evidence in the Qumran *Community Rule* as efforts to manage reactions to ingroup deviants as well as accentuating the outgroup homogeneity in situations where ambiguity may have prevailed.

Jokiranta first explores clear rules of when the deviant member can and cannot be excused in line with the social psychological predictions. The more difficult cases are the passages on the "people of injustice". These people are similar to novices in that they should not be in direct contact with the full members in matters of purity, knowledge, and possessions. On the other hand, they are like deviant members, who also had to keep a distance to the full members. Lastly, in 1QS, the people of injustice clearly represent the outgroup with whom the insiders should not mix. Separation from the outgroup or threatening ingroup members always concerned practical everyday issues, but grew also to include ideological distinctions and essentialisation of the outgroup.

Elisa Uusimäki studies a wisdom text from Qumran, *4QBeatitudes* (4Q525) in "Wisdom, Scripture and Identity Formation in 4QBeatitudes". Uusimäki argues that macarisms and the cursing account in 4Q5252 are not descriptions of the present reality, but they create the future social reality; they do more than describe. Uttering and performing such divisions of the world have social and spiritual aims. They invite the recipients to see the world in a particular way and to enhance the coherence of the ingroup's internal worldview by polarization. The distinction between two groups of people – the wise and the foolish – was probably based on having (or not having) Torah piety. Uusimäki further draws implications on understanding such teaching in the setting of the Qumran movement. Group leaders typically employed shared cultural knowledge and "received wisdom" as resources in their attempts to efficiently construct new group identities.

Rikard Roitto explores in his "Forgiveness, Rituals, and Social Identity in Matthew: Obliging Forgiveness" the role of the divine and the interpersonal forgiveness in the formation of the Matthean social identity and gives special attention to rituals related to forgiveness. Roitto maintains that forgiveness is an ongoing process in Matthew's covenantal and salvific identity narrative and explores the conceptualizations of sin in the Gospel of Matthew with the aid of insights from cognitive linguistics.

Of particular importance is the role of forgiveness in ritual activities – the Lord's Prayer, intercessory prayers for sinners, and the Eucharist. Roitto uses ritual theory to explore how these rituals contributed to identity formation in the Matthean community and points to the contribution of the ethics of forgiveness – non-retaliation and love of enemies, forgiveness of brothers – to inter- and intragroup dynamics.

In his "The Johannine Community as a Constructed, Imagined Community", Raimo Hakola takes issue with recent attempts to deny that the New Testament Gospels were addressed to distinct early Christian communities and argues that it is still meaningful to trace how these writings construct distinct early Christian identities. Hakola applies the social identity approach and concepts related to the symbolic construction of communities and imagined communities to explain how an ideal portrait of the community of Jesus' followers is created in the Gospel of John. Hakola contends that this portrait constructs social reality rather than reflects it in any transparent way.

Hakola demonstrates how John anchors his story of Jesus to mythical beginnings and uses various dualistic polarities to express a clear demarcation between Jesus' followers and the rest of world. In the Gospel, the knowledge of God communicated only by Jesus and the mutual love between Jesus' disciples function as strong symbols of belonging for Jesus' followers but also create an imagined boundary between them and those who have not received Jesus' revelation. Hakola argues that the Gospel writer has embedded his story of Jesus in a mythical framework in order to naturalise and essentialise a distinct early Christian social identity that was actually blurred and in the making.

Nina Nikki argues in her "Contesting the Past, Competing over the Future: Why is Paul Past-Oriented in Galatians and Romans, but Future-Oriented in Philippians?" that in the letters to the Galatians and the Romans Paul is more interested in the past than in his letter to the Philippians. Nikki suggests that the distinct temporal orientations are due to the different historical situations behind the texts: In both Galatians and Romans Paul is faced with Jewish Christ-believers, who subscribe to a particular view of the Jewish past, whereas in Philippians a Gentile audience is in view, with no previous Jewish historical narrative to be contested. With the use of the social identity approach, and the concepts of *possible future and past social identities*, Nikki clarifies the way Paul constructs identity on a temporal level and demonstrates how Paul's references to the past and the future exemplify the role of history as a domain of social contest in various intergroup conflicts.

According to Nikki, Paul contests his opponents' view of scriptural history in Galatians by claiming that Gentile believers are the legitimate heirs of this history without the demand of circumcision and the observance of the Law. In Romans, Paul tries to incorporate Jewish and non-Jewish addressees of the letter into one group by reminding them that they have a shared past but can also anticipate jointly the transformation of the whole creation (Rom 8:19–39). In Philippians 3, on the other hand, Paul does not really reinterpret a common understanding of the Jewish past but simply negates it by presenting himself as having renounced his earlier Jewish life. In this way Paul identifies with Philippian believers who have rejected their Gentile past just like Paul has done away with his Jewish past.

In his "Covenant, Conflict and Collective Identity: The Relationship between Hebrews and 1 Clement", Martin Wessbrandt investigates the construction of collective identity in the letter to the Hebrews and *1 Clement* and argues against the consensus opinion which maintains that the two writings originated in a similar social context in Rome around the turn of the 1st century. Using Richard Jenkins' theories concerning collective identification, especially issues concerning boundary-making, Wessbrandt points to the problems arising with the consensus view once we realize how different these letters are in matters concerning collective identity construction, specifically in their relationship to Judaism.

According to Wessbrandt, the author of Hebrews is involved in an intra-Jewish conflict, seeking to establish that his Christ-believing community represents something so radically different from other Jewish communities that one cannot participate in it and at the same time be a part of others. The author distances his group from Jewish institutions related to Jerusalem and creates a new collective identity for his group around the concept of a new covenant. The author of *1 Clement* was familiar enough with the letter to the Hebrews to quote from it and allude to it in dozens of places throughout his own letter but seems unaffected by the way Hebrews presents the notion of a new covenant, its rejection of the Levitical cult and the special role it gives to Jerusalem. The things that were central to the collective identity in Hebrews are ignored in *1 Clement.*

Most of the articles of this volume were originally presented at the conference "Memory, Orality, and Identity" at the University of Lund, Sweden, 14–16 November 2013. The conference was a joint meeting with the Nordic Network "Socio-Cognitive Perspectives on Early Judaism and Early Christianity" at the University of Helsinki. The editors would like to thank the head of the network, Prof. Petri Luomanen, and the staff at the University of Lund for organizing the conference. We also wish to thank Dr. Nina Nikki for her careful work in the copyediting of the manuscript, the editors of the Novum Testamentum et Orbis Antiquus for accepting the book for publication in this series, and Christoph Spill (Vandenhoeck & Ruprecht) for helping in the final editing of the book.

Raimo Hakola, Samuel Byrskog and Jutta Jokiranta

I Social Memory

Samuel Byrskog

Philosophical Aspects on Memory: Aristotle, Augustine and Bultmann

Memory in Perspective

During the last decades NT scholarship has seen a significant shift in the way it discusses the notion of memory and recollection in Greek, Roman and Jewish antiquity and in early Christianity.[1] While previous scholarship reacted to old form criticism and focused on the capacity of each person's memory to learn by heart and on the oral forms of conveying stored information almost unaltered in disciplined processes of transmission,[2] more recent scholarship, with some notable exceptions,[3] rarely discusses the memory and memorization of individuals but elaborates theoretical agendas for mnemonic activities in social contexts. The discussion ensuing from Maurice Halbwachs' (1877–1945) groundbreaking studies of the social ramification of collective memory and Jan Assmann's culturally imbedded investigation of communicative memory,[4] and from many other theoretical reflections,[5] has received increasingly more attention and resulted in several attempts to clarify the mnemonic negotiations and commemorations of the early Christians.

The previous investigations of memory were under-theorized but grounded in ancient discussions; more recent scholarship is theoretically more sophisticated but not always sufficiently based on what the ancient sources actually say about memory. There is an unfortunate gap between the theorized

1 In what follows I will use the term "memory" in a comprehensive way including both the faculty and content of memory as well as the processes of recollection. The two often overlap, despite Aristotle's attempt to make a distinction, and I will separate them only when necessary.

2 The groundbreaking reaction to form criticism from the perspective of memory is B. Gerhardsson, *Memory and Manuscript: Oral Tradition and Written Transmission in Rabbinic Judaism and Early Christianity* (ASNU 22; Lund: Gleerup, 1964).

3 E.g. R.K. McIver, *Memory, Jesus, and the Synoptic Gospels* (SBLRBS 59; Atlanta, GA: Society of Biblical Literature, 2011).

4 M. Halbwachs, *Les cadres sociaux de la mémoire* (Paris: Presses Universitaires de France, new ed. 1952); idem, *La mémoire collective* (Paris: Presses Universitaires de France, 1950); J. Assmann, *Das kulturelle Gedächtnis: Schrift, Erinnerung und politische Identität in frühen Hochkulturen* (München: C.H. Beck, 1992).

5 For introduction and overview of the theoretical issues of social and collective memory, see B.A. Misztal, *Theories of Social Remembering* (Philadelphia: Open University Press, 2003); A. Kirk, "Memory", in W.H. Kelber/S. Byrskog (ed.), *Jesus in Memory: Traditions in Oral and Scribal Perspectives* (Waco, TX: Baylor University Press, 2009) 155–72.

approaches to memory of present day scholarship and earlier less theoretical but more source-oriented investigations. The two approaches are not incompatible, because the ancient sources can be analyzed from the perspective of modern theoretical agendas, but the powerful influence of scholarly traditions has resulted in a somewhat polarized situation concerning the way we approach the mnemonic processes of early Christianity.

The prospect of bridging this gap might not yet be sufficiently recognized and revolves around the polarization between the individual or cognitive aspects of memory studied in earlier scholarship and the social and collective memory studied broadly today.[6] When in the late 1990s I worked on some theories of social and collective memory within the general framework of oral history, I was impressed by their potential to enhance our understanding of tradition and transmission as social constructions, but I could not escape the idea that individual consciousness matters also in collectively conditioned contexts and that strictly speaking only individuals remember.[7] I developed these insights in later publications and tried with the help of cognitive sociology to link the cognitive aspects of memory evident in personal recollection to theories of social and collective memory.[8] I affirmed indeed the idea that memory is social, I also affirmed the idea that memory is individual, and I argued that social memory is closely related to the cognitive aspects of each person's memory. Biblical scholars, in reviewing the book where I first indicated my view, often missed the point of trying to combine both perspectives and, with some exceptions, thought that oral history is an agenda for reconstructing the past from the retentive memory of passively observing eyewitnesses, neglecting to realize that it highlights history as a social construction embodied in the stories of eyewitnesses and that is to it is deeply interlocked with memory as both retentive and individualistic as well as social and collective.[9]

6 The expression "cognitive aspects of memory" is perhaps better than "individual memory", granted it describes aspects that are broader than the mere intellectual activity of remembering. See Alan Kirk's discussion in the present volume and part one in I. Czachesz/R. Uro (ed.), *Mind, Morality and Magic: Cognitive Science Approaches in Biblical Studies* (London: Routledge, 2014), with references to further literature. In previous publications I have used the theoretical framework of "sociomental typography" presented by the cognitive sociologist Eviatar Zerubavel, at first in his article "Social Memories: Steps to a Sociology of the Past", *QS* 19 (1996) 283–99; and more fully in his book *Time Maps: Collective Memory and the Social Shape of the Past* (Chicago: Chicago University Press, 2003). I used this terminology for the first time in "A New Quest for the *Sitz im Leben:* Social Memory, the Jesus Tradition and the Gospel of Matthew", *NTS* 52 (2006) 319–36.

7 S. Byrskog, *Story as History – History as Story: The Gospel Tradition in the Context of Ancient Oral History* (WUNT 123; Tübingen: Mohr Siebeck, 2000), 255.

8 I did not include theories taken from psychology, mainly because I did not see a feasible link to theories concerning the social construction of memory.

9 E. Eve, *Behind the Gospels: Understanding the Oral Tradition* (London: SPCK, 2013), 135–43, is unfortunately unfamiliar with my more recent attempts to link "the eyewitness model" to theories of social and collective memory.

Today's scholarship is intensely occupied with the social ramifications of memory, to the extent that the individual specificity of memory fades into the background. In his last major study, published in 2000, Paul Ricoeur (1913–2005) addressed this problem and discussed a host of issues relating to personal memory versus collective memory, including a critical section on Halbwachs' contribution.[10] Ricoeur is unsatisfied with the intrusion of sociology and the appearance of the concept of collective consciousness as this has resulted in a polemical situation where a younger notion of objectivity opposes the ancient ideas of reflexivity, so that individual memory and collective memory are placed in a position of rivalry creating separate universes of discourse estranged from each other. Neither Plato nor Aristotle nor any other ancient author, according to Ricoeur, held the concept of collective consciousness to be prior to knowing who remembered. Ricoeur's own attempt to find the region where the two discourses intersect focuses on the linguistic subjects of the ascription of memories: the ascription to oneself, to others and to our closest relations.

Ricoeur pointed to an impasse that is prevalent also in NT scholarship. Here the crucial questions have to do with the hermeneutical challenges emerging from our attention to social and collective memory and their intrinsic implications for notions of history and time. One way of beginning to move beyond the present scholarly situation is to analyze the theoretical discussions concerning the cognitive aspects of each person's memory in the ancient sources and relate them to modern hermeneutical reflections on how individuals and groups negotiate with the past in the present. This is what I intend to do here, indicating also the consequences of this for understanding the early Christians' mnemonic processing of the Jesus tradition. As I hope to show, the cognitive aspects of memory disclosed in each person's process of recollection are deeply social in that they profoundly relate to human existence in history and time.

As for the ancient sources, I am not thinking of the well-known advices for how to memorize. These techniques, whether we think of the mnemonic *loci* mentioned by Greek and Roman authors and traced back to Simonides of Ceos of the sixth century BCE (Cicero, *De Orat.* 2.86.352–53) or the rabbinic ideals of written and oral transmission emerging during the tannaitic period of the late first and second century CE or the preliminary exercises of Theon of Alexandria and others that include recommendations for how to remember and recite the *chreia* with clarity, have received considerable attention in the discussion of the historical reliability of the gospel tradition but contain almost no theory of memory and relate only vaguely to today's interest in theories of social and collective memory. Of more significance are those texts

10 P. Ricoeur, *La mémoire, l'histoire, l'oubli* (L'ordre philosophique; Paris: Seuil, 2000). For an English translation, see P. Ricoeur, *Memory, History, Forgetting* (transl. K. Blamey/D. Pellauer; Chicago: The University of Chicago Press, 2004), here pp. 93–132.

that betray a philosophically informed meta-reflection on memory. The intense interest in the social and collective dimension of memory in modern NT studies still lacks a profound philosophical basis that could be fruitfully compared with what ancient authors had to say, in spite of the fact that Halbwachs studied under the famous French philosopher Henri Bergson (1859–1941), who in 1896 published an influential book defending memory as something both material and spiritual,[11] and was himself as much a philosopher as a sociologist. In antiquity memory was not articulated in terms of its social and collective ramifications. Although helpful as a heuristic tool of understanding, sociology is after all a modern invention. Rather, the theoretical agenda of the Greek and Roman antiquity was taken from philosophy and when memory was to be discussed in theoretical terms it was philosophy that set the parameters. Memory had to do with life – she was the mother of the muses – and its philosophical implications had to do with how to live in the midst of time. To be more precise, in order to begin grasping the hermeneutical dimensions of memory through ancient philosophy, I will focus on things that have deep implications for the existential function of memory, namely, the individuality of memory, the notions of time and narrative, the importance of the present "now", and the use of mnemonic images.

Two highly educated persons in the ancient world stand out as especially significant for such reflections on memory, namely, Aristotle (384–323 BCE) and Augustine (354–430 CE). No other ancient author provides a comparable systematic reflection on memory and time. Despite the vast temporal and cultural distance between them and regardless of their different understandings of the transcendent realities, they both betray a significant awareness of the nature and functions of memory and recollection. As for modern philosophical and hermeneutical reflections on the nature of history and time, no one has been more prolific and influential among Biblical scholars than Rudolf Bultmann (1884–1976). To be sure, Bultmann did not discuss memory, neither its role in the gospel tradition nor its potentials of mediating existentially between the past and the present, but his life-long interest in human existence and its crucial relation to history and time reflects modern philosophical concerns issuing from the awareness of how competing temporal horizons shape human existence and are reconciled individually and collectively. It is true that other philosophically oriented authors discuss memory in antiquity and in modern times as well, from Plato to Bergson, Ricoeur and further on, and they do so with much philosophical finesse, but these three have been especially important for the emerging mnemonic

11 H. Bergson, *Matière et mémoire. Essai sur la relation du corps à l'esprit* (Paris: F. Alcan, 1896). For an English translation of the 5th edition from 1908 (with a new introduction by Bergson), see H. Bergson, *Matter and Memory* (transl. N.M. Paul/W. Scott Palmer; London: George Allen and Unwin, 1911).

trajectories of the early Christians and the early Church as well as for today's discussion of history and time in NT scholarship.

Aristotle, *De Memoria et Reminiscentia*

While neglected at first, Aristotle's brief work that has come down to us under the Latin title *De Memoria et Reminiscentia* came to strongly influence medieval philosophical thinking on memory.[12] It forms one of the seven treatises of the *Parva naturalia* discussing the natural capacities common to the body and soul of living beings. It also relates closely to Aristotle's more extensive *De Anima*, which reflects on the kinds of souls possessed by living things according to their different activities.

Its location in *Parva naturalia* and its relation to *De Anima* is an important indication of a significant difference between Aristotle's philosophically based notion of memory and recent theorizing about the psychological and social condition of memory. It shows in itself, without further scrutiny of his reasoning at this point, that Aristotle considered memory and recollection to be closely connected with his notions about the material or physical structure of things.[13] Just as he already at the out-set of the treatise indicates that people have different capacity to remember, he also, towards the end of the treatise discussing the nature of recollection, points out that the affection of memory is corporeal (σωματικόν) and that recollection depends on the concrete physical factors of the body ($453^{a}14$–$453^{b}7$). In Aristotelian thinking mnemonic functions cannot be reduced to psychologically and socially conditioned features of the mind but are intrinsically dependent on the nature of body and soul. Regardless of how we will further define Aristotle's idea of memory and recollection and its theoretical implications for modern hermeneutical reflections on history and time, the fundamental material and physical aspect of memory and recollection must remind us that the cognitive mnemonic processes were part and parcel of what it meant to be a living being with body and soul.

Aristotle's treatise was probably a reaction to Plato's ideas about memory presented in connection with, for instance, the discussion of knowledge (*Theatetus*) and pleasure (*Philebus*).[14] This reaction, although difficult to trace

12 Cf. R.A.H. King, *Aristotle and Plotinus on Memory* (QSP 94; Berlin: de Gruyter, 2009); D. Bloch, *Aristotle on Memory and Recollection: Text, Translation, Interpretation, and Reception in Western Scholasticism* (PA 110; Leiden: Brill, 2007).

13 Bloch, *Aristotle*, 56.

14 For discussion of Aristotle's understanding of memory and recollection, cf. R. Sorabji, *Aristotle on Memory* (2nd ed.; London: Duckworth, 2004); J. Anna, "Aristotle on Memory and the Self", in M.C. Nussbaum/A. Oksenberg Rorty (ed.), *Essays on Aristotle's* De Anima (Oxford: Clarendon Press, 1992) 297–311. For critique of Sorabji and Anna, see Bloch, *Aristotle*, 110–18.

in detail, has interesting implications for Aristotle's reflections on memory and time. For Plato, memory (μνήμη) was, in the words of Socrates, the preservation of perception or sensation (σωτηρία αἰσθήσεως; *Phil.* 34ᵃ10) and operated independently of the body to unify various physical affections. Helen S. Lang, an expert on Greek and medieval philosophy, has suggested that Aristotle was critical of Plato's idea that memory applies equally to sensations of the past, the present and the future and that he was concerned to distinguish memory of the past (μνήμη) from the present recollective process (ἀνάμνησις).[15] At the beginning of his treatise, he points out that the future is not possible to remember but is a matter of judgment (δοξαστός) and expectation (ἐλπιστός) and that we know the present by perception (αἴσθησις). "But memory is of what has happened",[16] he adds (*Mem.* 449ᵇ15). Being more of an empiricist and skeptical of the idea that knowledge is a mnemonic recollection of another reality, he maintains that only objects of past perception can be objects of memory and that only such objects can be recalled, because they have been impressed onto the mind as a seal is impressed onto a wax tablet and have produced mental images serving as copies of absent objects from a past reality.

The crucial factor in this notion of memory is time. Only those living beings that perceive time have memory. Memory is subsequent to perception and is a state (ἕξις) of sensation or conception or an affection (πάθος) that senses the lapse of time (449ᵇ25). "All memory is therefore 'with' time",[17] Aristotle insists at the outset of his discussion of memory (449ᵇ28). Things not "in time" (ἐν χρόνῳ) cannot be grasped "without time" (ἄνευ χρόνου), he adds (450ᵃ8–9).

For Aristotle, time has to do with change and movement (κίνησις). He discusses time and what it is to be "in time" at some length as part of his philosophy of nature in *Physica* 219ᵇ1 and defines it as "a number of change/movement according to the before and after."[18] Just as nature is subject to change, so time is the number of change and movement. Aristotle's idea of time does not correspond to notions of an abstract entity governing all existence but has a relativistic and yet fundamental coloring to it. Time helps us to identify our perception of things that have passed and things that will come from the perspective of the present moment. By defining time as the number of change and movement, Aristotle does not claim that time measures according to fixed numbers, but that it is the means in the present to make sense of something that is in constant flux. Time is not change and movement in itself; it is the number or counting (ἀριθμός) of change and movement. This countable ordering takes place at the present moment, in the existing "now", and thus becomes itself part of the change and movement. "And the now

15 H.S. Lang, "On Memory: Aristotle's Corrections of Plato", *JHP* 18 (1980) 379–93, on p. 385–9.

16 ἡ δὲ μνήμη τοῦ γενομένου.

17 διὸ μετὰ χρόνου πᾶσα μνήμη.

18 ἀριθμὸς κινήσεως κατὰ τὸ πρότερον καὶ ὕστερον.

measures time" (*Physica* 219^{b}12),[19] Aristotle states. The "now", in other words, measures that which numbers or counts the change and movement. The "now" is the essence of time, while holding it together also being captured by it, and it is therefore in transition, always evasive and, so to say, in becoming.[20]

With his notion of time, Aristotle realizes that while the affection induced by perception is present, the thing itself is absent, and he ponders how it is conceivable that what is not present is at all possible to remember (*Mem.* 450^{a}25–451^{a}14). What is produced is "a sort of picture" (οἷον ζωγράφημα) that has been imprinted like a seal as the result of the change and movement sensed in the soul. This result indeed leaves open the possibility of remembering only the affection and not the absent past, because the picture might be merely a figure and not a copy (εἰκών). Aristotle does not give a clear-cut solution to this dilemma but realizes that we sometimes make a switch from thinking of an image as something in itself to contemplating it as a representation of something else, especially if we exercise memory by repeated reminding.

In order to make this move from the imprinted mental picture to the absent thing, it is necessary to have a sense of time. Aristotle develops this discussion towards the end of the second part of the treatise dealing with recollection. "And the most important thing is to cognize the time",[21] he states (*Mem.* 252^{b}7). Again the notion of change and movement (κίνησις) becomes important. The crucial statement is found in *Mem.* 452^{b}23–24: "Thus, whenever the change/movement of the thing and of the time occurs together, then one exercises memory."[22] Although there is always the possibility that a person is deceived and only thinks that s/he remembers the past, Aristotle seems to argue that each person's conception of the change and movement of the things of the past must correspond with the counting of the time-lapse between these interrelated things and the present moment.

This discussion of time implicitly directs the attention to the closely related notions of temporality and narrativity. In the *Poetica* Aristotle discusses narrative and mimesis in tragedy, epic and comedy and insists that plot has to do with cause and effects, but without linking narrativity to memory.[23] In *De Memoria et Reminiscentia*, however, it is evident that he believes that the chain of thought ending in recollection is connected to the well-known threefold

19 τὸ δὲ νῦν τὸν χρόνον ὁρίζει.

20 For extensive discussion, cf. U. Coope, *Time for Aristotle: Physics IV. 10–14* (Oxford Aristotle Studies; Oxford: Oxford University Press, 2005); T. Roark, *Aristotle on Time: A Study of the Physics* (Cambridge: Cambridge University Press, 2013).

21 τὸ δὲ μέγιστον, γνωρίζειν δεῖ τὸν χρόνον.

22 ὅταν οὖν ἅμα ἥ τε τοῦ πράγματος γίγνηται κίνησις καὶ ἡ τοῦ χρόνου, τότε τῇ μνήμῃ ἐνεργεῖ.

23 For a profound analysis of time and narrative in Aristotle, including the notions of plot and mimesis, see P. Ricoeur, *Temps et Récit* (Paris: Seuil, 1983–85). For an English translation, see P. Ricoeur, *Time and narrative* (transl. K. McLaughlin/D. Pellauer; 3 vols; Chicago: University of Chicago Press, 1984–88).

laws of association: similarity, contrast, and contiguity: "Therefore we hunt the next thing, thinking from the present or from something else, and from similar or contrary or contiguous. Through this recollection takes place" (*Mem.* 451^b18–20).[24]

When Aristotle insists that all memory involves time, even that it depends on things being "in time", and returns to the discussion of memory as crucial for recollection, he is thinking of how memory navigates in the present "now" between different and differently interrelated images of the past and senses the order of their changes and movements creating an inner affection of temporality. Just as time is relative to the present "now" and yet also the fundamental means of creating order among ever-changing impressions of what was before and what might come after, so memory resides in the present existence and negotiates with the past with a sense of temporality. This temporality, by being linked to a notion of time as the present counting and ordering of movement and change and to Aristotle's laws of association, especially the law of contiguity, has an inherent narrative dimension that relates things to each other according to various chronologically determined patterns. Memory is, in other words, dependent upon the possibility to sense the narrative temporality of the past and combines historical persons and events with each other in a certain order that often have to do with narrative causality. Even things that are not "in time" can only be mnemonically apprehended when we imagine them to exist "in time" and when they possess qualities that relate them to some kind of narrative order.

Augustine, *Confessiones*

Augustine's notion of memory, while reflected also in *De Trinitate* from the early 5th century CE, becomes the subject of sustained discussion in *Confessiones* 10.[25] Perhaps his thinking is here indirectly influenced by Aristotle's ideas, which were available to him through the neo-Platonic philosopher Plotinus (205–270 CE) composing the six Enneads. The fourth Ennead discusses sense-perception and memory in the sixth treatise. Plotinus also touches on the same topic when he discusses the soul in treatises three and four of the same Ennead.

R.A.H. King, an expert on Aristotle, has compared Aristotle's and Plotinus' notions of memory and argues with a number of scholars that a member of

24 διὸ καὶ τὸ ἐφεξῆς θηρεύομεν νοήσαντες ἀπὸ τοῦ νῦν ἢ ἄλλου τινός, καὶ ἀφ' ὁμοίου ἢ ἐναντίου ἢ τοῦ σύνεγγυς. διὰ τοῦτο γίγνεται ἡ ἀνάμνησις.

25 For discussion and references to Augustine's discussion of memory in other writings and to scholarly literature, see P.E. Hochschild, *Memory in Augustine's Theological Anthropology* (OECS; Oxford: Oxford University Press, 2012).

Plotinus' immediate circle, and probably also Plotinus himself, had read Aristotle's *De Memoria*, in spite of the minimal verbal echoes and the different metaphysical convictions in the *Enneads*, and that there are similarities especially in the idea that the absent thing is represented in memory.[26] The difference was mainly that Plotinus was interested in the unchanging soul, the *logos* of everything capable of innate thoughts as forms of memory, and that he therefore located memory and mnemonic representation in the soul alone, because the motivation for Plotinus' discussion of memory was in the importance of the soul to rediscover and recollect where it comes from. Aristotle, by contrast, linked memory and representation to the perception of a real thing, being more of an empiricist, as we noticed, and insisted that memory is a corporeal and physically conditioned affection about the past. From this perspective, it is likely that Augustine reflects the Aristotelian thinking on memory indirectly and with the modifications of Plotinus' neo-Platonic reasoning, illustrating how Aristotle's empiricist tendency was received and revised to fit the new philosophical and theological landscape of the fourth and fifth century CE.

In the *Confessiones*, commonly regarded as the first introspective autobiography written in 397 CE, Augustine, at the age of 43, looks back over the events and reorientations of his past and couples the autobiographical ambition with profound and extensive philosophical and theological reflections. The narratively autobiographical section ends with Book 9, after the account of his baptism by Ambrose, the death of his mother Monica and his friends Nebridius and Vecundus, and the telling of the abandonment of his studies of rhetoric.[27] It is followed by some personal reflections on memory in Book 10, on creation, eternity and time in Book 11, on the material and spiritual creation in Book 12, and on revelation and time in Book 13. Almost half of the *Confessiones* thus lacks the prolific autobiographical character. The first half of his work functions as the mnemo-historical basis for his more philosophical and theological discussions, where Augustine turns from reflecting on what he has been to speaking of what he is, from the exterior to the interior life.[28] Book 10 on memory belongs to these discussions and follows immediately after the account of his previous life, providing a crucial link between the report of his experiences and his wish to comprehend these experiences more systematically.

This part of his work, while much more reflective than the previous one, is basically an attempt to understand himself and how he should find God in his

26 King, *Aristotle and Plotinus on Memory*. For a discussion of Plotinus and memory, see also J. Coleman, *Ancient and Medieval Memories: Studies in the Reconstruction of the Past* (Cambridge: Cambridge University Press, 1992), 63–79; Hochschild, *Memory in Augustine's Theological Anthropology*, 45–61.

27 For discussion of Augustine's life, see P. Brown, *Augustine of Hippo: A Biography: A New Edition with an Epilogue* (Berkeley and Los Angeles: University of California Press, 2000).

28 Hochschild, *Memory in Augustine's Theological Anthropology*, 138.

memory,[29] taking up anew the grand theme with which the *Confessiones* opened, "grant me Lord to know and understand" (1.1.1).[30] After having asked what he loves when he loves God and explained how he will pass beyond that which binds him to his body, he drastically exclaims, "and I come to the field and large palaces of memory" (10.8.12),[31] beginning his long meditation on memory. Again, after having discussed memory at some length, he cries out, "great is the power of memory",[32] and relates the idea of memory to his own mind and to himself, asking, "what am I then, my God, of what nature am I" (10.17.26).[33] The conclusion of this section reveals his concern: "If I find you without my memory, then I have no memory of you. And how shall I find you, if I do not remember you" (10.17.26)?[34] Somewhat later it becomes clear that he finds rest only where his own self meets God, in the *beata vita* that, after all, can be recalled from memory (10.20.29–10.23.34). While memory will always remain a mystery to him, he is convinced that God resides there: "You certainly dwell in it, since I have remembered you from the time I learned to know you, and I find you in it when I recall you" (10.25.36).[35] Memory was for Augustine thus truly individual and focused on his own existence, an anthropological category determining his very mind and self.

Although Augustine's training in rhetoric certainly had made familiar with the mnemonic techniques used to improve the retentive capacities of memory, it is evident that memory was to him much more than the individual's ability to mechanically relate to the past and also much more than a social construction of what happened. Memory was the crucial and divinely inspired means to reach beyond human existence in this world and to recall and know the transcendence that lies hidden within each human being and makes possible the truly joyous life with God. Memory has, according to Augustine, to do with anthropology and theology in conjunction, the human self in relation to God, with theological anthropology. Augustine elsewhere goes as far as to argue that memory together with intellect and will corresponds to the trinity and form the trinitarian union of thought (e.g. *Trin.* 11.8.14).[36] Towards the end of his long discussion in *De Trinitate*, composed a few years after the *Confessiones*, he concludes significantly that man's memory (*memoria hominis*) has some sort of likeness in this image of the trinity (*hac imagine trinitatis*) to the Father (*Trin.* 15.23.43).

29 J.J. O'Donnel, *Augustine Confessions* (3 vols; Oxford: Clarendon Press, 1992), 3:174.

30 *da mihi, domine, scire et intellegere.*

31 *et venio in campos et lata praetoria memoriae.*

32 *magna vis est memoriae.*

33 *quid ergo sum, deus meus? quae natura sum?*

34 *si praeter memoriam meam te invenio, immemor tui sum. et quomodo iam inveniam te, si memor non sum tui?*

35 *habitas certe in ea, quoniam tui memini, ex quo te didici, et in ea te invenio, cum recordor te.*

36 For discussion of memory in *De Trinitate*, cf. Coleman, *Ancient and Medieval Memories*, 101–16; Hochschild, *Memory in Augustine's Theological Anthropology*, 189–224.

In line with this theological purpose, Augustine discusses in the *Confessiones* the nature of memory. A prominent feature in his thinking is the subject of memory. What is it that forms the content of memory? According to Augustine, the subject of memory does not consist only of images representing past experiences of historical reality, as Aristotle stressed, but also of different kinds of physical sensations and of things that are solely inherent to the human mind. The outline of his discussion in chapters 8–14 of Book 10 reveals a line of thought that accounts for the diverse contents of memory. Already immediately after having mentioned the entry into the palaces of memory and briefly expressed its amazing power in chapter 8, he points out that memory contains various things that have to do with the senses of seeing, hearing, smelling, tasting and feeling with your whole body. "All these does that great receptacle of memory receive in its numberless secret and indescribable windings, to be recalled and brought out at need, each entering by its own door and stored in it" (*Conf.* 10.8.13).[37]

He continues in chapters 9–13 to explain the contents of memory that have not entered into it through any of the senses just mentioned, such as literature confirming what is hidden in memory and the laws of numbers and dimensions. These are intrinsic to memory and, as it were, have resided there without having ever entered through any of the bodily senses. Emotions – joy, sadness, fear, pain, etc. – present a special case, as he points out in chapter 14, because they are remembered without bringing back the actual experience of the emotion. Memory encompasses all the cognitive capacities and is the repository of all of a person's experiences and knowledge, being central to the self and the sense of personal identity.

Intersected with this discussion of the subject of memory is his idea that memory recalls the images (*imagines*) of things rather than the things themselves. He states it already at the beginning of chapter 8: in the field and palaces of memory there are not simply memories, but "the treasures of countless images" (*thesauri innumerabilium imaginum*) that have been imported into it (10.8.12). This is similar to Aristotle's idea of mental images, but it becomes more sophisticated and theologically loaded in Augustine's *Confessiones* due to his conviction that memory contains also things that do not correspond to concrete objects and his ambition to find knowledge of God in memory.

After having pointed to the different subjects of memory, Augustine continues in chapters 15 and 16 of Book 10 to reflect on the presence of images of things absent. He mentions images of a stone, the sun, of pain, health and numbers, emphasizing that the images rather than the things themselves are present when he remembers them. This applies not only to physical objects

37 *haec omnia recipit recolenda cum opus est et retractanda grandis memoriae recessus et nescio qui secreti atque ineffabiles sinus eius: quae omnia suis quaeque foribus intrant ad eam et reponuntur in ea.*

but also to all the other things that are recalled. An image can be visual, conceptual or linguistic and is part of complex mental and mnemonic processes of producing pictures and, as it were, of fictionalization.

The idea of remembering memory itself leads him in the chapters that follow to reflect on the paradox of remembering to have forgotten something. This paradox attests to the idea that he remembers the image of forgetfulness itself as it was imprinted on his memory at the moment he forgot the real thing, because otherwise he would have forgotten even to have once remembered. He is left in wonder about this strange paradox, yet he is certain to remember forgetfulness: "In some way or other, even though it is incomprehensible and inexplicable, I am still certain that I also remember forgetfulness, by which we remember that something is blotted out" (10.16.25).[38] Augustine is here moving beyond what he had learned about memory as a rhetorician, where he had probably become acquainted with the mnemonic *loci* mentioned by Cicero and others and of similar techniques used to fight embarrassing lapses of memory at the moment of oral delivery. Forgetfulness cannot be counteracted with training, he realizes, but must be acknowledged for what it is. For Augustine, the notion of memory and forgetfulness is not to be reduced to various ideas about mnemonic techniques; it is ultimately a theological concern about how to find God, as we noticed in the quotation above: "If I find you without my memory, then I have no memory of you. And how shall I find you, if I do not remember you" (10.17.26)?[39] If he remembers to have forgotten, there is after all a possibility that the image of God is hidden somewhere in the field and large palaces of memory.

It is significant that the discussion of memory is immediately followed by Augustine's reflections on creation, eternity and time in Book 11.[40] If he knows God by remembering to have learned of his eternal presence, then there is a problem of time, because Augustine lives within time while God has created time and exists beyond time. Realizing that creation and time coexist and that human knowledge is determined by the temporality of human existence, Augustine is concerned to understand the mystery of creation *ex nihilo* and to find the unity between the temporal conditions of bodily existence and eternity. In the eternal everything is simultaneously present, while, as he states, "no time is all at once really present" (11.11.13).[41] All time past is forced

38 *et tamen quocumque modo, licet sit modus iste incomprehensibilis et inexplicabilis, etiam ipsam oblivionem meminisse me certus sum, qua id quod meminerimus obruitur.*

39 *si praeter memoriam meam te invenio, immemor tui sum. et quomodo iam inveniam te, si memor non sum tui?*

40 For discussion of Book 11, see E.P. Meijering, *Augustin über Schöpfung, Ewigkeit und Zeit. Das elfte Buch der Bekenntnisse* (PP 14; Leiden: Brill, 1979); Hochschild, *Memory in Augustine's Theological Anthropology*, 155–68, with references to further literature. The unpublished MA dissertation by P. Corkum, "*Et Mirum si Non Ipsius Animi:* On Augustine, *Confessions*, Book XI" (Dalhousie University, Halifax, 1994), was not available to me.

41 *nullum vero tempus totum esse praesens.*

to move on by the incoming future and all future follows from the past; and all, past and future, issues from that which is forever present. Augustine senses strongly the tension between the eternity and the temporality of time, insisting that the two should not be confused and realizing the difficulties of grasping the eternal God – who precedes all times past and extends beyond all future times (11.13.16) – within the conditions of time: "Who will hold the heart of man that it may stand still and see how the eternity which always stands still, neither future nor past, expresses itself in times future and past" (11.11.13)?[42]

Although never providing a precise definition of time,[43] Augustine seems to think of it as a constant process. It never stands still and is like a dripping water-clock – in 11.2.2 he speaks of "drops of time" (*stillae temporum*). Time could be said to consist of the past, the present, and the future. Yet, strictly speaking only the present time exists. The past is no more and the future is yet to come. The present time, moreover, exists only until it passes into the past, always tending towards non-being (11.14.17). For Augustine, time passed and time future can be apprehended and estimated as being long or short only from the present moment of the temporal existence moving instantly from existence to non-existence.

Within this context of temporality, memory becomes important as the crystallization of the three dimensions of time.[44] Augustine refers to it in Book 11 as something out of which images being formed on the basis of the perceptions in the past are drawn and takes his own childhood as an example (11.18.23). His argument is that the past and the future exist only in the present, because we can grasp them only in time present. Somewhat later he mentions again memory and tries to come to a conclusion:

> Perhaps it might be said: 'there are three times, present of things past, present of things present, present of things future'. For these three do exist somehow in the soul, for otherwise I do not see them, present of things past: memory; present of things present: contemplation; present of things future: expectation (11.20.26).[45]

The soul senses the three dimensions of time through *memoria*, *contuitus* and *expectatio*, which together constitute each individual's temporal experience in the transient "now". It is through this inner experience that time, strangely enough, can be measured.[46] The movement of the sun or the moon or the stars

42 *quis tenebit cor hominis, ut stet et videat, quomodo stans dictet futura et praeterita tempora nec futura nec praeterita aeternitas?*

43 For a recent discussion of Augustine's notion of time, see D. van Dusen, *The Space of Time: A Sensualist Interpretation of Time in Augustine,* Confessiones *X to XII* (SST 6; Leiden: Brill, 2014).

44 Cf. M. Mendelson, "*venter animi/distentio animi:* Memory and Temporality in Augustine's *Confessions*", *Augustinian Studies* 31 (2000) 137–63.

45 *fortasse proprie diceretur: tempora sunt tria, praesens de praeteritis, praesens de praesentibus, praesens de futuris. sunt enim haec in anima tria quaedam, et alibi ea non video praesens de praeteritis memoria, praesens de praesentibus contuitus, praesens de futuris expectatio.*

46 G.J.P. O'Daly, "Augustine on the Measurement of Time: Some Comparisons with Aristotelian

or any other body outside the human mind cannot measure time (11.23–24). It is *vice versa:* their movement is measured by time. The measurement of time is something different, because, "time is nothing else than extendedness" (11.26.33);[47] and what is being measured is, strictly speaking, "time passing, not time passed" (11.26.33).[48] Time is defined as extendedness (*distentio*) and its measure is a subjective inner feeling of the soul,[49] which senses the passing of time so that, "the past is increasing by the diminution of the future until by the consumption of the future all is past" (11.27.36).[50] Memory is enlarged as time passes, Augustine continues and refers again – somewhat differently – to the threefold temporal experiences of the mind: "For it expects, it attends, it remembers; so that what it expects passes into what it remembers by what it attends" (11.28.37).[51] Memory is thus for Augustine the comprehensive cognitive presence of the ultimate pastness of both what is already past and, paradoxically, what is still future.

By thinking of time as an inner sense of extendedness contrary to the everlasting presence of eternity and arguing that the constant passing of time increases memory, Augustine places temporality and, by implication, narrativity at the very center of human existence and memory. It is not so much Aristotle's idea of time as a means of ordering the present according to the ever-changing impressions of what was before and what might come after that creates this mnemonic narrativity as the idea that time is always in a flux and makes memory into a place in the transient "now" where experiences and expectations become images located in narrative sequences that are variously extended as long or short. Time and narrative have for Augustine no clear nuance of ordering according to certain laws of association or plots, as they had for Aristotle. They appear instead to be a subjective, almost mystic, sensation where everything that was, that is and that will be is constantly fused into feelings of temporal extendedness constituting the human predicament of existing in the present "now" and of vaguely grasping in – and beyond – memory what was before time existed.

and Stoic Texts", in H.J. Blumenthal/R.A. Markus (ed.), *Neoplatonism and Early Christian Thought: Essays in Honor of A.H. Armstrong* (London: Variorum, 1981) 171–9. Cf. idem, *Augustine's Philosophy of Mind* (Berkeley and Los Angeles: University of California Press, 1987).

47 *nihil esse aliud tempus quam distentionem.*

48 *praetereuntia tempora, non praeterita.*

49 Cf. G.J.P. O'Daly, "Time as *distentio* and St Augustine's Exegesis of Philippians 3:12–14", *REAug* 23 (1977) 265–71.

50 *deminutione futuri crescente praeterito, donec consumptione futuri sit totum praeteritum.*

51 *nam et expectat et attendit et meminit, ut id quod expectat per id quod attendit transeat in id quod meminerit.* Cf. also 12.15.18.

Bultmann, *Jesus* and *The Presence of Eternity*

The influence of Martin Heidegger's philosophy on Bultmann's notions of history and time is well known and evident already in Bultmann's early publications. Experts on Heidegger agree that Heidegger was deeply influenced by both Aristotle and Augustine, not least by Augustine's thinking about time.[52] Bultmann's book *Jesus*, especially the introduction, written shortly after Heidegger arrived at Marburg and published only one year before the first part of Heidegger's *Sein und Zeit*,[53] betrays Bultmann's shift away from the old reconstructionist tendencies of the so-called liberal school and the Rankean *Historismus* to a more hermeneutically informed view of history.[54] Bultmann later recalled to have discussed the introduction with Heidegger.[55] Bultmann read widely and was himself also influenced by Augustine's *Confessiones*, but Heidegger probably provided the means to integrate his reading into more profound hermeneutical reflections on history.

Two studies form an *inclusio* to Bultmann's life-long reflections on history.[56] While the introduction to his book *Jesus*, which he published in 1926 at the age of 42, is the earliest statement on his ideas of history, the Gifford lectures *History and Eschatology* or *The Presence of Eternity* that he held in Edinburgh in 1955 at the age of 71 and published two years later reflects the mature synthesis reminiscent of the ideas presented almost 30 years earlier.[57]

52 See F. Van Fleteren (ed.), *Martin Heidegger's Interpretations of Augustine: Sein und Zeit und Ewigkeit* (Collectanea Augustiniana 6; Lewiston: Edwin Mellen Press, 2005), especially part one dealing with Heidegger's understanding of *Conf.* 10; and C.J.N. de Paulo (ed.), *The Influence of Augustine on Heidegger: The Emergence of an Augustinian Phenomenology* (Lewiston: The Edwin Mellen Press, 2006).

53 M. Heidegger, *Sein und Zeit* (Halle: Niemeyer, 1927). Also published in *Jahrbuch für Philosophie und phänomenologische Forschung* 8 (1927) 1–438. I have not been able to evaluate fully the influence of Heidegger on Bultmann. For discussion, see J. Macquarrie, *An Existentialist Theology: A Comparison of Heidegger and Bultmann* (London: SCM, 2012 [1955]).

54 R. Bultmann, *Jesus* (Tübingen: Mohr [Siebeck], 1926). For discussion of the background of Bultmann's work on this book, see K. Hammann, *Rudolf Bultmann. Eine Biographie* (2nd ed.; Tübingen: Mohr Siebeck, 2009), 179–92. The 2012 edition of Hamman's biography of Bultmann was not available to me.

55 This is what Bultmann claimed in a letter to Hans Hübner, dated June 5, 1972, and in conversation with Günther Bornkamm in early 1976. See Hübner, "Bultmanns 'existentiale Interpretation' – Untersuchungen zu ihrer Herkunft", *ZTK* 100 (2003) 280–324; Bornkamm, "In memoriam Rudolf Bultmann. * 20.8.1884 † 30.7 1976", *NTS* 23 (1977) 235–42, on p. 239.

56 For discussion of Bultmann's notion of the historical Jesus and history, see my "The Message of Jesus", in B.W. Longenecker/M.C. Parsons (ed.), *Beyond Bultmann: Reckoning a New Testament Theology* (Waco, TX: Baylor University Press, 2014) 3–22; and "What is Historical about the Mission of the Historical Jesus? Rudolf Bultmann and the Hermeneutics of Memory", in S. Byrskog/T. Hägerland (ed.), *The Mission of Jesus: Second Nordic Symposium on the Historical Jesus, 7–10 October 2012* (WUNT II 391; Tübingen: Mohr Siebeck, 2015) 41–58.

57 R. Bultmann, *History and Eschatology: The Gifford Lectures 1955* (Edinburgh: The University Press, 1957). The lectures were also published as *The Presence of Eternity: History and Escha-*

Although he touched on the subject in several other publications and alluded to it in most of his hermeneutical discussions and his program of demythologization, these two studies indicate Bultmann's deep and life-long interest in the nature of history and betray a profound sensitivity to the time-bound existence of human beings and to history as being relative to the "now" of each person.

The book *Jesus* indicates on the very first page a stance to the historical Jesus that breaks with the old notions of historicity and gives prominence to the idea that each person is always involved in the history s/he aims to study and reconstruct. We cannot simply observe history at a distance if we truly want to understand its essence.[58] As soon as we say something about history, we say something about ourselves. The key concept for Bultmann is dialogue with history, but not in the sense that the dialogue occurs after history has been reconstructed, but as a means to confront history throughout.[59] This does not imply that the present time of the historian takes over. The dialogue is not a simple subjective game. History has a voice of its own and our questions to and conceptions of history challenge the presence of our existence. To be sure, the allegedly objective approach to history that limits its perspective to a particular scientific method of historical reconstruction is also essential, Bultmann acknowledges, but it is caught within the subjectivity of the method, misses the essence of history, and detects nothing new about human beings and their history. History, in other words, exists as a relationship between the past and the present, so that the present time both determines and is determined by what happened in a dialectical process of dialogue between the two temporal horizons.

With this notion of history Bultmann also modified narrow conceptions of the historicity of the Jesus tradition. Quite early scholars noticed that in his book *Jesus* he employed material that he in his analysis of the synoptic tradition, originally published a few years earlier, did not trace back to Jesus.[60] Julius Schniewind called Bultmann's procedure "Querschnittexegese".[61] Bultmann moved quite easily between that which he had established as part of the kerygmatic mythmaking and that which he had argued came from past tradition and Jesus himself.

tology. The Gifford Lectures 1955 (New York: Harper & Brothers, 1957). I have used the American edition.

58 "Denn eine Grundvoraussetzung der folgenden Darstellung ist die, daß man die Geschichte, wenn man ihr Wesentliches erfassen will, nicht 'betrachten' kann" (Bultmann, *Jesus*, 7).

59 "Vielmehr vollzieht sich die wirkliche Begegnung der Geschichte von vornherein nur im Dialog" (Bultmann, *Jesus*, 7).

60 R. Bultmann, *Die Geschichte der synoptischen Tradition* (FRLANT 29; Göttingen: Vandenhoeck & Ruprecht, 1921).

61 J. Schniewind, "Zur Synoptiker-Exegese", *TRu* 2 (1930) 129–89, on pp. 172–4.

It is probably a mistake to understand this feature as a blunt contradiction.[62] Bultmann comments on it briefly in the introduction to his book *Jesus* and maintains that it is ultimately the conceptions reflected in the earliest layer of the tradition that are of interest to him and assumes that the ascription of them to Jesus probably is correct, although adding that nothing would change if things were different and someone else had uttered them.[63] The reason for this significant addition is probably twofold. Firstly, as is well known Bultmann was not interested in the person (or personality) of the historical Jesus. As a reaction against the previous reconstructions of Jesus, he avoided to enhance the person of Jesus and regarded the proclamation of God's kingdom to be the crucial historical and eschatological event, whether it came from Jesus or not. What is less known is that it probably also, secondly, has to do with his sophisticated approach to history. It is precisely the mutual dialogue between the past and the present that is prominent both in Bultmann's notion of the modern historian's approach as well as in his evolutionary and diachronic account of the synoptic tradition, where history moves back and forth between the past and the present dimension of tradition, as if history were a dialogue and relationship rather than an object to be reconstructed. The seeming dissolution of historical fact and interpretation reflects a similar idea that the past and the present are inextricably intertwined in historical constructions. He did of course realize that there was a dimension of pastness in the early Christians' mythmaking and that their eschatological existence also, just like that of the modern historian, involved a dialogue between the horizon of the past and of the present in the midst of time.

Bultmann maintained his notion of history throughout his life. His relationship to Heidegger changed, partly due to the turmoil and political upheavals during the War,[64] but almost three decades after the publication of his book *Jesus* the old Bultmann lectured on the break with the *Historismus* of his youth, traced the view of history from the ancient Greek and Roman historians up to his own time, and presented his own synthesis, focusing on the shift from the old cyclical interpretation of history to teleological and eschatological alternatives. Developing what he indicated already in 1926 under influence from the young Heidegger, but now with fuller awareness of the philosophical discussions concerning human existence and of Ernst

62 I comment on this more fully in discussion with James Dunn and Anthony Le Donne in my article "What is Historical".

63 "Sollte es anders gewesen sein, so ändert sich damit das, was in dieser Überlieferung gesagt ist, in keiner Weise" (Bultmann, *Jesus*, 14).

64 See A. Standhartinger, "Bultmann's *Theology of the New Testament* in Context", in B.W. Longenecker/M.C. Parsons (ed.), *Beyond Bultmann: Reckoning a New Testament Theology* (Waco, TX: Baylor University Press, 2014) 233–55, on pp. 236–7; eadem, "Modernisierte Theologie. Zeitgeschichtliche Reflexionen in Rudolf Bultmanns Theologie des Neuen Testaments", *TRu* 29 (2014) 161–89, on p. 167.

Käsemann's reopened quest for the historical Jesus,[65] Bultmann challenged the teleological approach and brought history and eschatology together in the historical event of Christ confronting the human being in her existence in history and time. Because history exists in relation to human existence and can be fully perceived only from the present time of each individual, the eschatological moment that makes history meaningful slumbers in the present. "Always in your present lies the meaning in history", he concludes.[66]

Since Bultmann emphasized the Christian thought that the present historical existence is crucial and invaded by eschatology and eternity, the notion of time became more urgent here than in his book on *Jesus*. If we wish to understand the two alternative titles of his lectures – *History and Eschatology* and *The Presence of Eternity* – from the perspective of Augustine's notion time and eternity, Bultmann seems to think that the eschatological moment beginning with the historical appearance of Jesus Christ manifested in preaching and in faith, makes God's timeless eternity present and abolishes the enslaving temporality of time, arguing that past, present and future are crystallized in the eschatological and historical "now" of each person.

Bultmann admired Augustine for his concept of history and time and his groundbreaking autobiographical way of seeking God. While the ancient authors understood history and time by analogy with the cyclical process of nature, Augustine believed in divine creation and therefore, according to Bultmann, argued that time has a beginning and an end. The decisive reason for this is Augustine's understanding of the human being unfolded in opposition to the ancient manner of thinking and grounded on the idea that s/he is distinct from the world and a free individual aiming at the future and something ultimate. Augustine's *Confessiones* introduces autobiography and shows that history is always experienced from the perspective of individual experiences, so that history is moved by the personal self-understanding of the persons who are acting within history.[67] This fits into Bultmann's idea of history and implies that time was for him not only a dimension of existence independent of events and existence but also and fundamentally an entity locked into the present and into each individual's horizon and experiences of her/his temporality and "historicality".

Bultmann did not explicitly connect this notion of history and time to Augustine's extensive reflections on memory and time. As we have seen, for Augustine memory was closely related to what is hidden in his own inner being and to his almost mystical experience of time. Bultmann takes to my knowledge no notice of this. He also failed to account for Halbwachs' idea of collective memory, despite stressing elsewhere the importance of the joint activities of the Christian community for understanding the development of

65 E. Käsemann, "Das Problem des historischen Jesus", *ZTK* 51 (1954) 125–53.
66 Bultmann, *The Presence of Eternity*, 155.
67 Bultmann, *The Presence of Eternity*, 59–60, 146–7.

the synoptic tradition. Instead he developed his hermeneutics of history and time without taking into account the mnemonic explanation of how the past enters into and is conquered by the present time of the remembering individual and group and without detecting the potentials of the theories of social and collective memory for grasping the notions of eschatology and of the presence of eternity in the now of each believer.

Notwithstanding this neglect, his understanding of history and time has similarities to the ancient philosophical notions of memory. Just as memory according to Aristotle and Augustine depends on each individual's experience of time, be that in terms of the number of change and movement or the subjective feeling of extendedness, history was for Bultmann essentially and intrinsically related to the existence and temporal horizon of each individual. Just as memory according to Aristotle and Augustine exists in and is determined by the evasive "now" of each person and negotiates with the past with a sense of temporality, which is an idea that recurs in today's theories of social and collective memory, Bultmann stressed that history must be heard and understood as a dialogue between the present time of the individual and the pastness of history. Just as Aristotle and Augustine realized that memory creates its own images of the past, be that as copies of what really happened or sensations of the human mind, Bultmann insisted that history consists of a configuration and mixture of images reflecting the presence of an absent past and the creative reformulation and invention of historical myths. Although Bultmann has been blamed for not realizing the importance of memory for the transmission of the synoptic tradition, he entertained through-out his life notions of history and time that are reminiscent of ancient philosophical discussions of memory.

Conclusions

What is there to learn from all this for present day scholarship on the historical Jesus and the Jesus tradition? Are the theories of Aristotle and Augustine obsolete granted the former was not as influential in Greek and Roman antiquity as in medieval times and today and granted the latter was dependent on neo-platonic ideas and more interested in the memory of the soul than the memory of the past? The presupposition here is that the two philosophers represent how ancient people in the Greek and Roman world with a significant intellectual training conceived of memory in the daily life of themselves and others and hence indicate how early Christians might have sensed the presence of the past when they negotiated with the Jesus event mnemonically. The reconstructive tendencies of modern Jesus research, invaluable as it is, capture only part of the ancient notions of memory; and the recent interest among Jesus scholars in the social and collective memory of the early Christians, while often bypassing the specificity of memory, might be reconciled with philosophical and hermeneutical thinking about history. I have tried to provide an account of Aristotle's and Augustine's notions of memory and followed their discussion as it unfolds their writings. A few concluding remarks will bring out some common traits of the two philosophers and relate them to the most influential and philosophically sophisticated NT scholar of last century, indicating also how the early Christians made sense of the past in the present through memory. These traits, as we have seen, have to do with the individuality of memory, the notions of time and narrative, the importance of the present "now", and the use of mnemonic images.

It is a remarkable fact that while the ancient authors experienced and tried to cope with seen and unseen realities in a milieu where the importance of the group and the collective mentality overshadowed the sense of the individual self, *memory was philosophically always part of the individual* and her/his own personal experiences and thoughts. As we have seen, Aristotle considered memory and recollection to be conditioned by the physical structure of things and thought that memory was corporeal and that recollection was dependent on the concrete bodily facilities of each person. Augustine chose autobiography as a means of theologizing about memory, aiming to present the human self in relation to God and to find God in his own memory. The idea that memory was social and only collectively conditioned was not invented and did not occur as an explanation of its character. Bultmann, while ignorant of the emerging theories of social and collective memory, relied on contemporary Heideggerian philosophy influenced by Aristotle and Augustine and oriented towards the individual and was deeply sympathetic to the convictions of Augustine. This is not to deny the importance of the theories of social and collective memory that are widely employed today. But as I have repeatedly tried to point out elsewhere, we should make a distinction between collective memory, which is social in that it includes those memories and processes of recollection of a group that are shared by all of its members, and social memory, which is social in that it deals with the social aspects of each person's memories and cognitive act of remembering.[68] Social memory, we could say, is interested in the memory and recollection of individuals in social contexts that are larger than the individual and yet closely related to the individual. So, *the ancient focus on the individual is not opposed to the social approaches to memory but brings us back to the personal traits and individual specificity of all memories and mnemonic processes.*

Aristotle's and Augustine's reflections on the memory and recollection of each person provide an unrecognized potential of balancing the explanatory

68 Recently in S. Byrskog, "Theissen, Form-Criticism, and Social Memory: Ways to Reconfigure Jesus the Galilean", in P. von Gemünden/D.G. Horrell/M. Küchler (ed.), *Jesus – Gestalt und Gestaltungen. Rezeptionen des Galiläers in Wissenschaft, Kirche und Gesellschaft. FS für Gerd Theißen zum 70. Geburtstag* (NTOA/StUNT 100; Göttingen: Vandenhoeck & Ruprecht, 2013) 499–513, on p. 506.

monopoly of modern sociology minimizing the individuality of the individual and recur in today's theories through the notions of time and narrative, the importance of the present "now", and the mnemonic images discussed by Aristotle and Augustine and endorsed, in his own way, by Bultmann. Aristotle and Augustine realized, both with different emphases, that *the understanding of memory implies an understanding of time and narrative.* They defined time in different ways, Aristotle by referring to the number of change and movement and Augustine to the feeling of temporal space and extendedness. Aristotle was emphatic by pointing, as we have seen, stressing that all memory is "in time" and that the most important thing for memory and recollection is to cognize the time. Being an empiricist, he thought of time as part of nature rather than metaphysics and made it dependent on the change that takes place outside the human mind. But the numbering of change and movement cannot take place without the mind, which means that no time exists outside of the human mind, according to Aristotle, despite the constant changes taking place in nature independent of time. Augustine also realized that memory depends on time and was eager to distinguish it from eternity, where everything is simultaneously present. Different from Aristotle, however, he thought of it solely as an inner feeling of extendedness that senses, so to say, the passing of time and measures it subjectively as something analogous to space, as a distention of the mind that enabled him to perceive duration. Therefore, according to Augustine, the three dimensions of time cease to exist or – better – coexist in the soul as a sensation of space experienced through *memoria, contuitus* and *expectatio.*

Since memory is related to temporality, the notions of past, present and future were mnemonic conceptions. Memory was identified as memory by its capacity to navigate between the horizons of time. *This intrinsic temporal character of memory implies a profoundly narrative dimension.* Ricoeur pointed out that although the notion of sequence and chronological time might be an illusion, the solution is not a recourse to a-chronological models but, with Heidegger, one that relates time to narrative, taking "temporality to be that structure of existence that reaches language in narrativity and narrativity to be the language structure that has temporality as its ultimate referent".[69] This is not explicit in Aristotle's and Augustine's discussion of memory, and Ricoeur is closer to Augustine than Aristotle in speaking of time, thinking of narrative more in terms of repeated configurations than a series of episodes, but Aristotle realized that memory links events "in time" to each other according to narrative patterns and Augustine made the narratively autobiographical section of his *Confessiones* the basis of the philosophical and theological deliberations on memory and placed narrativity at the center of memory by thinking of time as a constant fluctuation creating feelings of temporal extendedness.

69 P. Ricoeur, "Narrative Time", *Critical Inquiry* 7 (1980) 169–90, on p. 169.

The two notions of time and narrative come together in the idea that *the "now" is the essence of the temporal existence experienced in memory.* Memory is always in and of the present. It is only from the perspective of the present that time can be measured or acknowledged as an extension; and it is only from the present that the past can be mnemonically ordered according to narrative patterns or felt to be part of a narrative flow. But *time is constantly moving.* Augustine was most emphatic, sensing strongly the human imprisonment in time and hoping that memory would bring back his knowledge of God in and beyond time. While everything is instantaneously present in eternity, where time does not exist, the "now" of human existence is both that which actually exists and that which constantly passes into the past and tends towards non-being. *Memory belongs to this transient "now" and is therefore unstable,* being more than merely a chamber of mnemonic images and enlarged by the future as time passes, encompassing the evolving presence of things that existed a moment ago and – paradoxically – of the lost memories of something forgotten.

Since memory exists in the transient "now" and produces a present narrative configuration of the past, *it designs the past through available pictures and images.* Both Aristotle and Augustine realized this, Aristotle with more focus on the possibility of regarding the picture as a copy of past reality and Augustine emphasizing the cognitive process of remembering also things that do not correspond to concrete objects and the configuration of visual, conceptual and linguistic objects. The common idea is that the reality of the past is forever gone and can be recaptured only indirectly through cognitive processes that interact with the present process of recall and the remembering individual's capacity to create mnemonically relevant images.

As we have seen above, Bultmann neglected to discuss memory but entertained a profound interest in history and time and was deeply influenced by Augustine. The similarities with the ancient philosophical notions of memory come to the fore in his understanding of what history is, that is, in its implications for notions of time, the present "now", and the mnemonic images. Just as memory depends on each individual's experience of time, *history is for Bultmann related to the temporal horizon of each individual.* Just as memory is determined by the evasive "now" of each person, *history should according to Bultmann be understood as a dialogue between the present time and the pastness of history.* Just as memory creates its own images of the past, *history consists according to Bultmann of a configuration and mixture of images reflecting the presence of an absent past and the creative reformulation and invention of historical myths.* In Heidegger's philosophy Bultmann found a theologically relevant reasoning that defined being by non-being and time by death and that was appropriate as a hermeneutical framework for the idea that each human being, imprisoned in history and time and faced with the inevitable death, waits for the eschatological future of God to enlighten her existence, reminding us of Augustine's idea that memory is the crystallization of the three dimensions of time and the present sensation of the past that is no more and the future that is yet to come.

What is lacking in comparison to both Aristotle's and Augustine's notion of memory is a clear idea that time implies narrative. To be sure, Bultmann was interested in narrative mythmaking, and these narratives were part of history because they used mythological language to depict and confront something as if it had happened in the past and built on traditional elements that interacted with the concerns of the transmitting Christian community. But being a convinced form-critic, he endorsed the idea that the words and the deeds of Jesus' mission were separate items of tradition. This is evident in his study of the synoptic tradition in particular, but also in his studies of Jesus, and it betrays his lack of interest in how memory functions cognitively. His Jesus certainly said things and did things, but people, he believed, initially recalled or created the words and the deeds as separate items until someone ingeniously placed his words within episodal frames through kerygmatic processes of mythmaking.

Scholars of memory, from Aristotle and Augustine up to the present time, see things more clearly and note that memory always tends to arrange the past in series of small or large episodes taking place at a certain time and place. To the extent that memory is autobiographical, episodic memory may be distinguished from the broader, wide-ranging notion of semantic memory.[70] *People think of themselves as temporal beings*, linking their personal experiences to past events and regarding episodes of their lives as belonging to particular times and places, so that their creation of stories of the past in which they were involved play an important part in how they build and maintain a personal sense of belonging.[71]

The modes of analysis informed by theories of collective memory as well as those informed by the criteria of authenticity need to consider more fully the role of the individual and the functionalities of memory, such as the ones highlightened by Aristotle and Augustine, for grasping historical realities. It is not by accident that the historical sensibility of ancient historians has parallels to what is today commonly called oral history.[72] This approach takes seriously the individual who experiences and interprets the past in her/his memory and regards the ensuing story of an eyewitness or someone else as a social construction constituting in and of itself a history that is "truer" and more "faithful" to the past than the ones reconstructed from the stories. Time and narrative are essential components of the individual's narrative reconfigura-

70 E. Tulving, "Episodic and Semantic Memory", in E. Tulving/W. Donaldson, *Organization of Memory* (New York: Academic Press, 1972) 381–403; D.C. Rubin, *Autobiographical Memory* (Cambridge: Cambridge University Press, 1986).

71 Cf. L.P. Hinchman/S.K. Hinchman (ed.), *Memory, Identity, Community: The Idea of Narrative in the Human Sciences* (Albany, NY: State University of New York Press, 1997).

72 The classic introduction to oral history is P. Thompson, *The Voice of the Past: Oral History* (3d ed.; Oxford: Oxford University Press, 2000).

tion of the past, the present "now" determines her/his perspective on what happened, and the images used to explicate it are mnemonic aids and conceptions taken from her/his socially constructed system of meaning. Perhaps *oral history, when understood as propagating a social construction of the past from the perspective of an eyewitness, presents a symbiosis of Aristotle's and Augustine's individualistic notions of memory and Bultmann's existential idea of history* and could function as a bridge between divergent modes of analysis of history.

Bultmann's idea of history seems closer to the philosophical discussions of memory in antiquity than today's scholarly attempts to reconstruct the Jesus who once lived. The early Christians were not unconcerned about the facts of the past; and the well-studied techniques of memorization in the Greek, Roman and Jewish milieu are important indication of their ambition to preserve the memories of what had happened. But the preservation of the past had also – and primarily – a function in the present and interacted with rhetorical elaborations (of *chreiai* and other forms) for the sake of clarity and relevance and with the creation of new versions of what happened. When the early Christians recalled the decisive Jesus event, they did so from the perspective of their present existence and the eschatological moment opening up the imprisoning temporal boundaries of their earthly life. The memory of the past was a matter of perception and sensation and of deeply felt experiences. To remember and report what Jesus was and what he did and what happened to him was to say something crucial about themselves and their own existence in the present.

After years of reconstructing the historical Jesus as an intangible object recoverable behind that which was remembered about him, and after a century or so of discussion of the historical reliability of oral and written traditions, *it is vital in today's scholarly landscape to fully account for the existential notions that were intrinsic to memory and always intruded into the transmission process*, such as the sense of time and the ensuing narrativization of the past, the feeling of an evasive "now", the mnemonic sensations, the construction and conception of the individual self, the use of images and imagination, the rhetorical need for clarity and relevance, etc., and to incorporate into our thinking of the Jesus tradition consideration as to how history interacted with the present life and the "historicality" of the early Christians when they recalled it individually and commemorated it at collective ritual celebrations of mnemonic synchronization. A vast field of unexplored possibilities opens up, with the need to pay more attention to factors such as the formation and elaboration of the mnemonically important *chreia*, the temporal dimension of the verbs used in the Gospel units, the variegating narrative order of the Gospel stories, the temporal and conceptual point of view from which the story of Jesus is told, the awareness of fictionality in the Jesus tradition, the mnemonic and synchronizing role of rituals such as baptism and Eucharist, and much more. This would bring us closer to how ancient people in the Greek and Roman world conceptualized and experienced memory and add a significant dimension to the old question of the reliability of the Gospel tradition. Granted memory normally contains all these elements, the memory of Jesus was even more existentially loaded. The early Christians did not recall and commemorate items of little importance but the words and deeds and fate of someone who meant everything to them. The way back to the historical Jesus is not by stripping off their memory that which was intrinsic to it, but to see it as the multifaceted prism through which the historical reality was variously reflected, interpreted and existentially embodied.

Alan Kirk

The Formation of the Synoptic Tradition: Cognitive and Cultural Approaches to an Old Problem

Research on the cognitive and cultural aspects of memory calls in question the sharp distinction the form critics made between memory and tradition. Conceiving memory as individual "reminiscence", Bultmann and his followers seemed to have good grounds for ruling out any significant role for memory in the history of the tradition, for the observable features of the synoptic tradition have little in common with individual eyewitness recollection. Form criticism shared in the widespread conceptual paradigm that separated the "individual" and the "psychological" from the "social" and the "cultural". Wang and Brockmeier note that ever since Durkheim distinguished between "collective" and "individual" representations, and thereby separated the sociological from the psychological, "memory has been seen as either individual (i.e. mental, neuro-cognitive) or collective (social, historical, cultural)".[1] Though hardly influenced by French sociology, form criticism was similarly predicated on this split between the individual and the sociological. The tradition was emergent in the sociological forces of the Sitz; its existence had only tangentially to do with memory.

Cognitive science and experimental psychology continue to study mental and neurological processes in isolation from social and cultural factors, and sociology and anthropology continue to resist encroachment by biology and psychology into explanations of social and cultural phenomena.[2] But criticisms of this divide have been advanced and efforts made to replace it with more integrative approaches. According to anthropologists Claudia Strauss and Naomi Quinn,

> the private/public (i.e. inner/outer or subject/world) divide ... is problematic ... We think that the inner world or psyche and the world outside of persons are not isolated realms and that too large a gulf has been posited between them in current theorizing.[3]

1 Q. Wang/J. Brockmeier, "Autobiographical Remembering as Cultural Practice: Understanding the Interplay Between Memory, Self, and Culture", *Culture and Psychology* 8 (2002) 45–64, on pp. 59–60. See É. Durkheim, "Individual and Collective Representations", in É. Durkheim (ed.), *Sociology and Philosophy* (London: Cohen and West, 1953 [French original 1898]) 1–34.

2 C. Strauss/N. Quinn, *A Cognitive Theory of Cultural Meaning* (Cambridge: Cambridge University Press, 1997), 253; Wang/Brockmeier, "Autobiographical Remembering", 60.

3 Strauss/Quinn, *Cognitive Theory*, 8; similarly A. Norenzayan/I. Choi/K. Pen, "Perception and

Philosopher and cognitive scientist John Sutton laments "the ongoing and damaging lack of contact between the cognitive and the social sciences", arguing that "[t]he time is ripe for integrative work to close these gaps", first and foremost in the field of memory.[4] This essay is an effort in that direction, clarifying how the synoptic tradition, a cultural artifact, emerges at the interface of the cognitive and cultural operations of memory. It will explore the interpenetration of cognitive and cultural factors along a spectrum that runs from memory (as a neurobiological phenomenon) to a cultural tradition, showing that this interface accounts for the formation of the synoptic tradition and for a number of its emblematic features.

Mental Schemas, Cultural Schemas, and Memory Formation

Lambros Malafouris urges us to "see culture as the enactive process that brings forth, envelops, and partially constitutes human cognitive and emotional lives."[5] Culture penetrates right down to the neural encoding of memories. This is evident in the cognitive operations that filter salient elements out of the diffuse flux of perceptual experience, encoding these elements in neural networks organized in accord with a set of economical patterns, or "schemas". This large-scale reduction of complexity to simple schematic forms is a practical matter of efficiency – shedding the vast amounts of detail that under conditions of total recall would induce cognitive paralysis.[6] It delivers, in Conway's words, "the optimum amount of information for the minimal amount of cognitive effort".[7] The schematic patterns that organize memories

Cognition", in S. Kitayama/D. Cohen (ed.), *Handbook of Cultural Psychology* (New York: Guilford, 2007) 569–644, on p. 607. In a 1975 essay Daniel Sperber expressed concerns about the pernicious split between psychology and anthropology ("Anthropology and Psychology: Towards and Epidemiology of Representations", *Man* 20 [1975] 73–89).

4 J. Sutton, "Remembering", in P. Robbins/M. Aydede (ed.), *The Cambridge Handbook of Situated Cognition* (Cambridge: Cambridge University Press, 2009) 217–35, on p. 224. Elsewhere he states: "[W]e must find a general framework for the sciences of memory in which the concepts of social or 'collective' memory ... will be integral parts of cognitive science, rather than social constructionist myths" ("Representation, Reduction, and Interdisciplinarity in the Sciences of Memory", in H. Clapin/P. Staines/P. Slezak (ed.), *Representation in Mind: New Approaches to Mental Representation* [London: Elsevier, 2004] 187–216, on p. 204).

5 L. Malafouris, "The Brain-Artefact Interface (BAI): a Challenge for Archaeology and Cultural Neuro-science", *SCAN* 5 (2010) 264–73, on p. 264.

6 S.J. Schmidt/S. Weischenberg, "Mediengattungen, Berichterstattungsmuster, Darstellungsformen", in K. Merton/S.J. Schmidt/S. Weischenberg (ed.), *Die Wirklichkeit der Medien: Eine Einführung in die Kommunikationswissenschaft* (Opladen: Westdeutscher Verlag, 1994) 212–36, on p. 213.

7 M.A. Conway, "Remembering: A Process and a State", in H.L. Roediger III/Y. Dudai/S.M. Fitzpatrick (ed.), *Science of Memory: Concepts* (Oxford/New York: Oxford University Press, 2007) 237–41, on p. 241; similarly, S.J. Schmidt, *Kognitive Autonomie und soziale Orientierung: Kon-*

exist as neural networks (engrams) constituted of conventionalized sequences, or "nodes". These "are so strongly interlinked that activating any one of them necessarily activates them all."[8] In memory encoding, elements filtered from the flow of incoming perceptual information are conformed, as noted, to the representational structure of the schema. When the thus encoded memory is recollected, schematic elements perhaps not present in the original experienced realities may be filled by default through activation of the conventional nodes of the schema. The supplied elements are therefore conventional, or "typical". Experiences unfold in unpredictable, diffuse ways, rarely schematically, but in memory they will be organized and recalled as such.[9] Cognitive schemas are already at work in perception: one perceives a "tree" schematically, as a cognitive unity, not all the branches and leaves individually. But just as it would be perverse to regard this as a defect in perception, it is perverse to regard the consolidation of memories in cognitive schemas as a defect of memory.

Moreover, it is through filtering and mediation into schematic patterns that remembered experiences receive *intelligibility*.[10] Cognitive schemas and scripts possess an innate conceptual or sequential logic, but they also filter experiential input for *salience*, directing perceptual attention to elements that are significant.[11] Sub-schematic elements of a situation – details irrelevant to the operative schema or lacking salience – have a low probability of being encoded in memory. "The schema", Mandler says, "prepares the person to see certain kinds of things; consequently, little attention need be paid to those things that match expectations, leaving attentional resources free to devote to the more unusual, and therefore, more informative, items."[12] Schematically similar memories will over time blend into a generic memory. These operations bring us back to the mass shedding of detail in conforming

struktivistische Bemerkungen zum Zusammenhang von Kognition, Kommunikation, Medien und Kultur (3rd edn; Münster: Lit Verlag, 2003), 173.

8 E.R. Smith/S. Queller, "Mental Representations", in M.B. Brewer/M. Hewstone (ed.), *Social Cognition* (Oxford: Blackwell, 2004) 5–27, on p. 21.

9 J.M. Mandler/N.S. Johnson, "Remembrance of Things Parsed: Story Structure and Recall", *Cognitive Psychology* 9 (1977) 111–51, on pp. 134, 149; J.M. Mandler, *Stories, Scripts, and Scenes: Aspects of Schema Theory* (Hillsdale, N.J./London: Erlbaum, 1984), 47–8; Smith/Queller, "Mental Representations", 17. See also F.C. Bartlett, *Remembering: A Study in Experimental and Social Psychology* (Cambridge: Cambridge University Press, 1995 [original 1932]), 52–4, 312–13.

10 H. Welzer, *Das kommunikative Gedächtnis: Eine Theorie der Erinnerung* (München: Beck, 2002), 30.

11 Mandler/Johnson, "Remembrance", 112; Welzer, *Gedächtnis*, 172.

12 Mandler, *Stories, Scripts, and Scenes*, 105. She gives the example of the script, "ordering in a restaurant": schema-accordant features of this event include being seated, scanning a menu, the appearance of the waiter after a decent interval, and so forth. These schematic aspects would be encoded by default, while "low level details" such as "where the waiter parts his hair" would not be noticed nor remembered. But an unusual feature of the scene, e.g., "a ten foot tall waiter", would be noticed and encoded (102–3).

memories to mental schemas: the drive toward cognitive efficiency is at the same time a drive toward maximum intelligibility. Koriat and his colleagues describe this as achieving "maximal compactness within a [neural] trace system while suffering only a minimal loss of information".[13] Memory-encoding therefore amounts to abstracting from originating occurrences. The effect is to give memories a *representational* relationship to the experiential realities that are their grounds.[14]

A good example of a cognitive schema is the "life script," studied by Bernsten and Rubin, that organizes autobiographical memories. The life script is a "shared cognitive structure"; more precisely, "culturally shared expectations as to the order and timing of life events in a prototypical life course".[15] It accounts for the "reminiscence bump", that is, the curious concentration of autobiographical memories into the period between an individual's late adolescence and thirties, for it is in this period that most of the significant life-transitions that make up the "life script" occur. "[L]ife scripts structure retrieval ... and for this reason events that fit into the life script are more easily recalled than events that do not."[16] Notably, the "life script" is both a *cognitive* and a *cultural* schema. The cognitive schemas that mediate memory formation are drawn from a *cultural repertoire* of schemas and scripts that have been internalized through socialization. Welzer points out "daß die Einspeicherung und der Abruf von Erinnerungen kulturellen Schemata folgt (was bedeutet, daß der Erinnerungsvorgang selbst kulturell organisiert ist)".[17]

Here we see hints of the cognitive and cultural interface that will be implicated in the formation of tradition. Cognitive schemas and tradition forms overlap in a number of respects. Both are schematic, mnemonically efficient formats, culturally grounded, that stabilize content and facilitate retrieval and reenactment. Both "verleihen unseren Vorstellungen Festigkeit und Dauer".[18] Schema-supplied organization gives to memories as well as to tradition a good measure of *typical* elements. Both exhibit economy, converging on high-salience elements. Both reduce diffuse phenomena to unitary cognitive entities. Both are significance-laden, symbolically dense entities. Cognitive schemas and scripts are culturally transmitted and

13 A. Koriat/M. Goldsmith/A. Pansky, "Toward a Psychology of Memory Accuracy", *ARP* 51 (2000) 431–587.

14 L.R. Squire/E.R. Kandel, *Memory: From Mind to Molecules* (New York: Scientific American Library, 1999), 206.

15 D. Berntsen/D.C. Rubin, "Cultural Life Scripts Structure Recall from Autobiographical Memory", *M&C* 32 (2004) 427–42, on p. 427.

16 Berntsen/Rubin, "Cultural Life Scripts", 440.

17 Welzer, *Gedächtnis*, 146; also Strauss/Quinn, *Cognitive Theory*, 49; Schmidt, *Kognitive Autonomie*, 169.

18 Schmidt/Weischenberg "Mediengattungen", 213.

acquired: they are already a form of tradition.[19] We will have more to say about this memory/tradition convergence in due course.

Schematic encoding does not mean that memories are static entities, like files retrieved from a computer hard drive. The activation of any memory is matter of approximate pattern re-creation across a network of neuronal connections dynamically open to associative connections with other memory networks. The strength of these neural connections – their "weight" – is a variable that depends upon conditions affecting initial encoding, and then by the history of subsequent activations. None of the neural activations of a specific memory is precisely identical to any other activation of that memory, for each is sensitive to immediate contextual cues that have stimulated the recollection and also to other, concurrent patterns of activation.[20] Memories, Smith and Queller note, "are not explicitly 'stored' anywhere. Instead, the network stores connection strengths that allow a range of patterns to be reproduced given the right cues."[21] In other words, remembering is *situated:* memories are activated in response to cues of immediate contexts, while persisting in their existence as neuronal entities distinct from those contexts. Strauss and Quinn describe this as the "distinction between relatively stable cognitive networks and the ever-changing reactions that are the response of these networks to particular events".[22] It is by connecting present experience to stable schematic patterns laid down in memory that memory carries out its indispensable function of rendering present experience intelligible.[23]

The stability of memories is a matter of the connection strengths of their neural networks.[24] What factors affect encoding strength? The leading variable in strong as opposed to weak encoding is the *motivational state* of the

19 Berntsen/Rubin, "Cultural Life Scripts", 430; see also R. Zimmermann, "Formen und Gattungen als Medien der Jesus-Erinnerung: Zur Rückgewinnung der Diachronie in der Formgeschichte des Neuen Testament", in O. Fuchs/B. Janowski (ed.), *Die Macht der Erinnerung* (*JBTh* 22; Neukirchen-Vluyn: Neukirchener Verlag, 2008) 131–67, on p. 145.

20 Smith/Queller, "Mental Representations", 10–13; Sutton, "Remembering", 219–20; Welzer, *Gedächtnis*, 20; F.I.M. Craik, "On the Making of Episodes", in H.L. Roediger III/F.I.M. Craik (ed.), *Varieties of Memory and Consciousness: Essays in Honour of Endel Tulving* (Hillsdale, NJ: Erlbaum, 1989) 43–57, on p. 43; D.L. Schacter/K.A. Norman/W. Koutstaal, "The Cognitive Neuroscience of Constructive Memory", *Annual Review of Psychology* 49 (1998) 289–318, on p. 312; Squire/Kandel, *Memory*, 73–4.

21 Smith and Queller, "Mental Representations", 10.

22 Strauss/Quinn, *Cognitive Theory*, 54; similarly Welzer, *Gedächtnis*, 203, and J. Sutton/C.B. Harris/P.G. Keil, "The Psychology of Memory, Extended Cognition, and Socially Distributed Remembering", *PCS* 9 (2010) 521–60, on p. 544.

23 Memory pioneer Frederic Bartlett referred to this as "utilization of the past in the solution of difficulties set by the present" (*Remembering*, 225); see also Smith/Queller, "Mental Representations", 10; Sutton, "Remembering", 219–20; Welzer, *Gedächtnis*, 20; Craik, "On the Making of Episodes", 43 l.

24 N.E. Spear, "Retrieval: Properties and Effects," in *Science of Memory*, 215–19, on pp. 216–17; similarly Smith/Queller, "Mental Representations,"13–14.

subject, which determines the *attentional resources* devoted to the task.[25] Not surprisingly, subjects are more highly motivated to encode information that is *salient* – that *matters* – to them, and conversely, to filter out the many details of perceptual input that do not.[26] *Affect level* frequently correlates to salience: "emotionally arousing" events will be more durably encoded, and recollecting them will re-excite the affective response.[27] Likewise, what DiMaggio calls *moral salience* is a leading factor in differential encoding: elements charged with moral significance, thus that excite evaluative attention and affective response (itself an evaluative reflex), have a higher probability of being selected out of the morass of details and deeply encoded, together with the accompanying moral judgments and their emotional coloring.[28] Morally – and affectively – signified memories will be more frequently recollected and ruminated, further strengthening the connections of the schematic patterns in which they are encoded.[29]

Let us pause to take stock. Rather than getting caught the trap of talking about "individual memory" we have looked at the *cognitive* aspects of memory formation. Thus we have avoided dead-end dichotomies and seen ways that the cognitive workings of memory intersect with cultural media. Though we are still a long way from being able to talk about the formation of a tradition, we have begun to see overlap between memories as *cognitive artifacts* and tradition forms as a *cultural artifacts:* schematic, scripted structure; filtering out of detail; convergence upon salient elements within generic spatio-temporal contexts. Both memories and tradition are economical bearers of judgments, evaluations, and affects. The enactment of tradition and the recollection of memories occur in and for present contexts. We will see now that when memories are externalized into the social realm through communication, they rise to a still more tangible level of culturally-mediated, narrative expression.

25 Craik, "On the Making of Episodes," 55–6; Strauss/Quinn, *Cognitive Theory*, 47; Koriat/Goldsmith/Pansky, "Memory Accuracy", 496. Koriat et al. cite S.T. Fiske: the rememberer is "a motivational tactician, choosing among a number of possible strategies, depending on current goals" (S.T. Fiske, "Social Cognition and Social Perception", *Annual Review of Psychology* 44 [1993] 155–94, on p. 172).

26 Craik, "On the Making of Episodes", 55. DiMaggio labels this phenomenon "deliberative cognition" ("Culture and Cognition", *ARS* 23 [1997] 263–87, on p. 271). Paul Thompson says that "[a]ccurate memory is much more likely when it meets a social interest and need" (*The Voice of the Past: Oral History* [3rd edn; Oxford: Oxford University Press, 2000], 132).

27 D.L. Schacter, *The Seven Sins of Memory: How the Mind Forgets and Remembers* (Boston/New York: Houghton Mifflin, 2001), 179; also Craik, "On the Making of Episodes", 53–4; Strauss/Quinn, *Cognitive Theory*, 93.

28 DiMaggio, "Culture and Cognition", 271; also Welzer: "Emotionen sind die zentralen Operatoren, mit deren Hilfe wir Erfahrungen als gut, schlecht, neutral, usw. bewerten und entsprechend in unserem Gedächtnis abspeichern" (*Gedächtnis*, 136). See also Schmidt on the "gefühlsmäßiger Aspekt" of cognitive schemas (*Kognitive Autonomie*, 170).

29 Welzer, *Gedächtnis*, 21.

Memory in Communications Media: Genres, Gattungen, Forms

Memories are socially mediated through communication. To this end they are conformed to formulaic and narrative patterns drawn from the repertoire of genres absorbed from the ambient culture. Genres are "[zugleich] kognitive und kommunikative Schemata"; they are "überindividuelle, intersubjektive wirksame Ordnungsmuster oder kognitive Programme" that by mediating between the cognitive and social spheres make successful social interaction and communication possible.[30] Genres, moreover, act back upon cognition: memory encoding and consolidation occur in and through communication.[31] Memory, Bruner and Feldman explain, "become[s] public by being based on narrative properties such as genre and plot type that are widely shared within a culture ... In this way private experiences ... are constituted meaningfully into a public and communicable form."[32] Welzer puts the point as follows:

> Gespräche ... scheinen also direkt die Organisation dessen zu beeinflussen, was aus der Menge des Wahrgenommenen eingespeichert wird und später abrufbar ist. Durch das gemeinsame Sprechen bekommt das Wahrgenommene eine strukturierte und kohärente Form – und diese Form scheint auch den Abruf der Erinnerung zu erleichtern.[33]

As internalized cognitive schemas genres help reduce diffuse experience to mnemonically efficient organization. They filter for salience and contribute to the distillation of affective, moral, and conceptual signification.[34] Oral historian Paul Thompson gives the example of retired Turinese workers who had been active in socialist movements. When sharing their memories, they "adopted the traditional form of a life-story similar to that used for saints ... and some of them even referred to this 'self-hagiography' as 'my confession'."[35] Much input to cognition from the social world is already

30 Schmidt, *Kognitive Autonomie*, 170; also Strauss/Quinn, *Cognitive Theory*, 49, and A. Erll/K. Seibel, "Gattungen, Formtraditionen und kulturelles Gedächtnis", in V. Nünning/A. Nünning (ed.), *Erzähltextanalyse und Gender Studies* (Weimar: Metzler, 2004) 180–208, on p. 189.

31 Welzer, *Gedächtnis*, 98; W. Hirst/D. Manier, "Remembering as Communication: A Family Recounts its Past", in D.C. Rubin (ed.), *Remembering Our Past: Studies in Autobiographical Memory* (Cambridge: Cambridge University Press, 1996) 271–90, on p. 271; similarly Q. Wang/M. Ross, "Culture and Memory", in *Handbook of Cultural Psychology*, 645–67, on p. 661 (prelinguistic children fail to form enduring memories).

32 J. Bruner/C. Fleisher Feldman, "Group Narrative as a Cultural Context of Autobiography", in *Remembering Our Past*, 291–317, on p. 293.

33 Welzer, *Gedächtnis*, 98.

34 Schmidt, *Kognitive Autonomie*, 168; C. Fleisher Feldman, "Genres as Mental Models", in M. Ammaniti/D. Stern (ed.), *Psychoanalysis and Development: Representations and Narratives* (New York: New York University Press, 1994), 111–22, on p. 117; also Erll/Seibel, "Gattungen", 190–91.

35 Thompson, *Voice of the Past*, 277–8; also E. Tonkin, *Narrating our Pasts: The Social Construction of Oral History* (Cambridge: Cambridge University Press, 1992), 86.

shaped by cultural patterns, scripts, and genres, so this is not a matter of cognition impressing cultural and conceptual form upon wholly amorphous perceptual data. Cultural genres stabilize unstable cognitive processes, and owing to their dedicated communicative functions they give memories intelligible and durable form.[36]

Zimmermann points out the connection to tradition-formation: "Gattungen haben als Erinnerungsmedien also eine traditionsstiftende Funktion."[37] The genres implicated in the cognitive formation of memory belong to the repertoire of genres and narrative scripts one also finds in a body of tradition, though naturally we are still some way from describing the emergence of a normative body of tradition. Our next step, therefore, is to discover something about the emergence of shared memories within groups.

From "Collaborative Remembering" to Tradition Artifacts

Researchers increasingly take the view that what is called "collaborative remembering" is best studied in genuine communities rather than in nominal subject groups constituted ad hoc for lab experiments.[38] Analysis has shown, for example, that when collaborative remembering occurs in real communities, the problem of "social contagion" – false memories of one member infecting the memories of all the members – "is greatly reduced or even eliminated."[39] Community identity is grounded in a shared past. Remembering is a high stakes activity: commemoration.[40] Family memory is a diagnostic case. Welzer explains:

> [D]ie kommunikative Vergegenwärtigung von Vergangenem in der Familie ist kein bloßer Weitergabe von Erlebnissen und Ereignissen, sondern immer auch eine

36 Schmidt, *Kognitive Autonomie*, 168. Memory latency refers to memory in an unactualized state. As Vittoria Borsò points out, there is more to memory than what is brought to a public symbolic, communicable form ("Gedächtnis und Medialität: Die Herausforderung der Alterität. Eine medienphilosophische und medienhistorische Perspektivierung des Gedächtnis-Begriffs," in V. Borsò/G. Krumeich/B. Witte [ed.], *Medialität und Gedächtnis: interdisziplinäre Beiträge zur kulturellen Verarbeitung europäischer Krisen* [Weimar: Metzler, 2001], 23–54, on p. 53). See also Aleida and Jan Assmann's distinction between "bewohnte" and "unbewohnte Erinnerungen" ("Das Gestern im Heute: Medien und soziales Gedächtnis", in *Wirklichkeit der Medien,* 114–40, on p. 122).

37 R. Zimmermann, "Gleichnisse als Medien der Jesuserinnerung: Die Historizität der Jesusparabeln im Horizont der Gedächtnisforschung", in R. Zimmerman (ed.), *Hermeneutik der Gleichnisse Jesu: Methodische Neuansätze zum Verstehen urchristlicher Parabeltexte.* (WUNT 231; Tübingen: Mohr-Siebeck, 2008), 87–121, on p. 109.

38 C.B. Harris/H.M. Paterson/R.I. Kemp, "Collaborative Recall and Collective Memory: What Happens When We Remember Together", *Memory* 16 (2008) 213–30, on p. 223

39 Sutton/Harris/Keil, "Psychology of Memory", 548–9.

40 Welzer, *Gedächtnis*, 151.

gemeinsame Praxis, die die Familie als eine Gruppe definiert, die eine besondere Geschichte hat.[41]

The social and emotional bonds that hold communities together, Wang points out, are particularly reliant upon commemorative practices.[42] Groups employ specific strategies to subsume individual contributions into shared representations.[43] But these representations display *emergent* rather than additive properties; that is, they are not an aggregate of individual recollections. Rather, they distill out the existential and moral significance of an experienced event into an integral, shared representation.[44] Emergent representations thereby overcome the limitations of unreflective, notoriously unstable eyewitness memories with their fragmented, idiosyncratic perspectives. Commemorative remembering converges on elements salient to the social and moral identity of the community; thus it is a simple matter of course that discrete individual recollections with their particularistic elements get filtered out.[45] Commemorative remembering interacts with the wider cultural field of symbols, master narratives, genres, and topoi. These shape emergent representations and infuse them with rich cultural signification and intelligibility.[46]

Here we are coming within view of a normative tradition, mediated in conventional cultural forms, emerging out of commemorative remembering. In the anthropological literature one occasionally finds real-time descriptions of this process. Maurice Bloch's sudden return to his adoptive Madagascar village after an unexplained absence of three years triggered an explanatory crisis for the community: his absence had to be given moral intelligibility in a culturally scripted way. Shortly after his return his adoptive village family hosted a series of formal social calls by individual residents of the village, during which Bloch recounted the story of his departure and return. He found

41 Welzer, *Gedächtnis*, 151.

42 Q. Wang, "On the Cultural Constitution of Collective Memory", *Memory* 16 (2008) 305–17, on p. 309.

43 Sutton/Harris/Keil, "Psychology of Memory", 547–8; see L.M. van Swol, "Performance and Process in Collective and Individual Memory: The Role of Social Decision Schemes and Memory Bias in Collective Memory", *Memory* 16 (2008) 274–87, on p. 275.

44 Sutton/Harris/Keil, "Psychology of Memory", 547–8.

45 Harris/Paterson/Kemp, "Collaborative Recall", 225–6; DiMaggio, "Culture and Cognition", 271. R. Thomas (*Oral Tradition and Written Record in Classical Athens* [Cambridge/New York: Cambridge University Press, 1989]) analyzes how in ancient Athens family tradition "grows up from the reminiscences of one relative to another" (97). Along the way, "casual reminiscences" related to the salient event are shed as those aspects of the memories that resonate with the moral traditions of the polis move to the fore (118).

46 E. Reese/R. Fivush, "The Development of Collective Remembering", *Memory* 16 (2008) 201–12, on p. 202; also Tonkin, *Narrating Our Pasts*, 60; and Erll, *Memory in Culture*, 106: "[T]he creation of collective-autobiographical memories always takes place against the backdrop of existing cultural semantics."

that members of the family were actively coaxing his iterations of the narrative into a stereotyped, condensed, and increasingly invariable form. He explains:

> At every repetition what I could say and could not say became clearer and clearer ... This [emergent narrative] transformed the total arbitrariness of my coming ... into an apparently inevitable and morally appropriate sequence ... The narrative was very poor on information but very strong on the reestablishment of order ... [T]he construction of the narrative abolished the specificity of time by reordering and making the past follow a predefined pattern [and] it did this by dissolving the specificity of events into a prototypical present.[47]

The script enacted by the narrative conformed to the *Tantara* genre, a story that emphasizes morally significant elements of a past event at the expense of specific details and thus takes on timeless, exemplary qualities.[48] Elizabeth Tonkin notes that the harrowing experiences of British paratrooper William Deakin, who parachuted into Montenegro to assist Yugoslav partisans, were cast by the locals into the "existing rhetoric" of the "local epic tradition".[49] The anthropologist Liisa Malkki observed tradition formation occurring in real time in refugee camps in Tanzania, among Hutu who had just fled from the genocide in Burundi:

> Accounts of these key events very quickly circulated among the refugees, and, often, in a matter of days, acquired what can be characterized as "standard versions" in the telling and retelling ... they were accounts which, while becoming increasingly formulaic, also became more didactic and progressively more implicated in, and indicative of, something beyond them.[50]

These became "moral ordering stories" in the post-genocide moral universe of the refugees.[51]

We see that tradition artifacts, emerging out of commemorative enterprises, function as *cultural symbols:* dense concentrations of social and moral signification, freed of all but the barest historical contextualization, stabilized in expressive media forms. Symbols – to use Sapir's definition – are "condensations" of meaning, or in Geertz's fuller formulation, "vehicles for a conception ... abstractions from experience fixed in perceptible forms,

47 M.E.F. Bloch, *How We Think They Think: Anthropological Approaches to Cognition, Memory, and Literacy* (Boulder, CO: Westview Press, 1998), 104–5.

48 Bloch, *How We Think They Think*, 108: "What the Malagasy stress most about Tantara is its categorical 'truth' which also conveys its moral value."

49 Tonkin, *Narrating Our Pasts*, 60: "[T]he teller 'codes' memories or reports of remembered events into existent stereotopic forms."

50 L.H. Malkki, *Purity and Exile: Violence, Memory, and National Cosmology among Hutu Refugees in Tanzania* (Chicago/London: University of Chicago Press, 1995), 106. Jan Vansina writes, "[G]roup traditions can be created quite rapidly after the events and acquire a form which strikingly makes such a tradition part of a complex of traditions" (*Oral Tradition as History* [Madison: University of Wisconsin Press, 1985], 20).

51 Malkki, *Purity and Exile*, 244. See also Wang, "Cultural Constitution of Collective Memory", 309.

concrete embodiments of ideas, attitudes, judgments, longings, or beliefs."[52] Tradition artifacts are symbolic entities that express and disseminate, or as Jan Assmann puts it, make "visible … permanent, and transmittable", the defining elements of a community's moral universe.[53]

Here let us pause again to take stock. Evolutionary psychologist Merlin Donald remarks on the apparent "simplicity" of "the underlying cognitive processes that support the emergence of complex human cultural features".[54] Having started with cognitive processes in the formation of memory we find ourselves, without crossing any great divide, in the external realm of cultural artifacts. Having traced the line from cognitive processes to cultural artifacts, we are now in a position to enquire more fully into the *converse* effects of mediated cultural artifacts back upon cognitive processes.

Cognitive-Cultural Coupling: Tradition as Cybernetic Memory

"Cognitive-cultural coupling" is shorthand for the ways in which neurobiological cognition co-opts cultural artifacts to greatly extend its cognitive capacities. "Brain-artefact interface" is Malafouris's term for the same phenomenon.[55] "The very simplest cases [of cognitive-cultural coupling]", writes Andy Clark, "are those that involve the use of external symbolic media to offload memory onto the world."[56] Consolidating memory representationally in external media – or "exograms", in Merlin Donald's coinage[57] – drastically reduces the cognitive load on the brain. These symbolic artifacts in turn are appropriated right into the internal cognitive apparatus: they take on a cognitive existence and functionality. This is seen most clearly in the case of language, a symbolic cultural artifact. Clark explains:

> Understanding language … involves getting to grips with a special kind of coordination dynamics: one in which the actual material structures of public language … play a key and irreducible role … involving a complex interplay between

52 E. Sapir, *Selected Writings of Edward Sapir* (Berkeley/Los Angeles: University of California Press, 1949), 564; C. Geertz, *The Interpretation of Cultures* (New York: Basic Books, 1973), 91.

53 J. Assmann, "Form as Mnemonic Device: Cultural Texts and Cultural Memory", in R.A. Horsley/ J.A. Draper/J.M. Foley (ed.), *Performing the Gospel: Orality, Memory, and Mark* (Minneapolis: Fortress, 2006) 67–82, on p. 70.

54 M. Donald, "Hominid Enculturation and Cognitive Evolution", in C. Renfrew/C. Scarre (ed.), *Cognition and Material Culture: The Archaeology of Symbolic Storage* (Cambridge: MacDonald Institute for Archaeological Research, 1998) 7–18, on p. 13.

55 Malafouris, "Brain-Artefact Interface (BAI)", 264–73.

56 A. Clark, *Being There: Putting Brain, Body, and World Together Again* (Cambridge, MA: MIT Press, 1997), 201.

57 M. Donald, *Origins of the Modern Mind: Three Stages in the Evolution of Culture and Cognition* (Cambridge, MA: Harvard University Press, 1991), 315–16.

internal biological resources and external non-biological resources. Language ... occupies a wonderfully ambiguous position on any hybrid cognitive stage, since it seems to straddle the internal-external borderline itself, looking one moment like any other piece of biological equipment, and at the next like a particularly potent piece of external cognitive scaffolding.[58]

This is a matter of "the *complementary* action of actual material symbols (and the image-like encodings of such symbols) and more biologically basic modes of internal representation."[59] Tradition is likewise a symbolically-dense cultural artifact, emerging out of cognitive processes, and circulating in oral, written, ritual, and material media. In its enactment it acts recursively back upon the neural plasticity of the brain. This brings about, as Malafouris describes it, an "extensive structural rewiring either by fine-tuning of existing brain pathways or by generating new connections within brain regions."[60] The cognitive effect is to "drive, sculpt, and discipline the internal representational regime."[61] Memory engrams are relatively unstable: a matter of reconstructive pattern completion across plastic and associative neural networks constituted by variable connection weights. These connection weights, however, can be strengthened. Encounters with external memory representations, mediated in stable cultural formats, shape and stabilize the corresponding neurobiological memory networks.[62] The result is enduring modifications to one's cognitive

58 A. Clark, "Material Symbols", *Philosophical Psychology* 19 (2006) 291–307, on p. 293.

59 Clark, "Material Symbols", 304; Sutton makes a similar point: "[N[either ... must artefacts operate in precisely the same way as brains do nor exactly mimic neural processing profiles" ("Material Agency", 41).

60 Malafouris, "Brain-Artefact Interface", 266; similarly J. Sutton, "Material Agency, Skills, and History: Distributed Cognition and the Archeology of Memory", in C. Knappett/L. Malafouris (ed.), *Material Agency: Toward a Non-anthropocentric Approach* (New York: Springer, 2007) 37–55, on pp. 37–8; A. Clark, "Word, Niche, and Super-Niche: How Language Makes Minds Matter More", *Theoria* 54 (2005) 655–68, on p. 264.

61 Clark, "Word, Niche, and Super-Niche", 264. It would be remiss not to mention the contemporary debate among cognitive scientists and philosophers of mind (with members of both disciplines found on both sides of the debate) over the problems of "cognitivism". Cognitivism is the attempt to explain meaning, abstraction, and symbolic capacities reductively as neurological states ("embodied cognition"). The problem is how meaning, i.e., symbolic representation, which involves abstraction and intentionality, can be grounded in neurological, physical, states. A good introduction to this debate is A. Gomila, "Mending or Abandoning Cognitivism?" in M. de Vega/A.M. Glenburg/A.C. Graesser (ed.), *Meaning and Cognition* (Oxford: Oxford University Press, 2008) 357–74. Closely related is the running debate between Clark, Sutton, and others who take the "extended mind" position, and critics like Adams and Aizawa who question whether external artifacts can bear the "mark of the cognitive", and to what extent posited cognitive-cultural couplings are empirically tractable (e.g. F. Adams/K. Aizawa, "Defending the Bounds of Cognition", in R. Menary [ed.], *The Extended Mind* [Cambridge, MA.: MIT Press, 2010] 67–81).

62 J. Sutton, "Exograms and Interdisciplinarity: History, the Extended Mind, and the Civilizing Process", in *The Extended Mind*, 189–225, on p. 205.

apparatus.[63] Indeed, the commemorative production and dissemination of tradition artifacts is a cultural strategy for stabilizing and ensuring the transmission of salient memory. These materials, moreover, are now immanent to cognitive operations in the stabilized representational format afforded by their cultural mediation.[64] Tradition is an exemplary case of cognitive-cultural coupling. It emerges as a set of meaning-laden forms out of cognitive memory processes and circulates externally in various media forms apt for cycling back into cognition. Tradition can with justice be called *cybernetic memory.*

Whatever Happened to the Eyewitness Memories?

Our discussion thus far has been carried out very much at the theoretical level. But let us pause to look at a problem that directly connects our theorizing to the synoptic tradition: the absence in the tradition of recognizable traces of individual eyewitness testimony, an issue in recent years taken up again in studies by R. Bauckham, R. McIver, and others.[65] This absence seems to confirm the categorical distinction form criticism made between memory and the tradition, between the individual and the social.[66] Cognitive-cultural coupling allows us to give an economical explanation of this absence and at the same time confirms the sound intuition that memory must somehow have been a principal factor in the origins of the tradition.

The reason is that tradition is neurally assimilated such that it *displaces* individual eyewitness memory: tradition becomes the cognitive basis for individual recollection. This displacement effect, or more precisely, inhibition effect, has been observed in empirical studies. In one a group was given the task of collaborative remembering of shared experiences. In subsequent *individual* recall the participants easily retrieved the *collaboratively*-recon-

63 Sutton, "Remembering", 229; also Clark, *Being There*, 61, 198–9; E. Hutchins, "Material Anchors for Conceptual Blends", *JP* 37 (2005) 1555–77, on p. 1575.

64 L. Malafouris/C. Renfrew, "The Cognitive Life of Things: Archaeology, Material Engagement, and the Extended Mind", in L. Malafouris/C. Renfrew (ed.), *The Cognitive Life of Things: Recasting the Boundaries of the Mind* (Cambridge: MacDonald Institute of Archaeology, 2010) 1–12, on pp. 6–7.

65 R. Bauckham, *Jesus and the Eyewitnesses: The Gospels as Eyewitness Testimony* (Grand Rapids & Cambridge: Eerdmans, 2006); R. McIver, *Memory, Jesus, and the Synoptic Gospels* (Atlanta: SBL Press, 2011). For analysis of these and other recent efforts toward restoring the link between the tradition and eyewitness memory see A. Kirk, "The Memory-Tradition Nexus in the Synoptic Tradition: Memory, Media, and Symbolic Representation," in T. Thatcher (ed.), *Memory and Identity in Ancient Judaism and Early Christianity: A Conversation with Barry Schwartz* (Atlanta: SBL Press, 2014) 131–60.

66 See D.E. Nineham, "Eyewitness Testimony and the Gospel Tradition", *JTS* n.s. 9 (1958) 13–25, 243–52; *JTS* n.s. 11 (1960) 253–64.

structed memories. But now they had difficulty retrieving their *personal* recollections that had not been taken up into these shared representations. In other words, individual recollection converges on shared representations.[67] Subjects in another experiment learned information from two domains, then rehearsed the information from just one of those domains. Unsurprisingly they best recalled information from the rehearsed domain. But the surprising finding was that memory for "unrehearsed information from the same domain as the information that was rehearsed is now worse than the information from the (other) domain that wasn't rehearsed at all." In other words, "retrieving some information ... induces forgetting of associated information ... as a result of either interference or inhibition."[68] Commemorative remembering in a community is a powerful means of reinforcement; it has "enduring and transformative effects on the participants' individual memories, which converge on the same shared representation of the past."[69] Through rehearsal tradition artifacts take on a stable cognitive existence, displacing, overwriting, or fine-tuning an individual's unstable and less integrated personal memory traces.[70]

This *cognitive* phenomenon has a value-added *cultural* effect. It clears away the clutter of a person's less relevant individual memory traces. Conversely, it selects for salience: the constitutive elements of shared representations are those that are highly salient to the groups that rehearse them.[71] Tradition becomes the cognitive basis for memory. In becoming the cognitive basis for memory, it becomes the cognitive basis of an individual's cultural identity.[72] Solitary individual remembering is exchanged for participation in a moral community formed by a shared past.

67 Harris/Paterson/Kemp, "Collaborative Recall", 220.

68 Sutton/Harris/Keil, "Psychology of Memory", 545.

69 Sutton/Harris/Keil, "Psychology of Memory", 546 (in reference to collaborative remembering studies); see also Welzer, *Gedächtnis*, 99.

70 Loveday Alexander says in reference to Xenophon's *Life* of Socrates: "Xenophon could justly claim to be writing on the basis of his own personal recollection of Socrates. But a glance at Xenophon's work makes it clear ... that even within one generation, memory, however personal in origin, is already molded by the literary forms and expectations of the larger society" ("Memory and Tradition in the Hellenistic Schools", in W.H. Kelber/S. Byrskog (ed.), *Jesus in Memory: Traditions in Oral and Scribal Perspectives* [Waco: Baylor University Press, 2009] 113–53, on p. 121).

71 L. Hasher, "Inhibition: Attentional Regulation of Cognition", *Science of Memory*, 291–4, on p. 292.

72 Strauss/Quinn, *Cognitive Theory*, 123. Culturally-acquired schemas are already active in the formation of individual memories, so the distinction between the two is already indistinct. Note that the transmutation and eliding of individual memories in commemorative remembering, and then the assimilation of the shared representations back into individual cognition, confirms the *symbiotic* nature of the relationship of "episodic" memory (specific events, times, places) with "semantic" memory (generalized knowledge). It shows how memory and tradition can be intimately connected at the same time as it accounts for why the synoptic tradition does not retain features of individual episodic memory.

Cognitive displacement does not mean that an eyewitness's personal memories are erased. Under other conditions, not defined by the commemorative *Sitz*, and with the appropriate cues, such individuals might well be capable of remembering in the genre of an *ad hoc* personal account.[73] But the latter has little cultural value. It does not carry in itself the symbolic weight and significance of events. It is transient, except as it has been taken up into the tradition of the community. Hence eyewitnesses themselves might not give much importance to their personal memories.[74]

Tradition as an Autonomous Cognitive System

The media forms of a tradition, cognitively internalized, stabilize and shape neurobiological memory processes. We have seen that tradition artifacts are meaning-laden symbolic entities. The assimilation of tradition into memory creates the conditions for higher-order cognitive operations, for conceptual and moral reasoning, utilizing this internalized system of symbols.[75] Stability of mental representations is essential to advanced cognition.[76] Tradition formation is a process of abstracting salient, normative elements and patterns from originating realities and resolving these into simple representational wholes, in turn cycled back into memory. The effect, as Terrence Deacon puts it, is an "increasingly indirect linkage between symbolic mental representation and its grounds of reference".[77] Clark describes this aptly as "fix[ing] the ideas at a high level of abstraction from the idiosyncratic details of their proximal origins in sensory input".[78] The indirect, representational relationship of the tradition to its historical grounds vastly reduces the load on memory and by the same token greatly extends the scope for cognitive operations – now directly with the tradition. As symbolic entities, tradition artifacts operate at two levels of reference: *indirectly* and *implicitly* to their

73 Bloch, *How We Think They Think*, 107–8.

74 We note that if the history of the synoptic tradition proceeded, as form criticism supposed, without a vital connection to memory, and, accordingly, was formed by extensive *de novo* creation and importation of materials, then the absence in it of traces of eyewitness recollection would on cognitive grounds be inexplicable, for such a tradition could not cognitively displace individual memory. We can say this without begging the question of the historicity of the tradition.

75 Clark, "Word, Niche, and Super-niche", 263–4; idem, *Being There*, 209.

76 E. Hutchins, "Material Anchors", 1557. E.J. Lowe argues that symbols are artifacts that represent and embody concepts, and thus enable abstract thought and analysis ("Personal Experience and Belief: the Significance of External Symbolic Storage for the Emergence of Modern Human Cognition", in *Cognition and Material Culture*, 89–96).

77 T.W. Deacon, *The Symbolic Species: The Co-Evolution of Language and the Brain* (New York/London: Norton, 1997), 454.

78 Clark, *Being There*, 210.

empirical (i.e. historical) referents, but *directly* with one another as a configurable system of symbols.[79] This is the much-remarked *autonomy* of the tradition. Tradition maintains its indexical reference to historical realities but operates free from them, at what Deacon calls a "superordinate" level. Tradition amounts to symbolic mediation of the past: it subsumes normative elements of the past freed of all but barest spatio-temporal contextualization. This intensifies the cultural effects of the formative historical realities exponentially. Tradition's decoupling from its originating contexts is what renders it capable of ongoing normative engagement with the shifting historical and social horizons of its tradent communities. It frees cognition from being tied down to laborious and pointless recapitulation of past events in all their diffuse detail. Higher-order cognitive operations can now be performed with this stable yet versatile system of symbolic representations.[80] In short, it is by virtue of its autonomy, its coalescing in mnemonically efficient, durable representational forms loosened from originating historical contexts, and made proof against the vagaries of individual memory, that tradition is able to operate, much like language itself, as an internally ordered, "superordinate" system of symbols, as a living cognitive system, the elements of which are capable of being brought into new combinations and mobilized to meet new challenges that arise with shifts in a community's historical and social horizons. Tradition makes it possible for a community to engage in higher-order cognitive reflection on present predicaments. It makes available the moral resources for comprehending and mastering present realities, and thereby it ensures the transmission of a cultural identity.

Oral and Written Media

The oral medium and the written medium extend cognition in overlapping but different ways. Rubin has shown that the genres of an oral tradition are mnemonic systems of cues and constraints that exploit memory's cognitive efficiencies for ease of mental encoding and activation.[81] The stabilization afforded when a tradition is disseminated in a material, visual medium – such as writing – opens it up to a more complex range of cognitive operations. "Problems that are too complex to hold in mind as a cultural model", Hutchins

79 Deacon, *Symbolic Species*, 301–2.
80 Hutchins, "Material Anchors", 1573–4.
81 D.C. Rubin, *Memory in Oral Traditions: The Cognitive Psychology of Epic, Ballads, and Counting-out Rhymes* (New York/Oxford: Oxford University Press, 1995): "Oral tradition must, therefore, have developed forms of organization (i.e., rules, redundancies, constraints) and strategies to decrease the changes that human memory imposes on the more casual transmission of verbal material" (10).

explains, "… can be expressed and manipulated in material structure."[82] Clark elaborates on the media effects of writing on cognition:

> By writing down our ideas we generate a trace in a format that opens up a range of new possibilities. We can then inspect and re-inspect the same ideas … We can hold the original ideas steady … and safely experiment with subtle alterations. We can store them in ways that allow us to compare and combine them with other complexes of ideas … [T]he real properties of the physical text transform the space of possible thoughts.[83]

Even here though a still deeper level of cognitive interface with material artifacts becomes possible. Hutchins continues:

> A final turn in this path is that when a material structure becomes very familiar, it may be possible to imagine the material structure when it is not present in the environment. It is even possible to imagine systematic transformations applied to such a representation … Beginning as external representations physically embodied and operated on with manual skills, we learn to imagine them and to operate on the imagined structures.[84]

In other words, written artifacts can themselves be internalized and operationalized in memory. For those of us interested in the written transmission of the gospel tradition this brings to mind scribal competencies and practices, though we cannot pursue that line of enquiry further here.

Making Sense of the Synoptic Tradition

We have approached the formation of the synoptic tradition by stepping back and reflecting upon tradition as a cognitive and cultural phenomenon. Naturally, it is impossible to go back and observe the emergence of the synoptic tradition. But its profile indicates that it owes its formation to the cognitive and cultural operations that we have described. We have accounted for two of its most striking features – the absence in it of traces of eyewitness testimony, and its remarkable autonomy (recognized but misunderstood by the form critics). The cognitive/cultural model would also predict that the forms of the tradition correspond to different Jewish and Hellenistic genres, such as the *chreia*, and also its shaping and deep coloring by the "Great Tradition", that is, its permeation by the ambient biblical and early Jewish

82 Hutchins, "Material Anchors", 1574.

83 Clark, *Being There*, 208; similarly R.A. Wilson/A. Clark, "How To Situate Cognition: Letting Nature Take Its Course", in *Cambridge Handbook of Situated Cognition*, 55–77, on p. 64.

84 Hutchins, "Material Anchors", 1575; also Clark, *Being There*, 198–9; Malafouris, "Cognitive Basis of Material Engagement", 57.

narrative and moral tradition. Commemorative remembering, the matrix for an emergent tradition, always draws upon deep sources of cultural signification, a cognitive process facilitated by the dynamism of neurological networks: the rapid forming of associative connections between new memory patterns and established ones. Indeed, the Jesus tradition is so deeply connected into scriptural and corollary cultural tradition that the boundaries between them can be difficult to draw.

Cognitive analysis calls into question one-sidedly homeostatic views of the tradition – of the sort that make out the synoptic tradition to be largely the product of contemporizing theological and social interests, and its connection to the past little more than an ideological construct. Cultural schemas, artifacts, and representations shape cognition at a deep level. These cultural patterns take on a deep-seated neuronal existence.[85] Innovation can only occur along the lines of these existing cognitive patterns, otherwise it will fail to get any cognitive traction, any cognitive foothold for intelligibility, in the tradent group. "Even when intent on reinventing themselves", Strauss and Quinn observe, "people do not pluck new cultural forms out of the air ... [N]ew forms are still always incorporated, rejected, and remade in terms of previous schemas."[86] Present realities are only cognizable through existing cultural schemas: tradent communities think and act through their tradition. The synoptic tradition can therefore scarcely be reduced to a byproduct of sociological processes at work in community *Sitze*.

The cognitive/cultural model also helps account for the synoptic tradition's curious patterns of variation and agreement. The stabilization tradition affords to memory does not cancel the context-sensitivity of memory activation. Rather, it disciplines and channels it. What Clark says of the cognitive effect of language can similarly be stipulated of tradition:

> [S]treams of words act as reliable signposts to recovered meanings, while still allowing those meanings to shift and color according to context. Sustaining this balance between rote retrieval and anarchic context-sensitivity is ... the key trick that public language performs for minds like ours.[87]

Strauss and Quinn characterize neural network activity grounded in cultural schemas as "regulated improvisation": *improvisational* because reactivations of neural patterns are always context-sensitive; *regulated* because these activations "are guided by previously learned patterns of associations".[88] This aptly describes how tradition brings the normative weight of the past to bear upon contemporary contexts of the tradent community, and it is a principal factor in the rise of patterns of variation and agreement in the tradition.

85 Strauss/Quinn, *Cognitive Theory*, 90.
86 Strauss/Quinn, *Cognitive Theory*, 25–6.
87 Clark, "Word, Niche, and Super-Niche", 264.
88 Strauss/Quinn, *Cognitive Theory*, 54.

A cognitive and cultural approach to the history of the tradition also gives potential leverage on source-critical problems. We noted briefly that the cognitive assimilation of written artifacts, and their operationalization as memory artifacts, connects to well-attested scribal practices. This suggests that synoptic source-critical problems might be become more tractable if reframed within a scribal *Sitz.*

Finally, when Luke or Matthew for example transpose the order of Markan episodes, or when John displaces the Temple Cleansing from the end to the beginning of Jesus' ministry, they are treating their tradition as a configurable, autonomous system of symbols. At the same time, it is the connection of this system of symbols to its grounds in the formative past that licenses actions of this sort and indeed makes them possible.

We began by noting the initiative in a number of disciplines to overcome the dichotomy of the individual and the social, the cognitive and the cultural, a dichotomy that has been a definitive feature of the form-critical model for the synoptic tradition. The synoptic tradition is a paradigm case of cognitive-cultural interface, "a privileged area" (to borrow Bloch's words) "for seeing how public, historically created cultural representations join private representations".[89] Without gainsaying the enduring importance of many of the insights of form criticism, it is hoped that this analysis has contributed to putting our working models for the origins and history of the tradition on more solid theoretical ground.

89 Bloch, *How We Think They Think*, 82. In this respect the analysis has contributed, I hope, to the critique of the neurological reductionist program of what Sutton describes as the "narrower forms of evolutionary psychology" (Sutton, "Exograms", 192), and Malafouris as the "sterile neurocentrism" that reduces cultural and cognitive phenomena to neuroimaging scans of brain activity (Malafouris, "Brain-Artefact Interface", 270).

Sandra Huebenthal

Reading the Gospel of Mark as Collective Memory

The appearance of social memory theory in Biblical Studies is something that can be regarded as good news. A lot of work has been done in the recent years, especially in the realm of hermeneutics – the introduction of Maurice Halbwachs' and Aleida and Jan Assmann's works to an audience of Biblical scholars, for example, the coining of models and suggestions how to apply their trajectories to biblical texts.[1] Despite all of this effort, the memory approach seems to have gained much more currency in Jesus research than in traditional exegetical work and, even if applied to New Testament texts, questions are rather directed towards what actually happened than to the memory of those events.[2]

What seems to make matters even more difficult is the fact that the memory approach has lately become occupied by a certain strand of Jesus research, which uses recent neuro-scientific research on group memory to foster the hypothesis that the Early Christians were reliable eyewitnesses whose testimony is treasured in the Gospels. This approach aims to form eyewitness-models which rest on positivist foundations and is, thus, prone to return to the idea that the Gospels are reliable and objective testimonies or reports on how things really happened.[3] It would be obvious to point out that this

1 The research field was at first charted by Alan Kirk and Tom Thatcher, following the ideas of Werner H. Kelber. Cf. A. Kirk/T. Thatcher (ed.), *Memory, Tradition, and Text* (Semeia Studies 52; Atlanta: Society of Biblical Literature, 2005). Following their lead, an enormous number of studies on various aspects of the question has emerged.

2 Samuel Byrskog has rightly observed that "Social memory approaches are frequently being used in the humanities and social sciences. By contrast, despite the intriguing comments by Dunn and others, they have rarely been employed in the scientific works with the Jesus tradition and the Gospels. The scholars who advocate a social memory approach to the Jesus tradition fail to pursue it consistently and mostly refer to the flexible phenomenon of oral performance. Those interested in reconstructing the identity of the Gospel communities make no distinction between subgroups within the community and the social setting of authorship and the intended audience. They insist on the redaction-critical modes of historical reconstruction and read the Gospels as one-dimensional imprints of social realities. The sociological study of the Jesus tradition and the Gospels has been amazingly uncritical of its form- and redaction-critical basis and allegorizing tendencies". S. Byrskog, "A New Quest for the *Sitz im Leben:* Social Memory, the Jesus Tradition and the Gospel of Matthew", *NTS* 52 (2006) 319–36, on p. 320.

3 For a first impression cf. R.K. McIver, "Eyewitnesses as Guarantors of the Accuracy of Gospel Traditions in the Light of Psychological Research", *JBL* 131 (2012) 529–46; for the discussion of the ideas cf. J.C.S. Redman, "How Accurate are Eyewitnesses? Bauckham and the Eyewitnesses in

approach fails to take into account the overall constructivist condition of recollection and memory. What I find somewhat disturbing is the fact that that the question whether we are dealing with the contributions of eyewitnesses at all is rarely critically asked. If one engages in a discussion of whether or not the eyewitnesses could have been reliable witnesses, one may quite often be misunderstood as having accepted this assumption from the outset. When it comes to the task of understanding the Gospels *memorywise*, the eyewitness debate is only a side show, even though at times a very noisy one. It is nevertheless time to focus the attention back to the main stage and address the question of what it actually means to read and interpret biblical texts as memory texts. If we take seriously Samuel Byrskog's notion that "the social memory approach may provide a 'memory-critical' repertoire which opens up a new framework for studying the social dynamics reflected in the Gospel narrative",[4] we need to consider other hermeneutical and methodological steps.

This contribution aims to read the Gospel of Mark as a memory text, or, to be more specific, as an externalization of collective memory. As I have recently lined out my understanding of *social memory theory and biblical texts* elsewhere,[5] I limit myself here to a brief hermeneutical sketch before I turn to an exemplary reading of Mark as collective memory, and reflections about the possibilities for the reader(s) to familiarize. After a second glance at the technical side of the narration, my considerations will close with a brief evaluation of whether or not Mark's idea worked out.

Social Memory Theory and the New Testament

Memory does not preserve the past as such, but only parts in a certain perspective, which can be learned both from neuro-sciences and cognitive

the Light of Psychological Research", *JBL* 129 (2010) 177–97; J.S. Kloppenborg, "Memory, Performance, and the Sayings of Jesus", *JSHJ* 10 (2012) 97–132. How difficult and at times disappointing the discussion of this approach can be could also be gathered from a paper Joseph Verheyden gave in the newly installed seminar "Memory, Narrative, and Christology in the Synoptic Gospels" at the SNTS Meeting in Szeged (2014), in which he raised some serious questions and received answers by Robert McIver that both he and the majority of the audience found quite unsatisfactory.

4 Byrskog, "A New Quest", 321.

5 Cf. S. Hübenthal, *Das Markusevangelium als kollektives Gedächtnis* (FRLANT 253; Göttingen: Vandenhoeck & Ruprecht, 2014); S. Hübenthal, "Social and Cultural Memory in Biblical Exegesis. The Quest for an Adequate Application", in P. Carstens et al. (ed.), *Cultural Memory in Biblical Exegesis* (Perspectives on Hebrew Scriptures and its Contexts 17; Piscataway: Gorgias, 2012), 191–216. Further: S. Hübenthal, Articles "Social Memory", "Communicative Memory", "Collective Memory" and "Cultural Memory", in T. Thatcher/C. Keith/R.F.Jr. Person/E. Stern (ed.), *Dictionary of the Bible in Ancient Media* (London: T&T Clark, 2016, forthcoming).

studies. When these parts are recalled, they will not be re-found but constructed anew according to the needs of those who recall them.[6] This also implies that the construction of the past, regardless of whether it is undertaken by an individual or a group will not manage without creative elements in line with the social environment or framework where the past is actualized. Recollection and memory have a deeply pragmatic side to them: the past is always constructed according to the (needs of) the present.

According to Halbwachs, this social framework consists of *mémoire collective* or *collective memory.*[7] The individual locates his/her memories within this frame in order to be able to understand, interpret and communicate them. The act of remembering itself is not transferred from the individual to the group during this process; the group only provides the frame for perception and judgment. Therefore, the following is essential: in the same way as a single event only gains its place and meaning when it is seen in the context of other events, a structure can only develop when several events are connected.[8] The interdependence of event and structure also entails the changeableness of social frames – and thus implicitly the changeability of memory. Because the structure is determined by the events, new or recent events always have the potential to change the structure as well as the frame.

Halbwachs' findings achieve two goals. On the one hand, they explain the existence of social frames and how the need to place events within these frames may change the individual recollection of events. This process is called *social memory.*[9] On the other hand, they explain how social frames add to the (re-)construction of events or how mnemonic groups semanticize events though their frames. This process is called *collective memory.* Both processes

6 Jan Assmann nicely sums up Halbwachs' argument when he states "Die Vergangenheit existiert nur als soziale Konstruktion. Sie wird nur erinnert rekonstruiert, insoweit sie gebraucht wird". J. Assmann, "Halbwachs, Maurice", in N. Pethes/J. Ruchatz (ed.), *Gedächtnis und Erinnerung. Ein interdisziplinäres Lexikon* (Hamburg: Rowohlt, 2001) 247–9, on p. 248.

7 Initially introduced in M. Halbwachs, *La mémoire collective* (Bibliothèque de l'Évolution de l'Humanité 28; Paris: Presses Universitaires de France, 1949/1950). Exemplifications of the idea are to be found in M. Halbwachs, *La Topographie lègendaire des Èvangiles en Terre Sainte* (Paris: Presses Universitaires de France, 1941).

8 Cf. N. Pethes, *Kulturwissenschaftliche Gedächtnistheorien. Zur Einführung* (Hamburg: Junius, 2008) on p. 55: "Tatsächlich gewinnt eine individuelle Erinnerung ihren Inhalt erst durch Einordnung in eine kollektive Struktur, während die kollektive Struktur aus der Verallgemeinerung der Gemeinsamkeiten einzelner Inhalte entsteht. Jede Erinnerung gehört damit zugleich zwei Bereichen zu: demjenigen des individuellen Erinnerns und demjenigen seiner sozialen Bedeutung". In this context, Pethes also mentions that sociology, following Niklas Luhmann, only recently made explicit the logical relation of event and structure.

9 As Harald Welzer, one of the protagonists of German-speaking research on social memory puts is, its realm consists of the "Gesamtheit der sozialen Erfahrungen der Mitglieder einer Wir-Gruppe". H. Welzer, "Das soziale Gedächtnis", in H. Welzer, *Das soziale Gedächtnis. Geschichte, Erinnerung, Tradierung*, (Hamburg: Hamburger Edition, 2001) 9–21, on p. 15. Welzer refers back to P. Burke, "Geschichte als soziales Gedächtnis", in A. Assmann/D. Harth (ed.), *Mnemosyne. Formen und Funktionen kultureller Erinnerung* (Frankfurt: Fischer, 1991) 289–304, on p. 392 ff.

have in common that they deal with the placement of memories within social frames.

A pivotal innovation of Halbwachs' idea is that the concept of memory itself is detached from the idea of memory as a storehouse, which keeps all recollections in an irreversible place.[10] This paves the way to imagine both the composition and management of memories in a dynamic way. Halbwachs, thus, already conceived theoretically what empirical surveys on the construction of identity have shown much later both for individuals and intimate memory groups. In both cases, the actualization of the past is shaped according to the needs of the present. Memory is not an image or a decal of the past but a perspective and selective construct in which remembering and forgetting are equal partners.

The Halbwachsian distinction between *collective memory* and *social memory* consists also of the notion that *social memory* is a non-intentional dealing with the past while in *collective memory* the past is consciously recalled and shaped, as Harald Welzer has noted.[11] Media of *social memory* are more of an oral nature and usually not created in order to shape tradition, although they draw from the past and transport history. What divides them from actual texts is the fact that they do not consciously recall or actualize the past. A personal diary would thus be regarded as a medium of *social memory* while a family chronicle would rather pass as a medium of *collective memory.* The distinctive criterion is the intention to create a tradition, which plays a certain role – as is the case, for example, in the diaries of politicians. When it comes to New Testament texts, it is disputable whether even the authentic Pauline Letters fall into the realm of *social memory*, for they do not create history *en passant.* Even the First Epistle to Thessalonians can be read as recalling and shaping past events according to certain needs.[12]

Another distinction between *social memory* and *collective memory* is the scope. *Collective memory* is usually applied to larger groups in which all the members do not know each other personally. Aleida Assmann points out the constructive nature of *collective memory* when she observes that such larger groups do not *have* a common memory but rather *create* it with the help of symbolic means such as texts, images, monuments, anniversaries, or rites of communication. Collectives thus create a *We*-identity based on shared points of reference within their lore or cultural tradition. This *We*-identity is not an event of the individual's origin or ancestry but gained by forms of learning,

10 For different types of *storage metaphors* cf. A. Assmann, *Erinnerungsräume. Formen und Wandlungen des kulturellen Gedächtnisses* (München: Beck, 1999), 150–78 and N. Pethes, "Gedächtnismetapher", in N. Pethes/J. Ruchatz (ed.), *Gedächtnis und Erinnerung. Ein interdisziplinäres Lexikon* (Hamburg: Rowohlt, 2001) 196–8.

11 Cf. H. Welzer, "Das soziale Gedächtnis", 9–21.

12 Cf. S. Alkier, "Der 1. Thessalonicherbrief als kulturelles Gedächtnis" in G. Sellin/F. Vouga, Logos *und Buchstabe. Mündlichkeit und Schriftlichkeit im Judentum und Christentum der Antike* (TANZ 20; Tübingen: Francke 1997) 175–94.

participation in rites, identification and other forms of exercised membership.[13] The fact that Early Christian documents were and are still read in congregations and the idea that the Gospels might have been written with the purpose of using them for catechesis help to illustrate and understand the concept of collective memory.

In a nutshell: in the case of *social memory* identity formation takes place within a social frame while *collective memory* fabricates and provides the frames for future processes of identity formation. Although the application of *social memory theory* on biblical texts has been developed a lot further, for the sake of the perceivability of the argument, I have chosen to limit the considerations presented here to this one assumption: *The Gospel of Mark when read and understood as collective memory provides a frame for identity construction by remembering and narrating encounters and experiences with Jesus from a certain perspective.*

How can this process be imagined? The memories externalized in the Gospel of Mark, which now serve as a larger frame, have developed from individual memory episodes: from the rather daily and not institutionalized narratives of *social memory*, where they had a certain meaning depending on their carriers and their contexts. In this stage, the episodes were much more flexible and could change form, structure and message depending on the situation in which they were recalled.[14] The treasure of episodes in the stage of *social memory* formed a loose narrative net that consisted of chronologically and causally unrelated little stories ("episodes"). Each episode could be referred to according to the needs of the moment without the need of reflecting upon the question of when it happened or whether the additional information (from other episodes) is necessary to understand it. The truth of these episodes is, as recent research on family memories has proven, a social agreement.[15] Stories will only be retold and passed on when they are socially accepted and convey a certain meaning.

The recalling of episodes in *social memory* can be pictured in analogy to family gatherings or regular meetings of former classmates or alumni: recalling one episode leads to recalling another and the whole process of

13 Cf. A. Assmann, *Einführung in die Kulturwissenschaft. Grundbegriffe, Themen, Fragestellungen* (Grundlagen der Anglistik und Amerikanistik 27; Berlin: Erich Schmidt, ^{2}2008), 191.

14 This understanding offers a plausible explanation not only for different versions of the same parables in the Synoptics, but also for the gospel material in general. Parallel traditions can be explained satisfactory by alluding to the fact that the same episode could have been edited quite differently in order to match the needs of different contexts and that these variants might well have materialized as different versions of the same event in different texts.

15 Cf. H. Welzer, "Das gemeinsame Verfertigen von Vergangenheit im Gespräch", in H. Welzer, *Das soziale Gedächtnis. Geschichte, Erinnerung, Tradierung*, (Hamburg: Hamburger Edition, 2001) 160–178. See also K. Gergen, "Erzählung, Moralische Identität und historisches Bewusstsein", in J. Straub (ed.), *Erzählung, Identität, Historisches Bewusstsein* (Frankfurt am Main: Suhrkamp, 1998) 170–202 and A. Keppler, *Tischgespräche. Über Formen kommunikativer Vergesellschaftung am Beispiel der Konversation in Familien* (Frankfurt am Main: Suhrkamp, ^{2}1995).

sharing memories affirms the group identity. It is easy to imagine that the gatherings of early Jesus followers would not have been very different. Even though there were individuals with a better standing or a larger authority within this group, it would not have been possible for them to impose certain versions of episodes on the other members, if their truth was not a shared truth.

The shift from *social* to *collective memory* involves significant alterations. The ephemeral episodes are transformed into a more stable form, which no longer depends on its carriers, but on its function. When individual episodes are put into a larger narrative frame, these episodes and their overall narrative frame interact with each other. This has been observed for the shaping of memories in a social frame.[16] The choice and alignment of certain episodes adds to a particular character of the overall narration just as the formation of the overall story shapes the perspective and understanding of each episode. In a logically and chronologically adjusted narrative composition, it is – in contrast to a loose net of episodes – no longer arbitrary when an episode is recalled. For example, the story of the Syrophoenician woman (7:24–30) receives a specific interpretation because of its location in the course of the Gospel.[17]

When individual Jesus-memory-stories were transferred into the larger narrative frame of the Gospel of Mark, they also became contextualized and subordinate to an overall perspective. They received a place and a time, not only within the narrative composition but also in the *narrated world* of the Gospel. Even if an episode was initially told and passed on without a reference

16 What makes working with the terms "episodes" and "frame" a bit awkward is the fact that these categories have a history in Markan Scholarship. Dating back to Karl Ludwig Schmidt's times, "Episode" and "Rahmen" were coined in the form-critical approach which distinguished between the original historical episodes and the later composed secondary frame. I admit that it is a challenge not to blend both ideas, but to neatly keep apart form-critical "Episode und Rahmen" and "episode and frame" according to social memory theory. It is more or less a consensus view that the Gospel of Mark is narrated episodically. Nevertheless, the form-critical paradigm of episode and frame cannot be left unchallenged. Neither does the Gospel have an outer narrative frame as for instance the book of Job into which the inner narration is embedded, nor is it possible to isolate a constant narrative strand into which single episodes became "hooked". And this is not all: on the one hand, the insights of memory theory clearly show that mnemonic episodes are constantly reworked and restructured, especially if they are to enter a new framework and, on the other hand, the analysis of the Markan text shows that singling out episodes is not as easy as the theory proposes. Where the beginning and the end of an episode is seen, is very often decided according to ambiguous criteria. The idea of ideal forms or *Gattungen* is only one of the myths memory theory helps to overcome.

17 This can be seen nicely when Mark is compared to Matthew. In Mark, the episode of the Syrophoenician woman opens a longer set of scenes that present Gentile characters experiencing with Jesus similar kinds of events as Jewish characters have experienced before. In his Gospel, Matthew has reduced the episode to an individual episode which even sharpens the contrast between the Jew and Gentile groups by mentioning also Sidon, by describing the woman as Canaanite and by having Jesus make the point that he was only sent to the lost sheep of the house of Israel (Matt 15:24).

to a certain time or place, its narrative context will now provide both time and place. In the *narrated world* of the Gospel of Mark, the house of Simon is located in Capernaum (1:29) and the *Feeding of the four thousand* takes place in Gentile territory (8:1–10).[18]

Episodes with traditions of specific places such as Capernaum, Jericho, or the Sea of Galilee could not only have been preserved, but might as well have attracted other episodes that are either similar or just nicely fit the overall perspective of the narration. Nevertheless, it stands to reason that traditions referring to specific places are not just invented, but were preserved in the text and changed or complemented in the course of the linguistic-narrative formation of these traditions. It can be assumed that there is a core in these traditions, which was reworked and complemented over and over again and can no longer be made visible in its original shape: "From the perspective of social memory, the Jesus of history emerges through a process that transmitted tradition *and* reconfigured him narratively on the basis of conventional plot structures and shared mnemonic patterns".[19] In the Gospel of Mark, we thus find literarily edited memories of Jesus, which are socially shaped and oriented towards culturally given forms and interpretative models.

As an identity constitutive *founding story*, the text offers both individual traditions and a collective draft of the group's identity, which is open to familiarization for those who are willing to join. The narration is based on the encounter with Jesus as the constituting moment. It explains the present as the group understands it and is oriented towards the future. As a founding story, it reflects not so much the events themselves but their significance for the group. In this way, the Gospel provides a frame for identity construction, not only for the members of the group but also for newcomers who are invited to understand their own encounters and experiences with Jesus according to the provided patterns.[20]

18 Both Matthew and Luke agree with Mark on the location of Simon's house in Capernaum, but the case is different with the feeding of the four thousand. Luke does not narrate this episode at all and Matthew (14:32–39) locates it right after a healing summary which happens at the Sea of Galilee, on a mountain (14:29). According to Matthew, the participants of this shared meal are thus the people mentioned before, those who praised the God of Israel (14:31).

19 Byrskog, "A New Quest", 326.

20 Cf. Bysrkog, "A New Quest", 326: "A significant part of identity formation has to do with mnemonic identification and narrativity. Identities are projects and practices, not properties, and emerge from the ways we are positioned by and position ourselves in the narratives of the past. Remembering becomes part of the ever-ongoing search for belonging. To be part of a community means to situate oneself in relation to its past, be that a story about Jesus or other mnemonic narratives, and negotiate one's own mnemonic identity in relation to the history of that group".

Reading Mark as Collective Memory, or: what does the Gospel of Mark narrate beyond the story of Jesus?

As collective memory, the Gospel of Mark remembers and narrates Jesus as the Messiah and the Son of God who, through his teaching, healing and miracles, opened the way into the coming of βασιλεία τοῦ θεοῦ as a possible new world. Jesus invited people to actualize this new world and thus inhabit in it.

In the overall narration of the Gospel, the theme εὐαγγέλιον Ἰησοῦ Χριστοῦ is closely linked to the character Jesus and his message that the Kingdom of God is at hand. Immediately at the beginning of the narrative, μετάνοια and πίστις are introduced as the right answer to Jesus' invitation (1:15). This programmatic summary is narratively unfolded along two questions: *How is the* βασιλεία *at hand concretized* and *What is the proper attitude to this situation?*

The treatment of these questions is closely connected to the character Jesus, who contrary to the other characters of the story shows that he has an answer to both questions. In the course of the narration, it becomes increasingly clear that the βασιλεία at hand is substantiated paradigmatically in Jesus' words and deeds, and his behavior introduces a pattern that the other characters can relate to. In the story of the Gospel, the fact that the βασιλεία is at hand is expressed primarily through Jesus' deeds (i.e. healings and miracles), while the proper attitude is mediated though his teaching activity and additionally supported by the concept of discipleship.

Although the question of how Jesus is to be understood adequately has already been answered for Mark's recipients in the opening verses of the Gospel, the *way* that leads to this answer is told once again. Different images of Jesus are introduced and discussed in the *narrated world*, i.e. on the level of the characters. The Gospel tells how Jesus' family, the disciples, bystanders and opponents struggle to understand the "phenomenon Jesus", while the readers of the Gospel have a clear advantage over against the characters as the right answer to the question τίς ἄρα οὗτός ἐστιν; (4:41) has already been revealed to them. The intriguing question is whether they will make use of this advantage and live in an adequate and efficient mnemonic community of Jesus' followers. What this adequate and efficient mnemonic community of Jesus' followers would look like, is of course not explained in the prologue of the Gospel. It has to be deduced from the actual narration. The answer to the question of how the ideal community of followers is structured is narrated similarly to the elucidation of the right image of Jesus. Here, too, the right answer is supposedly reflected back into the *narrated world* so that this answer can be deduced from it as a role model. It can be guessed that here, too, Jesus will be the main interpreter while the opponents (Scribes, Pharisees, Herodians, Sadducees, and the high council) will rather represents counter concepts. It can further be suspected that the disciples will show ambivalent behavior and that the minor characters might give interesting insights.[21]

The above-mentioned ideas are presented in the narrative in two different ways. On the one hand, Mark is about the (accurate) understanding of Jesus. This narrative strand is unfolded through the introduction and negotiation of different images of Jesus which take place in the more public scenes. On the other hand, the text is about the constitution and organization of an adequate community of followers, which is established through a common life and meal praxis and collective rituals. This narrative strand can be grasped better in the more private scenes of the inner circle.[22] The emphasis of the first part of the Gospel (1:16–8:26) lies stronger on the question of how the community of followers is *constituted*, while the emphasis of the second part (8:27–11:10) lies on the question of how they are *organized.* The third part (11:11–15:37) deepens and carries on both topics.[23] It seems logical that the first part, dealing with the *constitution* of the community, also addresses the issue of *who* belongs to and *how* the admission can be achieved. These themes are relevant both on the level of the characters and the recipients.

Before the actual story begins, the prologue (or the first part of the frame; 1:1–15) narrates Jesus' baptism and his "calling" by the voice from heaven. This part precedes the rest of the narrative in the same way as the story that is told took place before people became members of the community of followers. The encounter with the εὐαγγέλιον takes place prior to the *constitution of the community of followers.* The fact that this encounter is narrated also for the main character Jesus and that it is even narrated as an experience connected with baptism is hardly a coincidence and can thus be understood paradigmatically. Similar things happen later within the story: the encounter with the εὐαγγέλιον marks the beginning of the community of followers and this is first exemplified by Peter, Andrew, James and John (1:16–18, 19–20) and later repeated in Jesus' meeting with Levi (2:14) and the calling of the Twelve (3:13–19). Unlike Jesus and the recipients, these characters are not baptized – a tiny detail which might well strengthen the emotional bond between Jesus and the recipient.

The constitution of the circle of the Twelve through personal encounter and calling is followed by episodes dealing with Jesus' relatives and their attitude

21 Cf. M. Ebner, "Im Schatten der Großen. Kleine Erzählfiguren im Markusevangelium", *BZ* 44 (2000) 56–76, on pp. 66–76, and E.S. Malbon, "Fallible Followers. Women and Men in the Gospel of Mark", *Semeia* 28 (1983) 29–48.

22 It is most striking that the Markan Jesus (and those following him, including the disciples) apparently never seems to find time to eat. Nevertheless, food, eating and commensality play a major role in the narrative.

23 For a more detailed argument for the structuring the Gospel in five parts, *prologue* (1:1–13), *caesura I: focus on Jesus* (1:14–15), *part I: in and around Galilee* (1:16–8:26), *part II: the way to Jerusalem* (8:27–11:10), *part III: in and around Jerusalem* (11:11–15:37), *caesura II: focus on the followers* (15:38–41), *epilogue* (15:42–16:8), cf. S. Hübenthal, *Markusevangelium*, 165–76.

towards him (3:20–21, 31–35). In addition to the question of the adequate understanding of Jesus, these episodes also address the question of the composition of the community of followers. This group is not constituted through family ties but through the auxiliary construction ὃς [γὰρ] ἂν ποιήσῃ τὸ θέλημα τοῦ θεοῦ (3:35). Taking up Bernhard Giesen's terminology, the *primordial code* is abandoned here in favor of a *traditional code.*[24] However, overcoming family ties is not the only issue. In 6:1–8:26, another demarcation is overcome, too, namely religious affiliation. The community of followers is thus constituted *neither* via kinship *nor* via religious affiliation. On the level of the narration, Jewish and Gentile groups are in fact not merged, but because they share similar experiences of exorcisms (1:23–28, 32–34; 9:14–29//5:1–20; 7,24–30), healings (1,29–31, 40–45; 2:1–12; 3:1–5; 5:21–43; 6:55 f; 10:46–52// 7:31–37; [8:22–26][25]) and meals (6:35–44//8:1–9) with Jesus, there is no fundamental difference between them.[26]

It can thus be concluded that the access to the mnemonic community of followers is regulated by the right understanding of Jesus. This access is not dependent on the origins of a person but on his/her attitude to the βασιλεία τοῦ θεοῦ. This attitude can be seen in the person's relation to Jesus in πίστις. This faithful relation to Jesus also determines whether a person belongs to the inner circle or τοῖς ἔξω (4:11). Nevertheless, calling does not protect against dropping out, as Jesus' conversation with the disciples in the boat to Betsaida indicates (8:14–21). But the obduracy theory (*Verstockungstheorie*) as introduced in 4:11–12 and resumed in 8:14–21 is only one facet of the theme of *attitudes towards the Gospel.* Jesus' opening words, μετανοεῖτε καὶ πιστεύετε ἐν τῷ εὐαγγελίῳ, sketch the right answer and this answer is echoed whenever the πίστις of one of the characters is mentioned, starting with 2:5 through 4:40; 5:34, 36; 9:23 f and 10:52 until 11:22–24.

If the first part of the Gospel (1:16–8:26) provides the reader with insights into the *constitution* of the community of followers, the second part (8:27–11:10) focusses on the *organization* of this group. The relationships among the followers are expected to be shaped according to the patterns Jesus has exemplified through his own life. The individual and his or her relation to God is the core. This relationship models the individuals' relationships both to fellow humans and the environment in accordance with the βασιλεία τοῦ θεοῦ. The relation to the fellow humans is further shaped according to the Torah, thereby the human being itself – and not a (religious) command – is regarded as the focal point (3:22 ff; 7:6, 18; 10:18 ff; 12:28–34). Whatever separates the individual from God and fellow humans has to be overcome. The idea of

24 For the distinction between the different codes, cf. B. Giesen, *Kollektive Identität* (Die Intellektuellen und die Nation 2; Frankfurt am Main: Suhrkamp, 1999), 32–69.

25 Although Betsaida was predominantly Gentile, it is far from clear, whether this man was also Gentile. The episode just presents a human being in all his neediness.

26 This special character of Mark's version, which is mostly conveyed through the structure, the succession and the location of the individual episodes, is lost in the other Synoptics.

10:21ff could also be understood in the way that *possessions* (χρήματα 10:23) should not be allowed to stand between the individual and the βασιλεία τοῦ θεοῦ.[27] The members of the community encounter each other as equal in rank (9:34ff; 10:41–45) and their relationships are not polluted in the sense of 7:20–23.

However, it is also obvious that things are not as simple as they seem to be. The disciples and their "failures" exemplify how difficult these simple axioms are to persevere with (9:33–34, 38; 10:13, 28, 35–41). The positive side of the disciples' "failures" (which the narrator does not hesitate to comment on, cf. 6:52; 9:6) is that they also indicate that being a member of the community of followers is a process. The community itself is *on the way*, grows, is led astray but also understands and learns. When it comes to familiarization, the portrait of the community given in Mark is much easier to relate to than a perfect model group – especially in times of crisis, insecurity or persecution.

Please join in: How the Gospel invites recipients to become part of it

Considering the question of familiarization – how the recipients can make the text their text – we need to take a second look at the prologue. I have shown that the beginning of Jesus' story provides a link to the recipients' own experiences. It might be surprising, but this second look reveals that before his story is told, the protagonist – Jesus himself – is introduced as the role model and figure for identification, and not – as we will see – the disciples.[28]

In the prologue (1:1–15), Jesus is at first announced to be a special character – 'Ιησοῦς Χριστός υἱὸς θεοῦ – then introduced as an ordinary Galilean (1:9) who joins his fellows from Judea and Jerusalem (1:5) and lines up at the banks of Jordan for the baptism of repentance. The turning point is narrated in connection with the baptism itself. The character experiences something very special and the readers are invited to witness. The change of perspective from the author to the inside view of the character Jesus might already indicate the preferred perspective for familiarization. There is a narrative gap in 1:8 because the words *he will baptize you with the Holy Spirit* are left unfulfilled. For the character Jesus, however, this gap is closed in the following verses where Jesus' baptism is described. The offer to familiarize can hardly be

27 The mirror-inverted episode to this idea would be 12:41–44.

28 Cf. N.S. Petersen, "Die 'Perspektive' in der Erzählung im Markusevangelium", in F. Hahn (ed.), *Der Erzähler des Evangeliums. Methodische Neuansätze in der Markusforschung* (SBS 118/119; Stuttgart: Katholisches Bibelwerk, 1985) 67–91, on p. 74: "Beides, die gemeinsame Perspektive von Erzähler und Hauptfigur und die Dramatisierung der Geschichte, veranlaßt den Leser, sich nicht nur mit dem Erzähler zu identifizieren und sich ihm anzuvertrauen, sondern auch der Hauptfigur".

overlooked, for baptism is a crucial turning point for everyone on the ὁδός of following Jesus.

After the baptism, the character Jesus is thrown into an ἔρημος, a desert or solitude. Recipients might also be able to identify with this experience, even though we must not psychologize the scene as showing the social isolation of the newly baptized. The narrative structure, baptism/experience of vocation – desert/latency – onset of proclamation/onset of the ὁδός of following, is much more interesting to note and relate to.[29] The character Jesus, unlike some of those whom he has healed, does not take his personal turning point as the starting point for his "mission" but begins to pass on his experience only after the time in the desert.[30]

It is significant that Jesus takes up his task only after a time of withdrawal and reclusion. The text is not quite clear whether the beginning of his public activity is directly connected to his return from the ἔρημος or whether some time passes before Jesus begins his proclamation. The way this part of the story is told nevertheless leads to the suspicion that it is not the experience in the desert but that of an actual crisis (1:14) which leads to Jesus' public activity and proclamation. John the Baptist was handed over and arrested (παραδοθῆναι, cf. 3:19; 14:10 f, 42) but this was not the end of his mission. If we take this observation into account, we can fill the narrative gap at the end of the Gospel. This is exactly what the young man in the tomb (16:7) calls the women to do: to go forth and proclaim that the Jesus-story has not come to an end, but will continue.[31] As the Gospel of Mark is a *progressive story* told in a *regressive* way,[32] this call is extended to the recipients. Just like the character Jesus, who reacted to the experience of an existential crisis by proclamation and like the women who are called to overcome the experience of crisis by proclamation, the recipients, too, are asked to overcome their experiences of crisis by applying the same strategy.

If read in this way, the role of the disciples in the story changes. According to their own history, they are not so much depicted as role models and figures for identification but rather as examples for the experience and the (not very successful) handling of crises and failure. Instead, the recipient is directed to the minor characters. Their emergence and their stories speak of possibilities

29 Cf. K.M. Schmidt, *Wege des Heils. Erzählstrukturen und Rezeptionskontexte des Markusevangeliums* (NTOA 74; Göttingen: Vandenhoeck & Ruprecht, 2010), 530: "der Lektüreplan des Markusevangeliums sieht vor, dass man die eigene Geschichte im Leben Jesu entdeckt".

30 Jesus' withdrawal to the desert or to solitude is a motif that occurs in the narrative several times and illustrates one aspect of his attitude towards the world. Something similar could be suspected for the women at the end of the Gospel who *at first* do not speak because they are afraid. For the understanding of the aorist εἶπαν cf. S. Alkier, "Auferweckung denken. Oder: wie das Markusevangelium mit seinen Wundergeschichten seine Leser theologisch bildet", *BiLi* 84 (2011) 258–67, on p. 261.

31 Like an ironic support to the violation of the commands to keep silent (1:45; 7:36–37), it is the command not to keep silent that is violated here.

32 For the theoretical background cf. Gergen, "Erzählung" 170–202.

to become members of the mnemonic community of followers at different moments in time. It is always their personal situation which makes them come to Jesus, and very often their turning to him is accompanied by πίστις, showing an approving perception of the βασιλεία at hand and its realization in the Son of Man.[33] It is irrelevant whether the minor model characters are with the group from the very beginning like Peter's mother-in-law (1:29–31) or join on the ὁδός as for instance Bartimaeus (10:46–52). Or whether they have a stable location as Levi (2:14), are on the way as the women (15:41) or whether they appear only at the very end like Josef of Arimathea (15:43–46). The only thing that counts is their turning to Jesus and the βασιλεία.

This makes a strong argument that the community of followers is constituted through the individual's relation to Jesus and his or her advocacy for the βασιλεία τοῦ θεοῦ – and not through kinship, a certain group membership or religious affiliation.[34] This is especially noticeable in the episode where the disciples try to hinder a foreign healer and exorcist to cast out demons in Jesus' name, because he does not follow them (9:38ff). Jesus' answer indicates that whoever works in the name of the anointed one (9:41), is a member of the mnemonic community of followers, even though s/he might not be a member of a certain group. On the level of the story this also applies to the scribe (12:28–34) and Josef of Arimathaea (15:43–46). This could also be considered to apply to the healed man at Gerasa who is called to proclaim to his people (5:19–20).[35]

Technical observations, or: how does the narration achieve its goals?

If we take a technical look at the narration, two observations are essential. On the one hand, the text seems to have a preference for individual scenes, which are predominantly structured episodically. On the other hand, it seems to offer a clear fragmentation of roles. Because of the allegedly restrained style, it seems that the narrator just describes the world while the characters are responsible for the interpretation and evaluation of the events themselves. The

33 This explains why Jesus cannot perform δύναμαι in his hometown (6:5): there is only ἀπιστία (6:6), no πίστις.

34 See also P. Dschulnigg, "Grenzüberschreitungen im Markusevangelium. Auf dem Weg zu einer neuen Identität", *MThZ* 52 (2001) 113–20; L.E. Vaage, "An Other Home: Discipleship in Mark as Domestic Ascetism", *CBQ 71* (2009) 741–61.

35 Especially if 7:31–37 is taken seriously as taking place in Gentile territory. The question how people learned about Jesus would have a very simple answer: according to 5:20, there was proclamation in these regions. On the level of the story, where Jewish and Gentile characters share the same experiences with Jesus without becoming one body, this makes sense, but, of course, it should not be taken literally.

argument would thus take place on the level of the characters and not on the level of the narration. Compared to the other Gospels, the Markan narrator is indeed remarkably restrained. Apparently, the recipient's perception of the characters is not predefined by evaluative insights nor is s/he guided to a certain understanding of the narrated events though reflexive quotations (Reflexionszitate).[36]

However, it should be asked whether a text that introduces itself as the *founding narrative* and serves as a frame for identity construction would really leave it completely open to the recipients how they should respond to the texts and its claim? Of course not – but it is also obvious that the *Leserlenkung* is neither on the level of the characters nor as obvious as in e. g. in the Gospel of Matthew. It must be found elsewhere.

We must take into consideration that one of the characteristics of *collective memory* is that it provides a structure that connects the individual episodes and assigns them a certain place within the overall narrative framework. Therefore, it is this framework that directs the interpretation of the readers.

The Gospel of Mark might thus be read on two different levels: on the level of the actual story, the world of the characters and what is said, thought, and done there, and on the level of the narration and what is communicated and evoked there. If we observe carefully how the story of the Gospel is told and structured, it soon becomes clear that the question of how the reader should respond and behave is anything but open, even though the narrator is seemingly restrained.

The narrator has obviously great sympathy for the character Jesus and presents him as the primary role model and figure for identification. Jesus is introduced as *Christ* and *Son of God* (1:1), announced as the one to come (1:7–8), and the reader is drawn into his perception, to see with his eyes (1:10 f) and to follow his teaching (1:15). This is the first position the reader meets with. Technically speaking: the reader is given an insight into *Jesus' world*[37], and his worldview reaches him/her with the *primacy effect*[38]. The narrator's preference for Jesus and his world can also be deduced from the way

36 Leaving aside Mark 1:1–3 and 15:23 f, quotations from the Scriptures can only be found in the characters' direct speech.

37 For a brief theoretical introduction cf. C. Surkamp, "Die Perspektivenstruktur narrativer Texte aus der Sicht der possible-worlds-theory. Zur literarischen Inszenierung der Pluralität subjektiver Wirklichkeitsmodelle", in A. Nünning/V. Nünning (ed.), *Multiperspektivisches Erzählen. Zur Theorie und Geschichte der Perspektivenstruktur im englischen Roman des 18.–20. Jahrhunderts* (Trier: Wissenschaftlicher Verlag 2000) 111–32, for an application to the Gospel of Mark cf. S. Hübenthal, *Markusevangelium*, 326–53.

38 For theoretical foundation and method cf. A. Nünning/V. Nünning, "Multiperspektivität aus narratologischer Sicht. Erzähltheoretische Grundlagen und Kategorien zur Analyse der Perspektivenstruktur narrativer Texte", in A. Nünning/V. Nünning (ed.), *Multiperspektivisches Erzählen. Zur Theorie und Geschichte der Perspektivenstruktur im englischen Roman des 18.–20. Jahrhunderts* (Trier: Wissenschaftlicher Verlag 2000) 39–77. For an application to the Gospel of Mark cf. S. Hübenthal, *Markusevangelium*, 326–53.

the other characters are presented. When the Scribes appear for the first time in 2:6–7, the reader has already been introduced to them and remembers from 1:22 that they – unlike Jesus – have no ἐξουσία. In a similar way, most of the characters and events are evaluated – sometimes long before or after they appear, but almost never in the situation itself. Sometimes, the narrator's assessment is hidden in the thoughts of one of the characters.[39] This technique is not easy to see through at first, but as soon as it becomes clear that the narrator's hints or the thoughts of a character have no relevance for the course of the narrated events, it is only logical that they serve a purpose in the narration rather than in the *narrated world* of the text. Mark's narrative technique is particularly powerful because the strong direction of the recipient remains mostly unnoticed but is hard to escape.[40]

In the *narrated world*, the character Jesus advertises his world view and it is told how the other characters relate to it. He and his message meet both acceptance and rejection. The *possible world* Jesus proclaims is unique and in many aspects runs counter to the convictions of the other characters or the mainstream of the *narrated world*. The most remarkable points are the proclamation of the βασιλεία τοῦ θεοῦ which is supposedly at hand and Jesus' self-introduction as *Son of Man*. Both terms are only used by the character Jesus and must thus be part of his *world*. A main part of the Gospel's plot, both on the level of the characters and the narration is how the other characters and the recipients will react.

Just like the characters in the *narrated world are invited to response to Jesus*, there is an invitation to the recipients of the Gospel of Mark to become part of the community of commemoration and narration which affirms its memory and its self-concept on the basis of the text. The narrative thereby becomes a self-testimony that is literarily reflected back in time and serves the purpose of fostering the identity construed on the basis of the narrative. As Halbwachs already noted, the movement goes in the two directions at the same time. On the one hand, common history constructs a common identity and, on the other hand, common identity is fostered by referring back to or drawing from this common history. It is the gamete of the community to narrate this (hi)story over and over again and to refer back to it. The group as such is not a closed circle but open for newcomers who recognize themselves and their experiences in the experiences memorialized and narrated in the Gospel. The steady growth of the community of followers, which is based on the Twelve and extends beyond social, religious or family ties is a development preinscribed in the text.

If the narrative is read in this way, it is further not surprising that the

39 Cf. Mark 2:6–8; 12:34; 15:10.

40 R. Zwick, *Montage im Markusevangelium. Studien zur narrativen Organisation der ältesten Jesuserzählung* (SBB 18; Stuttgart: Katholisches Bibelwerk, 1989), on p. 595, concludes: "Der Leser kann sich kein vom Erzählerwillen unabhängiges 'Bild' der Ereignisse machen".

narrative does not present the disciples as the role model but Jesus. People who achieve πίστις and become members of the community experience the beginning of their way with Jesus possibly very similarly to Jesus himself. Like him, they are baptized and experience the closeness to God or even being God's child and community, but also incomprehension, hostility and the necessity of withdrawal. The coming βασιλεία as the *possible world* that Jesus has proclaimed is the new reality the recipients seek to realize in their lives. In this process, they take over Jesus' perspective, not the perspective of the disciples.

The community of commemoration might well recognize itself in the fears, miseries and doubts of the disciples. Nevertheless, they are invited to outgrow the disciples and follow Jesus more consistently. They are standing chronologically in the succession of the disciples and are invited to accept their inheritance. Thereby the members of the community are called to set off with the disciples, but not to repeat their mistakes. The disciples serve as a model from which the readers can both learn how to do it and how not to do it, while the real role model to be identified with is Jesus himself.

A closer look at the levels of communication helps to clarify the difference. The way the disciples and their "failures" are portrayed makes clear that the differences between the level of the characters (the *narrated world*) and the level of the narration are indeed stunning.

In Mark in 8:17, 21, the character Jesus asks the disciples whether they still have not understood or whether even their hearts were hardened. This should be understood as a real question, not as a rhetorical one. On the level of the characters, this question has up to now not been addressed. On the level of the characters and according to the standards of the *narrated world*, the disciples do not react surprisingly or incomprehensibly in light of the first part of the Gospel (1:16–8:26). This can easily be gathered from the reactions of the other characters, who also try to understand Jesus and make sense of his words and deeds as, for example, the people of his home town (6:1–6a). The disciples and their reactions only appear incomprehensible in light of the cross and the resurrection, because only then full perception and full testimony are possible for them. In the *narrated world*, the disciples have a pre-Easter perspective and thus understand Jesus and the events in the narrative almost naturally differently than the narrator who has a post-Easter perspective. The narrator can thus depict the disciples to be on the way but states at the same time that they have not gained full perception yet. In this way the narrator makes sure that the disciples are received as credible characters by the readers of the narrative.

In Mark 6:52, the narrator had already stated that the disciples have not understood but that their hearts were hardened. Although this comment coincides with the reader's understanding of the disciples – especially as the evaluation is narrated long before Jesus's question and placed in a similar situation in the boat on the way to Betsaida –, the alleged lack of comprehension on the part of the disciples is not a feature of the *narrated* but of the *narrator's world.* The narrator uses Jesus' question as a reminder of his/her own idea about the disciples, but also makes use of the opportunity to describe the disciples in a way that they can be memorialized both as credible witnesses and still remain a solemn warning to the community. In the post-Easter perspective of the narrator, the inability to perceive Jesus as the Son of Man, the Messiah and the Son of God can only be understood as obduracy and as having a hardened heart. The two level reading of the narrative can thus also explain why the Gospel remains silent about the fact that the disciples did not stay dispersed and silent, but rather trusted in the reality of the βασιλεία and bore witness to it.

Concluding remarks: Was the Markan concept successful?

In this conclusion, I summarize what reading Mark as collective memory might tell us about those who remember Jesus and about their ideas and needs. In the Gospel, the community of Jesus' followers is structured according to family ties but also extends these ties. Among the disciples, there are two pairs of brothers, but the new family ties quickly sidestep these relationships when those who do God's will and follow his ways become brothers and sisters (3:35 and 10:30). The immediate family is not entirely excluded from this tendency – towards the end of the Gospel, Mary is not depicted as a family member of Jesus but as one of the women who are already his followers in Galilee. This does not necessarily mean that the "old" family ties are overcome. Rather they are seen in the context of the new reality of the βασιλεία at hand.

The community thus constructs itself beyond the usual and familiar frame without disrupting it. Boundaries such as clean/unclean, Jewish/Gentile, rich/poor, sick/healthy or inside/outside are overcome in and by Jesus and are made irrelevant. This can be seen nicely as Jewish and Gentile characters share the same experiences with Jesus but do not add up to one single community. Over and over again Jesus turns towards people who for a variety of reasons find themselves excluded. He exercises commensality with sinners and tax-collectors, touches the sick and the unclean, actively addresses Gentiles, and even eats with them. Resistances, distinctions, purity requirements and socio-religious boundaries of all sorts are overcome in and by Jesus. The "others" are not "the Jews" or "the Gentiles", but those "ἔξω" (4:11) who do not follow the way. Religion and ethnicity do not appear as identity constituting factors. Identity is constructed through relating to Jesus. In the βασιλεία as the *possible new world,* other categories than the relation to Jesus are not or no longer relevant and thus ignored in favor of a more general notion of *catholicity.* The symbol for this is the βασιλεία understood as an eschatological and messianic concept that manifests itself especially in commensality – the multiplication of the loaves becoming the counter image of Herod's banquet – and healings. The mnemonic group or the *Mark People* are directed towards Jesus and share his vision of the βασιλεία. Their agreement is to live in the βασιλεία and thus to realize the *possible world* Jesus has proclaimed. The mnemonic group thus understands itself to be following Jesus' path. Their memory of Jesus, his proclamation and his deeds, is the binding factor. It proves again that a *Bindungsgedächtnis,* as Jan Assmann calls it, is less about the events themselves than about their significance for the memory group. This *collective memory* is externalized as a text, and thus provides a frame for future processes of identity construction.

On the basis of the Jewish tradition, the *Mark People* are on the way into the new reality of the βασιλεία. It envisions itself as a group living and walking (7:5) in the way Jesus went ahead, but also in the line of the disciples who time and again had their problems and doubts with this reality. The major and minor crises of the group are thereby taken seriously in the *narrated world* and the Gospel describes exemplary strategies for how these crises can be overcome. These strategies serve as a model for the characters in the narrative even though not every character takes every step within the model. Even though fear is legitimate, continuous stepping out of the world is not an option as Jesus' example shows. There is no final withdrawal into private life or 'behind the gates', even in situations of crisis. The invocation to newcomers could thus sound: *Be open for the possible new world of Jesus and strive to live in the coming* βασιλεία τοῦ θεοῦ *without being discouraged by crises and failures.*

Equally important is the notion that the Gospel of Mark can be actualized both within a Jewish and a Gentile encyclopedia.[41] The individual episodes as well as the overall narration offer various motives and references to contemporary texts and genres, which can be connected with both encyclopedias. It is probably one of the great advantages of the text that both Jewish and Gentile recipients can recognize their experiences and their sense of the *narrated world.* One of many examples for this is the comprehension of Jesus as υἱὸς θεοῦ, which is constructed differently on the basis of the Jewish Scripture or Roman imperial propaganda. However, even though the narrative is apparently open to other frames of reference, it remains deeply rooted in the Jewish tradition. There is a basic openness to other readings, but there is no way beyond Israel's Scripture. Even though the Gospel of Mark might not share every tradition or halacha with other early Jewish groups, the reader is never in doubt that there can be no adequate perception of Jesus beyond Israel's tradition. It is the *cultural memory* that they all share.

Last but not least: Until the Gospel of Mark was written, the term εὐαγγέλιον denoted an oral proclamation. The concept of an oral message as it can also be

41 For the term "encyclopedia" cf. U. Eco, *Lector in fabula. Die Mitarbeit der Interpretation in erzählenden Texte,* (München: dtv, 3rd ed. 1998), 94–106.

encountered in Paul's letters underwent significant change when it became *collective memory*. When Mark wrote it down and dissolved it from its original social context and thus transferred the oral gospel onto a new written medium, he inevitably but (accidently) started a new *Gattung* of memory texts: The written Gospel as an externalized oral memory text about the εὐαγγέλιον. In the headline of Mark's Gospel, the beginning of Jesus' oral Gospel turns into the beginning of a new kind of memorialization and proclamation of this Gospel.[42]

This new kind of memory artifact was obviously successful. The acceptance, extension and adaption of Mark by both Matthew and Luke not only reveal a common process in *collective memory*, but can also be read as another stage in the process of negotiating early Christian identities. It can be said that Mark created a first proposal, which did not perish, but was enhanced and adjusted to other social situations and needs.[43]

If performance criticism has its arena, then this is exactly its place: Mark was performed and, in this situation of secondary orality, adjusted and further modeled according to both the needs of different audiences and the principles of oral traditions *and* social memory theory. The different versions in the manuscripts can fruitfully be read as testimonies to this process. On the surface, we see the emergence of Matthew and Luke.

42 In his forthcoming book, *The Fourfold Gospel*, Francis Watson presents a similar thought: "At the beginning of Mark's narrative, Jesus preaches the Gospel in Galilee; as it draws towards its close, a future is envisaged, in which the gospel is preached to all nations, in all the world, and to the whole creation. That, then, is the context, when the evangelist applies the term 'gospel' to his own written text, as he announces 'the beginning of the Gospel of Jesus Christ...' (1.1). The underlying idea is that his text is the embodiment and continuation of the original apostolic preaching. In writing the gospel, the evangelist ensures that the original apostolic testimony is extended to future generations". F. Watson, *The Fourfold Gospel* (Grand Rapids: Baker Academic, 2016) in the first chapter.

43 Cf. S. Byrskog: "The Markan narrative was the decisive site of memory. It was heard, memorized and performed anew. This kind of re-oralization generates negotiation for shared meaning and cohesion. The Gospel of Matthew may be seen as a mnemonic moment of the re-oralization of the Markan narrative. The social identity thus has a strong mnemonic and narrative dimension to it. The retelling of Mark as a kind of narrative orality points to a performance which positions itself mnemonically to the narrative past which it retells". Byrskog, "A New Quest", 335 f.

Kari Syreeni

Eyewitness Testimony, First-Person Narration and Authorial Presence as Means of Legitimation in Early Gospel Literature

Introduction

The concept of memory has attracted keen interest in recent Jesus research. In a way, all Jesus research is and has been the study of the remembered Jesus. What sets the recent trend apart from previous research is the focus on memory as a key concept. To choose this concept as a focal point implies that it is regarded as somehow more promising than its alternatives. Hence it is instructive to note that simultaneously there is a decline of scholarly confidence in finding the original words and deeds of Jesus through a meticulous application of authenticity criteria, and a growing suspicion towards literary and source-critical hypotheses, such as the Q hypothesis. Instead, the memory approach makes use of oral studies, comparative cultural approaches, sociological and now even cognitive-scientific perspectives. Perhaps there will come a time for a renewed interest in the literary inquiry into the early Jesus material, but until then we do well to take all the aid we can get along the memory trend and its methodological allies. Meanwhile, though, we should not forget that our principal evidence from the early Jesus tradition is written texts.[1] Any hypothesis concerning pre-Gospel developments, no matter on how advanced sociological, cognitive or other models they are based, must cohere with the literary remains – the memory that we actually have.

Eric Eve, in his *Behind the Gospels*,[2] discerns five approaches to oral Jesus traditions after form criticism. Eve labels one of them "the memory model", which in fact seems shorthand for the social memory model. He adds that two other models – Kelber's media contrast model and Bailey's informal controlled tradition model – "converge on a broadly similar approach".[3] Thus, by implication, he would exclude Birger Gerhardsson's "rabbinic" model and the "eyewitness model" represented by Samuel Byrskog and

1 B. Gerhardsson, *The Reliability of the Gospel Tradition* (Grand Rapids: Baker Academic, 2010), 92–5 distinguished between inner and outer tradition. The former denotes mental phenomena (beliefs, values, and views), while outer tradition includes verbal, behavioural (practical), institutional, and material tradition. With the partial exception of material tradition (archaeological evidence), early Christian traditions are only available through texts.

2 E. Eve, *Behind the Gospels: Understanding the oral tradition* (London: SPCK, 2013).

3 Eve, *Behind the Gospels*, xiv.

Richard Bauckham from the contemporary mainstream approach. This is to some extent conceivable but also quite misleading. While there are obvious ideological and research-historical connections between Gerhardsson, Byrskog and Bauckham, all these scholars very decidedly address the question of memory: Gerhardsson in his pivotal study *Memory and Manuscript*,[4] Byrskog through his concern for autopsy in *Story as History – History as Story*[5] and through his concept of an early Christian "mnemonic trajectory"[6] – and finally Bauckham in his colossal *Jesus and the Eyewitnesses*.[7]

I make no secret of the fact that my own preferences diverge considerably from the above mentioned three scholars. Yet I do think that their works – especially Byrskog's – deserve careful consideration. In the present paper, I study the written Gospels, canonical and non-canonical, and ask how possible hints of eyewitnesses or explicit eyewitness testimonies should be evaluated. Such hints are difficult to assess, and the choice of examples that I discuss may be the most vulnerable part of the analysis. However, to the extent that there are *hints* at all, there must be something specific that alerts the reader or hearer to the possibility of an eyewitness backup. A comprehensive list of possible hints cannot be given, but at least the *naming* of characters in the story, the *mention* of what they saw, heard and remembered, and other *details* concerning *involved* characters are of interest. The use of first person singular or plural by the narrator is a direct device. The various forms of authorial presence, ranging from the real author's self-presentation to heavy authorial fiction, are also important indicators. In observing such devices, my question concerns the kind of legitimation they seek to provide.

The concept of legitimation comes basically from the sociology of knowledge, where it is understood as a means of maintaining a shared symbolic universe, typically in a situation where the second and subsequent generations need explanations for the existing order.[8] However, I think that the concept also applies to the immediate concerns of establishing and

4 B. Gerhardsson, *Memory and Manuscript: Oral Tradition and Written Transmission in Rabbinic Judaism and in Early Christianity* (ASNU 22; Lund: Gleerup, 1961). See also the follow-up booklet *Tradition and Transmission in Early Christianity* (CB 20; Lund: Gleerup, 1964), where he clarifies his position and defends it especially against Morton Smith's critique. My references are to the 1998 combined edition which includes both studies (Biblical Resource Series; Grand Rapids: Eerdmans, 1998).

5 S. Byrskog, *Story as History – History as Story: The Gospel Tradition in the Context of Ancient Oral History* (WUNT 123; Tübingen: Mohr Siebeck 2002).

6 S. Byrskog, "From Memory to Memoirs: Tracing the Background of a Literary Genre", in M. Zetterholm/S. Byrskog (ed.), *The Making of Christianity: Conflicts, Contacts and Constructions* (FS Bengt Holmberg; CBNTS 47; Winona Lake: Eisenbrauns, 2012) 1–21; the precise term is used on p. 18.

7 R. Bauckham, *Jesus and the Eyewitnesses: The Gospels as Eyewitness Testimony* (Grand Rapids and Cambridge: Eerdmans, 2006).

8 P.L. Berger/T. Luckmann, *The Social Construction of Reality: A Treatise in the Sociology of Knowledge* (Garden City, NY: Anchor Books, 1966), 110–46.

propagating a new group's symbolic universe.[9] From the viewpoint of addressees it can also function as a means of strengthening group identity in relation to outgroups. A third aspect of legitimation is rhetorical: to establish the trustworthiness of the speaker or writer, and his or her subject matter.

Mark

Mark, in all likelihood the oldest survived Gospel is consistently written in third-person narration. The author does not present himself,[10] we only hear the narrator's voice. The narrator is omniscient and comments on the events by referring to Scripture and by adding some explanatory remarks for his Gentile audience. There is no explicit reference to eyewitness testimony. It is, though, tempting to regard some characters in the story as possible eyewitnesses. Perhaps the best case can be made for Mark 15:21:

> They compelled a passer-by, who was coming in from the country, to carry his cross; it was Simon of Cyrene, the father of Alexander and Rufus. (NRSV)

Here a character who is intimately involved in the passion story is not only *named*, but also his home town and two sons are mentioned. It would seem as if the author here occasionally and almost inadvertently, informs his readers about an involved eyewitness whose offspring can still – in Mark's own day – affirm their father's testimony. Bailey's theory of an informal but controlled – or rather, controllable – tradition seems to triumph here, and those who regard the whole Markan passion story as a literary invention have hard times in explaining this detail. Martin Dibelius considered Mark 15:21, together with the anonymous young man in Mark 14:51, as hints of eyewitnesses. Interestingly, Byrskog is less confident that the two instances are meant primarily as eyewitness hints on the final Gospel's level: the fleeing young man is "probably not, as Dibelius thought, without significance in the Markan story itself" and "(t)he listing of [Simon's] sons may simply have served to distinguish him from other men of the same name".[11] Byrskog sees in both cases an indication of eyewitnesses on the level of the pre-Markan tradition. This is not uncontestable, however. The fleeing young man may have a literary-theological function (in conjunction with the young man in the tomb) rather than a real-life reference.[12] Simon of Cyrene and his sons probably refer to real persons, but the historicity of the incident is not thereby verified.

9 Similarly P.F. Esler, *Community and Gospel: The Social and Political Motivations of Lucan Theology* (SNTSMS 57; Cambridge University Press, 1987), 17–18.

10 Or *herself*; we never know.

11 Byrskog, *Story as History*, 66.

12 The simplest way of describing the symbolism is the following interpretation: "The young man who ran away in the garden becomes the messenger for Jesus' resurrection." A. Moore,

Another salient case with *named* eyewitnesses is the three named women who were among the women who *saw* the crucifixion of Jesus from a distance and later *visited* the empty tomb and *received* a message from the young man in the tomb (Mark 15:40; 16:1–18). Clearly the mention of the women is crucial to the Markan plot, indeed to its overarching message. How the evangelist understood their function is not quite clear, however. Gerhardsson thought that they were originally meant as "witnesses to whom the curious listener might turn and interrogate".[13] Byrskog, however, concludes that for Mark and his audience the presence of the women was just "part of the traditional material of the passion narrative",[14] which seems wise, because the Markan readers were likely unable to go and interview the women. What Mark knew or concluded from his tradition may well have been, partly, that "some women" (v. 40) who had followed Jesus to Jerusalem (v. 41) were present at the crucifixion, and partly, that the named women were important persons in the early community.

It may be significant that the two most conspicuous cases of name-dropping appear precisely in the Markan passion narrative.[15] One possible explanation is that the evangelist thought this final part of the Gospel had lower advance credibility among the audience and thus in need of special rhetorical persuasion. Such an explanation would cohere with the observation that the evangelist has sought to support the passion storyline with several legitimating devices: the passion story is full of scriptural testimony and is anticipated early on and repeatedly in the preceding narrative, both through the narrator's comments and by the protagonist himself.

Considering the named witnesses in the passion story, the anonymity of the man with the sword (14:47) and the fleeing young man (14:51–52; cf. 16:5) in the arrest story are not easily explained as being due to protective anonymity, as Gerd Theissen has suggested.[16] Theissen's hypothesis was granted by

"Enigmatic Endings and Delayed Signs: The Ending of Mark's Gospel", in J.H. Ellens (ed.), *Text and Community: Essays in Memory of Bruce M. Metzger, Vol. 1* (NTM 19; Sheffield: Sheffield Phoenix Press, 2007) 103–20, on p. 119. I would see a bit more pronounced baptismal symbolism that has to do with the changed clothing of the young man, but this is not the place to develop the theme.

13 B. Gerhardsson, "Mark and the Female Witnesses", in H. Berens/ D. Loding/ M.T. Roth (ed.), *Dumu—E2-Dub-Ba-A* (FS Åke W. Sjöberg; OPSNKF 11; Philadelphia: The Samuel Noah Kramer Fund, 1989) 217–26, on p. 217.

14 Byrskog, *Story as History*, 82 n. 165.

15 The healing of blind Bartimaeus (Mark 10:36–42) is thematically embedded in a passion context, placed as it is between Jesus' "ransom" saying (v. 45) and the entry into Jerusalem. G. Theissen, *The Gospels in Context: Social and Political History in the Synoptic Tradition* (Minneapolis: Fortress, 1991), 101 observes that Bartimaeus is singled out as a *follower* of Jesus, which might make him plausible as an informant-eyewitness. However, it is also possible that the evangelist is developing his favourite themes (faith in Jesus, following Jesus).

16 Theissen, *The Gospels in Context*, 184–9.

Bauckham, who expanded it to explain other unnamed characters.[17] The woman who anointed Jesus in Mark 14:3–9 is an intriguing case because of Jesus' concluding words (vv.8–9): "She has done what she could; she has anointed my body beforehand for its burial. Truly I tell you, wherever the good news is proclaimed in the whole world, what she has done will be told in remembrance of her." How should we interpret "in remembrance of her" (εἰς μνημόσυνον αὐτῆς)? Read carefully, this can only mean that the woman will be remembered for what she *did*, namely, that she anointed Jesus' body for burial. It is sometimes suggested that the anointing had messianic connotations which would endanger the safety of the woman if she were named. However, the text seems more concerned with the approaching death and burial of Jesus. Every time the gospel is preached, the act of the woman, pointing to Jesus' death and burial, should be mentioned – or else one does not preach *the gospel.* One more named and actively involved character in the passion story is Joseph of Arimathea.[18] Here, too, we have signs of the evangelist's interest in witnesses to Jesus' actual death:

> When evening had come, and since it was the day of Preparation, that is, the day before the sabbath, Joseph of Arimathea, a respected member of the council, who was also himself waiting expectantly for the kingdom of God, went boldly to Pilate and asked for the body of Jesus. Then Pilate wondered if he were already dead; and summoning the centurion, he asked him whether he had been dead for some time. When he learned from the centurion that he was dead, he granted the body to Joseph. Then Joseph bought a linen cloth, and taking down the body, wrapped it in the linen cloth, and laid it in a tomb that had been hewn out of the rock. He then rolled a stone against the door of the tomb. Mary Magdalene and Mary the mother of Joses saw where the body was laid. (Mark 15:42–47 NRSV)

Another intriguing feature is Mark's pejorative view of both the relatives of Jesus (who thought Jesus was mad, cf. Mark 3:21) and the group of the twelve disciples, including Peter, who most of the time did not understand Jesus. Various reasons for this attitude have been suggested, but since the family of Jesus and the Twelve are among the best candidates for a reliable tradition, it is strange that the oldest evangelist treats them as he does. Apart from the named witnesses in the passion story, Mark shows little interest in eyewitness testimony as a means of legitimating his message; usually scriptural testimony was enough. Peter is certainly a salient figure in Mark, and the anecdote about

17 Bauckham, *Eyewitnesses*, 183–201.

18 To my mind, two hypotheses about the historical background are worth considering: either Joseph of Arimathea was a member of the council whose responsibility was to take care of the burial of executed criminals (thus, e.g., Matti Myllykoski), or the name is due to pre-Markan midrashic interpretation (Roger David Aus). See my article, "Resurrection or Assumption? Matthew's View of the Post-Mortem Vindication of Jesus", in W. Weren/H. van de Sandt/J. Verheyden (ed.), *Life Beyond Death in Matthew's Gospel: Religious Metaphor or Bodily Reality?* (Biblical Tools and Studies 13; Leuven: Peeters, 2011) 57–77, on pp. 66–8.

the healing of Peter's mother-in-law might have a Petrine origin. However, Jesus also called Peter "Satan" and was denied by him three times.[19] It takes a lot of unwarranted psychologizing to explain how such narratives might have been told by Peter himself to John Mark mentioned in the Acts and in 1 Peter. Neither is there any sign of appearances of the risen Jesus in Jerusalem, where John Mark lived according to Acts – to the contrary, the disciples and Peter are to go to Galilee. Byrskog concludes that "only a minority of the Markan chreiai actually go back directly to Peter".[20] All things considered, the traditional identification of the author as John Mark is unlikely, and in any case the author does not seem to *legitimate* the message of the Gospel through his acquaintance with Peter.[21]

Matthew

Matthew, by most exegetes considered the next Gospel in order, is equally silent about its author. It seems that early church historians sought for its writer in the list of apostles, where "Matthew the tax collector" is mentioned in the place of Mark's "Matthew" (Mark 3:18/ Matt 10:3) and identified with the man whom Jesus called according to Matt 9:9 (cf. Mark 2:14 where the man is called Levi son of Alphaeus). Matthew was, of course, a suitable candidate, because as a tax collector he could be presumed to be literate. The fact is, however, that the author does not present himself in the Gospel. At the same time, there is a strong community presence in Matthew (cf. Matt 16:16–18 and the community discourse in ch. 18). The mission commission displays the idea of a teaching tradition from Jesus through the eleven disciples to all nations (28:18–20).

Much of Matthew's Gospel is based on Mark, and the additional speech material, especially the well-structured Sermon on the Mount (Matt 5–7), reflects scribal and catechetic tradition rather than historical survey. It is therefore difficult to trace individual eyewitnesses behind Matthew other than those who might have contributed to his narrative predecessor.[22] For Matthew,

19 Cf. my article, "Satanic Disciples: A Narrative and Cognitive Analysis of Two Gospel Scenes", in J.A. Ramos/P.R. Davies/M.A. Travassos Valdez (ed.), *From Antiquity to the Present: the 2008 European Association of Biblical Studies Lisbon Meeting* (Lisbon: Centro de História da Universidade de Lisboa, 2008) 69–80.

20 Byrskog, *Story as History*, 291.

21 I do not discuss Bauckham's (*Eyewitnesses*, 124–7) constrained argument about the *inclusio* of eyewitnesses, i. e., the *naming* of the principal eyewitness in the beginning and at the end of the work. For criticism, see Eve, *Behind the Gospels*, 144–6.

22 Byrskog (*Story as History*, 293) is eloquent but hardly convincing (observe the several caveats) in suggesting "a cumulative argument" in favour of eyewitnesses behind Matthew: "Yet, considering all we are now in a position to know about the vital importance of oral history and oral tradition in antiquity, including early Christianity, we can indeed, at this point of our inquiry, ask somewhat programmatically whether it is not likely, after all, that the stories of an eye-

Jesus is ideally the only Teacher (23:8) whose teaching is mediated through the eleven apostles, perhaps especially through Peter, and it is valid for all times. The role of the disciples as eyewitnesses is taken for granted (13:16–17). In seeing Petrine influence behind both Mark and Matthew, Byrskog confronts the difficulty that the two Gospels display rather dissimilar attitudes to the law. Byrskog suggests that "what we have in Mark reflects Peter before Antioch; what we have in Matthew reflects Peter after Antioch".[23] This is to beg the question, inasmuch as Peter's personal influence behind Mark and Matthew should first be established. In addition, the explanation rests on a doubtful construction of Peter's changing attitudes, harmonizing Acts 10 and 15 with Gal 2:11–13. The type of explanation Byrskog suggests is curiously reminiscent of a biblicist strategy. If Mark and Matthew relied on Peter but differed from each other, then "each author adhered to one of the different attitudes of Peter".[24] But perhaps Byrskog is actually referring to traditions *about* Peter, which is quite another matter than dependence on Peter's changing attitudes.

Traditions *about* Peter may and indeed do diverge, and it is certainly conceivable that there were Matthean community members who claimed to represent a "Petrine" stance in halakhic matters. In the pericope on the temple tax (Matt 17:24–27), found only in Matthew, Peter plays an important role as issuing, as it seems, the disciples' halakhic decision about the matter. Jesus, however, does not seem quite content with Peter's simple "yes", but explains that in principle the sons are free from paying the tax – they only pay it in order not to cause offence. Similarly in 18:21–22, a narrative intrusion in the community discourse, Peter enters the scene to propose a "sevenfold" forgiveness – but again Jesus must correct him. Thus Peter's authority is strangely ambivalent in Matthew. Obviously Matthew knew of Peter's special status from a tradition that was backed up by one group within the community. The evangelist was critical of this tradition, however, and confronted allegedly Petrine traditions with the only valid teaching – *Jesus'* teaching.[25]

When the Matthean Jesus refers to "all that I have commanded you" (28:19), the reference is back to the Gospel itself, which – rather than any Petrine or other tradition – is the criterion valid for all times. As Gerhardsson notes –

witness played some role also as the Matthean author collected information and composed his narrative. There is a cumulative probability that such was, as a matter of fact, the case." Where is the beef? Byrskog only cites Matt 16:13–20. But even if we agree that "the nucleus of the notion of Peter's authorization as tradition carrier was known in the Matthean community already before the gospel story took shape" (p. 294), this is no evidence that Matthew used "the stories of an eyewitness" in composing his work.

23 Byrskog, *Story as History*, 297.

24 Byrskog, *Story as History*, 296.

25 See my article, "Peter as Character and Symbol in the Gospel of Matthew", in K. Syreeni/D. Rhoads (ed.), *Characterization in the Gospels: Reconceiving Narrative Criticism* (Sheffield: Sheffield Academic Press, 1999) 106–52, on pp.134–44.

adding, perhaps too confidently, that the same idea appears to underlie the Gospel tradition *as a whole* – the Matthean Jesus is programmatically the *only* teacher (Matt 23:8–10).[26] This is so only ideally, however; certainly there were many teachers in Matthew's community, and among them the evangelist himself was the most influential one, as it was *his* Gospel that petrified the teaching of Jesus.

Luke

Luke, the third and probably latest of the so-called Synoptic gospels, opens with an authorial self-presentation in first person singular (Luke 1:1–4; cf. Acts 1:1–3). The author does not reveal his name, however, nor does he present himself as an eyewitness, although he asserts that the chain of tradition ultimately goes back to eyewitnesses and involved participants:

> Since many have undertaken to set down an orderly account of the events that have been fulfilled among us, just as they were handed on to us by those who from the beginning were eyewitnesses and servants of the word, I too decided, after investigating (?) everything carefully from the very first, to write an orderly account for you, most excellent Theophilus, so that you may know the truth concerning the things about which you have been instructed. (Luke 1:1-4 NRSV)

Loveday Alexander has shown that the general structure (including first person presentation without further dwelling on the author's identity) conforms to the conventions of Hellenistic "scientific" prefaces.[27] Alexander finds eyewitness terminology more typical of medical and other "scientific" treatises than of historiographical works,[28] but Byrskog stresses that seeing with own eyes was also a historian's virtue. Irrespective of whether we describe Luke as a historian, a biographer in the "scientific" tradition or a creative developer of the gospel genre, it is clear that Luke presents his story (διήγησιν, v. 1:1) as being based on reliable eyewitnesses. At the same time, the mention of several predecessors indicates that the Gospel is in fact dependent on written sources. The author need not have seen here any tension; he may have thought that his predecessors had had access to eyewitness, and by comparing, combining and editing his sources he would be at least as truthful to the original witnesses as his sources.

The rendering "after investigating (everything carefully)" in the above quotation is probably inaccurate. Alexander proposes "having followed" as a compromise between two possible interpretations, namely, "being thoroughly

26 Gerhardsson, *Tradition and Transmission*, 41–2. Compare also *Memory and Manuscript*, 332.

27 L. Alexander, *The Preface to Luke's Gospel: Literary convention and social context in Luke 1.1–4 and Acts 1.1* (SNTSMS 78; Cambrigde: University Press, 1993).

28 Alexander, *Preface*, 34–41.

familiar with the whole affair" or "having followed them [*scil.* the eyewitnesses as sources] all".[29] The expression is thus best understood

> either as a claim to thorough and accurate understanding ... or possibly as a claim to be "following in the footsteps" of the sources already identified in verse 2. Either way, what we have here is a claim to fidelity and comprehension in transmission rather than to any personal contribution by the author.[30]

Apart from the prologue, Luke's Gospel is thoroughly third-person narration. In the Acts, however, the "we" passages give the impression that the author was Paul's travel companion.[31] To my mind, the literary interpretation suggested by Vernon K. Robbins seems the most plausible.[32] Robbins observes that the "we" passages appear in the context of sea voyages, a context where first person plural narration was a well-known stylistic device since Homer's *Odyssey.* Robbins's interpretation is also enlightening in connecting the "we" to the prologue of Luke's Gospel, where apparently the whole story of Luke-Acts is depicted as "the events that have been fulfilled among *us*". With Paul, the gospel is finally making its way to "us", that is, to the Roman Gentile Christians of Luke's day. Understood in this way, the "we" passages are neither eyewitness notes nor the gravest, deceptive kind of authorial fiction, but a stylistic and hermeneutical device, indicating that the story is basically "our" story. In this way, the "we" style is used as a means of legitimating Luke's and his audience's symbolic universe.

Before focusing on Paul's mission, Luke stresses the role of the apostles as witnesses. In the beginning of Acts (1:8), Luke has the risen Jesus himself say that the apostles "will be my witnesses in Jerusalem, in all Judea and Samaria, and to the ends of the earth". As Byrskog points out, for Luke the decisive criterion was that the person must have been among Jesus' followers from the beginning, namely from John the Baptist's ministry and until the day of Jesus' ascension (Acts 1:21–22). In line with this, Peter's testimony in front of Cornelius's household highlights the function of the apostles as witnesses: "We are witnesses to all that he did both in Judea and in Jerusalem. They put him to death by hanging him on a tree; but God raised him on the third day and allowed him to appear, not to all the people but to us who were chosen by God as witnesses, and who ate and drank with him after he rose from the dead." (Acts 10:39–41 NRSV)

29 Alexander, *Preface*, 128–30. Referring to Moessner, Byrskog (*Story as History*, 231) too rejects the translation of παρηκολουθηκότι as "having investigated".

30 Alexander, *Preface*, 134.

31 "The only certainty is that by using 'we' the author attempts to convey the impression of an eyewitness account." H. Conzelmann, *Acts of the Apostles* (Hermeneia; Philadelphia: Fortress, 1987), xl.

32 V.K. Robbins, "By Land and By Sea: The We-Passages and Ancient Sea Voyages", in C.H. Talbert (ed.), *Perspectives on Luke-Acts* (PRSMS 5; Macon, Ga: Mercer Univ. Press and Edinburgh: T.& T. Clark, 1978) 215–42.

Luke's pattern of thought is clear: there is an unbroken and uniform testimony about the earthly and the risen Jesus by the group of the twelve apostles. If Luke's picture is historically correct, Birger Gerhardsson's hypothesis of an authoritative Jerusalem *collegium* of apostles guaranteeing the reliability of the Jesus tradition would seem justified. Luke goes even further in stressing the reliability of his account of "the things that have been fulfilled among us". On the way to Emmaus, the risen Lord met two of his disciples and "beginning with Moses and all the prophets, he interpreted to them the things about himself in all the scriptures" (24:27). According to Acts (1:3), the same Jesus appears to his eleven disciples during 40 days, "speaking about the kingdom of God". The chain of tradition and testimony goes on with Paul, whose "seeing" the risen Jesus is told three times, and whose testament to the Ephesian elders admonishes the church to "remember" the words of the Lord Jesus (Acts 20:35).

What is noteworthy, however, is that Luke's mnemonic language is a *literary* device. Byrskog remarks that the Lukan author "presents the mnemonic activity in a somewhat odd way".[33] The two examples Byrskog gives are Luke 24:6–8 and Acts 1:5, cf. 11:16. In both cases Luke's reference to remembering is unfortunate within the narrated world. In the first case, the women should remember Jesus' words that they do not seem to have heard before. In the second case, Peter remembers Jesus' words that according to Luke 3:16 were uttered by John the Baptist. But as soon as we realize that Luke is addressing his readers, the narrative lapses become understandable. The *reader*s have learned Jesus' prophecy although the women may not have heard it. The *readers* know that John's words about Jesus were true, so of course the risen Jesus could confirm them and Peter could remember them as words of the Lord. And why could not Paul remember a saying of Jesus not recorded in the Gospel (Acts 20:35)!

All in all, Luke puts much effort in legitimating the Christian tradition through Scripture, a uniform apostolic testimony, the risen Jesus' own teaching, and Paul's testimony to the future church. Throughout in Acts, Luke also stresses the Spirit's guidance. A closer examination of Luke's work would show additional means of legitimating the Christian symbolic universe, above all his presentation of the church as the legitimate heir of Israel's ancestral faith. For this, too, Luke provides a paradigmatic eyewitness: old Simeon, a pious Jew, who has seen God's promises to Israel and the nations fulfilled with his very eyes (Luke 2:25–32). It is most convenient that this eyewitness is about to die (*nunc dimittis*) and is only accessible through Luke's writing.

The question, of course, is precisely the reliability of Luke's work as historical account. *All story is not history*, after all. If Luke was dependent on Mark and other predecessors, it is not obvious why he should have been better informed than these sources about what actually happened in Jesus' lifetime.

33 Byrskog, "From Memory to Memoirs", 11.

Moreover, it is doubtful whether Luke is always trying to show the eyewitness backup of his tradition apart from and beyond his general point that the apostles are trustworthy witnesses. In some cases, as with Simeon and another worthy representative of the old Israel – "a prophet, Anna the daughter of Phanuel, of the tribe of Asher... a widow to the age of eighty-four" (Luke 2:36–38) the precise naming might signal such an attempt, although the legendary nature of the narrated incidents hardly convinces a modern reader. But when, e.g., it is said of Jesus' mother that she "treasured all these words and pondered them in her heart" (2:19; cf. 2:51), it is more likely that the evangelist is just offering his readers a paradigm of proper hearing and understanding, as he certainly does in 10:38–42 (Martha and Mary).

John

The main bulk of the Gospel of John is third-person narrative with an omniscient narrator. However, already the prologue introduces a confessing "we" (1:14–18). Both there and in 3:11–12, where the "we" sentence appears abruptly, the theme of eyewitness testimony is present. So it is also in John 21, the postscript of the Gospel, which seems to be added after the completion of John 1–20.[34] If one compares the new ending in 21:24–25 to 20:30–31, one observes that the testimonial and authorial complexity has grown: a "we" group testifies to the reliability of the testimony of the anonymous disciple who has also written the text; finally an "I" adds a comment which seems reminiscent of the earlier ending.[35] Thus the theme of testimony is especially emphatic in the latest redaction of the Gospel. It is tempting to regard 1 John 5:6–12 as the culmination of the Johannine idea of testimony: no human testimony (as John the Baptist's in John 1:17), not even the Beloved Disciple's or the community's testimony (John 21:24–25) is enough. The Spirit and the water and the blood testify, and eventually God himself testifies to Jesus. At the same time, the believers have the Spirit's assurance and guidance; in a way, then, they as charismatics bear a testimony in themselves. Here at the latest it should be evident that the concept of testimony is deeply theological or more precisely, both dogmatic and charismatic. It has little to do with a careful handing down of eyewitness reports or learning Jesuanic sayings by heart.

34 Although John 21 seems a postscript and may reflect a slightly altered situation in the Johannine community, it is not necessarily much later than the final redaction of John 1–20. The new ending rounds off the final redaction by bringing the story of the Beloved Disciple to an end and by resolving the tension between Peter and the Beloved Disciple that is created in John 13–20.

35 Bauckham, *Jesus and the Eyewitnesses*, 369–83, argues that the "we" in Johannine literature often, and also in John 21:24–25, is the "we" of authoritative testimony and is used instead of "I". In that case the author of the Gospel must have forgotten the words of Jesus which he records at John 5:31 (NRSV): "If I were to testify on my own behalf, my testimony would not be valid."

In the Gospel of John, the curious combination of dogmatism and charismatic claim has not yielded such extremes. In John, human testimony – in the form of eyewitness testimony or as "seeing" and proper "understanding" – is valued. As in Luke, so also in John remembrance is tied to the idea of eyewitnesses. However, the peculiarities in Luke's mnemonic language are relatively trivial in comparison with John. When Jesus has cleansed the temple in chapter 2, the narrator tells: "His disciples remembered that it was written, 'Zeal for your house will consume me.'" (2:17 NRSV). Why was it necessary to speak of the disciples' remembrance, when Scripture alone could have been quoted? A few verses later we are told: "After he was raised from the dead, his disciples remembered that he had said this; and they believed the scripture and the word that Jesus had spoken." (2:22 NRSV). The saying the disciples remembered was, as the narrator explains, about destroying and building the temple – but only the scriptural reference guided the disciples to understand that the temple was Jesus' body. Thus, the remembrance was about the passion of Jesus. Jesus' entry into Jerusalem is narrated as follows:

> The next day the great crowd that had come to the festival heard that Jesus was coming to Jerusalem. So they took branches of palm trees and went out to meet him, shouting, "Hosanna! Blessed is the one who comes in the name of the Lord – the King of Israel!" Jesus found a young donkey and sat on it; as it is written: "Do not be afraid, daughter of Zion. Look, your king is coming, sitting on a donkey's colt!" His disciples did not understand these things at first; but when Jesus was glorified, then they remembered that these things had been written of him and had been done to him. (John 12:12–16 NRSV)

What exactly did the disciples remember in retrospect? It is first said that they did not understand or know these things (ταῦτα οὐκ ἔγνωσαν), but afterwards they "remembered that these things ... had been done to him (ταῦτα ἐποίησαν αὐτῷ)". Taken at face value, this means that the disciples not only understood that the event was a fulfillment of Scripture but that they "remembered" the very event of Jesus' entrance.[36]

The surprising "remembrances" in John 2 and 12 both have to do with the passion and resurrection tradition. It is therefore interesting that the Johannine passion story introduces a disciple who not only "remembered" afterwards but was a mindful eyewitness to the passion, death and the empty

36 T. Thatcher, "Why John Wrote a Gospel: Memory and History in an Early Christian Community", in A. Kirk/T. Thatcher (ed.), *Memory, Tradition, and Text: Uses of the Past in Early Christianity* (Semeia Studies 52; Atlanta: SBL, 2005) 79–97, theorises about John 12:12–16 as follows (p. 83): " ... John's assertion that they 'did not know these things' must mean that their initial sensory experience differed from their later understanding. In other words, the disciples' initial neurological impressions were flawed, and were reconfigured and corrected in light of subsequent events." I just wonder if we really need neural science to explain the *literary* means by which the Johannine redactor legitimates the passion story.

tomb. This Beloved Disciple[37] enters the stage at the last supper, reclining "in the bosom" of Jesus. The same expression was used in the prologue depicting Jesus "in the bosom" of the Father and presenting him as the only one who makes God known. This bold application of the prologue lends the Beloved Disciple the function of a trustworthy witness to, and interpreter of, Jesus. He has other related functions, too, such as being a symbol of a spiritual authority that exceeds Peter's. At the last meal, Peter had to ask for his help to identify the traitor. After Jesus' arrest, the Beloved Disciple helped Peter to come in to the courtyard of the high priest, so Peter was able to deny Jesus three times. A comparison with Mark shows that the character of the Beloved Disciple is a secondary feature in both cases. Later, we are told, the tandem disciples ran to the empty tomb, with the Beloved Disciple running faster but politely letting Peter go into the tomb first; but of course it was the Beloved Disciple who first believed (in Jesus' *resurrection* after his *death*; 20:8).[38] In the appendix of the Gospel, the two are once more together in the company of the risen Jesus. Peter is pardoned and receives leadership in the church, but in the end both men become blood witnesses: Peter through his foretold martyrdom and the Beloved Disciple through being a remaining eyewitness to Jesus' betrayal, arrest and death. The Beloved Disciple was at the cross together with Jesus' mother, and obviously he is the one who testifies to the water and blood that came out from the dead body of Jesus:

> Then the soldiers came and broke the legs of the first and of the other who had been crucified with him. But when they came to Jesus and saw that he was already dead, they did not break his legs. Instead, one of the soldiers pierced his side with a spear, and at once blood and water came out. (He who saw this has testified so that you also may believe. His testimony is true, and he knows that he tells the truth.) These things occurred so that the scripture might be fulfilled, "None of his bones shall be broken." And again another passage of scripture says, "They will look on the one whom they have pierced." (John 19:32–37; NRSV)

Scripture could testify to the unbroken bones and the piercing, but the Beloved Disciple was needed to account for the blood and the water. Here we must recall the three witnesses in 1 John 5. The issue is about the implications of the incarnation of Jesus as the Logos of God. The dogma of the Johannine community, as taught by the author of 1 John, is that Jesus came "*not* with the water *only but* with the water *and the blood*" (1 John 5:6 NRSV; my emphasis).

37 See my article, "The Witness of Blood: The Narrative and Ideological Function of the 'Beloved Disciple' in John 13–21", in A. Mustakallio (ed.), *Lux Humana, Lux Aeterna: Essays on Biblical and Related Themes in Honour of Lars Aejmelaeus* (PFES 89; Helsinki: Finnish Exegetical Society/Göttingen: Vandenhoeck & Ruprecht, 2005) 164–85.

38 The Beloved Disciple is first and foremost a (fictional) witness of the *passion* story; but the passion storyline, by narrating Jesus' *death*, also involves his *resurrection* (rather than disappearance or ascension) – so it is vital that the trustworthy Disciple can also be a witness of and a believer in Jesus' resurrection.

About water – the water of Jesus' baptism that occurred simultaneously with the outpouring of the Spirit – there was a pan-Johannine and probably pan-Christian consensus; what was at stake was the blood. Was Jesus God incarnated even at his death? Yes he was, states the author of 1 John. The final Gospel of John employed the Beloved Disciple to confirm this; the author of 1 John even took recourse to a divine authority.

Thus, the Gospel of John employs first person singular and plural testimony in order to legitimate the symbolic universe of a Johannine group, especially the right understanding of incarnation, against another Johannine group. The identity of the Beloved Disciple is kept in secret, and even though he may not be a purely fictional character, the symbolism he carries seems more important than his person. The figure of the Beloved Disciple may have been inspired by a real person, but Byrskog seems very reluctant to discuss the historical question.[39] Bauckham has more to say, but his portrayal of a relatively unknown person who was outside the circle of the twelve and in need of legitimating his role as a Gospel author by means of careful narrative rhetoric, hardly concurs with the picture of a disciple who reclined nearest to Jesus at the last meal, was a friend of the high priest, was the sole disciple at the cross, took care of Jesus' mother after the crucifixion, was the first male disciple at the empty tomb, appeared later in the fishing company of Peter, and if Bauckham is right in interpreting John 1:35, even became a disciple before Peter.[40]

The relationship between the Beloved Disciple and the Paraclete is much discussed. They have some common functions, especially that of witnessing to and reminding of Jesus, but the Paraclete is a divine figure – the Spirit of God and of Jesus – and "the presence of Jesus when Jesus is absent",[41] while the Beloved Disciple is a human witness to the earthly Jesus and his passion. The two characters may belong to different paths of Johannine tradition-history, because the Paraclete only figures in Jesus' farewell speeches (John 14–16) and the Beloved Disciple is a witness to Jesus' passion, becoming the author of the Gospel only in 21:24.[42]

39 Byrskog, *Story as History*, 237–8, formulates very carefully: "... it is evident that at a certain stage someone preferred to compose ... another account of the life and deeds of a historical person. That writing needed a legitimating foundation. The editor(s) adding 21:24–25 took refuge in a person who, they believed, had been an eyewitness to the ministry of Jesus."

40 Perhaps this rather unlikely combination of characteristics motivates Bauckham's dwelling on the *semantics* of witness and his keen approval of Byrskog's idea of eyewitnesses as *interpreters*.

41 R.E. Brown, "The Paraclete in the Fourth Gospel", NTS 13 (1966–67) 113–32, on p. 128.

42 See also my article, "Testament and Consolation: Reflections on the Literary Form of the Johannine Farewell of Jesus", in J. Pakkala/M. Nissinen (ed.), *Houses full of all Good Things: Essays in Memory of Timo Veijola* (PFES 95; Helsinki: Finnish Exegetical Society, 2008) 573–90.

The Gospel of Thomas

Gerhardsson, Byrskog and Bauckham hardly pay notice to the non-canonical Gospels.[43] This is regrettable, since a broader look at early Christian Gospel literature will enable us to see clearer some tendencies and developments that begin with the canonical documents from the first and early second century[44] but become more obvious in the second century and later. Of course, canonicity is no guarantee against a mild or a grave sort of pseudonymity. The deuteropauline letters perhaps are in the former category, while 2 Peter 1:16–18 – a pseudonymous "Peter" referring to his autopsy and auditory experience on the mountain of Jesus' transfiguration – is a striking example of the latter.

We have already seen that the later canonical Gospels – Luke and in particular John – are much more concerned about eyewitness testimony than Mark and Matthew. This is so in spite of the fact that these later canonical Gospels are less likely based on direct eyewitness memories than Mark's Gospel. In the last chapter of John, the eyewitness is even made the author of the Gospel. As we look at a sample of early non-canonical Gospels, we see this trend continued and getting stronger.[45] As in John 21, we can often observe a secondary ascription of the text to an assumed eyewitness or an original follower of Jesus. In addition, narration in first person is increasingly used to strengthen the authorial fiction.[46]

Let us begin with the second-century Gospel of Thomas (GThom), sometimes called the "fifth" Gospel because of its importance as a source to Jesus traditions. The Gospel is mainly third person narration, although the narrative elements are very scanty and the literary form with Jesus' sayings and short dialogues with the disciples have an air of immediacy and direct address. However, the heading counteracts the impression of immediacy by referring to the writing and authorship of the document: "These are the secret sayings that the living Jesus spoke and Didymos Judas Thomas recorded."

43 Gerhardsson, *Memory and Manuscript*, has none, while Byrskog, *Story and History*, has one reference to the Gospel of Thomas and one to the Gospel of the Hebrews (both in the same footnote). Bauckham, *Jesus and the Eyewitnesses*, has a few more references.

44 I cannot discuss here the dating of the canonical Gospels, but I assume that Mark and Matthew come from the second half of the first century (ca 70–75 and 80–90 CE), while John and Luke(-Acts) come from the last years of the first century or from the first quarter of the second century. My hypothesis, for which I cannot argue here either, is that Luke-Acts is later than and dependent on John.

45 In what follows, space does not permit a discussion of all the Nag Hammadi documents, but certainly we can observe the trend there, too.

46 It is an interesting fact that first person narrative and authorial fiction do not go hand in hand in the four canonical Gospels. The author of Luke-Acts is not the storyteller in his work apart from the "we" sections, and the Beloved Disciple only appears in third-person narration (so even in John 21:24).

The heading is not incidental, for the Gospel grants Thomas a special relation to Jesus (log. 13). Thus, although the authorial presentation is clearly fictional, there may be a tradition-historical connection between the figure of Thomas and the Gospel who bears his name. At the same time, the possible connection seems weaker than in the case of John and the Beloved Disciple, because there is no explicit "we" group joining the testimony of Thomas. GThom also incorporates another tradition, which has James as the leading figure (log. 12).

It is interesting that the temporal and local setting of Jesus' instructions to his disciples remains obscure. In view of the later Gnostic dialogue Gospels, it might seem as if the implied setting here, too, is after Jesus' public career and after his (seeming) crucifixion and death, as Bertil Gärtner thought at an early stage of Thomasine research.[47] It is, however, not advisable to interpret GThom in light of later Gnostic texts, because the Gnostic character of this Gospel is anything but certain. Instead, we should observe that GThom *does not specify* the time and place of the deliverance of Jesus' words. That the speaker is the "living" Jesus might in principle indicate a Post-Easter (or post-departure) setting; but in log. 12 the disciples say to Jesus, "We know that you are going to leave us." This reminds of the Johannine farewell speeches, which are in their present context strangely "out of place" (cf. John 17:11: "I am no longer in the world").

I concur with Ismo Dunderberg, who rejects the hypothesis that the Gospels of John and Thomas are engaged in a direct dialogue, although the appearance of Thomas in some crucial scenes in John does point to a similar early Christian milieu.[48] It seems that the authorial fiction in both of these documents reflects a situation where an appeal to Peter or the twelve could not legitimate the community's special tradition.

The Gospel of Peter

The fragment of the (late?) second-century Gospel of Peter is mostly narrated in third person by an omniscient narrator. However, on two occasions the story is told in first person: after the crucifixion, when the disciples mourn, and right at the end of the survived fragment, after the women's visit at the empty tomb and the disciples' return to their homes, as Peter – a spokesman for the apostles – is fictively presented as the narrator:

> But I began weeping with my friends…

47 B. Gärtner, *Ett nytt evangelium: Thomasevangeliets hemliga Jesusord* (Stockholm: Diakonistyrelsens bokförlag, 1960), 128–9.

48 I. Dunderberg, *The Beloved Disciple in Conflict? Revisiting the Gospels of John and Thomas* (New York: Oxford University Press, 2006).

> But we, the twelve disciples of the Lord, continued to weep and mourn, and each one, still grieving on account of what had happened, left for his own home. But I, Simon Peter, and Andrew, my brother, took our fishing nets and went away to the sea. And with us was Levi, the son of Alphaeus, whom the Lord...

The shift between first and third person narration seems clumsy, and it is likely that the use of first person is secondary. Whether Peter is also presented as the author of the Gospel must remain uncertain, because there are no hints of his writing activity and still less of the circumstances of his writing. The redactor did not bother to give the impression that the story as a whole was based on Peter's or the disciples' memories. It is said that the disciples hid themselves and fasted, mourned and swept night and day until the Sabbath, and at the end we find the disciples still mourning, so obviously they are not presented as eyewitnesses in the intervening narrative. One of the most astonishing scenes in the Gospel is the nightly incident with huge men coming from the tomb and a cross that spoke – but only the Roman soldiers witness it. As far as we can conclude, first person narration seems to occur redactionally in dramatic turns where the focus is on the emotions and inner thoughts of Peter and his company.

The Gospel of Mary

The early or mid-second century Gospel of Mary[49] is third person narration, but like Thomas and later Gnostic dialogue gospels it is essentially based on a discourse between Jesus and his disciples. The beginning of the text (probably six pages) is missing from the Coptic manuscript and the two Greek fragments do not help here, but the narrative situation is clearly a post-resurrection appearance of Jesus. After a more philosophical discourse, where Peter is singled out as a speaker (BG 7), there follows a more "canonical" scene. Jesus greets the disciples ("Peace be with you") gives a mission commission with final advice, then departs – but the disciples are still distressed and weeping. From this moment (BG 9), Mary becomes the most prominent character. She stands up, encourages the disciples and is asked by Peter to tell the words of the Saviour (BG 10). So she does: "What is to you unknown and I remember I will tell you..."[50] Interestingly, although the Gospel presupposes that Mary knew

49 For the Coptic and Greek texts with translations and commentaries, see C.M. Tuckett, *The Gospel of Mary* (*Oxford Early Christian Gospel Texts*; Oxford: Oxford University Press, 2007). As for a date, the Gospel very likely comes from the second century. Tuckett suggests that "perhaps a date in the first half the second century might fit the data in the gospel slightly better than a date in the second half (or the last quarter) of the century" (p. 12).

50 So the Greek text (POxy 3525). The Coptic manuscript (BG 8502) reads just: "I will inform you about what is hidden from you." Instead, the Coptic text has the theme of remembrance in Peter's question to Mary: "Tell us the words of the Saviour which you remember, which you know but we do not, and which we have not heard."

well the earthly Jesus, her remembrances render the contents of her visionary encounter with the (risen?) Savior. Thus the "remembrance" language does not seem to refer to a recollection of Jesus' earthly words and deeds. Despite the framing third person narration, Mary's speech is conspicuous enough to render the text, in a qualified sense, a "testimony" of Mary – a testimony debated and eventually accepted by one of the apostles (so the Greek text), or by all (Coptic).

While the remembrance theme in the Gospel of Mary may seem slender, the document testifies to another kind of remembrance, namely, the memory of the Gospel of John. Ismo Dunderberg argues convincingly that there are several reminiscences of the Fourth Gospel in the Gospel of Mary.[51] Dunderberg's most interesting observations concern the narrative setting, which – although post-resurrectional – resembles thematically the Johannine farewell section.[52] Mary's role is not just one of Jesus' beloved (cf. the Beloved Disciple in John), but she also fulfils some functions of the Paraclete by reminding the disciples of Jesus' words and by comforting them when they were distressed and in fear. Although the Johannine reminiscences are not overwhelmingly clear, there is enough to suggest that the author of the Gospel of Mary remembered a farewell situation – not from the life of Jesus but from a *literary scene* in John.

Jewish Christian Gospels

The so-called Jewish Christian Gospels[53] have only been preserved in very fragmentary quotations, and the confusing statements of the church fathers make it extremely difficult to conclude even the number of the individual Gospels. From the evidence we have, we may surmise that the narration was mostly in third person, leaving the authorship unanswered, but a few fragments might indicate a tendency to make Jesus a direct narrator of the story. In what is usually considered a fragment of the Gospel of the Hebrews, Jesus tells about his ecstatic experience: "A moment ago my mother, the Holy Spirit, took me by one of my hairs and brought me to the great hill, the Tabor." However, it is risky to draw far-reaching conclusions, since for example Luke occasionally, in an otherwise third-person narrative, has Jesus describe his ecstatic vision (Luke 10:18).

51 I. Dunderberg, "Johannine Traditions and Apocryphal Gospels", in J. Schröter (ed.), *The Apocryphal Gospels within the Context of Early Christian Theology* (BETL CCLX; Leuven – Paris – Walpole: Peeters, 2013) 67–93, on pp. 82–91.

52 The blending of a pre-passion farewell address and a post-resurrection scene is noteworthy. What makes the blending understandable is that both scenes deal with Jesus' departure and "testament".

53 The cited translations of these Gospel fragments come from P. Luomanen, *Recovering Jewish-Christian Sects and Gospels* (VCSup 110; Leiden – Boston; Brill, 2012), 245–52.

Another fragment, thought by Epiphanius to be from the "Hebrew Gospel" but according to Petri Luomanen's analysis might derive from the epilogue of the Gospel of the Ebionites or from an introduction to an Ebionite Acts of the Apostles, has a peculiar mixture of first person plural and Jesus' speech. The fragment also makes use of authorial fiction, making Matthew the author or at least the narrator of the story:

> There was a man called Jesus, about thirty years old, who chose us. And came to Caphernaum, he entered the house of Simon, also called Peter, and opened his mouth and said: "When I went by the Sea of Tiberias I chose John and James, the sons of Zebedee, and Simon and Andrew and Thaddeus and Simon the Zealot and Judas the Iskariot and you Matthew, who was sitting at the custom-house; I called you and you followed me. I wish you to be twelve apostles for the testimony to Israel."

In the Synoptic Gospels (and in John), the calling of the apostles is narrated in third person by an external omniscient narrator. Here Jesus himself apparently reminds his disciples of how he chose them. The text seems a bit confusing, but its combined effect is that the events are turned into eyewitness stories and at the same time into Jesus' direct address to the eyewitnesses (and to the alleged author).

Infancy Gospels

Two infancy gospels deserve mention. The mid-second century Infancy Gospel of James,[54] or The Birth of Mary as its oldest title seems to have been, is mainly third person narrative. In a short middle part of this text (chapters 18–21), Joseph speaks in first person singular ("Now I, Joseph..."). It is conceivable that this is a stylistic device (cf. the "we" in Acts), but more probably the sudden change reflects the composition history of the text.[55] Thereafter the narrative continues in third person, until a fictional first-person author presents himself in the epilogue:

> Now I, James, am the one who wrote this account at the time when a disturbance arose in Jerusalem at the death of Herod. I got away into the wilderness until the disturbance in Jerusalem was over. I will, however, praise the Lord, who gave me the wisdom to write this account. Grace will be with all those who fear the Lord. Amen.

54 See S. Pellegrini, "Das Protoevangelium des Jakobus", in C. Markschies/J. Schröter (ed.), *Antike christiliche Apokryphen in deutscher Übersetzung, Band 1/2* (Tübingen: Mohr Siebeck, 2012) 903–29. For convenience, I quote the Scholars Version in R.J. Miller (ed.), *The Complete Gospels* (Sonoma: Polebridge, 1992), 376–89.

55 Pellegrini, "Das Protoevangelium des Jakobus", 907 n.18.

The authorial fiction in this document is unrealistic and may well be secondary, but it is interesting that here even the fictional circumstances of the writing are recorded, as also, e.g., in the Secret Book of James (see below).

The Infancy Gospel of Thomas may be younger than that of James, but hardly later than the third century.[56] The main narrative is in third person by an omniscient narrator, but it is framed by an authorial fiction in the heading and the prologue:[57]

> Heading: "The Words of Thomas the Philosopher about the Youthful Deeds of the Lord."
>
> Prologue: "I, Thomas the Israelite, make this proclamation to all of you, gentile brothers, to make known the wondrous youthful deeds of our Lord Jesus Christ that he performed after being born in our land. It begins as follows."

The conclusion of the Gospel reads as follows: "Jesus got up, followed his mother, and was obedient to his parents. His mother remembered all these events. Jesus grew in wisdom and age and grace. To him be glory for ever and ever. Amen." The conclusion is derived from Luke (2:51–52), where Mary's remembrance was also mentioned. Luke's paradigmatic portrayal of Jesus' mother as one who remembered all that happened has by now become a literary cliché.

Conclusion: "The Mnemonic Trajectory" in a Literary and Socio-Cognitive Perspective

In sum, as we have gone through several early Gospels from the first centuries, a trend emerges to the effect that authorial fiction, coupled with first person narration, becomes a literary commonplace and seems increasingly unrealistic. In later texts authorial fiction could even make Jesus an author. How should we explain this development?

Samuel Byrskog, in his *Story as History*, recognizes that the notion of autopsy first occurs after Mark and Matthew, and finds that one reason to the development is apologetics. Another reason is simply the lapse of time. These two factors go hand in hand, Byrskog contends, motivating "elaboration, but not forgery".[58] This clearly does not pertain to the non-canonical gospel literature, or the canonical 2 Peter. In the case of the Beloved Disciple in John, the concept of elaboration must be stretched to its limits. If we resist the

56 U.U. Kaiser, "Die Kinderheitserzählung des Thomas", in *Antike christliche Apokryphen* (see note 53), 930–59, thinks that the terminus ad quem is "das vierte Jahrhundert oder sogar das Ende des dritten Jahrhunders" (p. 936).

57 The quotations are again from *The Complete Gospels*, 365–72.

58 Byrskog, *Story as History*, 252.

canonical bias, we see that the Beloved Disciple shares company with a number of privileged disciples.[59] To be sure, John's authorial fiction is exceptional in that the eyewitness-author remains unnamed. It is even possible that a real person has somehow inspired the formation of this literary character. But clearly the lapse of time does not explain the growing number of bizarre authorial and eyewitness fiction.

Already Mark and Matthew sought to legitimate their message by various means, however not by authorial fiction. Luke took some further steps, but was still content with referring to the apostolic witness, and with creating an impression of being Paul's contemporary: the living Paul, whose voyages "we" had followed, is still proclaiming the gospel. John, instead, wanted to link "us" to Jesus, even by means of his word as in Matthew, but also through the testimony of the Beloved Disciple – hence the authorial fiction – and through the Paraclete's testimony and the risen Jesus' dwelling in "us". Even if the perceived time span between then and now was the hermeneutical prerequisite for the need of legitimation, the differences in legitimating devices call for an explanation.

My discussion points to some possible factors. The relatively heavy authorial fiction in John is understandable in light the Gospel's social dynamic. The Gospel's legitimation required a man of authority, more precisely, "our" man – not the first best man from the list of the twelve or eleven apostles but a representative of the Johannine group. Another, related factor was the need to legitimate the right understanding of the Johannine Jesus traditions over against a competing Johannine interpretation. In this inner strife, the Beloved Disciple's eyewitness role, together with the other disciples' recovered memory of the passion story, was useful. When we move to second century and later gospels, the "sectarian" factors still play a role in Thomasine literature and for example in the use of Mary or Judas as privileged disciples. At the same time, however, the phenomenon of literary *habitualisation* gains more importance: the group of the twelve – with some variation in names – becomes a literary cliché.

To what extent can we assume that the earliest Gospels are based on eyewitness testimonies? Byrskog would obviously like to describe the (canonical) gospels as "the memoirs the apostles", a description found in Justin Martyr near the middle of the second century. But Byrskog himself notes that there are apologetic reasons for Justin's coinage, and Justin knew well that "the gospel(s)" was the usual term for this kind of literature. What Justin's terminological innovation is supposed to prove, besides the probability that Justin thought the Gospels or some of them were apostolic memoirs, is not quite obvious.

Byrskog pays much attention to the *chreia* form, which is typical of Mark. Since third person narration is the rule in *chreiai*, and also throughout Mark's

59 Dunderberg, *The Beloved Disciple*, 175–80.

Gospel, this observation only underlines the fact that we do not have access to first person eyewitness testimonies. Byrskog's conclusion that

> Within these stories we see the encoded traces of living people interacting with the past in a context of orality, we see their use of texts in a constant and dynamic process of re-oralization, we see people cherishing their own memories and recalling the past within the frames of their conceptual world, we see other people eagerly interrogating them for information, etc., etc.[60]

must therefore be deemed conjectural. We cannot "see" that much. The closest we safely get to the narrative memory of Jesus in the Gospels is not eyewitnesses who tell what they recall, not even people eagerly interrogating eyewitnesses, but third person stories about Jesus, stories that already conform to rhetorical – and thus socio-cognitive – *conventions* in order to be *memorised.*[61] And even if we by chance had access to eyewitness testimonies, we still have the question posed by John Dominic Crossan in a chapter of his *The Birth of Christianity:* "Does Memory Remember?"[62] This question is all the more urgent if we subscribe to Eric Eve's remark that "it may well be that in future research memory will turn out to be a more useful category than oral tradition".[63] If so, then despite my criticisms not only social memory, but also the question of eyewitnesses will have to remain on the scholarly agenda.

60 Byrskog, *Story as History*, 252–3.

61 We should remember that *chreia* as a mnemotechnic structure was principally an aid for keeping in mind and retelling something that was already told: "Why is the *chreia* an *apomnemoneuma?* Because it is kept in mind (*apo-mnemoneuetai*) in order that it may be quoted." Third century CE Pap. Oxy. 85, quoted in M.C. Moeser, *The Anecdote in Mark, the Classical World and the Rabbis* (JSNTS 227; Sheffield: Sheffield University Press, 2002), 65.

62 J.D. Crossan, *The Birth of Christianity: Discovering What Happened in the Years Immediately After the Execution of Jesus* (New York: HarperCollins, 1998), 59–68.

63 Eve, *Behind the Gospels*, 185.

Dan Nässelqvist

Dual Conventions: The Oral Delivery of New Testament Writings in Light of First-Century Delivery Practices

At least since the publication of Werner Kelber's *The Oral and the Written Gospel*,[1] orality studies have presented a significant contribution to exegesis, in part by turning attention to the importance of oral performances in antiquity. Despite a focus on the multivalence of form and content in oral delivery, however, the conception of the oral performances themselves has been strangely uniform. When different types of performances are distinguished, they are nevertheless explained as functioning in the same way.

In what follows I will question this uniform picture of oral delivery in antiquity, distinguish between delivery of oral texts ("oral performance") and written texts ("public readings"), and argue that they were accompanied by different conventions. Oral texts may well have been recited from memory whilst standing up and employing gestures, movements, facial expression, and tone of voice. Against the consensus of scholars working within the field of performance criticism I will show, however, that pictorial and textual evidence from antiquity indicate that written texts were delivered in another manner. The reader was frequently seated and read directly from a manuscript held in his hands, whilst communicating the text with fitting vocal expression, yet without gestures or mimicry. These findings demonstrate that notions about the function and effect of oral performance must be related to – and contingent upon – a deeper understanding of different types of oral delivery that were prevalent in antiquity.

The Uniform Model: Oral Performance

Orality studies have had a considerable influence upon biblical studies during the last three decades. Consequently, an increasing number of publications focus upon various aspects of orality in the context of early Christianity and a specific discipline ("performance criticism") that focuses upon oral performances has emerged.[2] Orality studies deepen our understanding of the

1 W.H. Kelber, *The Oral and the Written Gospel: The Hermeneutics of Speaking and Writing in the Synoptic Tradition, Mark, Paul, and Q* (Philadelphia: Fortress, 1983).

2 Among the more influential studies are W. Shiner, *Proclaiming the Gospel: First-Century Per-*

complexities involved in ancient media culture, in which orality and textuality cannot be completely separated. They also illustrate the active and creative use of memory in antiquity and the variation inherent in performances shaped by audience participation. As mentioned above, however, the descriptions of such changeable oral performances are remarkably monolithic and rarely scrutinized.

This traditional model of oral performances in antiquity, which I will describe below, originates in folkloristic studies from Milman Parry and Albert Lord onwards and has occasionally been uncritically embraced by biblical scholars.[3] The almost axiomatic understanding, therefore, has been that all types of texts, including New Testament writings, were orally delivered in the same manner. A single model is thus used to describe performances of Homeric poetry, the handing over of oral Jesus traditions among the earliest apostles, and the oral delivery of New Testament writings in early Christianity.

The traditional model describes oral performances as a lively recitation of a previously memorized text with a standing performer who employs gestures, facial expressions, movements, and tone of voice to convey the text. Pieter Botha expresses the view clearly:

> Reading in antiquity was not experienced as a silent scanning, mainly mental activity. It was a performative, vocal, oral-aural event. The reader literally recited, with vocal and bodily gestures, the text that one usually memorized beforehand.[4]

According to this view, which is repeatedly asserted by scholars engaged in performance criticism,[5] the advent of the New Testament writings as written texts made no difference to how they were orally delivered. "Reading" is thus interpreted as an act of oral performance from memory. Richard Ward and

formance of Mark (Harrisburg: Trinity, 2003); W.D. Shiell, *Reading Acts: The Lector and the Early Christian Audience* (Boston: Brill, 2004); D. Rhoads, "Performance Criticism: An Emerging Methodology in Second Testament Studies: Part I", *BTB* 36 (2006) 118–33; D. Rhoads, "Performance Criticism: An Emerging Methodology in Second Testament Studies: Part II", *BTB* 36 (2006) 164–84; H.E. Hearon/P. Ruge-Jones/T.E. Boomershine, *The Bible in Ancient and Modern Media: Story and Performance* (Eugene: Cascade Books, 2009).

3 A.B. Lord, *The Singer of Tales* (Cambridge: Harvard University Press, 1960).

4 P.J.J. Botha, *Orality and Literacy in Early Christianity* (Eugene: Cascade Books, 2012), 91.

5 See, e.g., P.J.J. Botha, "'Publishing' a Gospel: Notes on the Historical Constraints to Gospel Criticism", in A. Weissenrieder/R.B. Coote (ed.), *The Interface of Orality and Writing: Speaking, Seeing, Writing in the Shaping of New Genres* (Tübingen: Mohr Siebeck, 2010) 335–52, on p. 338; Rhoads, "Performance Criticism: Part I", 123, 127; Rhoads, "Performance Criticism: Part II", 164–84; Shiell, *Reading*, 107; W.D. Shiell, *Delivering from Memory: The Effect of Performance on the Early Christian Audience* (Eugene: Pickwick, 2011), 3–4; Shiner, *Proclaiming*, 89–98, 103–4, 135–36. The same view is also expressed in earlier literature, although not as regularly. See, e.g., R.F. Ward, "Pauline Voice and Presence as Strategic Communication", in J. Dewey (ed.), *Orality and Textuality in Early Christian Literature* (Atlanta: Society of Biblical Literature, 1994) 95–107, on p. 95.

David Trobisch even state that ἀνάγνωσις consequently can be translated "to perform the Scriptures in public" rather than "reading [aloud]".[6]

Scholars engaged in performance criticism point to a number of literary and pictorial sources from antiquity that describe or depict the type of delivery that they describe as oral performance. Whitney Shiner refers to rhetorical treatises from antiquity and how these present different levels of "oratorical style".[7] He shows that the rhetoricians (he primarily refers to Quintilian) emphasize the use of memory, gestures, movement, facial expressions, and tone of voice.[8] William David Shiell turns to both literary and pictorial sources and finds evidence for the same aspects of delivery. He demonstrates that sculptures of Roman magistrates often portray them as giving a speech, yet with the text in a closed roll held in the left hand. He thus rightly draws the conclusion that "the closed roll iconographically indicates that he is performing a recitation".[9] He also points to images of ancient drama that present actors as using gestures and facial expressions to convey the text and evoke emotions.[10]

There is thus ample evidence in ancient literary and pictorial sources for the type of oral performances envisioned in orality studies. Such dramatic performances involved a performer who had previously memorized a text, which he or she communicated with gestures, movement, facial expressions, and tone of voice.

The problem with the notion of oral performances as proposed by performance criticism scholars is not that it lacks support from ancient sources, but rather that the evidence is applicable to such a small number of settings and genres. Scholars who adhere to this model rarely acknowledge differences between oral and written texts, nor between written texts of different genres.[11] I will return to this issue after considering another model that recognizes a greater variety of oral delivery in antiquity.

6 R.F. Ward/D.J. Trobisch, *Bringing the Word to Life: Engaging the New Testament through Performing It* (Grand Rapids: Eerdmans, 2013), xi.

7 Shiner, *Proclaiming*, 87. For an introduction to stylistic levels in antiquity (and how they are misinterpreted by Shiner and Shiell), see D. Nässelqvist, "Stylistic Levels in Hebrews 1.1–4 and John 1.1–18", *JSNT* 35 (2012) 31–53.

8 Shiner, *Proclaiming*, 83–5, 87–8, 104–9, 130–1.

9 Shiell, *Reading*, 34–51 (the quote is found on page 49).

10 Shiell, *Reading*, 62–83.

11 Note, for example, how Ward and Trobisch conflate terms such as "public reading", "recitation", "recital", and "performance" into a single activity that is characterized by "voice, gesture, impersonation, and movement" (Ward/Trobisch, *Bringing*, 16–18).

A More Diversified Model: Tellings and Public Readings

In a recent volume Anthony Le Donne and Tom Thatcher describe the media culture of the first century CE and present two types of oral performances: "individual tellings" and "public readings".[12] As I have indicated, however, among performance criticism scholars the term "reading" is regularly interpreted as an act of oral performance from memory. Le Donne and Thatcher do nothing to dispel this notion. Although their model distinguishes "readings" from "tellings" – and thus acknowledges the difference between oral texts and written texts – the two types are characterized in the same way, as "oral performances". Such performances lack an original to check the content of individual performances against. On the contrary, each performance produces a unique text which is adapted to individual live audiences: "oral performances can and will vary in content, gesture, metre, volume and tone based on the immediate presence and response of the aural audience."[13]

Although Le Donne and Thatcher are right in identifying two broad types of oral performances in antiquity, they neither clearly distinguish between the types nor make any use of the insight, but rather focus entirely upon the supposed similarities of "tellings" and "readings". They are probably right to affirm that even public readings lack clear original texts (considering the complexities of publication in antiquity and the inevitable variation between individual manuscripts),[14] although each individual reading has its original in the manuscript from which the reading is made. Similarly, the notion that oral delivery – regardless of type – produces a unique text is true for public readings as well, at least in the sense that the vocal expression is modified to fit not only the content, but also the listeners and the context in which the reading takes place. To accentuate these aspects is not the same as asserting that public readings "can and will vary in content, gesture, [and] metre", however, since reading aloud from a manuscript does not automatically mean that the reader changes the text found in it.

The two types described by Le Donne and Thatcher thus need to be more clearly distinguished. Such an undertaking should apply not only those ancient literary and pictorial sources that describe the first type of oral delivery (oral performances), but also those that portray the second (public readings).

12 T. Thatcher/A. Le Donne, "Introducing Media Culture to Johannine Studies: Orality, Performance and Memory", in T. Thatcher/A. Le Donne (ed.), *The Fourth Gospel in First-Century Media Culture* (London: T&T Clark, 2011) 1–8, on p. 5.

13 Thatcher and Le Donne, "Media", 5.

14 Cf. K. Haines-Eitzen, "The Social History of Early Christian Scribes", in B.D. Ehrman/M.W. Holmes (ed.), *The Text of the New Testament in Contemporary Research: Essays on the Status Quaestionis* (Leiden: Brill, 2013) 479–96, on p. 484: "the notion of the 'original' text owes its opacity in part to such complex processes."

Distinguishing the Types

While there is some evidence in ancient sources for the type of oral performance envisioned by scholars engaged in performance criticism, this is also true of oral delivery in the form of public reading.[15] Literary and pictorial sources from antiquity thus affirm the existence of at least two types of oral delivery: oral performance – or, in the vocabulary of Le Donne and Thatcher: "tellings" – and public reading. Although these types share some common features, they differ in most aspects and are also clearly distinguished in many ancient sources. More importantly for the application to early Christian writings, they can be differentiated according to the type and genre of text that is being orally delivered.

Oral Performance

The types of oral delivery that appear in sources describing ancient oratory and drama are, as we have seen, similar to oral performances envisioned in orality studies. Such performances involve a memorized text, which can be either oral or written in nature, and which is performed dramatically with the application of gestures, movement, facial expressions, and tone of voice. The performance and the text are adapted to the gathered listeners and influenced by their interaction.[16]

The ancient sources that describe such oral performances confine them, however, to a limited number of settings. First, the rhetorical treatises focus upon the oral delivery of speeches, primarily in a judicial setting. Second, pictorial sources portray oral performances both in the context of public speaking (depicting statesmen and orators delivering speeches) and the theatre (depicting actors performing drama).[17] Third, oral performances also occur as part of education in school settings, as students memorize and recite aphorisms, shorter texts, and speeches.[18]

Oral performances can thus only be found in a few settings and the number of literary genres delivered in this manner is even more limited. Aside from the

15 I will describe some of this evidence below.

16 On the role of the listeners in oral performances, see Shiell, *Delivering*, 23–8; Shiner, *Proclaiming*, 143–9.

17 Pictorial sources that show oral performance can be identified by the fact that they depict individuals engaged in oral delivery who do not use manuscripts, but rather deliver texts from memory.

18 See, e.g., Juvenal, *Sat.* 7.150–53; Quintilian, *Inst.* 2.7.1–4, Seneca, *Ep.* 33; Theon, *Progymnasmata* 66–67. On memorization of texts in education, cf. S.F. Bonner, *Education in Ancient Rome: From the Elder Cato to the Younger Pliny* (Berkeley: University of California Press, 1977), 39–40, 111, 307; D.M. Carr, *Writing on the Tablet of the Heart: Origins of Scripture and Literature* (Oxford: Oxford University Press, 2005), 178–83; M.L. Clarke, *Higher Education in the Ancient World* (London: Routledge & K. Paul, 1971), 22, 27.

special case of a school setting, in which all genres could be actualized through both oral performance and public reading, oral performances as described in ancient literary and pictorial sources are confined to oratory and drama.

The close connection between oratory and drama expressed itself not only in the fact that both genres were regularly delivered through oral performance, but also in the way orators anxiously tried to delimit themselves from the activities and disreputability of actors at the same time as they drew parallels to acting and actors.[19] In oratory as well as drama, the use of voice, movement, gestures, and facial expressions were important features of ὑπόκρισις or *actio*, the engaging delivery of an already memorized and internalized text.[20]

Oral performance of literary writings was thus largely confined to two genres, oratory and drama. Although there is no evidence as to the practical manner of how oral tradition about Jesus was transmitted, it may well have been orally delivered in the manner of oral performances as conceived by performance criticism.

Public Reading

Public reading involves oral delivery in the form of reading aloud directly from a manuscript, rather than from memory. The handling of the manuscript restricts the reader's possibility to communicate the text with gestures, movements, and facial expression. The reader is nevertheless expected to employ a fitting tone of voice to express the text clearly and faultlessly.[21]

Ancient literary and pictorial sources connect public reading with a wider range of settings in comparison to oral performances. Public reading thus occurs in private, semi-private, as well as public settings, such as during dinner, in reading communities (which include philosophical groups and early Christian communities), and in public recitals at large-scale venues.[22]

The range of literary genres delivered in public readings is also more extensive than what we find in oral performances. Literary sources mention public reading of history, poetry, letters, and technical treatises, but also of oratory and drama, which are thus genres not solely confined to oral

19 See, e.g., Cicero, *De or.* 3.220; Cicero, *Or. Brut.* 86; Quintilian, *Inst.* 1.11.1–14, 11.3.88–91, 11.3.122–24.

20 Cf. Cicero, *De or.* 3.220–25; Cicero, *Or. Brut.* 58–60; Quintilian, *Inst.* 11.3.14, 11.3.65–67. See also E. Fantham, "Orator and/et actor", in P. Easterling/E. Hall (ed.), *Greek and Roman Actors: Aspects of an Ancient Profession* (Cambridge: Cambridge University Press, 2002) 362–76.

21 H.Y. Gamble, "Literacy, Liturgy, and the Shaping of the New Testament Canon", in C. Horton (ed.), *The Earliest Gospels: The Origins and Transmission of the Earliest Christian Gospels: the Contribution of the Chester Beatty Codex P45* (London: T&T Clark, 2004) 27–39, on p. 35; D. Nässelqvist, *Public Reading in Early Christianity: Lectors, Manuscripts, and Sound in the Oral Delivery of John 1–4* (NovTSup 163; Leiden: Brill, 2015), 84–6.

22 Nässelqvist, *Public Reading*, 67–72.

performance. Suetonius relates, for example, how Terence read *Andria*, one of his comedies, aloud during a dinner at the household of Statius Caecilius.[23]

Pictorial evidence from antiquity depicts readers in a variety of settings. Many of these may portray individuals immersed in silent reading, although that was not the regular practice of reading in antiquity.[24] Despite this, there are also a number of images that depict public reading in a community setting. These include a famous school scene from Trier, which portrays a *grammaticus* and two pupils who appear to be reading aloud from book rolls; a fresco from the house of the Tragic Poet in Pompeii, which includes two scenes that depict a young man who reads aloud for a captivated audience; and the so-called "Plotinus sarcophagus", which portrays a seated man with an open book roll in his hands and two women at his sides, who appear to be listening intently.[25]

Literary and pictorial sources of public reading relate a coherent picture of public reading in antiquity. The reader, commonly a lector of servile status, is seated on a chair or a stool, holds the manuscript (which can include a writing of any literary genre) in his hands, and reads aloud from it with fitting vocal expression, yet without gestures, movement, and facial expressions.

Fitting New Testament Writings into the Picture

Given the fact that ancient sources affirm that – during the first century CE – literary writings were orally delivered in oral performance from memory or in public reading from a manuscript, the remaining question is where the New Testament writings fit into this picture. I will consider evidence both from the New Testament itself as well as from other early Christian writings.

At first glance, early Christian sources seem to indicate clearly that New Testament writings were orally delivered in the form of public reading in Christian gatherings, rather than in oral performances of memorized material. The oldest references are found in the New Testament itself:

> I adjure you by the Lord that this letter be read aloud [ἀναγνωσθῆναι] to all the brothers. (1 Thess 5:27)
>
> And when this letter has been read aloud [ἀναγνωσθῇ] among you [παρ᾽ ὑμῖν], have it read aloud also in the community of the Laodiceans. (Col 4:16)

23 Suetonius, *Vita Terenti* 2.

24 On the debate about silent reading vs. reading aloud, see the excellent summary in W.A. Johnson, "Toward a Sociology of Reading in Classical Antiquity", *AJP* 121 (2000) 593–627, on pp. 594–600. On the commonality of reading aloud, see G. Cavallo/R. Chartier, "Introduction", in G. Cavallo/R. Chartier (ed.), *A History of Reading in the West* (Oxford: Polity, 1999) 1–36.

25 All of these images can be found in H. Blanck, *Das Buch in der Antike* (München: C. H. Beck, 1992), 132 (fig. 72), 133 (fig. 73), 140 (fig. 77), 152 (fig. 87).

Until I arrive, give attention to the public reading [τῇ ἀναγνώσει], the exhortation, and the teaching. (1 Tim 4:13)

Blessed is the one who reads [ὁ ἀναγινώσκων] the words of this prophecy, and blessed are those who hear [οἱ ἀκούοντες] and attend to the words written in it. (Rev 1:3)

All of these passages indicate that New Testament writings were read aloud. The references to multiple people taking part ("all the brothers" in 1 Thess 5:27, "you" in plural in Col 4:16, and "those who hear" in Rev 1:3) make it clear that the reading consists of reading aloud in a community setting. The oral delivery event is described with the verb ἀναγινώσκειν, "to read (aloud)", and the noun ἀνάγνωσις, "a (public) reading".

Having seen these examples, how is it that scholars engaged in performance criticism argue that New Testament writings were memorized and delivered in oral performances with gestures, movements, and facial expressions? This is only possible if one takes both ἀναγινώσκειν and ἀνάγνωσις to refer to such an oral performance from memory. As seen in the quote from Ward and Trobisch above, they translate the phrase τῇ ἀναγνώσει in 1 Tim 4:13 as "to perform the Scriptures in public".[26] As we have seen, however, most literary writings in antiquity were orally delivered in public reading rather than performed from memory. To be sure that the primary meaning of ἀναγινώσκειν/ἀνάγνωσις, "read (aloud)"/"(public) reading", is truly applicable to the New Testament writings, let us nevertheless turn to another early Christian source that clarifies the point.

The *Acts of Peter* includes a passage that clearly indicates the manner in which a gospel is orally delivered in an early Christian gathering. Having related the event of how Peter is invited to a Christian community in the private home of Marcellus, the following is stated about the oral delivery:

When Peter came into the dining room he saw that the gospel was being read aloud [*legi*]. And rolling it up [*involvens*] he said: … Now I will explain that which has been read [*lectum est*] to you.'[27] (*Acts Pet.* 20)

The passage from the *Acts of Peter* portrays the oral delivery of the gospel text as a public reading directly from a manuscript, in this instance a book roll. Peter rolls it up as a way to signal that the reading is over and that he will commence with the interpretation of the text. The verb *legere*, "to read (aloud)", thus clearly denotes public reading and not a dramatic performance from memory.

Judging from the account in the *Acts of Peter* and in light of the fact that literary writings of other genres than oratory and drama regularly were orally

26 See footnote 6.

27 "*Introibit autem Petrus in triclinio et vidit evangelium legi. Involvens eum dixit: 'Viri, qui in Christo creditis et speratis, scitote, qualiter debeat sancta scriptura domini nostri pronuntiari. … Nunc quod vobis lectum est iam vobis exponam.'*"

delivered in the manner of public reading, there is no reason to doubt that the New Testament passages cited above refer to the same practice. The verbs for reading (aloud), ἀναγινώσκειν and *legere*, should thus not be taken as references to oral performances from memory, but rather to reading directly from a manuscript. The terms ἀναγινώσκειν and ἀναγνώστης ("reader"/ "lector") are used in this sense not only in the New Testament but also in 2 Clement, Justin Martyr, and in later Christian texts:

So then, brothers and sisters, after the God of truth I read to you an appeal that you turn towards that which has been written, so that you may save yourselves and the one who reads [τὸν ἀναγινώσκοντα] among you. (*2 Clem.* 19.1)

Then, when the one who reads [τοῦ ἀναγινώσκοντος] has ceased, the presider through a discourse admonishes and invites the imitation of these good things. (Justin, *1 Apol.* 67)

A reader [ἀναγνώστης] is installed when the bishop gives the book to him. He does not have hands laid upon him. (Hippolytus, *Trad. ap.* 11)

[I]f there is also a reader [ἀναγνώστης], let him too receive with the presbyters in honor of the prophets. (*Didascalia apostolorum* 2.28.5)

A Comparison of the Two Types

Having determined that the oral delivery of New Testament writings in early Christianity regularly consisted of public reading, I will relate in more detail how an oral delivery event comprising public reading differed from oral performance. These observations accentuate the problems of assuming that early Christian literary writings were delivered in dramatic performances from memory, as asserted by scholars engaged in performance criticism.

In terms of the skills required to present a certain text or tradition, the two types of oral delivery employ different techniques in enabling communication. In oral performances, the performer relies upon memorization and improvisation to deliver a text in a dramatic manner adapted to the present context. With the help of memorization, performers can identify material relevant to the current situation and audience, whereas improvisation aids the adaptation of both text and delivery to that setting. These demands match the material found in ancient rhetorical treatises. Aside from guiding students in composition, the treatises also stress the importance of memorization and of adapting the delivery through improvisation and bodily expression of the text (with the help of, for example, gestures and facial expressions, aspects that I will return to below).[28] Public reading, on the other hand, presupposes a

28 Quintilian, for example, spends the eleventh book of his *Institutio oratoria* on the study of appropriateness and adaptation (11.1), memory (11.2), and the bodily techniques of delivery (11.3). This book is immediately preceeded by a section on improvation (10.7).

different skill set. A lector needs the ability to quickly – albeit following thorough preparation – interpret the solid blocks of continuous letters, transform them into sound, and vocally express his interpretation of the text, while constantly looking ahead in the manuscript to what comes next.[29] Lectors thus rely upon preparation and a fixed text, rather than on improvisation around a memorized text. Regardless of the type of oral delivery, the difficulties involved and the contemporary conventions of what constituted acceptable delivery called for recurrent practice among the individuals responsible for oral delivery, in order to maintain the necessary skills

As indicated above, improvisation plays an important role in adapting an oral performance – both in terms of text and delivery – to the audience and the setting in which it occurs. In public reading, however, ancient scribal conventions precluded improvisation by producing manuscripts that were intentionally hard to use by other than trained specialists.[30] Lectors and other readers thus had few opportunities of embellishing or adapting the text during the reading, much less express it with bodily expression.

The manner in which manuscripts are used in the delivery event constitutes another clear dividing-line between the two types. Manuscripts are essential to public reading, which involves reading aloud directly from them. The features of a manuscript – such as column width, line spacing, punctuation, and other lectional signs[31] – thus affect the manner in which the text is delivered. In oral performances, manuscripts are regularly eschewed and performers focus instead on combining memory and improvisation.[32] At least in oral performances of speeches, however, a closed roll could be carried in the left hand to indicate the text being delivered.[33]

29 Cf. Gamble, "Literacy", 35.

30 Cf. Johnson, "Sociology", 609–12, 619–20. Larry Hurtado argues, however, that the manuscript tradition of early Christianity enfranchised a broader spectrum of readers by including a greater number of "reader's aids". Nevertheless, he does not draw the conclusion that these readers improvised around the texts that they now could read with somewhat less difficulty [L.W. Hurtado, "Manuscripts and the Sociology of Early Christian Reading", in C.E. Hill/M.J. Kruger (ed.), *The Early Text of the New Testament* (Oxford: Oxford University Press, 2012) 49–62]. On the contrary, in a recent article ["Oral Fixation and New Testament Studies? 'Orality', 'Performance' and Reading Texts in Early Christianity", *NTS* 60 (2014) 321–40] he strongly argues against the notion of oral performances from memory.

31 Most early Christian manuscripts comprise some lectional signs, such as apostrophe, ekthesis, and punctuation. See, for example, the lists of lectional signs found in a number of early manuscripts in S.D. Charlesworth, "Indicators of 'Catholicity' in Early Gospel Manuscripts", in C.E. Hill/M.J. Kruger (ed.), *The Early Text of the New Testament* (Oxford: Oxford University Press, 2012) 37–48, esp. 43–4. Note, however, that most manuscripts comprise more lectional signs than indicated by Charlesworth, who only includes those that indicate text division. Cf. Nässelqvist, *Public Reading*, 56–8.

32 Cf. Quintilian, *Inst.* 11.2.44–46.

33 See, e.g., statues of Titus and Tiberius, both of which have the right hand lifted in the adlocutio gesture of address while the left holds a closed roll (Shiell, *Reading*, 50 fig. 5).

When it comes to the position of the person who reads or performs, the difference between the two types is less clear. Pictorial evidence indicates that oral performance regularly involves a standing performer.[34] The extensive use of movements to express the text being performed seems to presuppose such a stance. The images of reading are less clear. Most readers in ancient pictorial sources are seated, yet we have to differentiate between reading in private (whether silent or aloud) and reading aloud for someone else – that is, public reading. Images of public reading regularly depict a seated reader.[35] A possible exception is found on a first-century CE relief which portrays Emperor Hadrian as he addresses the people. Hadrian has his right arm slightly raised in what may be a gesture, whereas his left land holds an open book roll.[36] It is possible that the relief portrays a public reading event with a reader who is standing up.[37] A similar arrangement is found on the funeral altar of the boy poet Quintus Sulpicius Maximus, who is also portrayed as standing up with an open roll in his left hand, in his case in the context of a poetry contest that he participated in.[38] The open roll with the midsection hanging limply between the beginning and the still unrolled end has been interpreted as an indication of "interrupted reading".[39] Hadrian and Sulpicius may therefore be examples that public reading was sometimes performed whilst standing up.[40]

The use of gestures, movement, and facial expressions are important features of a successful oral performance, especially for expressing and evoking emotions (an important feature of oratory and drama).[41] Such means

34 Cf. the images of orators and actors in Shiell, *Reading*, 39 fig 2, 50 fig. 5, 55 fig. 7, 63 fig. 10, 80 fig. 18.

35 For references, see footnote 24.

36 The relief can be seen from different angles in G. Davies, "Togate Statues and Petrified Orators", in D.H. Berry/A. Erskine (ed.), *Form and Function in Roman Oratory* (Cambridge: Cambridge University Press, 2010) 51–72, on p. 58 fig. 3, and in Shiell, *Reading*, 113 fig. 21.

37 This is the interpretation of Glenys Davis, who states that "Hadrian does appear here to be reading his text rather than speaking extempore" (Davies, "Statues", 57).

38 For images, see Davies, "Statues", 59 fig. 4; D.E.E. Kleiner, *Roman Imperial Funerary Altars with Portraits* (Rome: Bretschneider, 1987), plate XXVII, XXVIII; M. Nocita, "L'ara di Sulpicio Massimo: Nuove osservazioni in occasione del restauro", *BCACR* 101 (2000) 81–100, on p. 93 fig. 17 (detail of the open roll and the writing upon it). For a discussion of the implications of this monument for interpreting first-century reading culture, see D. Nässelqvist, "Contextualizing First-Century Education and Public Reading Practices: The Funerary Altar of Quintus Sulpicius Maximus", forthcoming.

39 T. Birt, *Die Buchrolle in der Kunst: Archäologisch-antiquarische Untersuchungen zum antiken Buchwesen* (Leipzig: B.G. Teubner, 1907), 181–96; Blanck, *Buch*, 72; G. Cavallo, "Between Volumen and Codex: Reading in the Roman World", in G. Cavallo/R. Chartier (ed.), *A History of Reading in the West* (Oxford: Polity, 1999) 64–89, on p. 71.

40 It is also possible to interpret these images as examples of what Quintilian describes as "brief notes and small books [*brevem adnotationem libellosque*] that can be held in the hand and that may be glanced at from time to time" (*Inst.* 10.7.31). If so, the images of Hadrian and Sulpicius do not portray public reading, but rather performers who use (or at least have access to) notes for oral performance.

41 Shiell, *Reading*, 47–82; Shiner, *Proclaiming*, 127–40.

of conveying the text are, however, rarely or never employed in public reading. Since lectors regularly are seated they cannot use movements to express the text that they are reading. The handling of the manuscript also means that the hands are occupied with holding it or – in the case of rolls – actually unrolling the book roll during reading. The continuous interpretation of *scriptio continua* lines renders extensive eye contact with the audience difficult and since gestures should be accompanied by corresponding movements of head and gaze (in the direction of the gesture),[42] public reading cannot be combined with gestures.

Despite the varying degrees to which the text can be conveyed through bodily expressions, both types of oral delivery are strengthened by ample use of vocal expression. Ancient literary sources indicate that ancient audiences expected not only a correct and clear pronunciation, but also one that was adapted to and expressed the content of the text being orally delivered.[43] The most basic requirement for a successful reading was a clear, faultless, and appropriate pronunciation and vocal expression of the text. This included knowledge of how to correctly pronounce each syllable, when to let the voice rise or fall, what to emphasize, and how to adapt the voice to bring out the character and meaning of a passage.[44]

Finally, the two types of oral delivery cannot both be combined with the use of furniture and tools. As indicated above, oral performances comprise dramatic delivery of a memorized text, which is conveyed by a standing, moving, and gesticulating performer. This leaves little room for furniture or tools in the form of roll holders. A lector performing public reading, on the other hand, makes use of furniture in different degrees. He or she is regularly seated in a chair or on a stool and the manuscript is either held in the hands or – as is occasionally the case with book rolls – in a portable roll holder. Such a roll holder, which consists of an open box of wood with low walls that protect the roll when it is used for reading, can be mounted on a small column to form a reading stand (much like a modern movable lectern) that allows for reading whilst standing up.[45] Portable roll holders can be held in one's hands, as in the school scene from Trier mentioned above, in which two of the students are reading from book rolls placed in roll holders, or it could be held by a servant or a slave, as in a relief from Como, in which the seated reader uses a *stylus* to follow the text in the manuscript.[46]

42 Quintilian, *Inst.* 11.3.68–70.

43 See, e.g., Aulus Gellius, *Noct. att.* 13.31.1–11; Cicero, *Or. Brut.* 55–59; Plautus, *Bacch.* 433–34; *Rhet. Her.* 3.20–27.

44 Botha, *Orality*, 101; Nässelqvist, *Public Reading*, 84–9.

45 Note, however, that although there are images of such furniture, they are not found in the context of public reading. See E.R. Knauer, "Roman Wall Paintings from Boscotrecase: Three Studies in the Relationship between Writing and Painting", *MMJ* 28 (1993) 13–46, on p. 25 fig. 30, where the reading stand is found in the background of a scene in which a woman is reading by herself.

46 Birt, *Buchrolle*, 140 fig. 77; Knauer, "Paintings", 23 fig. 26.

Conclusions

Literary and pictorial evidence from antiquity indicate that at least two broad types of oral delivery existed in the first centuries CE. The literary genres of oratory and drama (and, possibly, oral traditions) were presented in oral performances from memory by a performer who used gestures, movement, facial expressions, and tone of voice to convey the meaning and emotions. All other literary genres (and, at times, even oratory and drama) were commonly read aloud in public reading directly from a manuscript, with only vocal expression added to convey and express the text.

Contrary to the assertion of much of previous scholarship, especially within the field of performance criticism, oral performance and public reading did not function in the same way. They differed not only in terms of the techniques used, but also in the degree to which improvisation was used, the manner of bodily expression, the position of the performer/reader, etc. Below is a simplified summary of the differences – and the few similarities – between oral performance and public reading.

	Oral performance	Public reading
Required skills	memorization improvisation bodily expression vocal expression	fluent reading from *scriptio continua* manuscripts vocal expression
Use of improvisa-tion	yes	no
Use of manuscript	no (or rolled up in left hand)	yes, reading directly from it
Position of per-former	standing	seated (or less frequently: standing)
Use of gestures	yes	no
Use of movement	yes	no
Use of facial ex-pressions	yes	no
Use of vocal ex-pression	yes	yes
Use of furniture/ tools	no	yes, chair/stool, roll holder

Early Christian sources point clearly to the conclusion that as soon as the New Testament texts existed as writings, they were regularly read aloud in public reading and not delivered in dramatic oral performances from memory. Several of the earliest writings in the New Testament mention public reading in a community setting and the *Acts of Peter* even depict a scene of public reading of a gospel from a book roll, which took place at a Christian gathering in a household community.

In light of these conclusions, future discussions about the function and effect of oral delivery in early Christianity should take into account that not all delivery took the form of oral performances. On the contrary, there were at least two major types of oral delivery and the most common of these in early Christian contexts – and especially when it comes to the delivery of New Testament writings – was public reading from a manuscript.

II Social Identity

Cecilia Wassén

The Importance of Marriage in the Construction of a Sectarian Identity in the Dead Sea Scrolls

Introduction

The Qumran movement is often associated with celibacy, largely based on the characterization of the Essenes by the classical authors Philo, Josephus, and Pliny the Elder. In contrast, I will argue that marriage, not celibacy, was a prominent feature in the identity formation of the movement, which is evident especially in two texts that outline key halakhic issues, 4QMMT and the *Damascus Document* (D). These documents criticize outsiders for their wrong behaviour related to marital relations and thereby promote a self-understanding of the sect in which proper marriage practice makes up an important part. Informed by social identity and social categorization theories, I will analyse how the sectarian view on marriage contributes to the formation of identity in the D and 4QMMT. I will also address the question as to why marriage becomes an important issue in the formation of a sectarian identity.

Marriage has always posed a special problem for the identification of the Qumran people with the Essenes, since the descriptions of the Essenes by the classical authors appear to differ considerably on this issue compared to the information gleaned from the Dead Sea Scrolls. On the one hand, the classical authors describe the Essenes as male and celibate, with the notable exception of Josephus who mentions a married branch (Josephus *J.W.* 2.160–162). But the sectarian literature from Qumran, on the other hand, does not display any clear traces of a celibate praxis.[1] Instead, most of the rule texts, i.e., D, *Miscellaneous Rules* (4Q265), and the *Rule of the Congregation* (1QSa), reflect communities made up of families. The *Community Rule* (S), is conspicuous by its silence on women and families, but neither does it explicitly confirm the praxis of celibacy. Some scholars question the praxis of celibacy among the Qumran sectarians altogether, but this remains a minority opinion.[2] A

1 For an introduction to the issue of marriage versus celibacy, see C. Wassen, *Women in the Damascus Document* (Atlanta: SBL/Leiden: Brill 2005), 5–8.

2 Notably H. Stegemann, "The Qumran Essenes – Local Members of the Main Jewish Union in Late Second Temple Times", in J. Trebolle Barrera/L. Vegas Montaner (ed.), *The Madrid Qumran Congress: Proceedings of the International Congress on the Dead Sea Scrolls, Madrid 18–21 March 1991* (STDJ 11; Leiden: Brill, 1992), 2:83–166; L. Schiffman, *Reclaiming the Dead Sea Scrolls* (Philadelphia: The Jewish Publication Society, 1994), 127–43; and P. Heger, "Celibacy in Qumran

common solution to this problem has been to harmonize the evidence. So, the rules that reflect married life are used as evidence for the 'married branch' of Josephus, while S has been identified with an elite group, the *yaḥad* ('community'), living at Qumran.[3] This reconstruction of a two-tier system has been criticized by a number of scholars, including John Collins and Alison Schofield. I agree with them that the situation was likely much more complex.[4] Instead of two branches, we should rather envision the sectarians (whom I identify with the Essenes) living all around the country with a mix of married and non-married members in different kinds of living arrangements. Still, given that the sectarian literature overall simply presumes that marriage was the norm, we should accept that marriage was the common way of life in the Qumran movement and celibacy more rare. Concerning the claims about celibacy of the Essenes, I agree with Matthew Black's assessment, which I would extend also to Philo: "One cannot suppress the suspicion that Josephus's account may have been an exaggerated one. He may well be guilty of selecting the exceptions and making them the rule".[5] In addition, one may speculate that both Philo and Josephus were most familiar with the Essene community residing in Jerusalem. Since sexual intercourse was prohibited in Jerusalem, according to sectarian *halakhah* (CD 12:1–2; cf. 11Q19 45:11–12), the Jerusalem Essenes would likely be made up of mostly celibate men.[6] The

– Hellenistic Fiction or Reality? Qumran's Attitude toward Sex", *RevQ* 26/101 (2013) 53–90. These scholars argue that the movement as a whole was made up by families.

3 See e.g., J. Charlesworth's introduction to the *Rule of the Community:* "It has long been recognized that the Rule of the Community evolved in tandem with the needs of the Community, and reflects its ideological, social, and legislative thinking and practice as it developed over time, especially at Qumran"; "Rule of the Community", in E. Qimron/J. Charlesworth (ed.), *Rule of the Community and Related Documents* (The Dead Sea Scrolls: Hebrew, Aramaic, and Greek Texts with English Translations 1; Tübingen: Mohr Siebeck, 1994), 1–103, 2. He also argues (ibid., 3) that the members at Qumran were celibate, "which is the most obvious inference from studying the scrolls and the archaeological evidence".

4 J. Collins and A. Schofield reconstruct the movement as being quite heterogeneous and argue that it is misleading to assume a separation between two main branches based on whether or not members were married. See J. Collins, "The Yahad and the 'Qumran Community'", in C. Hempel/J.M., Lieu (ed.), *Biblical Traditions in Transmission: Essays in Honour of Michael A. Knibb* (JSJSup 111; Leiden: Brill, 2006) 81–96, on p. 94; *Beyond the Qumran Community: The Sectarian Movement of the Dead Sea Scrolls* (Grand Rapids, MI: Eerdmans, 2010), 65–9; A. Schofield, *From Qumran to the Yahad: A New Paradigm of Textual Development for the Community Rule* (STDJ 77; Leiden: Brill, 2009), 47–51.

5 See M. Black, "The Tradition of Hasidean-Essene Asceticism: Its Origin and Influence", in *Aspects du Judéo-Christianisme: Collogue de Strasbourg 23–25 avril 1964* (Paris: Presses Universitaires de France, 1965) 19–33, on p. 28; Wassen, *Women*, 9.

6 CD 12:1–2 reads, "Let no man lie with a woman in the city of the sanctuary to defile the city of the sanctuary with their pollution." Hypothetically, it is possible that the prohibition is part of the rule for the Sabbath, in which case it would only pertain to the Sabbath. Nevertheless, whereas the beginning of the Sabbath code is marked in the text (CD 10:14), it is less obvious where the section ends. The laws immediately before and after the law on sexual intercourse do not primarily relate to the Sabbath. According to Lawrence Schiffman (*The Halakhah at Qumran* [SJLA

community residing at Qumran appears to have been made up of a mix of single (celibate?) men and families, in light of the higher ratio of male than female skeletons at Qumran.[7]

Scholars have highlighted various models of sectarian self-constructions in order to explain the rationales for celibacy in the movement. They commonly point to the use of temple metaphors, arguing that these reflect the self-understanding of the sect as a pure priesthood serving in the temple and abstaining from sexual intercourse permanently.[8] I have previously disputed the interpretation that the temple metaphor (as well as some other models of

16; Leiden: Brill, 1975], 80–83), L. Doering ("New Aspects of Qumran Sabbath Law from Cave 4 Fragments", in M.J. Bernstein et al. (ed.), *Legal Texts and Legal Issues: Proceedings of the Second Meeting of the International Organization for Qumran Studies, Cambridge, 1995. Published in Honour of Joseph M. Baumgarten* [Leiden: Brill, 1997], 251–74), and A. Steudel ("The Houses of Prostration in CD XI,21–XII,1 – Duplicates of the Temple", *RevQ* 16 [1993] 49–63, on pp. 52–3), the section on the Sabbath laws ends in 11:18b. Also C. Hempel (*The Laws of the Damascus Document: Sources, Tradition, and Redaction* [STDJ 29; Leiden: Brill, 1998], 153–6, 189) distinguishes CD 11:21b–12:2a from the previous laws, labelling them "miscellaneous halakhah". The law in CD 12:1–2 is reminiscent of 11Q19 45:11–12, "And if a man lies with his wife and has an emission of semen, he shall not come into any part of the city of the temple, where I will settle my name, for three days". The assumption appears to be that no married couples live in the city of the sanctuary, i. e., Jerusalem, since they are prohibited from entering it. In contrast, if anyone has a nocturnal emission (which is involuntary) "he shall not enter into any part of the temple until [he will com]plete three days". In the latter case, the impure person remains in the city, but is restricted in his movements within it. In light of the law in 11Q19 45:11–12 it is reasonable to conjecture that married couples are supposed to live outside the holy city in CD as well. For the discussion on these laws see Wassen, *Women*, 97–102.

7 Both the sexing and the dating of the female skeletons are subject to debate. Out of the approximately 1200 graves of the cemetery at Qumran, Roland de Vaux excavated 43 and found the skeletons of eight women and six children. With subsequent analyses of the skeletons by Susan Sheridan (who determined that T7 was a male) and Olav Röhrer-Ertl (who revised the identification of several skeletons from male to female) the number of females from de Vaux's excavations is now ten: T22, T24b, T32–34, T35a–b, T37, TA, TS1. In the 1960's, Solomon Steckoll dug up ten graves which included four females and a child. Although his reports are commonly rejected due to his amateur status in archaeology, it should be noted that he used professional experts to determine the sex of the skeletons. Joseph Zias ("The Cemeteries of Qumran and Celibacy: Confusion Laid to Rest?" *DSD* 7/2 [2000] 220–53) dismissed all the evidence of female graves from Roman times claiming that some are later, Bedouin burials, while others are wrongly sexed. His attempts has been criticized by, among others, J. Zangenberg ("Bones of Contention: 'New' Bones from Qumran Help Settle Old Questions [and Raise New Ones]: Remarks on Two Recent Conferences", *The Qumran Chronicle* 9/1 [2000] 51–76). In 2001, Hanan Eshel excavated a structure which they interpreted as a 'mourning enclosure' in which they found the bones of two women in a secondary burial, dated by Carbon-14 testing to the Second Temple Period; see H. Eshel et al., "New Data on the East of Khirbet Qumran", *DSD* 9/2 (2002) 135–65. For a recent survey on publications on the Qumran cemetery, see R. Hachlili, "The Qumran Cemetery Reassessed", in T. Lim/J. Collins (ed.), *The Oxford Handbook of the Dead Sea Scrolls* (Oxford: Oxford University Press, 2000), 46–78.

8 There are many variations on this theme. Hannah Harrington (*The Purity Texts* [Companion to the Dead Sea Scrolls; London: T & T Clark 2004], 104), for example, states, "The Qumran Community was considered a temporary substitute for the Temple by its members, and this 'house of holiness' would certainly be compromised by sexual relations".

self-constructions) is related to celibacy, e.g., in light of the fact that priests were normally married and both ordinary Jewish men and women went to the temple.[9] In contrast to the many scholarly works that focus on the sectarian identity related to celibacy, my paper argues instead that the view of marriage and, by extension, the praxis of marriage, were crucial in the formation of a sectarian identity. In order to understand the appropriate context of the texts on marital laws in D and MMT, I will begin by providing an overview of the views on marriage found in the Scrolls.

General Views on Marriage and Sexual Relations

In general, the sectarian texts display a very positive view on marriage and sexuality. In his book, *The Dead Sea Scrolls on Sexuality*, William Loader surveys attitudes towards sexual relations in all the relevant literature from Qumran, including the rules, legal and liturgical texts, wisdom literature, and biblical expositions.[10] He convincingly demonstrates that there is a positive attitude towards sexual relations throughout the non-biblical literature in the DSS. He states that "the documents rather a generally positive attitude towards marriage and sexual relations within it, and significantly envision [marriage] as part of their future hopes and not as something which that holy time and place will exclude."[11] He points out the overtly positive view on sexuality between a husband and wife in 4QVisions of Amram, Genesis Apocryphon, 4/1QInstruction, and Jubilees.[12] Although these were likely not authored by sectarians, they were certainly used by them. As already mentioned, in the rule texts, D, 1QSa, and 4Q265, marriage is presented as the normal state of life for adults with regulations for various aspects of marital life.[13] According to 1QSa 1:8, men are expected to marry at twenty. D includes a

9 C. Wassen, "Women, Worship, Wilderness, and War: Celibacy and the Construction of Identity in the Dead Sea Scrolls", in J. Baden/H. Najman/E. Tigchelaar (ed.), *A Festschrift for John J. Collins in Celebration of His 70th Birthday* (JSJSup; Leiden: Brill), forthcoming 2015.

10 W. Loader, *The Dead Sea Scrolls on Sexuality: Attitudes towards Sexuality in Sectarian and Related Literature at Qumran* (Grand Rapids, MI: Eerdmans, 2009).

11 Loader, *Dead Sea Scrolls on Sexuality*, 376.

12 On 1Q- and 4QInstruction, see B.G. Wright III, "Wisdom and Women at Qumran", *DSD* 11/2 (2004), 240–61.

13 For general studies on women in the DSS and the evidence of women's participation in sectarian life, see E. Schuller, "Women in the Dead Sea Scrolls", in M. Wise et al. (ed.), *Methods of Investigation of the Dead Sea Scrolls and the Khirbet Qumran Site: Present Realities and Future Prospects* (Annals of the New York Academy of Sciences 722; New York: New York Academy of Sciences, 1994), 115–31; S. White Crawford, "Not According to Rule: Women, the Dead Sea Scrolls and Qumran," in S. Paul et al. (ed.), *Emanuel: Studies in Hebrew Bible, Septuagint, and Dead Sea Scrolls in Honor of Emanuel Tov* (VTSup 94; Leiden: Brill, 2003), 127–50; E. Schuller/C. Wassen, "Women: Daily Life," in L.H. Schiffman/J.C. VanderKam (ed.), *Encyclopedia of the Dead Sea Scrolls* (New York: Oxford University Press, 1999) 2.981–4.

great number of laws that concern women, such as whom not to marry, and purity rules within marriage. For example, a father is admonished to find a suitable husband for his daughter and is also under obligation to disclose any 'blemishes' a daughter might have to a prospective groom (4Q271 3 4–15).[14] Typical for Jewish society of the time, D reflects a strictly negative view on non-marital sexual relations, especially concerning women.[15] Thus, 4Q271 3 10–15 prohibits a man from marrying any woman who has had non-marital sexual relations and prescribes physical examination of a young woman who is accused of not being a virgin before the wedding. Other sectarian texts are worth mentioning, such as the fragmentary 4QpapRitual of Marriage (4Q502), in which marriage is affirmed and fruitfulness is seen as a blessing, and Hodayot, which entails a positive imagery of nursing (e.g., 1QH 15:24–25; 17:36).[16] Loader notes the absence of evidence for any "avoidance or embarrassment at things sexual or a will to deny sexual pleasure in the interests of a Stoic-like approach to intercourse and instilling strict control of the emotions".[17] But the prohibition against 'fornication' with a wife in 4QD[e] (4Q270 7 I 12–13), which likely relates to any form of sexual activity without the intention of procreation, implies a fairly restrictive view on sexuality also within marriage. Importantly, several texts indicate that family life and procreation is expected also in the eschatological era. This is the case with 1QSa and even 1QS in a passage promising abundant offspring, ופרות זרע 'multiplication of offspring' (1QS 4:7).[18]

There is no hint that impurity would be a concern in marital sexual relations or marital unions *per se*. Instead, the criticism in MMT and CD 4:13–5:11 focuses on the wrong unions of marriage and sexual wrongdoings, from which the sectarians must distance themselves. Through these examples

14 See Wassen, *Women*, 71–80.

15 Cf. 4Q159 2–4; on these regulations, see Wassen, *Women*, 80–88.

16 On 4Q502, see S. White Crawford, "Mothers, Sisters, and Elders: Titles for Women in Second Temple Jewish and Early Christian Communities", in J. Davila (ed.), *The Dead Sea Scrolls as Background to Postbiblical Judaism and Early Christianity* (STDJ 46; Leiden: Brill, 2003) 177–91. Loader (*Dead Sea Scrolls on Sexuality*, 257–60) interprets 4Q502 as a marriage ritual in agreement with the original editor.

17 Loader, *Dead Sea Scrolls on Sexuality*, 383.

18 Also 4QS[c] (4Q257) 5:4–5. Although scholars often interpret the promise as a metaphor (e.g., Schuller, "Women", 118), Loader (*Dead Sea Scrolls on Sexuality*, 194, 376–77), with support from Michael Knibb (*The Qumran Community* [Cambridge: Cambridge University Press, 1987], 100) disagrees. He points to similar expectations in *1 Enoch* 10:17–18: "...and they [the righteous] will live until they beget thousands" (trans. Nickelsburg). The expression appears in a list of promises for the eschatological era, including "healing and great peace in a long life", "everlasting blessings", "endless joy in everlasting life", a "crown of glory", and "attire in eternal light". Although metaphors are used in the list of promises to express a future, paradise-like existence, it is still hard to see how the "seed" can be a metaphor; in other words, what would be the target domain? The passage is cited in 4Q502 16 (or there may be a common source behind 1QS 4:4–6 and 4Q502; see Schuller, "Women", 137), i.e., a wedding ritual, or a liturgy for another family-oriented celebration of some kind, which appear to be a natural context for such a hope.

we gain insight into how improper sexual praxis and marital relations from a sectarian point of view are characteristic of the outsiders and thereby form a negative foil against which the sectarians can be drawn as a unified, homogenous, and perfect group. In this way, their own, proper marital praxis also becomes part of the construction of a sectarian identity.

4QMMT

Since its publication in the Discoveries in the Judaean Desert series in 1994,[19] 4QMMT has been subject to much debate concerning the genre, date, *sitz im leben*, as well as parts of the reconstruction.[20] According to the editors, 4QMMT should be dated to an early period in the history of the sect (an assessment which of course depends their reconstruction of that history).[21] The earliest MS (4Q395) is dated paleographically to the late Hasmonean or early Herodian periods. The document can be divided into three parts, A) a section on the calendar, B) a halakhic section, and C) a concluding hortatory or homiletical passage. Nonetheless, the calendar was likely not originally a part of the document.[22] The many divergent opinions about the document are partly due to the fragmentary nature of the manuscript remains and the mix of epistolary and halakhic elements, which makes the genre difficult to determine. The common hypothesis that MMT is a letter written by the Teacher of Righteousness is of course impossible to prove, especially since the name of a sender is not stated and we can only speculate about the *Sitz im leben*.[23] Nevertheless, I side with the initial opinion of the editors that MMT

19 E. Qimron/J. Strugnell, *Qumran Cave 4. V. Miqsat Ma'ase ha-Torah* (DJD 10; Oxford: Clarendon Press, 1994).

20 For an insightful overview of the content, the MSS, dating, and the debate concerning the genre, see H. von Weissenberg, "Miqṣat Maʿaśê ha-Torah (MMT)", in J.J. Collins/D.C. Harlow (ed.), *The Eerdman Dictionary of Early Judaism* (Grand Rapids, MI: Eerdmans, 2010), 952–4.

21 This assessment is based on the content and style of Hebrew; see Qimron/Strugnell, *Miqsat*, 108.

22 Due to the different genre of the calendar (A), compared to the halakhic part (B), and due to the fact that the calendar is attested in only one manuscript (4Q394 3–7); see Qimron/Strugnell, *Miqsat*, 203.

23 Also called "A Halakhic Letter", MMT addresses "you" in the singular (e.g., C 26 כתבנו אליך "we have written to you") but the group of the author is written in the first person plural, e.g., in B 80. A key question is whether this is a copy of a letter that was actually sent or a document produced solely for the ingroup, perhaps in the form of a letter of the Teacher of Righteousness. In the centre of the debate is the interpretation of 4Q171 (4QpPs[a]) 1–10 iv 7–9 which refers to the "Torah that he sent to him", i.e., in the narrative, a text sent from the Teacher of Righteousness to the Wicked Priest. For the former view, see Qimron/Strugnell, *Miqsat*, 119–20, but Strugnell later revised his initial conclusions on the genre, pointing to the lack of formal epistolary features; see J. Strugnell, "Second Thoughts on a Forthcoming Edition", in E. Ulrich/J. VanderKam (ed.), *The Community of the Renewed Covenant: The Notre Dame Symposium on the Dead Sea Scrolls* (Christianity and Judaism in Antiquity Series 10; Notre Dame, IN: Notre Dame,

originally was a letter which at one time was sent to someone in an authoritative position, possibly the high priest. Furthermore, from the very beginning, the letter must have been written with both the group of the addressee and the ingroup in mind, since at least one copy originally was preserved. Given that six copies of MMT (4Q394–399) were found at Qumran, it was evidently preserved within the movement as an important, foundational document.

The halakhic section (B) consists of a list of laws which, one can assume, differ in detail from the current praxis at the time. Many of the laws represent a similar position to that found in the *Temple Scroll* and D, as Lawrence Schiffman has demonstrated.[24] Most of the laws are related to the temple and the priesthood: for example, the handling of animal skins in the temple, tithing, and various aspects of sacrifices. Hanne von Weissenberg is likely correct in her assessment that this part reflects "inner-priestly disputes".[25] Interaction with Gentiles in general and intermarriage with them in particular are major concerns.[26] According to the reconstructed, composite text, B 39–49 refers to the different categories of people who are prohibited from entering "the assembly" in the tradition of Deut 23:1–8, i. e., the Ammonite, the Moabite, the *mamzer*[27], the one with crushed testicles or whose penis is cut off. The biblical categories "the Ammonite and the Moabite" in this case serves as a label for foreigners in general. The author makes the accusation that people from within these categories still marry Jewish women, stating that they "are entering into the assembly… to take [wives] and to [bec]ome one bone" (B 40–41).[28] The accusation implies that marriage with non-Jews is prohibited in

1995), 57–73, on p. 72. H. Eshel (*The Dead Sea Scrolls and the Hasmonean State* [Grand Rapids, MI: Eerdmans, 2008], 45–53) argues for the likelihood that 4QMMT is the letter mentioned in 4Q171.

24 L. Schiffman, "The Place of 4QMMT in the Corpus of Qumran Manuscripts", in J. Kampen/M. Bernstein, *Reading 4QMMT: New Perspectives on Qumran Law and History* (SBL Symposium Series 2; Atlanta, GA: Scholars Press) 81–98, on pp. 86–90.

25 von Weissenberg, "Miqṣat", 953.

26 The fragmentary, reconstructed passages B 3–5, 8–9 appear to prohibit the consumption of the grain of Gentiles as well as their grain sacrifices (cf. CD 12:8–9). B 8–9 uses the allegory of a whoring woman to condemn the sacrifice of Gentiles; See Qimron/Strugnell, *Miqsat*, 46–7; E. Qimron et al., "Some Works of the Torah: 4Q394–4Q399 (=4QMMT^{a-f}) and 4Q313", in J. Charlesworth, *Damascus Document Fragments, Some Works of the Torah and Related Documents* (The Dead Sea Scrolls: Hebrew, Aramaic, and Greek Tests with English Translations 3; Tübingen: Mohr Siebeck, 2006) 187–251, on pp. 234–5, 246–7.

27 This was a child that was considered illegitimate; i. e., a child born outside of a legal marital union or outside of any marital union considered illegitimate (e. g., incest); see Deut 23:2.

28 Whereas the prohibition in Deut "to enter the assembly" קהל according to Rabbinic *halakhah* concerns marriage (e. g., *Sifre Deut.* 246–9), the prohibition may have a double meaning in MMT, referring both to inter-marriage and entrance to the temple. Hence, Qimron has added the words "and they enter the sanctuary" ובאים למקדש in B 41. The expression "to enter the assembly" in Lam 1:10 refers to the temple. Similarly, Deut 23:2–3 is cited in *4QFlor* (4Q174) 1–2 i 3–6 in a passage concerning a future temple ("house") from which these and other categories of

line with the tradition of Ezra and Nehemiah (e. g., Ezek 9–11; Neh 13:23–30).[29] Although in this case, it is foreign men who pose a threat, not women. Nevertheless, the author returns to the subject of intermarriage in B 75–82 when the focus turns to the Jewish men.

B 75–82 introduces the practice of prohibited marital unions by labelling such forbidden unions as זונות: ועל הזונות הנעסה בתוך העם "And concerning the practice of illegal marriage that exists among the people".[30] In B 77–78 such illegal union is compared to that of *kila'yim*, the improper mixing of two different kinds (Deut 22:9–11; Lev 19:19).[31] The passage emphasizes the holiness of the people and the priests: "because they are holy and the sons of Aaron are the [holiest of the holy]" (B 79; cf. 75–76). The precise accusation in this section is unclear due to the poor condition of the fragments. While the original editors suggested that marriage between priests and women from non-priestly families is at stake here, Joseph Baumgarten persuasively argues that laymen and priests are accused of intermarrying with Gentiles, a suggestion that has received wide support.[32]

Genealogical concerns are often expressed in purity terminology, as in this case where the people and the priests are said to 'defile' ומטמאים their 'holy

people are excluded. Consequently, Schiffman ("The Place of 4QMMT", 94) contends that the Deuteronomic prohibition in MMT refers to both inter-marriage and entrance to the temple (B 44–46). Still, Moshe Bernstein highlights the fragmentary nature of the MSS, noting that there is no clear reference to the temple until B 49, which makes him hesitant about assuming any link to temple law. He concludes, "the simple sense of MMT is that the subject under discussion is the law of marriage, not of the Temple"; see Bernstein, "The Employment and Interpretation of Scripture: Preliminary Observations," in J. Kampen/M. Bernstein (ed.), *Reading 4QMMT: New Perspectives on Qumran Law and History*, SBL Symposium Series 2; Atlanta, GA: Scholars Press), 29–51 on p. 38. I. Werrett (*Ritual Purity and the Dead Sea Scrolls* [STDJ 72; Leiden: Brill, 2007], 199] supports Bernstein's caution in this matter. In my view the passage B 39–49 most likely concerns both topics given that B 49–50 (4Q394 8 iii; par. 4Q396 1–2 i 5–6) clearly relates forbidden unions (or "mixing") תערובת הגבר with the sanctuary. In addition, it is hard to imagine that the main problem posed by men with defect male organs (B 39) is that they marry Jewish women.

29 According to the reconstruction by Qimron, [ונשים] לוקחים [להיו]תם עצם "to take [wives] and to [bec]ome one bone" (cf. Gen 7:13); see Qimron, "*Some Works*", 240–41.

30 Qimron and Strugnell, *Miqsat*, 54–5.

31 The law of *kila'yim* is alluded to also in the exhortation to a father to choose a suitable husband for his daughter in D (4Q271 3 10); see Wassen, *Women*, 76–80.

32 See Qimron/Strugnell, *Miqsat*, 55 n. 75; 171 n. 178, where they refer to Baumgarten's interpretation (through personal communication). Baumgarten ("'Halakah' in Miqṣat Ma'aśê ha-Torah [MMT]", *JAOS* 116/3 [1996] 512–16) disputes the evidence that Qimron puts forward of the alleged prohibitions against priests marrying non-priests in Josephus, Philo, and Aramaic Levi Document. The lack of halakhic parallels significantly weakens the suggestion. Loader (*Dead Sea Scrolls on Sexuality*, 65–90) provides an in-depth analysis of the section and supports the view that the issue concerns inter-marriage with Gentiles. Christine Hayes similarly argues that the issue concerns intermarriage; see Hayes, *Gentile Impurites and Jewish Identities: Intermarriage and Conversion from the Bible to the Talmud* (Oxford: Oxford University Press, 2002), 83–4.

seed' (B 81).[33] In what way are Gentiles defiling? Jonathan Klawans suggests that foreigners commonly were considered morally impure because of their sins, especially because of their idolatry, which is the problem with foreign wives in Ezra and Nehemiah.[34] Such perspective permeates *Jubilees*, which like 4QMMT refers to Israel as the 'holy seed' (Jub 16:17–18; 4QMMT B 76), but also imposes death penalty on anyone who defiles the seed by intermarriage (Jub 30:7–15). Like 4QMMT, Jubilees also uses the root *z.n.h.* with regard to intermarriage (e.g., Jub 20:4–5; 30:8; cf. B 75). According to Christine Hayes, "For Jubilees, intermarriage is Pentateuchally prohibited *zenut*, an immoral act of sexual union with one of nonholy seed, generating a moral impurity that defiles the holy seed of Israel".[35] Hence moral impurity is a defiling force linked to Gentiles also in 4QMMT whereby the holiness of the people and its priests is contaminated by any intermarriage with Gentile women.[36] This sinful, impure condition is also irreversible in Jubilees and 4QMMT since there is no legitimate way for non-Jewish women to join the Jewish people by marriage. On the contrary, all marriages with non-Jewish women are presented as defilement of the "seed" (B 81–82) and Gentile women are portrayed as זונות. I agree with Hayes' conclusion that "4QMMT rejects Israelite intermarriage with foreigners of all stripes – converted as well as unconverted – because of the emphasis on genealogical purity", although I do not find "conversion" an adequate term for this time period.[37] It should be noted that

33 J. Klawans (*Impurity and Sin in Ancient Judaism* [Oxford: Oxford University Press, 2000], 43–6) highlights the purity terminology employed by Ezra (6:21; 9:1, 11–14) and Nehemiah (in Neh 13:30 divorcing the foreign wives is called purification). Similarly, Hayes (*Gentile Impurites*, 56) argues that in Ezra, Chronicles, and 1 Esdras (the rewritten account of the history from Josiah to Ezra written in 2nd Cent BCE) the synonymous use of terms related to impurity and abominable deeds suggest that "the 'uncleanness' or 'impurity' of aliens refers to their abhorrent and immoral practices rather than to an intrinsic or derived ritual impurity".

34 *Jub.* 22:16–22; 30:13–15; see Klawans, *Impurity and Sin*, 45–6.

35 Hays, *Gentile Impurites*, 76.

36 For the status of foreigners in the Dead Sea Scrolls in general see J. Jokiranta, "Conceptualizing *Ger* in the Dead Sea Scrolls", in K. De Troyer et al (ed.), *In the Footsteps of Sherlock Holmes: Studies in the Biblical Text in Honour of Anneli Aejmelaeus* (Contributions to Biblical Exegesis and Theology 72; Leuven: Peeters Publishers, 2014), 659–77 ; see also L. Schiffman, "Non-Jews in the Dead Sea Scrolls", in *Qumran and Jerusalem: Studies in the Dead Sea Scrolls and the History of Judaism* (Grand Rapids, MI: Eerdmans, 2010), 365–80.

37 Hayes, *Gentile Impurities*, 86. Steve Mason explains that "there was no 'religion' to which one might convert… It was a change of ethnic-ancestral culture, the joining of other people"; see Mason, "Jews, Judeans, Judaizing, Judaism: Problems of Categorization in Ancient History", *JSJ* 38 (2007) 457–512, on p. 491. In comparison, the *ger* (a resident alien) in the Hebrew Bible is accepted and protected in the society, and is required to adopt some rituals, but cannot change his or her status to become a full member of the people, i.e., a proselyte. According to popular interpretation of the fragmentary passages in 11QT 39:5 and 40:5–7, *gerim* were allocated to the third court until the fourth generation (see Schiffman, "Non-Jews", 372, 379). The *ger* similarly in some of the sectarian texts from Qumran (CD 13:11; 14:3–6) is accepted but ultimately not allowed the same status as others; see Jutta Jokiranta, "Conceptualizing *Ger*". Schiffman ("Non-Jews", 379), in contrast, argues that the sect "recognized the institution of proselytism, or

the negative view on Gentiles in 4QMMT appears more stringent than the view on foreigners and resident aliens (*ger*) elsewhere. It is noteworthy, for example, that in contrast to MMT, marriage with Gentile women is accepted in the *Temple Scroll* (11Q19) 63:10–15 (cf. 57:15–16).[38] Although Schiffman argues that the initial rites are in effect a "conversion", there is little similarity with conversion as it would develop later, especially in terms of conversion being a voluntary act. But, in the case of the Temple Scroll, through marriage a non-Jewish woman would be able to join the people.[39]

4QMMT is addressed to "you" in the plural in the legal section (B) and "you" in the singular in the final section (C); e.g., C 26 כתבנו אליך "to you". The group of the author is referred to in the first person plural (e.g., in B 80). There is also a group of outsiders, "them", i.e., those among the people and the priests who are accused of entering into illicit marriages. The people as a whole is thereby not condemned by the implied author. But non-Jews are considered as an unqualified threat to the holiness of the temple and the people as they are prohibited from entering the holy temple and from marrying into the holy people. The condemnation of illegitimate marital unions as a defilement of the holy seed rests on the assumption that ordinary and correct marriages in between Jews are part of what makes them holy. While the author accuses the people, including the priests for engaging in various wrongful practices, he clarifies that "we have separated from the mass of the [people and from all their impurity and] from mixing in these matters and coming together wi] th them (on) this principle" (C 7–8).[40] By clearly distinguishing between a "we-

religious conversion to Judaism, that apparently existed at this time". But at the same time he holds that the *ger* had a lower status in the community in spite of being circumcised. *4QFlor* 1–2 i 4–6 stands out in excluding the *gerim* from a future sanctuary all together.

38 A paraphrase of the laws in Deut 21:10–14 provides strict rules for marriage with a war bride, that is, clearly a non-Israelite. During the first month, the captive woman undergoes various rites, after which the husband may have sexual relations with her. Nonetheless, only after seven years is the woman fully accepted into the Jewish society with the rights to eat holy food. See L. Schiffman, "Laws Pertaining to Women in the Temple Scroll", in D. Dimant/U. Rappaport (ed.), *The Dead Sea Scrolls: Forty Years of Research* (Leiden: Brill/Jerusalem: Magness Press, 1992) 210–28, on pp. 218–20.

39 Although reflecting a later time, it is noteworthy that Josephus perceives circumcision as a conversion, an initiation act into the Jewish people, in other words in effect as an act that makes male Gentiles Jews. In comparison he shows no awareness of a corresponding conversion ritual for women. Nonetheless, Gentile women were still allowed to marry Jewish men (but not priests) as long as they adopted Jewish practices and did not lead men astray. But they were never considered Jews. See D.R. Schwartz, "Doing Like Jews or Becoming a Jew? Josephus on Women Converts to Judaism", in J. Frey et al. (es.), *Jewish Identity in the Greco-Roman World* (Ancient Judaism and Early Christianity 71; Leiden: Brill, 2007) 93–109. In comparison Luke in Acts only uses the term "proselyte" with reference to men (Acts 6:5; for a group of people in 2:11; 13:43) and prefers the label "God-fearers" and the like in connection to women (Acts 16:14). Nevertheless, it is hard to draw any conclusions form his limited use of these terms.

40 Qimron ("*Some Works of the Torah*", 247 n. 46) points out that the wording concerns purity practices.

group" and the "mass of the people", the implied author invites the listeners to identify with the characteristics of the "we-group". Implicit in the message is the conviction that, in the author's group, proper marriage unions are a natural feature and marriage between Jews is seen as fundamental for preserving the holiness of the people. A positive view on proper marriage unions therefore forms a part of a sectarian identity in 4QMMT.

Appealing to Israelite history as a shared common ground, as well as to the insight that the addressee has, the implied author expresses hope in the final section of MMT that this person will realize the correctness of the interpretations offered in the letter:

> And also we have written to you some of the works of the Torah according to our decision, for the good of you and of your people. For we have seen in you prudence and knowledge of the Torah. Consider all these (things) and seek him that he make straight your counsel, and that he remove from you evil thought and the counsel of Belial so that you may rejoice in the latter time, when you will find some of our pronouncements are true (C 26b–30; 4Q398 frgs. 14–17 ii 2–8).[41]

The addressee is thereby linked with the people, here called "your people", and appears, like the people, to have the potential to act correctly – that is, according to the sectarian *halakhah* – but the outcome is yet unknown. Whereas the *halakhah* expressed in the letter is understood as correct, the opposite views are declared to have their origin in Belial's influence. The addressee is thereby invited to decide between God and Belial, according to the parameters set by the author's group.

Social Identity Approach

In order to examine the possible function of the document in the formation of a communal identity, I will highlight a few insights from a social identity approach that are useful. Social identity theory was developed by the social psychologist Henri Tajfel.[42] His theories were based on both personal experiences during WWII when he spent time in a war prison with French soldiers and on subsequent, scientific experiments. Although the experiments were carried out in the modern, Western world they reveal underlying principles about the social and psychological dynamics that are at play in the

41 Translation from James H. Charlesworth and Henry W. M. Rietz (ed.), *The Dead Sea scrolls: Hebrew, Aramaic, and Greek texts with English translations. Vol. 3, Damascus Document II, some works of the Torah, and related documents* (Tübingen: Mohr Siebeck, 2006).

42 H. Tajfel, *Human Groups and Social Categories* (Cambridge: University of Cambridge Press, 1981); see biography of Tajfel by J.C. Turner, "Henri Tajfel: An Introduction", in P. Robinson (ed.), *Social Groups and Identities: Developing the Legacy of Henri Tajfel* (Oxford: Butterworth-Heinemann, 1996) 1–23.

formations of identities of groups, i. e., social identities. His theories served as a basis for John Turner's social categorization theory, which particularly focuses on the ways in which we as humans identify ourselves in relation to different groups and how this influences our behaviour.[43] Together, these theories can be called a "social identity approach".[44] Initially we may note that the drive to categorize different groups and define one's own may have been even more pronounced in the ancient Mediterranean culture compared to the Modern, Western world, since the former can be characterized as collectivistic compared to the latter more individualistic society.[45]

If we consider the original function of MMT as a letter to an authority figure in a priestly group, we may notice how the implied author points to their common values, which aim at invoking a perception of a shared social identity: the addressee is invited to share a negative evaluation of the mixed marriages that *others* are doing, that is, to join the author's group in creating boundaries towards those outsiders. The statement "[you know that] we have separated from the mass of the [people]" (C 7) also presumes that the addressee will share a positive value judgement of such distancing from the common masses. Again, what causes them to separate from the people has nothing to do with celibacy (the classical view about the community), but with mixed marriages. The addressee is also encouraged to endorse the author's interpretation of the Israelite history which they share, again, in effort to break up, or at least soften, the boundaries between the ingroup and the addressee (and his group). Like good kings in the past, the addressee can turn to God and be forgiven (C 9–26). From the perspective of an outsider, the invitation to embrace the position of the author does not appear sincere. In spite of the flattering statement concerning "the prudence and knowledge of Torah" of the addressee, the appeal to joint understanding is delivered with thinly veiled insults, which places the addressee in the camp of those who are in need of repentance and forgiveness, and possibly even within the sphere of influence of Belial (C 28–30). But from an insider's perspective, it may well be an honest attempt to reach an agreement that consists of the complete acceptance of the ingroup's *halakhah* by the addressee. From the perspective of the ingroup, they possess the correct *halakhah* through revelation, and everything else is

43 J.C. Turner (with M.A. Hogg, P.J. Oakes, S.D. Reicher, and M.S. Wetherell), *Rediscovering the Social Group: A Self-Categorization Theory* (Oxford: Basil Blackwell, 1987). For an introduction to both theories, see J. Jokiranta, *Social Identity and Sectarianism in the Qumran Movement* (STDJ 105; Leiden: Brill, 2013), 77–90.

44 Jokiranta, *Social Identity*, 78.

45 R. Hakola, "Social Identities and Group Phenomena in Second Temple Judaism", in P. Luomanen/I. Pyysiäinen/R. Uro (ed.), *Explaining Christian Origins and Early Judaism: Contributions from Cognitive and Social Sciences* (BibInt Series 89; Leiden: Brill, 2007) 259–76, esp. p. 263.

contrary to God's will. This conviction is expressed throughout the sectarian texts and makes up a firm group belief.[46] Hence, no compromises are possible.

When it comes to the function of MMT *within the group*, MMT plainly reflects an effort of the ingroup to distinguish itself from others. Social theorists argue that it is especially important for groups to distinguish themselves from those who are very close to them in order to facilitate their members' efforts of developing distinct social identities.[47] This tendency is evident in MMT, in that the author outlines halakhic rules that focus on the temple cult and make up key differences between his group and the temple priests. Raimo Hakola clarifies, that "similarity between groups may often cause intergroup conflicts" and points to the conflict between the Qumran movement and the Pharisees as one poignant example.[48] Given the priestly orientation of the Qumran movement from the very beginning and the priestly identity of the Teacher of Righteousness, we can surmise that part of the ingroup belonged to the same larger group of priests in the Jewish society whose membership were based on family origin.[49] All priests would naturally have shared common views on the holiness of the temple and the importance of the priests as servants of God in his abode and so forth. Given this common ground, social identity theory allows us to understand why it was particularly important to demarcate boundaries towards priests who were not part of the author's group. It also explains that, in the process of strengthening the social identity of the ingroup, it is natural to emphasize and often exaggerate the differences between groups as well as to downplay similarities in between them, a tendency which we see in MMT.[50] This also helps to explain why some of the details listed in MMT appear fairly minor (at least from an outsider's perspective): for example, handling of skins and eating sacred food after sunset. These halakhic differences were likely important markers of the differences between the groups from the perspective of the ingroup, and helped to set boundaries, distinguishing them from the temple priests. At the same time, the many similarities between the ingroup and the temple priests are subdued, although an appeal to common ancestors appears at the end of the letter.

In addition to the need to distinguish themselves from the priestly

46 On group beliefs, see Jokiranta, *Social Identity*, 90–92.

47 Hakola, "Social Identities", 263, 266–70.

48 Hakola, "Social Identities", 268.

49 1QpHab 2:8; 4QpPs^a 2:19; 3:15. I concur with the common view that there was an initial schism within priestly circles that led to the founding of a group that later developed into a sect under the guidance of a leader figure, called the Teacher of Righteousness. See e.g., Eschel, *The Dead Sea Scrolls and the Hasmonean State*, 29–61. Still, I find it quite likely that these events took place in the early first century BCE; see Collins, *Beyond the* Qumran Community, 88–121. The debate about the identity of the Teacher continues to be a hot topic; see e.g., G. Brooke, "The 'Apocalyptic' Community, the Matrix of the Teacher and Rewriting Scripture", in M. Popović (ed.), *Authoritative Scriptures in Ancient Judaism* (JSJSupp 141; Leiden: Brill, 2010) 37–53.

50 Hakola, "Social Identities", 264.

outsiders, the ingroup reflected in MMT also needed to establish their social identity vis à vis the general population. Since the regulations concerning the temple service were most likely outside of the sphere of influence and power of the author's group, they would have been prevented from manifesting their differences in praxis in this arena. But marriage was not limited in this way. Through marriage laws the sectarians could potentially mark their differences towards outsiders through their praxis, as we will see below in D. In this document the accusations concerning marriage praxis are more encompassing, in comparison to those found in MMT, in that they cover more subjects and involve the whole population. In addition, Belial's role is more pronounced. It is tempting to see a development in sectarian ideology in D as compared to MMT. By imposing an unbridgeable divide between the ingroup and the population, D allows for no reconciliation with outsiders; marital regulations play a pivotal role in the construction of such divide. Thus we see an increased polarization and antagonism towards the outgroup expressed in the sectarian ideology in D.[51]

Key texts in the *Damascus Document*

Ten copies of the *Damascus Document* were discovered in the caves at Qumran (Cave 4, 5 and 6), which indicates the great importance of the document in the Qumran movement.[52] The document was known before the discovery of the Qumran Scrolls through two medieval manuscripts found in the geniza of an old synagogue in Cairo. In contrast to S, the Qumran copies display only minor differences in the wording.[53] D consists of two main parts, a sermon-like, hortatory section called the Admonition, and a long legal section that consists of both communal regulations (e.g., a penal code) and *halakhah*, i.e., the community's interpretation of biblical laws. Many of the laws in this legal section concern marriage, which suggests that marriage was the common way of life of the addressees.[54] For the purposes of this paper, my analysis will focus on three passages concerning marriage in the Admonition, not the legal

51 William Loader (in an unpublished paper, "Sex and Conflict Development in Qumran Literature") detects a general development of conflicts concerning specific issues, as we see in in D and MMT, that later turns into a general attack on people. This pattern of a progression "from issue-based dispute to *ad hominem* polemics" not only relates to marital laws, but also to laws more broadly.

52 The oldest of the copies, 4Q266 (4QD[a]), is dated paleographically to 100–50 BCE. For a description of the manuscripts from Qumran, see J. Baumgarten, *The Damascus Document (4Q266–273): Qumran Cave 4, XIII* (DJD 18; Oxford: Clarendon Press, 1996), 1–22.

53 There are major variants between the two medieval manuscripts, CD A and B, in the section CD 7:9b–8:2a (MS A)/CD 19:5b–14 (MS B).

54 See Wassen, *Women*, 30–31, 197–205.

section, since it is in the former that the connection between marital praxis and identity formation is particularly evident. In two passages the people are associated with זנות, a term which here refers to illicit marital unions and wrongful sexual practices in a wide sense. CD 2:14–3:12 is an important passage, since it explains how זנות has been a part of human and Israelite history from the very beginning. Another key passage is CD 4:13–5:11, which is part of the larger discourse on the nets of Belial. Finally, CD 7:4–9 is relevant with its discourse that highlights the marital unions of those who live in "camps".

CD 2:14–3:12

The Admonition includes forceful accusations concerning illegal sexual relations among the people, but in contrast to 4QMMT, these do not focus on marriage between Gentiles and Jews. CD 2:14–3:12 provides a retelling of Israel's history as a series of failures to keep the covenant. Addressing the listeners as "sons", the speaker contrasts two ways for human life: one of "walking perfectly in all his [God's] ways" and one of straying from this path because of יצר אשמה ועני זנות "a guilty inclination and licentious eyes", or "lustful eyes", as Geza Vermes suggests.[55] The speaker also promises to provide the tools, to uncover eyes of the listeners (2:14) so that they will be able to follow the right path; he explains that "for many have failed due to them (guilty inclination and licentious eyes); mighty warrior have stumbled due to them, from the earliest times and until today". According to this text, then, the illicit sexual practices have been a main reason for the failure of humans to live by God's will from the very beginning. Those who stumbled have also been punished because of their sins, i. e., the Watchers, the sons of Noah, and the sons of Jacob. But Abraham, Isaac, and Jacob are presented as exceptions and true covenant partners (CD 3:2–4).

The discourse sharply divides Israel's people into those who follow God's will and the people who do not, with the aim of encouraging the listeners to oppose the outsiders who follow their own will (3:12) and, instead, identifying with the ingroup. It is never explained which kind of specific sin is entailed in following "licentious eyes" and a "guilty inclination", but in the case of the Watchers, the sin is well-known, i. e., sexual relations with human women (Gen 6:1–4). It appears then, that any illicit sexual relation, which is normally caused by lust, is condemned. Following one's lust and engaging in illicit sex provides a counter-image of what constitutes a true sectarian identity. Hence, this discourse highlights legitimate marriages and sexual relations, not celibacy, at the core of communal self-identity.

In a polarized fashion, the ingroup is perceived to be part of an ongoing conflict with the outgroup, which is all of Israel. The present conflict is traced

55 G. Vermes, *The Complete Dead Sea Scrolls in English* (New York: Penguin Press, 1997), 128.

back into Israelite history where the exemplary behaviour of the patriarchs is upheld as role-models or prototypes for the ingroup, predecessors with whom they can identify as legitimate parties of the covenant (CD 3:3–4; cf. the sect as heirs of the covenant, e.g., 3:13; 6:19; 7:5). The members of the ingroup are also expected to identify themselves with the remnant, the righteous minority of Israel to whom God has revealed his will and with whom he has established his covenant (3:20). As a righteous remnant they are to observe the correct laws, i. e., the *halakhah* of the sect. On the surface, the prototypical character of the patriarchs in relation to sexual conduct may not appear that convincing since Abraham and Jacob both had sexual relations with more women than a single wife, which constituted זנות according to CD 4:20–21. But here, the logic is rather the reverse: since the tradition holds them as righteous forefathers, they must have been so; hence the implied author can confidently state that they observed God's ordinances (CD 3:2–4). In order for prototypes to be meaningful they have to be reinterpreted depending on the context; often, they make up "a stable image upon which new elements are intermittently superimposed", as in this case.[56] In contrast, the outsiders are identified with the unfaithful part of the people who were punished. To present the patriarchs as prototypes thus serves to unify the ingroup, but also to claim superiority, since only the ingroup members represent the legitimate descendants of the forefathers. We may notice a similar claim by Paul in regard to Abraham in both Romans 4 and Galatians 4.[57] Furthermore, through connecting the present conflict with the outsiders to Israelite history and back to the time before Noah, the ingroup will view their present situation as part of larger, cosmic drama between good and evil, which adds significance to their situation. This will also add value to their belonging to the ingroup and make their distancing from the outgroup more meaningful. As Philip Esler explains, a collective memory is crucial in the forming of group identities: "part of the social identity we derive from belonging to groups inevitably includes the fact of their being situated in history, stretching backward and forward in time. In relation to the past, it is clear that group identities are nourished by collective memory".[58] It is noteworthy that the remnant in the past was commanded to "fill the face of the world with their seed" (CD 2:11–12). Hence procreation forms an important part of the purpose of the ingroup, which again demonstrates the importance of marriage for the community's self-identity.

56 R.K. McIver, *Memory, Jesus, and the Synoptic Gospels* (Atlanta: SBL, 2011), 88; C.A. Baker, "A Narrative-Identity Model for Biblical Interpretation: The Role of Memory and Narrative in Social Identity Formation", in J.B. Tucker/C.A. Baker (ed.), *T & T Clark Handbook to Social Identity in the New Testament* (London: Bloomsbury, 2014) 105–18, p. 111.

57 See P. Esler, "Abraham as Prototype of Group Identity", Ch. 8 in *Conflict and Identity in Romans* (Minneapolis, MN: Augsburg Fortress, 2003) 171–94; also Baker, "A Narrative-Identity Model", 109–11.

58 P. Esler, "An Outline of Social Identity Theory", in J.B. Tucker/C.A. Baker (ed.), *T & T Clark Handbook to Social Identity in the New Testament* (London: Bloomsbury, 2014) 13–39, on p. 37.

CD 4:13–5:11

CD 4:13–5:11 belongs to a section on the nets of Belial (CD 4:12–5:15) in which Belial traps the people, Israel. The discourse is a long exposition, or "pesher", of Isa 24:17, which is quoted in the text (CD 4:14).[59] Two of the three nets concern sexual sins, הזנות "illicit sexual relations" and טמא מקדש "defilement of the sanctuary". In contrast to the Isaiah passage, these traps appear as "three types of righteousness", whereby Belial is able to trick the people into sinning. CD 4:12–18 reads:

> But during all those years, Belial will run unbridled amidst Israel, as God spoke through the hand of the prophet Isaiah, son of Amos, saying, "Fear and a pit and a snare are upon you, O inhabitant(s) of the land" (Isa 24:17). Its interpretation: the three nets of Belial, of which Levi, the son of Jacob, said that he (Belial) entrapped Israel with them, making them seem as if they were three types of righteousness. The first is whoredom (הזנות), the second wealth (ההון), and the third defilement of the sanctuary (טמא המקדש).[60]

There are literary seams in the passage and the whole text appears appears disjointed which makes the specific accusations against outsiders somewhat difficult to decipher; e.g., the net of "wealth" is never explained in the text.[61] הזונות is explained as "taking two wives in their (masc.) lifetime" (CD 4:20–21), which clearly refers to polygyny, an interpretation that is supported by the subsequent proof texts (CD 4:21–5:2).[62] Whether or not the passage also condemns any second marriage, also after the death of a wife, is debated. Nevertheless, since divorce is accepted elsewhere in D (CD 13:16–17/ 4Q266 9 ii 5), it is unlikely that all kinds of second marriages are prohibited. Furthermore, a widowed woman is allowed to remarry in 4QD[f] (4Q271) 3

59 The quote is followed by the expression, "its interpretation" פשרו (CD 4:14).

60 Translation from James H. Charlesworth (ed.), *The Dead Sea Scrolls: Hebrew, Aramaic, and Greek Texts with English Translations. Vol. 2, Damascus Document, War Scroll and Related Documents* (Tübingen: Mohr Siebeck, 1995).

61 Loader (*The Dead Sea Scrolls on Sexuality*, 113), however, interprets the sin of riches in relation to polygyny, arguing that the accusation is about marrying several wives in order to gain their dowries. This link is not evident in the text and remains speculative. The passage appears to be made up of material from different sources as Philip Davies argues; see P.R. Davies, *Damascus Covenant: An Interpretation of the "Damascus Document"* (JSOTSup 25. Sheffield: JSOT Press, 1983), 110–16. Likely, the passage on the nets of Belial is derived from a source of general charges that is attributed to Levi, as the author also makes clear, which later has been expanded by the examples of transgressions that do not quite match the nets.

62 Cf. The Law of the king in 11Q19 56:12–59:21, which prohibits the king from marrying many wives (56:19), and stipulates that he only marry one who should be from his father's house and not from the nations (57:15–19). Only if she dies may he marry someone else.

10–12, which supports the position that remarriage was allowed according to D.[63]

The accusations concerning הזנות continue in CD 5:6, "And they also continuously polluted the sanctuary by not separating according to the Torah, and they habitually lay with a woman who sees blood of flowing דם זובה. And they marry each one his brother's daughter or sister's daughter" (CD 5:6–7). Marriage between an uncle and a niece was accepted broadly in the Jewish population at the time, but according to the sectarian interpretation it constituted incest.[64] The *halakhah* is supported by a gender-inclusive reading of Lev 18:13 (the ban on marriage between a man and his aunt), and the sectarian point of view is communicated very clearly in CD 5:8–11:

> But Moses said "You shall not approach your mother's sister; she is your mother's near kin." And the law against incest is written with reference to males but the same (law) applies to women; so, if a brother's daughter uncovers the nakedness of her father's brother, then she is his near kin.

However, the preceding accusation about lying with a woman who sees her "blood of flowing" is not as clear.[65] זבה is used for any kind of vaginal blood in Lev 15:19–31 and *4QTohorot A*, and a broad meaning can be assumed also in this case.[66] But this kind of sexual sin cannot in any way be construed as a type of righteousness (CD 4:17–18). To circumvent this difficulty one could speculate that the alleged crime concerns a differing interpretation of

63 See Wassen, *Women*, 114–18. J. Murphy O'Connor ("An Essene Missionary Document? CD II, 14–VI, 1", *RB* 77 [1970] 201–29, on p. 220) argues that any second marriage is prohibited, while Schiffman ("Laws Pertaining to Women", 217) holds that a man may remarry only after the death of his wife. Nevertheless, their studies came out prior to the publication of the 4QD texts with laws that are pertinent to the issue. According to Vered Noam ("Divorce in Qumran in Light of Early Halakhah", *JJS* 56/2 [2005] 206–23, on pp. 206–7), CD 4:20–5:1 prohibits divorce. Loader (*Dead Sea Scrolls on Sexuality*, 119) concludes that the passage is about having more than one wife at a time.

64 T. Ilan, *Jewish Women in Greco-Roman Palestine* (Peabody, MA: Hendrickson Publishers, 1995), 75–9; Wassen, *Women*, 120–22.

65 Loader (*Dead Sea Scrolls on Sexuality*, 120–21) draws attention to the similarity between the charge of אין הם מבדיל כתורה, which he translates, "they do not differentiate according to the Law", and the importance of differentiating between pure and impure in CD 6:17, ולהבדיל בין הטמא לטהור. He also points to a possible connection to Lev 15:31, which relates impurity to defilement of the temple (tabernacle): "Thus you shall keep the people separate from their uncleanness, so that they do not die in their uncleanness by defiling my tabernacle that is in their midst". Still, Lev 15:31 uses the verb נזר (to consecrate, separate; see J. Milgrom, *Leviticus 1–16: A New Translation with Introduction and Commentary* [The Anchor Bible 3; New York: Doubleday, 1991], 945), rather than בדל (to separate, distinguish).

66 See Lev 15:19, 24–25, and Milgrom, *Leviticus 1–16*, 948. Whereas Philip Davies points to menstruation as the underlying issue ("The Ideology of the Temple in the Damascus Document", *JJS* 33 [1982], 287–301, on p. 289), Hans Kosmala believes the expression refers to both menstruation and vaginal discharge; see Kosmala, "The Three Nets of Belial", *ASTI* 4 (1965) 91–113, on p. 99. See discussion by Wassen, *Women*, 118–20.

menstruation laws (perhaps in counting clean days),[67] but this appears contrary to the graphic description in the text (the woman *sees* her bloody discharge). Another suggestion, that the text implicitly criticizes intermarriage with foreign women who could not be trusted in this regard, also lacks support in the text.[68] Therefore, we are left with no other option than to accept the charge according to its literal meaning, i. e., that a couple deliberately engages in sex during menstruation in contradiction to biblical law. The lack of coherence within the discourse must then be explained as a result of the use of different sources by the author.

In the discourse on the nets of Belial, polygyny and marriage between relatives are viewed as evidence of Belial's rule over the people, the outgroup. The different interpretations of marriage *halakhah* between the ingroup and the outgroup are thus far from theoretical debates, from the perspective of the implied author, but instead make for a genuine difference between doing God's will and following Belial. The boundary between the ingroup and the rest of the people marks a division between good and evil, God's sphere and that of Belial, and the divide is presented as absolute. In terminology from social identity theory, the discourse encourages "social immobility", the perception that movement between the two social groups is impossible, which reflects a high intergroup tension.[69] Demonizing the outsiders is furthermore an effective way to establish distance to the outgroup. It serves as a means to unify the members of the ingroup by strengthening their common identity as a group who lives according to God's rule, not Belial's. The discourse mediates quite bluntly the positive value of belonging to the ingroup, which aims at strengthening the salience of its members. According to Esler, such stereotyping of outsiders is typical of groups that are in a situation of "intergroup extreme"; members of the ingroup "would try to ignore individual differences between outgroup members and treat them as undifferentiated items in a unified social category".[70] Similarly, in the discourse of the nets of Belial, all outsiders are presented as a unified group, who through various transgressions are all ruled by Belial. By associating sexual sins with the defilement of the temple, the discourse emphasizes the enormity of the people's crimes, which perhaps makes Belial's involvement appear more realistic.

The stereotyping in CD is quite extreme and exaggerated since people would live in different marital relations; although polygyny and uncle-niece marriages were accepted among the population in general, not all men would have multiple wives or take nieces as wives. Again, it can be explained in terms

67 E. g., Knibb, *The Qumran Community*, 43.

68 As suggested by me previously; Wassen, *Women*, 119–20. This aspect of my interpretation was criticized by Loader, *Dead Sea Scrolls on Sexuality*, 120.

69 P. Esler, "Group Norms and Prototypes in Matthew 5.3–12", in J.B. Tucker/C.A. Baker (ed.), *T & T Clark Handbook to Social Identity in the New Testament* (London: Bloomsbury, 2014) 147–71, on p. 161.

70 Esler, "An Outline", 18.

of the tendency of the ingroup tendency to homogenize the outgroup by attributing the same traits to all outgroup members.[71] Also the accusation that men are having sex during women's menstruation also appears much exaggerated since such behaviour is an ancient, Israelite taboo (Lev 15:24). Although scholars have attempted to relate the accusation about sex during menstruation to an underlying halakhic debate about how women calculated their menstruation cycles as mentioned above, the accusation likely represents a simple, vicious attack that lacks empirical basis (i. e., who would know when other people had sex?). Such tendency to embellish and embroider perceived negative characteristics of the outgroup is common in intergroup conflicts; it aims at discouraging interaction with the outgroup while strengthening social cohesion and salience of the ingroup.[72] Implicit in these accusations is the conviction that the behaviour of the ingroup according to these norms is legitimate and proper; this is evident in that the behaviour of the outgroup represents an inversion to that of the outgroup since the former is ruled by Belial and the latter by God.[73] As Eileen Schuller put it in 1998[74]:

> Although the way these three nets are explained is intricate and not always clear, it is striking that the issues of whom to marry or not to marry (not one's niece), of divorce and remarriage (forbidden)[75], and of sexual relations (in relation to menstruation) – all issues involving women – formed the core of the community's self-definition *vis-à-vis* the rest of the Jewish people who are accused of following corrupt practices on these points.

Marital laws are thus highly important in the formation of identity of the movement as part of the sect's efforts to differentiate itself positively from the outgroup. According to Esler, a group that is perceived to be or is perceiving itself as inferior, "can invent new characteristics that establish positively valued group distinctiveness".[76] In this case, when the sect could no longer compete over temple practices, since it likely had no influence over the

71 On the phenomenon of 'the outgroup homogeneity effect' see R. Hakola, "Pharisees as Others in the New Testament", in R. Hakola/N. Nikki/U. Tervahauta (ed.), *Others and the Construction of Early Christian Identities* (Publications of the Finnish Exegetical Society 106; Helsinki: The Finnish Exegetical Society, 2013) 13–65, on p. 43.

72 As Esler explains ("Group Norms", 162) in relation to the very anti-Jewish material in Matthew 23, "by alleging the worthlessness of that outgroup's values" it enhances intergroup differences.

73 On "ingroup inversion of outgroup values", see Esler, "Group Norms", 149, 163.

74 E. Schuller, "Women in the Dead Sea Scrolls", in P.W. Flint/J. VanderKam (ed.), *The Dead Sea Scrolls after Fifty Years: A Comprehensive Assessment* (Leiden: Brill, 1998) 2.117–44, on pp. 123–4.

75 Schuller has since changed her view that the text implies that divorce was forbidden in light of the fragments of D from Cave 4. That divorce was allowed is evident in 4QD[a] (4Q266) 9 iii 5/CD 13:17 in which the Examiner is to give counsel "to one who divorces"; see Schuller and Wassen, "Women: Daily Life."

76 Esler, "An Outline", 21.

running of the temple, marriage praxis provided an arena where they could compete and win – from the perspective of the ingroup.

CD 7:4–9

CD 7:4–9 refers to two groups within the ingroup who are encouraged to live perfectly. In a similar vein as the rest of the sermon, the narrator here contrasts those who follow Gods laws ("all those who walk in these [God's laws] in perfection"; 7:4–5) and those who do not, "those who despise" (7:9). Although scholars typically highlight the contrast between the non-married and the married ones and identify only the former with the men of perfection,[77] the two main groups who are polarized in the narrative are clearly those who observe God's laws and those who despise them.[78] Thereby, the former group includes both those who marry and who do not within the ingroup, who are both characterized by walking in perfection and by "staying away from הזונות" (7:1, 4). From this perspective, again, proper marital unions and sexual relations play a basic role in the formation of sectarian identity among those who married. In addition, there is no hint that marriage would be an obstacle for holiness; on the contrary, those who marry and do so "according to the rule of the land… and walk according to the Torah…" (7:7) are counted as part of the group characterized by observing the laws "in perfect holiness" (7:5). From the sectarian perspective, then, the marital unions within the sect are an important part of the construction of a sectarian identity.

The implied author asserts that the outgroup, "those who despise" (God's laws), will be punished at God's visitation (7:9–12), as the sinners have been punished before (7:13). The ingroup are assured of their reward, also by references to the past history of God's dealings with Israel (7:13–21). At the same time, the implied author strongly warns the readers of the real possibility that some may stray from the right way, in which case they will be severely punished (8:1–4); the sins of such rebels recall those in the discourse of the nets of Belial and sexual sins are again highlighted: (they) בדרכי זונות ובהון "wallowed in the ways of prostitutes and wealth" (8:5), and in "and each ignored the relation of his flesh and they drew near (one to another) for incest."

The reality behind the possibility that also members of the ingroup are capable of committing sexual sins is made clear in the penal code in which "fornication" with a wife is considered such a serious transgression as to

77 E. g., Qimron, "Celibacy in the Dead Sea Scrolls and the Two Kinds of Sectarians", in J. Trebolle Barrera/L. Vegas Montaner (ed.), *The Madrid Qumran Congress: Proceedings of the International Congress on the Dead Sea Scrolls, Madrid 18–21 March 1991* (STDJ 11; Leiden: Brill, 1992) 1.286–94, on pp. 290–91.

78 See Wassen, *Women*, 125–8; this aspect of my interpretation is supported by John Collins (*Beyond the Qumran Community*, 33).

warrant expulsion: "One who comes near to fornicate with his wife contrary to the law (ואשר יקרב לזנות לאשתו אשר לא כמשפט) shall depart and return no more" (4Q270 7 i 12–13). Fornication in this case likely refers to any sexual activity that cannot lead to pregnancy.[79] In addition to the severe penalty, also the term זנות demonstrates the seriousness of the crime. זנות alludes to the nets of Belial; this indicates that such illicit sexual activity by a member is seen as evidence that he belongs to the outgroup who are ruled by Belial. The penalty – which may be considered extremely harsh in relation to nature of the crime by any standard – is understandable in light of the importance of proper sexual conduct for the identity of the ingroup. Transgressions of sexual nature endangered the core of the self-identity of the sect in which the life of perfect holiness also encompassed the sexual activity of the members. Importantly, none of the rules indicate a preference for no sexual activity (celibacy).

Conclusion

In conclusion, we have seen how the issues related to marital laws lie at the heart of sectarian identity; by observing the correct *halakhah* in this regard, the sect differentiates itself from the rest of the population. A person's marital union and sexual practice to a large extent also determines whether or not a person belongs to the camp of Belial. Although both 4QMMT and the *Damascus Document* highlight the illicit marital practices of the outgroup, there are also important differences which reveal a development in the function of the marital *halakhah* within the sect in the process of developing a common identity.

Marital laws appear in a list of many halakhic stipulations in MMT where the ingroup has a different view compared to what is commonly practiced and most of the laws concern the temple cult and priests. The marital laws do stand out as particularly important issues since the topic is addressed twice. Thus marital laws contribute to the formation of the group's identity together with other halakhic topics. Instead of marking a boundary to all outsiders, the laws focus on the illicit martial practices of a few, both priests and laypeople, who marry non-Jews. It appears that they consider all mixed marriages wrong, also with "converted" Gentiles, which represent a stringent view compared to the general opinion. The implied author attempts to convince the addressees in the correctness of *halakhah* of the author's group, also when it comes to the view on mixed marriages. Hence the author aims at convincing the addressees to adopt the *halakhah* of the ingroup and thereby – in halakhic matters – create a common social identity between them. As part of this strategy he stresses that illicit marriages are practiced by others than the addressees – thereby finding joint "enemies" – and by pointing to a shared heritage.

79 Wassen, *Women*, 173–81.

The perspective changes drastically in D. There are now only two groups, "we" and "them". Mixed marriages are not condemned (perhaps in line with the Temple Scroll they are accepted), but marital laws and sexual relations are perceived as the core issues that distinguish the ingroup from the outgroup and has a central role in the formation of a common, sectarian identity. In D, we see how basic, halakhic differences concerning marital laws (polygyny and incest) have developed into exaggerated accusations about the scope of these 'transgressions', which in turn provide evidence of Belial's far-reaching power. Furthermore, illicit sexual behaviour (wilful sex during menstruation) that lack empirical basis is ascribed to the outgroup in an effort to vilify and demonize them. These accusations can be explained as a result of the tendency of ingroups to exaggerate "bad" traits of the outgroup, coupled with the trend to homogenize them. By polarizing the ingroup against the outgroup and presenting the conflict as part of a cosmic drama through history between good and bad, God and Belial, the implied author adds importance to the conflict and aims at strengthening the salience of the ingroup and their resilience against assimilation within the larger outgroup. To observe correct laws concerning marital laws and sexual practice is at the core of the self-identity of the ingroup according to D. The importance of the marital laws becomes especially evident in the penal code in which a man who engages in wrongful sexual relations with his own wife will face the most severe penalty of all, expulsion.

One may wonder why marital laws became central for the common identity of the sect. There are likely many reasons. From a social identity perspective, in a situation in which one group has lost status compared to another group – as is likely the case of the early Qumran movement – they may reinterpret their characteristics and actions as being superior to the outgroup in order to survive as a group. Since the sect reflected in D could not "compete" in temple practice (which appears to have been the initial battleground) they changed the playing field, by putting the focus on an area where they felt superior given their stringent regulations. In addition, by focussing on marriage and sex, the conflict could be expanded to encompass the whole population which was viewed as united on this issue. Thereby they could prove the sway of Belial on the entire population and argue that the temple was defiled due to the sins of the whole people. Hence this perspective would strengthen the cohesion of the ingroup in their common rejection of the evil practices of the outgroup and aid unifying the ingroup as they shared a conviction of their own marital practice as tangible evidence of them living in perfect holiness.

This analysis has implications for understanding the view on marriage and celibacy in the Qumran movement. Josephus' depiction of the marital branch as peripheral has been highly influential in scholarly reconstructions of the Qumran movement since the discovery of the Scrolls. Scholars have pointed to various symbolic models of self-understanding which they claim put celibacy at the core, e.g., the community as a temple. On the basis of the marital and sexual laws in D and MMT – core documents within the Qumran community – this analysis instead points to a self-understanding in which marriage lies at the heart of the communal identity.

Jutta Jokiranta

Black Sheep, Outsiders, and the Qumran Movement: Social-Psychological Perspectives on Norm-Deviant Behaviour

Introduction

The term "black sheep effect" in social psychological research was coined by José Marques and his colleagues in the 1980s to describe the phenomenon in which ingroup norm-deviance is viewed more harshly than the corresponding behaviour of outgroup members. Deviant ingroup members present a challenge to the positive identity of the ingroup which has to be somehow resolved.[1] "Outgroup homogeneity effect", on the other hand, refers to the social identity process whereby outgroup members are perceived to be more similar to each other than ingroup members among themselves, and the perception of the outgroup is often coloured by the most negative stereotype available.[2] In this article, I will ask if markers of these phenomena can be identified in the Community Rule of Qumran and what significance these social psychological processes have for our understanding of this particular rule text and, more broadly, the Qumran movement.

In general, identity is based on perceptions of sameness and difference. I assume that the gathering of people around common ideals of studying, providing counsel, worshipping and/or having meals together already established a shared ingroup identity for the people we may call the Qumran movement. In recent research, even the "sectarian" scrolls are no longer seen as reflective of only one strict community living on the shore of the Dead Sea, but rather of a wide socio-religious movement with internal variation and change.[3] When studying the identity of its members, it matters a great deal

1 J.M. Marques/V.Y. Yzerbyt/J.-P. Leyens, "The 'Black Sheep Effect': Extremity of Judgments towards Ingroup Members as a Function of Group Identification", *EJSP* 18 (1988) 1–16.

2 P.J. Oakes/S.A. Haslam/J.C. Turner (ed.), *Stereotyping and Social Reality* (Oxford: Blackwell, 1994), 160–85.

3 E.g. C. Wassén/J. Jokiranta, "Groups in Tension: Sectarianism in the Damascus Document and the Community Rule", in D.J. Chalcraft (ed.), *Sectarianism in Early Judaism: Sociological Advances* (London: Equinox, 2007) 205–45; John J. Collins, *Beyond the Qumran Community: The Sectarian Movement of the Dead Sea Scrolls* (Grand Rapids, MI: Eerdmans, 2009); A. Schofield, *From Qumran to the Yahad: A New Paradigm of Textual Development for The Community Rule* (STDJ 77; Leiden: Brill, 2009); J. Jokiranta, *Social Identity and Sectarianism in the Qumran Movement* (STDJ 105; Leiden: Brill, 2013); C. Hempel, *The Qumran Rule Texts in Context: Collected Studies* (TSAJ 154; Tübingen: Mohr Siebeck, 2013). In this research, scholars have addressed different questions, such as the relationship between different documents (the *Da-*

whether we imagine a group of people who lived together and whose everyday life in all details was governed by the sect, or a socio-religious movement based on small group gatherings and comprised of people who came together on a regular basis – perhaps in some cases only annually – and who basically led their life as families among other families.[4] If we pursue this task on the basis of the textual evidence, especially the rule documents like the Community Rule, the Damascus Document, and others, we have no reason to think that this movement was a small isolated community of people living and working in only one place. Rather, the movement seems to have been based on small groups coming together and also regulating the life of members outside of the assembly setting, and perhaps during larger, more infrequent meetings. The movement rules are first and foremost about assembling and sharing knowledge, not about communal units/enclaves.[5] This is a claim based on textual data. The members probably lived scattered around the land, and they needed to create forms of negotiating their identity among themselves and among outsiders. The study of the movement and the identity of its members no longer assumes a communal setting where all members lived, but rather a network setting where members created firm and established contacts but continued their (family) life.

The *Community Rule* (= *Serekh Ha-Yahad* [S]) is a title given by scholars to a handful of manuscripts, most notably the well-preserved Cave 1 manuscript 1QS (dated around 100–75 BCE) and various types of manuscripts from Cave 4 and 5, 4QS[a–j] (4Q255–264) and 5QS (5Q11).[6] The naming can be somewhat misleading, since none of the fragmentary remains of the 4QS and 5QS manuscripts preserve anything close to 1QS. Textual forms vary from manuscript to manuscript, and the inclusion and preservation of various

mascus Document and the *Community Rule*; the rule documents and the *pesharim*), the development within one literary tradition, and the relationship between shorter and longer *Community Rule* manuscripts, but the important thing to note is that even the most sectarian documents are not seen as reflective of one community only.

4 The question of celibacy in the movement is debated. Recently, C. Wassén, "Women, Worship, Wilderness, and War: Celibacy and the Constructions of Identity in the Dead Sea Scrolls", in J. Baden, et al. (ed.), *Festschrift in Honor of John J. Collins* (Leiden: Brill, forthcoming), shows that the scholarly models presented as the rationale for celibacy are mostly mistaken.

5 See further J. Jokiranta, "An Experiment on *Idem* Identity in the Qumran Movement", *DSD* 16, no. 3 (2009) 309–29. A. van der Kooij, "The Yaḥad – What is in a Name?", *DSD* 18, no. 2 (2011) 109–28, argues that the term *yahad* itself points to a type of national assembly.

6 P.S. Alexander/G. Vermes, *Qumran Cave 4 XIX: 4QSerekh Ha-Yahad* (DJD 26; Oxford: Clarendon Press, 1998); S. Metso, *The Textual Development of the Qumran Community Rule* (STDJ 21; Leiden: Brill, 1997); S. Metso, *The Serekh Texts* (Companion to the Qumran Scrolls 9; London: T&T Clark, 2007). Other manuscripts are closely related, but named differently (e.g. 5Q13: *5QCiting the Community Rule* or *5Q[Sectarian] Rule*); see the discussion on manuscript variation by J. Jokiranta/H. Vanonen, "Multiple Copies of Rule Texts or Multiple Rule Texts? Boundaries of the S and M Documents", in M.S. Pajunen/H. Tervanotko (ed.), *Crossing Imaginary Boundaries: The Dead Sea Scrolls in the Context of Second Temple Judaism* (PFES 108; Helsinki: Finnish Exegetical Society, 2015) 11–60.

textual sections vary greatly as well. We can safely say that no manuscript was identical to another, even though the fragmentary nature of the evidence does not allow us to be more specific about how. There is growing awareness that 1QS is in fact a quite unique manuscript, and although there is no consensus about its nature, it should be studied as an exemplar of existing rule traditions, not the only one, and perhaps not necessarily the major one.[7] Thus, it is not assumed here that this manuscript is the most representative of the Qumran movement membership, yet it is still held that this manuscript, along with other rule manuscripts, reflects some of the *promoted* contours and dynamics of membership, and it is therefore a useful example to study in terms of the identity issues at hand.

Another methodological note is in order here. To study ingroup/outgroup differentiation is a social-psychological question and not directly a historical question of members and their opponents. What a manuscript like 1QS offers is foremost an ingroup (ideal) perspective, but on which ingroup(s) and which situations? Social identity is always context-dependent, varying in terms of levels of abstraction (e.g. human/non-human, male/female, educated/non-educated, full member/novice), and it reflects an individual's perception of him/herself as a group member. To grasp how a member of the Qumran movement may have identified him/herself[8] in different situations and what was seen as most important in relation to social identity is another matter than reading about membership rules, ideals, and teachings, often in collectivizing language, as we are not even sure for which group and occasion this manuscript was intended. Here we have to theorize on the basis of *imagined communities*, or *textualized identities*.[9] We cannot get a full grasp of the sectarian identity in all possible situations. What we can get is texts that most

7 J. Jokiranta, "What is 'Serekh ha-Yahad (S)'? Thinking About Ancient Manuscripts as Information Processing", in J. Baden, et al. (ed.), *Festschrift in Honor of John J. Collins* (Leiden: Brill, forthcoming); Charlotte Hempel, "The Long Text of the Serekh as Crisis Literature", *RevQ* 27 (2015) 3–24. Already in *The Textual Development* (1997), Metso paid attention to the theological emphasis in 1QS. Traditionally, 1QS has been considered a model copy of some sort (e.g. D. Dimant, "The Composite Character of the Qumran Sectarian Literature as an Indication of Its Date and Provenance", *RevQ* 22 [2006] 615–30), but it is actually striking that there are no other manuscripts strictly imitating 1QS. $4QS^b$ comes closest in terms of the amount of similar sections preserved. Many scholars have understood 1QS as an instruction primarily for the leaders of the movement who then instructed others; see C.A. Newsom, *The Self as Symbolic Space: Constructing Identity and Community at Qumran* (STDJ 52; Leiden: Brill, 2004), 102–3. Newsom reads 1QS in terms of formation of "sectarian identity", arguing that the "document's function has more to do with formation than information" (p. 103).

8 Membership language in 1QS uses masculine forms and nouns, and I will discuss the issue in terms of this language when discussing the text passages. However, 1QSa and CD clearly reflect a family setting, and females had their obligations as well; see further C. Wassén, *Women in the Damascus Document* (Academica Biblica 21; Atlanta: Society of Biblical Literature, 2005).

9 This can be compared to how R. Hakola, "The Burden of Ambiguity: Nicodemus and the Social Identity of the Johannine Christians", *NTS* 55 (2009) 438–55, aims at understanding the *symbolic* world underlying the *textual* world of the Gospel of John.

probably sought to *achieve* further positive distinctiveness and stronger identification with the group. Thus, while social identity is not clearly and directly accessible through the textual evidence, to approach this evidence in terms of a social identity approach will raise new questions about the data and suggest new answers to the study of membership as well. It provides theoretical tools for thinking about the individual member (whose identity it was always about), the collective processes that have taken place over time, and the dynamism needed in order to talk about identity (being context-dependent, non-stable, and hierarchical) in the first place.

I will first study some central starting points from social identity research that provide basic concepts and a theoretical framework, starting with more fundamental issues (categorization and social cognition), moving towards more specific themes (outgroup homogeneity and the black sheep effect), and then analysing some of the S material in light of those perspectives.

Categorization

Categorization, including social categorization, is an ongoing human ability to make sense of the world. But what is it exactly and why does it take place? Revisiting this question, Penelope Oakes, Alexander Haslam, and John Turner argue that evidence is lacking for understanding categorization as simplifying information because of a limited capacity to process information.[10] Instead, they propose that perception always entails categorizing. Abundant information is meaningless if not placed in classes: "Categorization gives a stimulus meaning through placement."[11] Thus, categorization does not take place due to an overload of information, but because humans need more information than is available; categorization creates expectations about a stimulus, its properties and effects. By categorizing people into men or women, old or young, elite or not, rich or poor, religious or not, for example, humans obtain expectations of their behaviour. Categorization changes uncategorized stimuli into "objects and events with human relevance and elaborated meaning" at one level of abstraction.[12]

Furthermore, there are no fixed, determined theories of the world that promote the salience of certain properties against some other properties. The salience emerges in the interaction between context-based categories (theories of the world seen apt for a certain situation and purpose) and real material properties in the environment. "Information is what the perceiver needs to know at any given moment in order to construct a meaningful representation

10 Oakes, Haslam, and Turner (ed.), *Stereotyping and Social Reality*, 104–26.
11 Oakes/Haslam/Turner (ed.), *Stereotyping and Social Reality*, 108.
12 Oakes/Haslam/Turner (ed.), *Stereotyping and Social Reality*, 109.

of the reality, and to achieve their goals."[13] These perspectives are important for any study of human categories and social perception.

Social Cognition and Social Self

Social identity starts with categorization and perceiving oneself as more similar to one group of individuals than to another group of individuals: the differences with the outgroup members are greater than the differences among the ingroup members. In any given context, similarities between the ingroup members are regarded as greater and as more significant than their differences (accentuation of intragroup similarities and intergroup differences in terms of relevant properties).[14] Social identity theory further claims that the positive aspects of social identities are inherently comparative in nature. In order to achieve positive social identity, members of the group compare themselves to outgroup members and show a biased perception of themselves (thus being selective in the accentuation effect).[15]

As positive distinctiveness is established, the group creates social *prototypes* that represent the desired behaviour of a group member. Group prototypes maximize the inside-outside differences. However, inside differences also begin to emerge when members are evaluated according to their similarity to the group prototype. These differences are needed in order to best maintain the maximal difference from the outgroup and a sense of superiority.

13 Oakes/Haslam/Turner (ed.), *Stereotyping and Social Reality*, 113.

14 J.C. Turner, "Some Current Issues in Research on Social Identity and Self-Categorization Theories", in N. Ellemers et al. (ed.), *Social Identity: Context, Commitment, Content* (Oxford: Blackwell, 1999) 6–34, on pp. 10–11; J.M. Marques et al., "Social Categorization, Social Identification, and Rejection of Deviant Group Members", in M.A. Hogg/S. Tindale (ed.), *Blackwell Handbook of Social Psychology: Group Processes. First published 2001* (Oxford: Blackwell, 2003) 400–24, on p. 405. Social identity theorizing is based on pioneering work by Henri Tajfel; see H. Tajfel, *Human Groups and Social Categories: Studies in Social Psychology* (Cambridge: Cambridge University Press, 1981).

15 In light of these perspectives, the positive distinctiveness of a Qumran movement member in all likelihood was related to what degree that member compared the movement to other groups and identified with the movement, believing that social change was possible only through it. Members had different expectations for ingroup/outgroup members' behaviour on the basis of categorization and group distinction, and rule texts like 1QS contributed to these types of expectations.

Outgroup Homogeneity Effect

Studies suggest that, in general, people have more varied information about their ingroup than about the outgroup. In other words, people perceive the outgroup as more homogenous than the ingroup.[16] This is understandable as people are more familiar with the ingroup and can retrieve more information about it.[17] However, the homogeneity effect appears both with the ingroup and the outgroup in an intergroup context, that is, when the ingroup is being compared to the outgroup. Only in an intragroup context, when the focus is not on comparison but on the ingroup itself, do the lower-level categories become available and people see more differences between the ingroup members.[18]

Black Sheep Effect

As noted above, according to the social identity theory, people are biased in their social evaluations and generally favour ingroup members against outgroup members. However, the black sheep effect seems to defy this tendency, as ingroup deviant behaviour is judged more harshly than corresponding behaviour by the outgroup. How can this be explained?

Overall, members have two options of how to react to ingroup deviance: either to downplay the meaning of the deviance or to derogate/punish the ingroup member (black sheep effect).[19] Both strategies aim to interpret the deviant behaviour as not representative of ingroup behaviour overall. In the first option, undesired ingroup behaviour is often justified by external, situational reasons, whereas undesired outgroup behaviour is explained by dispositional (related to a person's character) reasons.[20] For the second

16 Oakes/Haslam/Turner (ed.), *Stereotyping and Social Reality*, 160–85.

17 For the suggestion that information about ingroup deviance is also processed differently from outgroup deviance, see G. Reese/M.C. Steffens/K.J. Jonas, "When Black Sheep Make us Think: Information Processing and Devaluation of In- and Outgroup Norm Deviants", *Social Cognition* 31, no. 4 (2013) 482–503.

18 Oakes/Haslam/Turner (ed.), *Stereotyping and Social Reality*, 160–85. Furthermore, a small outgroup is depicted more negatively than a larger one, even though the relative amount of negative properties attached to their behaviours would be the same; see Oakes/Haslam/Turner (ed.), *Stereotyping and Social Reality*, 174.

19 S. Otten/E.H. Gordijn, "Was It One of Us? How People Cope with Misconduct by Fellow Ingroup Members", *SPPC* 8, no. 4 (2014) 165–77; M. Rullo/F. Presaghi/S. Livi, "Reactions to Ingroup and Outgroup Deviants: An Experimental Group Paradigm for Black Sheep Effect", *PLoS ONE* 10, no. 5 (2015) 1–14, on p. 11. Rullo et al. are interested in asking if the black sheep effect produces only psychological, judgmental, and evaluative effects, or if it also increases aggressive reactions and behaviours.

20 Otten/Gordijn, "Was It One of Us? How People Cope with Misconduct by Fellow Ingroup

option, let us look at the black sheep effect more closely. Typically, members of one's ingroup are judged more harshly than outgroup members. "People differentiate more strongly between likeable and unlikeable ingroup members than between likeable and unlikeable outgroup members."[21] Even though members of the ingroup should generally be liked more than outgroup members, thus contributing to positive social identity (ingroup bias), deviant ingroup members cause a contradictory effect: since they risk the positive distinctiveness of the ingroup, they are disliked even more than outgroup members who might act in a similar way.[22] Later research has sought to identify further criteria when this effect emerges.

Marques et al. make the distinction between *descriptive* (denotative) norms that generate intergroup differentiation and *prescriptive* norms according to which such differentiation is legitimated and evaluated. Descriptive norms define the group prototypes and "are framed by criteria that apply to both ingroup and outgroup".[23] In contrast, prescriptive norms regulate ingroup expectations. Such prescriptive norms are often more reflectively and consciously held. "Once intergroup distinctiveness is established by a denotative norm, ingroup members can devote attention to prescriptive norms that ensure consensus on criteria for positive ingroup evaluation."[24] If an ingroup member behaves against the expected ingroup norms, it creates a situation of confusion and raises the possibility that a non-deviant ingroup member has mistaken the relevant ingroup norms. It leads to heightened self-focus, whereby the member needs to monitor the valued norms, maintain those norms, and actively establish normative influence on deviant members – thus not only supervising distinction from the outgroup but also conformity to norms within the ingroup. "Derogation of ingroup deviants reinforces

Members", 167. Typically, the positive behaviour of the ingroup member is explained by the person's positive character, whereas the positive behaviour of the outgroup member is explained by situational factors. And *vice versa*, the negative behaviour of the ingroup member is explained by situational factors, whereas the negative behaviour of the outgroup member is explained by their inherent properties.

21 J.M. Marques/D. Páez/D. Abrams, "Social Identity and Intragroup Differentiation as Subjective Social Control", in S. Worchel et al. (ed.), *Social Identity: International Perspectives* (London: Sage Publications, 1998) 124–41, on p. 129.

22 Deviant outgroup members are more likely to be taken as representatives of the entire outgroup (see discussion on outgroup homogeneity effect above), especially when ingroup social identity is threatened. There is also a correlation between the degree of identification with the ingroup and the willingness to include the undesirable (deviant) member in the representation of the outgroup. P. Hutchison et al. explain, "Including an undesirable member in the representation of the outgroup allows high identifiers to establish or maintain a positive distinction between the ingroup and the outgroup," P. Hutchison et al., "Getting Rid of the Bad Ones: The Relationship Between Group Identification, Deviant Derogation, and Identity Maintenance", *JESP* 44 no. 3 (2008) 874–81, on p. 880.

23 Marques et al., "Social Categorization", 410.

24 Marques et al., "Social Categorization", 411.

people's commitment to the group."[25] Research also suggests that the black sheep effect is not directed at deserting members who join the outgroup, but rather those deviant ingroup members who blur the ingroup/outgroup distinction.[26]

Sabine Otten and Ernestine Gordijn integrate results from previous studies to suggest three sets of factors that play a role in evaluating the deviant ingroup member (either by excusing the member's behaviour or by punishing the behaviour, such as by excluding the member).[27] The black sheep effect (i. e. judging undesired ingroup behaviour more harshly than the corresponding outgroup behaviour) is clearest when the norm-deviant ingroup behaviour is:

1) connected to ingroup-defining norms (rather than general behavioural norms that are shared by the ingroup and outgroup), and its intent is unambiguous,
2) performed by full members (rather than newcomers or marginal members), or by current or past leaders (rather than future leaders), or
3) judged by a member who identifies strongly with the ingroup (rather than by a member whose identification is weak) and who has cognitive resources to pass judgment (rather than a member whose cognitive capacity in the evaluation situation is occupied by other tasks).

On the contrary, deviant ingroup behaviour may be excused when: 1) it deals with general norms ("everyone can break that norm") and its intent is ambiguous ("it was a mistake"), 2) it is performed by a newcomer ("who did not know any better"), a marginal member ("who is not really one of us"), or a future leader ("to change things, one is allowed some exceptions"), and 3) it is evaluated by a member whose identification with the ingroup is weak ("I do not really care") or a member whose cognitive resources for evaluating the behaviour are limited ("I have other things on my mind").

I will next turn to the 1QS evidence in search of possible signs of the black sheep effect. This first demands a quick look at the sections of 1QS: the cosmic discourse on two spirits (1QS 3:13–4:26) is a tradition in its own right and colours the portrayal of the world in 1QS as having sharp contrasts, light and darkness, truth and falsehood. However, it is possible to read other sections of 1QS without this cosmic duality, and most probably many of its traditions were not originally connected to that tradition.[28] For the most part, 1QS gives

25 Marques et al., "Social Categorization", 417.

26 G.A. Travaglino et al., "How Groups React to Disloyalty in the Context of Intergroup Competition: Evaluations of Group Deserters and Defectors", *JESP* 54 (2014) 178–87, on p. 184.

27 Otten/Gordijn, "Was It One of Us? How People Cope with Misconduct by Fellow Ingroup Members", 165–77.

28 C. Hempel, "The Teaching on the Two Spirits and the Literary Development of the Rule of the Community", in G. Xeravits (ed.), *Dualism in Qumran* (LSTS 76; London: T&T Clark, 2010) 102–20; L.T. Stuckenbruck, "The Interiorization of Dualism within the Human Being in Second Temple Judaism: The Treatise of the Two Spirits (1QS III: 13–IV: 26) in Its Tradition-Historical

the impression that *internal* hierarchy and order were very important in the rules preserved. These rules are thus comparable to rules of voluntary association in general.[29] On the other hand, the liturgical framework of 1QS (the covenant renewal in the beginning, the hymn in the end) focuses on becoming a member, acting as an ideal member, and striving for an ever fuller understanding of what membership meant.

The discourse on the two spirits is omitted from this analysis as its ideological division is fairly abstract and the dualism can be approached from several angles (e.g. cosmic, ethical, anthropological).[30] It certainly invites members to identify with the right side, but it does not tell much about the nuances in between.[31] More significant for our purposes here are those rules in 1QS that give more concrete advice about how to deal with deviant behaviour and how to maintain distance from outsiders. Again it must be kept in mind that even these rules are not windows into the members' behaviour, but rather instructions intended to affect their attitudes and behaviour.

Context", in A. Lange et al. (ed.), *Light against Darkness: Dualism in Ancient Mediterranean Religion and the Contemporary World* (Göttingen: Vandenhoeck & Ruprecht, 2011) 145–68.

29 E.g. M. Weinfeld, *The Organizational Pattern and the Penal Code of the Qumran Sect: A Comparison with Guilds and Religious Associations of the Hellenistic-Roman Period* (NTOA 2; Fribourg: Éditions universitaires, 1986); Y. Moynihan Gillihan, *Civic Ideology, Organization, and Law in the Rule Scrolls: A Comparative Study of the Covenanters' Sect and Contemporary Voluntary Associations in Political Context* (STDJ 97; Leiden Brill, 2012).

30 J. Frey, "Different Patterns of Dualistic Thought in the Qumran Library: Reflections on their Background and History", in M. Bernstein, et al. (ed.), *Legal Texts and Legal Issues: Proceedings of the Second Meeting of the International Organization for Qumran Studies, Cambridge 1995* (STDJ 23; Leiden: Brill, 1997) 275–335.

31 One contrast in the two spirits teaching involves truth (אמת) and injustice (עולה). The latter term is especially frequent in 1QS 4:9, 17–24, where the perspective is future-oriented, anticipating a time when injustice will no longer be found and human deeds will be free of it. Note the form עולה, in comparison to the more frequent form עול (see below), possibly indicating a distinct tradition of עולה. This form is also used in a similar sense in the final hymn in the context of waiting for judgment day: "The multitude of people of the pit I shall not capture until the Day of Vengeance, yet my fury shall not abate from the people of injustice (מאנשי עולה), and I shall never be appeased until righteousness be established" (1QS 10:19–20). Freedom from sin is described in purity language in 1QS 4:20–22. This appears to me to be an eschatological vision, and it thus does not imply that all sins were seen as defiling. For the relationship between the two spirits teaching and *4QInstruction*, see E.J.C. Tigchelaar, *To Increase Learning for the Understanding Ones: Reading and Reconstructing the Fragmentary Early Jewish Sapiential Text 4QInstruction* (STDJ 44; Leiden Brill, 2001), 194–207.

Deviant Behaviour in the Community Rule: When to Excuse and When not to?

The penal codes in the Community Rule (esp. 1QS 6–7; parallels in 4QS[b,d,g,e]) and elsewhere in the rule texts[32] give information about non-normative types of behaviour in meetings and sometimes also outside the meeting context.[33] These penalties (temporary exclusion of non-reliable members and fines in the form of food reduction) were, in my view, most of all meant for maintaining order during meetings and trust in the reliability of collective counselling, but they probably also contributed to ingroup gradation: a member who often received penalties or received severe penalties was likely trusted less (i. e. there was a shaming effect involved).[34]

The sections that deal with breaking more foundational rules of the movement are interesting for our purposes, since they go directly to the heart of ingroup/outgroup differentiation. Some of these rules can be seen as conforming to the dynamics of the black sheep effect and reflecting the desire to regulate attitudes about when and when not to excuse deviants.

According to 1QS 8:16b–19, a member who deviates needs to be examined again and then re-integrated back into communal activities and decision-making; this person is thus treated like an initiate.

No one belonging to the people of *yahad*, the covenant of the *yahad*, who flagrantly deviates from any commandment is to touch the purity belonging to the people of holiness. Further, he is not to participate in any of their deliberations until all his works have been cleansed from injustice (עול), so that he is again able to walk blamelessly. They shall admit him into deliberations by the decision of the general membership; afterwards, he shall be enrolled at an appropriate rank. This is also the procedure for every initiate added to the *yahad*. (1QS 8:16b–19)[35]

32 In particular, the *Damascus Document* has similar penal code material (CD 14:18–23; 4QD[a] [4Q266] frgs. 10–11; 4QD[d] [4Q269] frg. 11; 4QD[e] [4Q270] frg. 7), as does the manuscript 4Q265 frg. 4.

33 C. Hempel, "The Penal Code Reconsidered", in M. Bernstein, et al. (ed.), *Legal Texts and Legal Issues: Proceedings of the Second Meeting of the International Organization for Qumran Studies, Cambridge 1995* (STDJ 23; Leiden: Brill, 1997) 337–48.

34 J. Jokiranta, "Social Identity in the Qumran Movement: The Case of the Penal Code", in P. Luomanen et al. (ed.), *Explaining Christian Origins and Early Judaism: Contributions from Cognitive and Social Science* (BibInt 89; Leiden: Brill, 2007) 277–89.

35 Translations are based on E. Tov (ed.), *The Dead Sea Scrolls Electronic Library: Texts and Images* (partially based on The Dead Sea Scrolls Reader, edited by D.W. Parry/E. Tov, morphological analysis by M. Abegg, Jr., produced by N.B. Reynolds, associate producer K. Heal; Leiden: Brill, 2006), but include my modifications. I have chosen to translate אנשי as "people of" rather than "men of", following C. Hempel, "The Community and Its Rivals According to the Community Rule from Caves 1 and 4", *RevQ* 81 (2003) 47–81. However, the masculine singular is the governing form in many rules, and these are translated by using the masculine "he".

This seems to be a moderate or even lenient position: the deviant can be excused, though he must change his behaviour and still be excluded from the common purity (probably special meals but also other possessions governed by the movement) until appropriate conditions are met. This is noteworthy given the suggestion that he acted deliberately ("flagrantly", lit. "with a high hand"). In a similar vein, the rules in 1QS 7:18b–21 first allow the deviant member "whose spirit deviates from the instruction of the *yahad*, so that he forsakes the truth and walks in the stubbornness of his heart" (1QS 7:18–19) to be re-established in his membership after repenting and going through a process of inquiry. The member is punished by exclusion for a time period and by being treated like a novice. These rules are thus comparable to the (other) penal code rules on deviating from assembly rules: the emphasis is on the function of the collective instruction (deliberations) of the members, not on distinguishing the members from outsiders. Anything that risks the natural flow of knowledge and authority of the counsel provided by the assemblies is discouraged by moderate penalties, exclusion, a ranking system, and the possibility of inquiry and reintegration.

However, directly after these rules, some additional conditions are found. The rule in 1QS 8:20–27 makes a distinction between an intentional sinner and an unintentional sinner against the Mosaic Laws – possibly referring to members who have passed their admission process since the language of "blameless holiness" is used of full members in 1QS 8:10–11. Only the unintentional sinner will be purified and granted the same chance as the initiate. The intentional sinner can never return, and none of the covenanters are to do any business with him. In comparison, 1QS 7:22–25 states that if the deviant member has been a member for ten full years, he must leave and never return, and no-one may share any pure things or possessions with him on pain of also being expelled.

The rules suggest that having a penal code of temporary exclusions and rules for the transgression of more foundational communal principles was insufficient: further distinctions needed to be made between types of deviance. The solutions offered distinguished between intentional sin and unintentional sin,[36] as well as between junior and senior members. The latter rule meant that the more the member was regarded as belonging to the "inner" circles, the more harshly his transgression was to be viewed. These texts are silent about the corresponding behaviour of the outgroup members. There are

36 The distinction in some part goes back to the sacrificial rules for unintentional sins (Lev 4; Num 15); see G.A. Anderson, "Intentional and Unintentional Sin in the Dead Sea Scrolls", in D.P. Wright, et al. (ed.), *Pomegranates and Golden Bells: Studies in Biblical, Jewish, and Near Eastern Ritual, Law, and Literature in Honor of Jacob Milgrom* (Winona Lake, IN: Eisenbrauns, 1995) 49–64, on p. 52. Anderson suggests that unintentional sins were connected to the category of "hidden laws", that is, to *halakhah* that was not obvious to everyone but was continuously being revealed in the sect. The distinction is further elaborated by Philo; see e.g. *De posteritate Caini* 10–11, *De agricultura* 180, *De fuga et inventione* 86.

no clear distinctions between intentional and unintentional sinners among the outgroup members.[37] Viewing the deviant behaviour of ingroup members negatively gives potential indications of the black sheep effect. Deviance was not excused since the non-normative behaviour was:

1) connected to ingroup-defining norms: the movement members had the ability to follow the instruction and *torah* as they were part of the counselling and revelation, whereas the outsiders did not;
2) its intent was unambiguous: done "intentionally" (by full members?) or performed by established members (having been members for ten years or more);
3) we may speculate that this deviant behaviour was judged in this manner by members of the movement (authors/editors of 1QS) who found themselves threatened (e.g. boundaries becoming blurred, defectors leaving the group, or competition of resources and followers between groups) and by members who identified strongly with the ingroup: thus the existence of these rules in 1QS reflects possible competition, defection, and a need for further inculcation of suitable attitudes.

There are also other rules in 1QS that potentially contribute to constructing especially negative attitudes towards undesired behaviour: cursing the insincere member (1QS 2:11–18) and deeming the purification and atonement of a person who refused to enter the covenant as non-effective (1QS 2:25–3:12).[38] It is possible that the annual covenant ritual, of which these rules are part, emerged precisely in order to address the threat of blurred boundaries and defectors, or at least developed in that direction.

Another relevant body of evidence to investigate is the strong thread in the *Community Rule* (both the 1QS and 4QS[b,d] manuscripts) on demanding *separation*, especially in relation to the group called the "people of injustice". I shall turn next to this evidence and the question of how to interpret these rules

37 Note that the black sheep effect in theory could also work in reverse – that is, a more positive perception of an ideal outgroup member than of a corresponding ingroup member – if the outgroup member supported the legitimacy of the ingroup norms. This is how Hakola, "The Burden of Ambiguity", 438–55, interprets the character of Nicodemus in the Gospel of John. No markers of such effect are visible in the *Community Rule*, however.

38 M. Himmelfarb, "Impurity and Sin in 4QD, 1QS, and 4Q512", *DSD* 8, no. 1 (2001) 9–37, on pp. 30–31, explains that 1QS 2:25–3:12 is describing a person who has shown interest in joining but then refuses; the person is condemned with impurity language that goes beyond the language in Leviticus, rendering the outsider as permanently impure and sinful. However, the person can actually be an insider who refuses to participate in the covenant ritual and its discipline: "he rejects the laws of God, refusing to be disciplined in the *yahad* of His council" (1QS 3:5–6). G. Holtz, "Purity Conceptions in the Dead Sea Scrolls: 'Ritual-Physical' and 'Moral' Purity in a Diachronic Perspective", in C. Frevel/C. Nihan (ed.), *Purity and the Forming of Religious Traditions in the Ancient Mediterranean World and Ancient Judaism* (Dynamics in the History of Religion 3; Leiden Brill, 2013) 519–36, on pp. 523–4, rightly stresses that, according to the passage, neither ritual nor moral purity can be obtained by human efforts and rituals, but by God's spirit.

in light of the black sheep effect and the outgroup homogeneity effect. Here 1QS will be compared to the parallel tradition in $4QS^{d}$.

People of Injustice in Community Rule: Outgroup, or Ingroup Deviants?

The "people of injustice" in the Community Rule represent the outgroup since ingroup members needed to be separated from them. However, the matter is not quite this simple. Scholars have noticed that this group is presented ambiguously as comparable to former members or to novices who do not yet have full status and may err.[39] Is this group actually part of the ingroup but presented in strong negative terms (as in the black sheep effect) since they act against the central group norms, or does the title represent the outgroup with whom boundaries need to be established? Both options are possible, but I shall argue that the latter is more likely, at least in the 1QS tradition.

First, I suggest that such rules in the *Community Rule* are not (only) reflective of *denotive* norms on the basis of which the group identity was established, as opposed to the outgroup, but rather of *prescriptive* norms for maintaining positive social identity in the face of threats, blurred boundaries, and norm-violations. The evidence in the *Community Rule* can be read as efforts to manage reactions to ingroup deviants as well as accentuating the outgroup homogeneity in situations where ambiguity may have prevailed, in terms of responding to deviance and determining in relation to which matters ingroup and outgroup members should be distinguished.

In the first place, the people of injustice are encountered in the basic opening statement of 1QS 5//$4QS^{b,d}$:[40]

39 Hempel, "The Community and Its Rivals According to the Community Rule from Caves 1 and 4", 47–81, and discussion therein. Hempel notes (p. 57): "Some of the language (touching the purity, wealth, law, judgment) is reminiscent of the admission process – cf. *1QS* VI,13b–23 – almost as though we are dealing with reversal of that process."

40 This is partly comparable to CD 15, which gives regulatations about the oath and the teaching but does not demand any separation.

4QS^d (4Q258) frg. 1a i, 1b 1–2 (par. 4Q256 frg. 4 1–2)	1QS 5:1–2
Instruction for the *maskil*[41] concerning the people of the *torah* who volunteer to turn from all evil, and to hold fast to all that He has commanded, and to separate themselves[42] from the company[43] of the people of injustice (לבדל מעדת אנשי העול) to be a *yahad* (יחד) in law and possessions.	This is the rule for the people of the *yahad* who volunteer to turn from all evil, and to hold fast to all that He, by His good will, has commanded, and to separate themselves from the company of the people of injustice (להבדל מעדת אנשי העול) to be together (ליחד) in law and possessions.

Separation is at the heart of the collective identity of the covenanters: at the same time as they are to be united in law and wealth, they are to separate themselves (or be separated) from people of injustice.[44] This characterizes the shared group beliefs in relation to which the ingroup members perceive themselves *vis-a-vis* the outgroup, but it also outlines more conscious, prescriptive norms legitimizing the differentiation. How clear was it in each setting who belonged to the people of injustice and what the existence of the *yahad* meant in terms of law and possessions? In the following passage, what this separation meant is more clearly laid out and expanded on. Let us first look at the shorter 4QS^d manuscript.

And everyone who enters the council of [the *yaha*]*d* shall t[a]ke upon himself with a binding oath to [return t]o the [*t*]*orah* of Mos[es] with all (his) heart and with all (his) soul (regarding) everything revealed from the *t*[*orah,* in accordance] with [the opinion of] the council of the peop[le] of the *yaha*[*d,* and to be separated from all the people of] injustice (אנשי העול). [T]hey shall not touch (pl. [וא]שׁר לא יגעו) the purity of the people of [holine]ss. Let no one eat (sg. ואל יוכל) with him (אתו) in [the *yahad.* No one (ואשר לא)] of the people of the *yahad* [shall give answer] in accordance with their opinion relating to any [*torah*] or judgement. [He (ואש]ר לא) shall not be united with him in possessions or in] work. Let no one (ואל) of the people of holiness eat [from their possessions, n]o[r (ולא) take from their hand anythin]g. They shall not depend (pl. ולא ישענו) on [any of the wor]ks of vanity (הבל), for vanity are all who [do not know His covenant, and all who despi]se His word He shall blot out from the world, and their works are a defilem[ent] bef[ore Him, and in al]l [their possessions is

41 R. Hawley, "On *Maskil* in the Judean Desert Texts", *Henoch* 28, no. 2 (2006) 43–77, arguing that the translation of *maskil* should instead communicate the titular use of the term, suggests an alternate translation: "A lesson. For insight" (p. 69).

42 Nif. could also be interpreted passively as "to be separated from".

43 This is the only place where people of injustice are characterized with the term עדה. Whether this signifies an established, organized (institutional) group ('congregation') or looser meaning of 'company' of people is not clear. Here, the looser translation is preferred.

44 Similarly, see Hempel, "The Community and Its Rivals", 52, 59.

impurity.] [...]*m* nations. Oaths and bans and vows in their mouths [...] (4Q258 frg. 1a i, 1b 5–12)

The separation rules are very practical. The rules mostly seem to be addressed to the one entering the covenant or to those already inside, and the rules of separation concern purity and meals, law and judgment, possessions and work. The negative view of the people of injustice comes to the fore only in the designation itself and possibly at the end of the section, which pronounces judgment on all who do not know the covenant and represent vanity.

However, the language demands a closer look. Whereas the passage begins with rules for the one entering the *yahad* fellowship, there is inconsistency in the use of the singular and plural forms, as well as the use of the אל+jussive and לא+imperfect. In three places, the pronoun ואשר appears at the beginning of the sentence.[45] The sentence "*they* shall not touch the purity of the people of [holine]ss" first stands out from its context with its plural verbal form. There are two options to interpret this: 1) the sentence refers to the preceding people of injustice who are not to touch the purity of the people of holiness, or 2) the sentence concerns the entrants who are not yet fully authorized members in terms of communal purity (cf. 1QS 6:15–23; 8:16b–17).[46] In light of the multi-stage entrance and re-entrance processes found elsewhere, it is conceivable that this rule originally referred to the novice (perhaps in the singular, as in 1QS; see below), but in this context came to refer to outsiders – or was added to make a link to the multi-stage process.

Most translators choose the first option without discussing the second. For example, Charlotte Hempel explains that this sentence bans the people of injustice from having any pure table-fellowship with members, and the following sentence, "let no one eat (sg.) with him in the *yahad*," forbids taking less formal meals together, outside of the communal setting.[47] Furthermore,

45 However, the first one (4Q258 frg. 1a i, 1b 7) is partly reconstructed, with *waw* in the beginning, but the preserved trace in the parallel 4QS[b] (4Q256 frg. 4 8) could, in my view, equally be read as part of an *alef* (thus only אשר). The second one (4Q258 frg. 1a i, 1b 8) is completely reconstructed in 4QS[d] (4Q258), but finds support in 4QS[b] (4Q256 frg. 4 9). The third one (4Q258 frg. 1a i, 1b 9) lacks the end.

46 The term "people of holiness" would then represent the full members of the movement. In this interpretation, the whole passage could be read as referring to the novice whose property and knowledge are not yet part of the communal pool, and they should not be used as such (see 1QS 6:17–23 and compare CD 15:10–11, which prohibits sharing knowledge about the laws with a novice). However, this reading seems to presuppose the long two-year entrance process, which is not preserved in 4QS[d] (4Q258). Alternatively, if the passage speaks of the people of injustice, the sentence "let no one of the people of holiness eat [from their possessions, n]o[r take from their hand anythin]g" can be understood as a stricter rule for full members, in distinction to the novices who were perhaps still allowed to accept gifts from outsiders.

47 There nevertheless remains the problem of the plural and singular: the people of injustice would have been referred to both by the plural ("*they* shall not touch") and the singular (one should not "eat with *him*"). Whether the latter sentence could have also been connected to the novice is uncertain, but conceivable: it would have banned the entrant from touching the purity of full members and from eating together with a member in the *yahad* (until granted full membership).

the later sentence "let no one of the people of holiness eat from their possessions, nor take from their hand anything" concerns a different issue, the mixing of property and benefitting from the (wealthier?) people of injustice.[48]

The other plural form in the end of the passage "*they* shall not depend on [any of the wor]ks of vanity..." can only be addressed to ingroup members or members becoming as such, since vanity is associated with all who do not know (and do not enter) the covenant. If the first "they" is understood to refer to the outgroup (the people of injustice) and the second "they" to the ingroup, the mixture of singular and plural forms is nevertheless present in the passage; one cannot interpret the text as running smoothly but has to determine the subject in each case. The plural forms of the final sentence "oaths and bans and vows in their mouths", which is only preserved in 4QS^{d} and not found in 1QS, is again interesting and ambiguous from this perspective: are these false oaths, bans, and vows in the mouths of the people of injustice, or are these desired commitments in the mouths of the ingroup members, possibly not to be shared with or heard by members of the outgroup?

For Hempel, the ambiguity as to who the opponents really are points towards their closeness to the covenanters (at least some of them), or possibly closeness in the past.[49] If the latter, it raises the possibility that the people of injustice were at one point seen to be "on the same side" with the covenanters, but later seen as deviating, to the extent that they needed to be separated. These sections in the *Community Rule* would then have been largely targeted against a particular outgroup.[50]

Let us go back to the beginning of the section. That the novice took the oath is usually taken as referring to the ingroup and outgroup distinction: ingroup members took the oath when coming together, whereas (presumably) the people of injustice did not. Whether this was a one-time occasion or repeated is not certain from this context (but cf. CD 15 where children take the oath when they come of age). However, what if the people of injustice also had taken the oath or been part of the fellowship but were seen as having broken it, due to some serious norm-deviance? How would the passage read then?

In this type of reading of the passage, the emphasis is on two directions that

48 Hempel, "The Community and Its Rivals", 47–81, on pp. 52–4.

49 Hempel, "The Community and Its Rivals", 53, 57, 80: "physical and/or institutional closeness at one point" (p. 80).

50 A similar scenario has often been suggested for the "liar" figure and his company in the *pesharim*, e.g. F. García Martínez/A.S. van der Woude, "A 'Groningen' Hypothesis of Qumran Origins and Early History", *RevQ* 14 (1990) 521–41; L.H. Schiffman, *Reclaiming the Dead Sea Scrolls: The History of Judaism, the Background of Christianity, the Lost Library of Qumran* (Philadelphia: The Jewish Publication Society, 1994), 232. However, the outgroup in S does not need to be an organized, competitive, or schismatic outgroup. The mere closeness in everyday interaction with these people was the cause for the need for separation. If the people of injustice remained in close proximity with the covenanters, with several points of continuing contact, separation was needed merely for the ingroup to preserve its sense of superiority and distinctiveness.

an ideal member is to follow: turning towards the *torah*, in the right counsel of the people of the *yahad*, and turning away from the people of injustice, who have committed some form of breach and are excluded from this council. Possibly there was a fear of being lured onto their suspicious path.[51] This type of reading may become more compelling if one reads the relative pronoun without the *waw*:[52]

ולהבדל מכל אנשי] העול	...to be separated from all the people of]
[וא]שׁ̊ר̊ לא יגעו	injustice who shall not touch the purity of the
לטהרת אנשי	people of [holine]ss. 4QS[d] (4Q258) frg. 1a i, 1b
[הקד]ש	7–8[53]

This would indicate that people of injustice are separated from purity, so one should also be separated from them. Such people were then associated with vanity: they may have become part of the movement, but in truth they "do not know His covenant". Possibly their reintegration back into the movement had failed: they "despise His word". In this interpretation, the question arises, if these are people who can still re-enter full fellowship, or if they are lost cases, people who can no longer re-enter. *The language of "injustice" in 1QS is associated both with the initial turning away from injustice upon admission* (1QS 6:13–15)[54] *and with repentance and cleansing of one's injustice when a member* (1QS 8:16–19[55]; 9:8–9[56]). In a setting where members came together to meet, "membership" should not be understood as an on/off thing, proven by a "membership card", but rather as related to the sharing of property, the right of speech in decision-making, and the transfer of knowledge – i.e. participation in "doing politics" to varying degrees. The concerns of the whole passage reveal that contacts not only took place in (formal) assembly meetings and meals, but that everyday life included opportunities to mix with these people, exchange views, do business, and have a meal with them.

51 Note that in CD 15:7–10, the rule on the oath is very similar to 1QS as regards turning to the *torah*; however, CD completely lacks the rule on separation.

52 See footnote 45 above.

53 The closest parallel is found in 1QS 8:17, which provides instruction on the re-entrance of a deviant member: before being cleansed "from all injustice (עול)," the deviant member must not touch the purity of the people of holiness (אל יגע בטהרת אנשי הקודש). Cf. 1QS 6:16–17 regarding the rule on a novice (during the first year of the two years process): לוא יגע בטהרת הרבים; 1QS 7:19 rule on the re-entrance of a deviant member (during the first year of the two-year process): לוא יגע בטהרת הרבים.

54 The more general statement also notes the separation from the people of injustice: "And when these are [in Israel,] they shall be separated fr[om the midst of the settlement of] the people [of injustice (אנשי העול), in order to prepare the way of the Lord in the wilderness. This is the study of the Tor]ah…" (4Q258 frg. 3a–d 6–7, par. 1QS 8:12–15).

55 A parallel is found in 4QS[d] (4Q258) frgs. 3a–d 8–10.

56 A parallel is found in 4QS[d] (4Q258) frgs. 4a i and 4b 7–9. However, the sentence in 1QS 9:8–9 again is ambiguous, as the "people of rebellion who have failed to cleanse their path by separating from injustice (עול)" could also be seen as outsiders.

The above discussion suggests at least three options for the general framework of the passage: the passage speaks of a novice (especially if the two-year process was followed) not yet in full fellowship standing and whose property and knowledge should thus not be mixed with that of the ingroup; the passage speaks of an outgroup, which has to be kept apart; or the passage speaks of deviant ingroup members who have possibly failed to be reintegrated back into the movement. Despite the ambiguities and incongruences of the passage, the general impression is that matters of separation have to do with material items associated with purity, concrete behaviour, and everyday practices. The shared knowledge acquired in the assemblies and the shared property enjoyed in the fellowship were not supposed to be accessible by any outsider or excluded insider. The *outgroup homogeneity effect* becomes pronounced at the end of the passage, as all those who stand outside this special sharing of knowledge and communion, are to be labelled as defiled in their works and possessions.

An even longer description about the people of injustice and what the separation entailed comes to the fore in 1QS. Any possible ambiguity is, to say the least, much weaker here: people of injustice are characterized as inherently the opposite of an ideal ingroup member and in no position to avoid judgment any longer. I have added titles to the four subsections in order to show their main contents:

(a) *Entrants into covenant must separate from people of injustice who bring upon themselves the curses of the covenant*

Each one who thus enters the covenant by oath is to separate himself from all of the people of injustice (להבדל מכול אנשי העול), they who walk in the wicked way, for such are not reckoned a part of His covenant. They "have not sought Him nor inquired of His statutes" (Zeph 1:6) so as to discover the hidden laws in which they err to their shame. Even the revealed laws they knowingly transgress, thus stirring God's judgmental wrath and full vengeance: the curses of the Mosaic covenant. He will bring against them weighty judgments, eternal destruction with none spared. *vacat* (1QS 5:10b–13a)

(b) *People of injustice/insincere member/novice (?) are not to be purified*

Let him (sg. ואל) not enter purifying waters to touch the purity of the people of holiness. Indeed, it is impossible to be purified without first turning away from evil, since impurity adheres to all who transgress His word. (1QS 5:13b–14a)

(c) *Covenanters (?) are not to mix with people of injustice (?) in work, wealth, or judgment*

No one (ואשר לוא) is to be united (ייחד) with him in his work or wealth, lest "he cause him to bear guilt" (Lev 22:16). On the contrary, one must keep far from him in every respect, for thus it is written: "Keep far from every false thing" (Exod 23:7).[57] No one (ואשר לוא) belonging to the *yahad* is to discuss with them matters of *torah* or legal judgment. No one (ואשר לוא) is to eat or drink what is theirs, nor to take anything from them unless purchased, as it is written "Turn away from mere mortals, in whose nostrils is only breath; for of what account are they?" (Isa 2:22). (1QS 5:14b–17)

(d) *Non-covenanters and vanity (≈people of injustice?) must be separated out*

Accordingly, all who are not reckoned as belonging to His covenant must be separated out (כול אשר לוא נחשבו בבריתו להבדיל אותם), along with everything they possess. A person of holiness must not depend on works of vanity (הבל), for vanity (הבל) are all who do not know His covenant, and all who despise His word, He shall blot out from the world, and their every work is a defilement before Him, and in all their possessions is impurity. (1QS 5:18–20a)

The passage again preserves several types of rules, which are woven together. The first section (a) contains the main accusation against the people of injustice: they are not interested in finding out God's will, and even when they know it, they do not hesitate to ignore it and go their own way. The second section (b) bans one[58] from entering into the same purification waters as the people of holiness, and it denies the efficacy of their purification in general. The third section (c) again addresses a covenanter (or covenanter-to-be) and bans him from uniting with the people of injustice (although not explicitly named) in any matter connected to work, wealth, law, judgment, and meals. This section is notable for its many scriptural quotations. The fourth section (d) plays with the similarity of the words עול 'injustice' and הבל 'vanity', as did the parallel in 4QS^d, and it instructs a person of holiness to actively separate – not himself this time but non-covenanters; it is about the covenanter creating distance, not taking distance.

In comparison to the 4QS^d version, sections (a) and (b) provide more information.[59] The characterization in section (a) gives further criteria for identifying whom to separate from and how to call them: the ignorant and the cursed. This emphasis strongly suggests seeing these people as outgroup members, inherently wicked and doomed. *Separation is also ideological,* not

57 The context of the Exodus quotation refers to several offences of twisting justice against the poor and the innocent.

58 The addressee remains ambiguous here: is it a person belonging to the people of injustice, an insincere member (cf. 1QS 2:11–18), or a member refusing to enter with others (cf. 1QS 2:25b–3:12a)? Note the singular in comparison to the plural in the 4QS^d version "they shall not touch" (see above).

59 Hempel, "The Community and Its Rivals", 47–81, has discussed at length the rivalry groups in the S traditions and compares in detail the 4QS and 1QS differences. She points out the continuity shown by these manuscripts: even though there are considerable differences between 1QS and 4QS, the injunction to separate from people of injustice is remarkably similar and consistent.

only physical or material. This sort of material in 1QS is often interpreted as later additions and reworkings.[60] If so, they provide extra evidence for the homogeneity effect and polarization of the outgroup. In the setting of 4QS^d where an ingroup member would have been advised to be careful not to share communal treasures (knowledge and righteous sharing of property) with those who were not fully part of the movement, the ingroup member could have acknowledged at least some variation in the outgroup members' behaviour and standing. But when the separation came to be determined by the inherent properties of the outgroup members, ingroup members were more strongly invited to see the outsiders as all inherently and essentially the same.

Section (b) not only contains the ban on touching the purity of the people of holiness, as in 4QS^d, but it explicates that the ban is about entering into their waters.[61] Differing from many translations, it is possible to again read here that the rule applies to the entrant into the covenant who is not yet a full member and is forbidden from entering the water with full members. The principle behind this is one according to which whoever breaks the rules must first repent and only then be re-established in his membership (1QS 7:18–21; 8:16–19). However, the last characterization in this section, "since impurity adheres to all who transgress His word", seems to take this one step further: the person does not repent because he is (inherently) impure. Thus this section is associated with the people of injustice who in the previous section were already seen as cursed by the covenant.

Besides scriptural quotations that emphasize the argument, section (c) also includes one significant element in comparison to 4QS^d: the rule not "to take anything from them *unless purchased*". This seems to be a more lenient position, as noted by Hempel,[62] as every exchange with the people of injustice was not banned but buying was allowed. Another clear difference is that all the rules of separation are lumped together and addressed to one from the *yahad*, unlike in 4QS^d where the first rules (regarding knowledge and judgment, work and wealth) were addressed to one from the *yahad*, and then the subsequent rule (regarding eating or taking) was for one of the people of holiness.[63] Instead, the people of holiness appear in 1QS in the last section (d). If there was

60 Metso, *The Textual Development*.

61 C. Hempel, "Who is Making Dinner at Qumran?", *JTS* 63, no. 1 (2012) 49–65, argues that "touching the purity" did not necessarily indicate a meal context but involvement with other pure items as well. C. Wassén, "Common Meals in the Qumran Movement with Special Attention to Purity Regulations", in D. Hellholm/D. Sänger (ed.), *The Eucharist – Its Origins and Contexts: Sacred Meal, Communal Meal, Table Fellowship in Late Antiquity, Early Judaism, and Early Christianity. Vol. 1* (Tübingen: Mohr Siebeck) 55–78, argues that not all (ordinary) meals in the movement required full purity.

62 Hempel, "The Community and Its Rivals", 54.

63 In contrast, the rule in 1QS 9:8–9 explicitly mentions the people of holiness: the wealth of the *people of holiness* was "not to be admixed with that of the people of rebellion (אנשי הרמיה), who have failed to cleanse their path by separating from injustice (להבדל מעול)".

once a distinction in the tradition between a novice and a full member,[64] at least in the 1QS version it does not appear to be present.

In conclusion, 4QS[d] is already seen as made up of several rules brought together into a new whole. It not only includes practical arrangements of whom to allow to participate in communal decision-making and provisions, but further essentialization and condemnation of the actions of outgroup/ excluded ingroup members. 1QS contains even more markers towards this tendency: the community's neighbours were now labelled as people of injustice, who were painted as inherently ignorant and intentionally sinful, thus drawing curses upon themselves. They were also unable to purify themselves and repent, suspected of twisting justice, to be avoided in order not to bear their guilt, and they carried defilement and impurity in all their deeds and things.[65] Even though such labelling may have started with viewing ingroup deviant members more harshly than outgroup members, in an attempt to preserve the positive distinctiveness of the ingroup, it came to serve as the overall perception of outgroup members as clearly worth separating from. Thereafter, explicit rules regarding the deviant ingroup member (studied at the beginning) were designed to more clearly manage attitudes towards ingroup deviants in situations where outside relationships were already highly regulated but assembly rules and temporary exclusions were insufficient to address the problem of such deviants: intentional sinners were also found inside the movement[66] and even a senior member could fail to meet expectations.

Conclusions

This study has sought to understand the evidence of attitudes towards norm-deviant behaviour in a setting where Qumran movement members most likely lived among non-members and former members.[67] The context in which separation from the "people of injustice" was demanded implied everyday interaction between covenanters and non-covenanters, which in normal circumstances meant doing business with them, having meals with them, exchanging views and opinions with them, etc. Problems could have arisen

64 Or between a normal member and an elite member, as suggested by Collins, *Beyond the Qumran Community*, 69–75.

65 H.K. Harrington, *The Purity Texts* (Companion to the Qumran Scrolls 5; London: T&T Clark International, 2004), 117, notes the power of such labelling through impurity language.

66 The rule on intentional and unintentional sin was also part of the 4QS[d] tradition: 4QS[d] (4Q258) 3a–d 8–12; 4a i and 4b 1–3 preserves some words in parallel to the rules in 1QS 8:16–27.

67 To live as a celibate among fellow celibates in a closed environment is another matter than to live as a family member in a city or village but trying to remain segregated from others. The scholarly image of the Qumran movement has clearly moved from the first image more towards the second.

when ingroup members did not see the outgroup and ingroup members as sufficiently different as regards their following of the torah; perhaps interaction risked ownership of the right view on torah, either when ingroup deviants blurred the boundaries or when deserters threatened the legitimacy and positive distinctiveness of the ingroup.

The passages studied here provide some clues to understanding how ingroup members were meant to evaluate themselves and outgroup members in different situations, as well as what manuscripts like 4QS^{d} and 1QS sought to do in managing the attitudes, opinions, and behaviour of ingroup members. In some other passages, deviance and separation do not play a similarly important role. For example, the famous characterization in 1QS 6 only outlines togetherness, not separation: "Together they shall eat, together they shall bless, together they shall exchange counsel" (1QS 6:2b–3a). Furthermore, the emphasis in many places is on the *hierarchy among* ingroup members (one is "more in" than some other members), not the distinction between ingroup and outgroup members. In this regard, the rules of separation from the people of injustice contributed to creating shared attitudes about outgroup members, accentuating their difference, and seeing all of them as equally avoidable. Discrimination towards outgroup members served the various purposes of creating a sense of virtual power, clear-cut and secure group identity, and confidence in the ingroup.

The exact person concerned in some of the passages studied here – novice, insincere member, deviant member, outsider – is not entirely clear. This ambiguity (or at least the similarity in the statements) suggests that such traditions were flexible and adjusted to various needs. The possibility that the designation "people of injustice" at some point or in some contexts referred to ingroup members (either those who were excluded for a period or expelled altogether) was explored here. It was found to be possible but not necessarily compelling in 4QS^{d} and less likely for 1QS, where the people of injustice were portrayed as inherently possessing undesirable properties.

The ambiguity, however, may also suggest that separation was seen as never fully completed but a continuous process: first, a person had to learn the ideal of always turning to the *torah* and separating from those people who, doing the opposite, followed injustice. As one learned this, one also learned about the greater range of situations where this applied, and the greater variety of ingroup members and their ability to achieve these ideals. There is always anxiety about not finding neat categories in real life.[68] Such anxieties would have been addressed by a further outgroup homogeneity effect: seeing

68 That there was indeed a need to *teach* what separation meant is seen in the instructions found in the final section of 1QS (titled with למשכיל, 1QS 9:12–10:4) and the hymn in the first person (1QS 10:4–11:22): the ideal member "should conceal the counsel of the *torah* (4QS^{d} reads "his counsel") when among the people of injustice (אנשי העול)" (1QS 9:17) and "teach them to separate from everyone who fails to turn his way from injustice (והבדל מכול איש ולוא הסר דרכו מכול עול)" (1QS 9:20–21).

outgroup members as increasingly similar to each other, often in terms of their worst example, and thus perceiving their inner character as a permanent, natural essence of sinfulness and impurity.

In that kind of situation, the black sheep effect – seeing ingroup deviants more negatively than the corresponding outgroup members – produced tangible rules about how and when to punish the deviant member, in order to preserve the credibility of the ingroup and its being perceived as attractive as possible. These rules were interested not in separation, but rather the reintegration of the member who could be excused (unintentional sinner or junior member) and expulsion of the member who had no excuse (intentional sinner or senior member). The annual covenant ritual (1QS 1:1–3:12) may also be significant from this perspective. Even the deviant member was required to participate in the restoration of covenant relationship, repentance, and ranking – if he did not, he would be an outsider. Furthermore, the inclusion of the two spirits discourse in the S literature (1QS 3:13–4:26) added another unique and strong layer of perceiving humanity as divided into two distinct categories, as defined by their internal essences.

Elisa Uusimäki

Wisdom, Scripture, and Identity Formation in *4QBeatitudes*[1]

Introduction

Wisdom literature has been difficult to locate in social terms due to its rather abstract character and interests. Yet such texts did not emerge in an intellectual vacuum. Accordingly, they contain various clues about their social functions. This article analyses how the language of the wisdom text *4QBeatitudes* (4Q525), found at Qumran close to the Dead Sea, mirrors the process of (group) identity formation.[2] 4Q525, preserved in fifty mostly small leather fragments, is a late Second Temple wisdom teaching which was unknown until its discovery in the mid-20th century. There is nothing to suggest a particularly sectarian provenance for the text,[3] but a certain sense of self-identity is nonetheless conveyed over the course of the instruction. How did 4Q525 seek to affect and construct the self-understanding of its audience?

The invitations to listen (frag. 5:7; frag. 14 ii 18, 24; frag. 24 ii 2), characteristic of wisdom literature, indicate that 4Q525 is directed at wisdom students with the aim of edifying them. The text teaches by doing; that is, it endorses a certain view of the world as the student recites and memorises the text in an educational setting of some sort, be it formal or informal. As I hope to show below, the text contains two performative elements that require special attention with respect to identity formation: the series of macarisms or beatitudes in fragment 2 ii (col. II) and the description of curses in fragment 15

1 This article summarises the discussion on the social function of 4Q525 in my book *Turning Proverbs towards Torah: An Analysis of 4Q52* (STDJ 117; Leiden: Brill, 2016). I wish to thank Dr Jutta Jokiranta and Dr Raimo Hakola for commenting on a previous version of the article and sharing their expertise on social-scientific biblical studies.

2 For the text, see É. Puech, "4QBéatitudes", in É. Puech (ed.), *Qumrân Grotte 4 – XVIII: Textes Hébreux (4Q521–4Q528, 4Q576–4Q579)* (DJD 25; Oxford: Clarendon, 1998) 115–78.

3 An exception is found in J.C.R. de Roo, "Is 4Q525 a Qumran Sectarian Document?" in S.E. Porter/ C.A. Evans (ed.), *The Scrolls and the Scriptures: Qumran Fifty Years After* (JSPSup 26; Sheffield: Sheffield Academic Press, 1997) 338–67, who has argued at length for its sectarian provenance. Due to the lack of explicitly sectarian features in 4Q525, however, her thesis has not received support among other scholars; see, for example, Puech, "4QBéatitudes", 116–9; J. Kampen, *Wisdom Literature* (Eerdmans Commentaries on the Dead Sea Scrolls; Grand Rapids: Eerdmans, 2011), 308.

(col. VIII).[4] It will be argued that these passages operate as social markers that can both construct and maintain the self-image of the audience.

Social Identity and Religious Texts

The concept of identity relates to the self-categorisation of a person on three levels: self as an individual, a group member, and a human being. The group level is crucial in terms of social identity: its formation typically causes depersonalisation of self-perception, which appears in the process of self-stereotyping (that is, perceiving oneself increasingly as a member of a group and decreasingly as an individual).[5] Such a proclivity for group formation is intrinsic to all human beings. The similarities and dissimilarities noted by people between themselves and others constitute social boundaries – the sense of "we" and "others" – that construct, develop, and protect one's own identity.[6]

This phenomenon is pertinent to religious texts because the authors of such writings tend to shape the intended addressees by strengthening their ingroup identity; the coherence of an internal worldview is enhanced by polarisation.[7] The process of identity formation is closely intertwined with the type of language that is being used. The language of a text reflects and creates social structures, for example, by transmitting values, defining roles, and manifesting behaviour patterns.[8] The identity formation of 4Q525's audience, and the social structure promoted by the text, are next analysed in light of the social purposes of macarisms and curses.

4 Column numbers in the parentheses are based on my material reconstruction of 4Q525, which includes the placement of remaining fragments in the original but now partly lost scroll, see Uusimäki, *Turning Proverbs towards Torah*, 23–46.

5 P.J. Oakes/S.A. Haslam/J.C. Turner, "The Role of Prototypicality in Group Influence and Cohesion: Contextual Variation in the Graded Structure of Social Categories", in S. Worchel et al. (ed.), *Social Identity: International Perspectives* (London: Sage, 1998) 75–92, on pp. 76–7.

6 See B. Lincoln, *Discourse and the Construction of Society: Comparative Studies of Myth, Ritual, and Classification* (New York: Oxford University Press, 1989), 9; C.A. Newsom, "Constructing 'We, You, and the Others' through Non-Polemical Discourse", in F. García Martínez/M. Popović (ed.), *Defining Identities: We, You, and the Other in the Dead Sea Scrolls. Proceedings of the Fifth Meeting of the IOQS in Groningen* (STDJ 70; Leiden: Brill, 2008) 13–21, on p. 13.

7 A. Klostergaard Petersen, "Wisdom as Cognition: Creating the Others in the Book of Mysteries and 1 Cor 1–2", in C. Hempel/A. Lange/H. Lichtenberger (ed.), *The Wisdom Texts from Qumran and the Development of Sapiential Thought* (BETL 159; Leuven: Leuven University Press, 2002) 405–32, on p. 413.

8 M.A.K. Halliday, *Explorations in the Functions of Language* (Explorations in Language Study; London: Arnold, 1973), 69.

Fortunate Ones and the Prospect of Eternal Curses in 4Q525

The series of five extant macarisms in fragment 2 ii consists of four antithetical macarisms on the pursuit of wisdom, although the beginning of the first macarism is now lost. The series is immediately followed by a single line that expands into another related poem on the behaviour of a wise person:[9]

[Fortunate is the one who...] 1 with a pure heart and does not slander with his tongue. *vacat*

Fortunate are those who hold fast to her statutes and do not hold fast to 2 the ways of injustice. *vacat*

Fortu[nate] are those who rejoice in her and do not pour out into the ways of folly. *vacat*

Fortunate are those who seek her 3 with pure hands and do not search for her with a deceitful heart. *vacat* Fortunate is the one who attains wisdom. *vacat*

He walks 4 in the Torah of the Most High: he establishes his heart in her ways. *vacat*

He restrains himself with her teachings and favours her chastisements const[an]tly.

5 He does not leave her in the face of [his] affliction[s], during the time of distress does not abandon her, does not forget her [in the day] of terror, 6 and in the humility of his soul does not despise [her].

But he reflects on her constantly, in his distress muses [on her and in al]l 7 his being [comprehends] her. [He sets her] in front of her eyes, lest walk in the ways of...[10]

9 For the major studies on 4Q525's macarisms, often in association with those found in the Gospels of Matthew and Luke, see É. Puech, "Un hymne essénien en partie retrouvé et les Béatitudes", *RevQ* 13 (1988) 59–88; G.J. Brooke, "The Wisdom of Matthew's Beatitudes", *ScrB* 19 (1989) 35–41; É. Puech, "4Q525 et les péricopes des Béatitudes en Ben Sira et Matthieu", *RB* 98 (1991) 80–106; H.-J. Fabry, "Der Makarismus – mehr als nur eine weisheitliche Lehrform: Gedanken zu dem neu-edierten Text 4Q525", in J. Hausmann/H.-J. Zobel (ed.), *Alttestamentlicher Glaube und Biblische Theologie: Festschrift für Horst Dietrich Preuß zum 65. Geburtstag* (Stuttgart: Kohlhammer, 1992) 362–71; J.A. Fitzmyer, "A Palestinian Collection of Beatitudes", in F. van Segbroeck et al. (ed.), *The Four Gospels 1992: Festschrift Frans Neirynck* (3 vol.; BETL 100; Leuven: Leuven University Press, 1992) 1.509–15; É. Puech, "The Collections of Beatitudes in Hebrew and in Greek (4Q525, 1-4 and Matt 5, 3-12)", in F. Manns/E. Alliata (ed.), *Early Christianity in Context: Monuments and Documents: Essays in Honour of Emmanuel Testa* (SBFCM 38; Jerusalem: Franciscan, 1993) 353–68; B.T. Viviano, "Eight Beatitudes at Qumran and in Matthew?" *SEÅ* 58 (1993) 71–84; J.H. Charlesworth, "The Qumran Beatitudes (4Q525) and the New Testament (Mt 5:3-11; Lk 6:20-26)", *RHPR* 80 (2000) 13–35.

10 The English translations of 4Q525 are my own, but they have been strongly influenced by the previous English translations of the text to which I owe. Particularly influential has been the translation of M. Wise et al., published in D.W. Parry/E. Tov (ed.), *The Dead Sea Scrolls Reader: Calendrical and Sapiential Texts* (6 vol.; Leiden: Brill, 2004) 4:246–65.

Based on my material reconstruction of the fragmentarily preserved scroll, the series of macarisms and the subsequent poem were located in the second column of the manuscript, following the prologue of which only fragment 1 remains.[11] The prologue sets a model for the audience to follow: the ideal person is said to walk on "her" path (that is, on the path of wisdom and/or Torah[12]), to seek "her", and not to forget "her" in difficult times. The blessings described later in the text (frags. 11–12, 14) depict the consequences of such acts of awareness.

The idiom of the macarisms draws on wisdom literature and psalms.[13] The impact of Proverbs 1–9 is particularly clear: the second macarism (2 ii 1–2), which reads אשרי תומכי חוקיה, "happy are those who hold fast to her statutes", alludes to Prov 3:18, while the fifth macarism (2 ii 3), אשרי אדם השיג חוכמה, "happy is the one who attains wisdom", nearly mirrors Prov 3:13.[14] As for the influence of psalms, two references to Psalm 15 appear in the partly preserved first macarism (2 ii 1), which begins with the phrase בלב טהור, "with a clean heart", and continues with the hemistich ולוא רגל על לשונו, "and does no slander with his tongue" (cf. Ps 15:2b–3a). Psalm 24 has affected the fourth macarism (2 ii 2–3): אשרי דורשיה בבור כפים ולוא ישחרנה בלב מרמה, "happy are those who seek her with pure hands, and do not search her with a deceitful heart" (cf. Ps 24:4, 6).

While the macarisms discuss the search for "her", the next poem proceeds to the consequences of achieving wisdom (that is, the life dedicated to wisdom). The first hemistich (2 ii 4) proclaims that the wise person בתורת עליון ויתהלך, "walks in the Torah of the Most High". The statement closely resembles the opening of Psalm 119 and suggests that the content of the poem resonates with and is to be read in light of such Torah-oriented traditions.

In spite of being allusive, the influence of scriptural texts on 4Q525 shapes its instruction in significant ways: the links to Proverbs highlight the text's participation in the ancient wisdom tradition, whereas those to psalms with liturgical and Torah-centric elements demonstrate that, in the late Second Temple era, wisdom teaching was closely tied to the religious tradition of Judaism.[15] Psalms 15 and 24 bring a subtlety of liturgical poetry into the

11 For the likely placement of fragment 2 ii in the original scroll, see Uusimäki, *Turning Proverbs towards Torah*, 37.

12 Note that the feminine suffix can and probably does refer to both wisdom and Torah, which have feminine grammatical gender.

13 I have discussed the influence of scripture on 4Q525 in my article "Use of Scripture in *4QBeatitudes:* A Torah-Adjustment to Proverbs 1–9", *DSD* 20 (2013) 71–97. In addition, Puech's brief comments in the official edition ("4QBéatitudes", 115–78) include numerous insightful remarks on the connections between 4Q525 and biblical and other ancient Jewish texts.

14 The third macarism (2 ii 2) אש[רי] הגלים בה ולוא יביעו בדרכי אולת, "fortu[nate] are those who rejoice in her and do not pour out into the paths of folly", might also be an allusion to Proverbs if the "paths of folly" refer to the ways of female folly (cf. Prov 7:25).

15 This has long been clear in the light of Ben Sira and the Wisdom of Solomon, while the evidence from Qumran has required further redefinition of Jewish wisdom literature. See, for example, J.J.

pedagogical setting, while the tone of Psalm 119 indicates that 4Q525 takes part in the spiritual formation of the audience as it promotes the idea of Torah as a source for a blessed life.

The severely damaged fragment 15, on the other hand, contains a description of curses rather than a list of curses directed to the second person. The passage appears later in the text, after various wisdom instructions and poems (frags. 2 iii and 5), descriptions of evil spirits and future judgement (frags. 6–10), and sections on divine protection and blessings (frags. 11–12, 14 ii). The theme of the passage is confirmed by the reference to "eternal curses" (אררות נצח) in 15:4. The material reconstruction of the manuscript suggests that the fragment belonged to the ninth column of (probably) thirteen columns in the original scroll.[16]

The statement לוא ישיגו אורחות חיים, "they shall not attain the paths of life", in 15:8 is a verbatim citation from Prov 2:19. This verse of Proverbs describes the destiny of those who choose the strange woman, warning that those who go to her will not be able to return or attain the paths of life. The quotation is deliberate and reveals the poem's theme and setting: it portrays events that take place in the underworld, where folly's house is located. The passage is further shaped by the fire and serpent imagery of the Song of Moses (esp. Deut 32:22).[17] The vivid depiction of evils that befall the person is striking insofar as such content is not often embedded in wisdom instruction.

The language of Deuteronomy has, therefore, been combined with the Proverbs' motif: according to 4Q525, the curses in folly's underworld residence are comparable to the divine wrath portrayed in the Song of Moses. The end result contains contemporary theological undertones: Deuteronomy 32 mentions vengeance and the day of calamity (32:35), but these are not related to end-times, while 4Q525's language of fire, darkness, and Sheol seems to have eschatological connotations (frags. 15–23).[18] The portrayal of curses also differs from the curses that precede Deuteronomy 32 in Deuteronomy 27–28. The curses of 4Q525 are imagined poetically as horrible events that take place in the fiery Sheol. The rich use of verbs in fragment 15

Collins, "Wisdom Reconsidered, in Light of the Scrolls", *DSD* 4 (1997) 265–81; M.J. Goff, *Discerning Wisdom: The Sapiential Literature of the Dead Sea Scrolls* (VTSup 116; Leiden: Brill, 2007).

16 For the most likely placement of fragment 15, see Uusimäki, *Turning Proverbs towards Torah*, 41.

17 Deut 32:22 mentions Sheol and fire (cf. 4Q525 15:6) while depicting wrath caused by disloyalty to God. The serpent and venom images of this verse also have notable parallels in fragment 15: in addition to רוש (15:1), both פתנים/פתן (15:2, 3) and חמת תנין/תנינים (15:4; 17:4) are mentioned twice. The latter expression occurs only once in the Hebrew Bible when enemies are compared to the poison of snakes (cf. Deut 32:32b–33). The impact of Deut 32 on 4Q525 15 was first recognised by Goff, *Discerning Wisdom*, 219–22.

18 See, for example, the statement "its bolts are the fasts of the pit/perdition" in 15:7, the reference to M/mastema in 19:4, and the mention of "the designated day" in 23:2.

indicates that the fragment contains a narrative poem that describes future events, whereas Deuteronomy attests to a liturgical set of curses.

The reinforcement of 4Q525's teaching with scriptural imagery is not a matter of literary creativity and embellishment alone, as the macarisms and the description of curses create a dramatic contrast. Why did the author employ them in a wisdom instruction? What are their roles in relation to the overall purpose of the text, and what do they tell us about its target audience? These questions are further nuanced by the link between macarisms and blessings, as well as by their antithetical relationship to the phenomena of woes and curses.

The Acts of Blessing and Cursing

The Hebrew formula אשרי derives from the root אשר, "to call someone fortunate/happy". Instead of an actual blessing, a macarism is a proclamation of happiness, a form of congratulations, and an expression of praise for salutary conditions. Despite being declarative, it is conditional and functions as an implicit exhortation, which makes it natural for pedagogical contexts.[19] K.C. Hanson has further highlighted the formula's link to the cultural values of honour and shame in the Mediterranean region, even suggesting that אשרי should be translated as "honourable" instead of the typical "blessed" or "happy".[20] While the content of the אשרי statement is certainly not exhausted by social connotations alone, Hanson's argument aptly points to the social aspects that pertain to the use of the formula. Its employment was likely to contribute to identity construction in a culture where the value and honour of a person were constantly challenged and depended on the views of other people.

In addition to its social roles, the macarism is essentially religious or spiritual in the sense that prosperous situations were thought to follow divine blessing.[21] Thus, the macarism pertains to an act of blessing with multiple meanings: granting and receiving favour, or expressing human aspiration towards goodness. Verbal elements are crucial in this attempt to form a bond between God and human beings by speaking, but semantic, social, and

19 See, for example, A. George, "La «forme» des béatitudes jusqu'à Jésus", in *Mélanges bibliques rédigés en l'honneur de André Robert* (TICP 4; Paris: Bloud & Gay, 1956) 398–403, on p. 400; G. Bertram, "μακάριος in the LXX and Judaism", in G. Kittel (ed.), *Theological Dictionary of the New Testament* (10 vol.; Grand Rapids: Eerdmans, 1967) 4.364–7.

20 K.C. Hanson, "How Honourable! How Shameful! A Cultural Analysis of Matthew's Makarisms and Reproaches", *Semeia* 68 (1994) 81–111. The view has been adopted, for example, by J.H. Neyrey, *Honor and Shame in the Gospel of Matthew* (Louisville: Westminster John Knox, 1998), 164–7.

21 W. Käser, "Beobachtungen zum alttestamentlichen Makarismus", *ZAW* 82 (1970) 235–50.

psychological elements are involved as well.[22] As W. Janzen describes, the content of blessing seems to constitute the basis for the macarism, but "'ašrê and related terms are not initiators or carriers of blessing; they are not power-filled words meant to effect that state".[23] The primary purpose of a blessing act is to cause good fortune, while macarisms reassure the state of blessedness and require the recipient to do certain things.

The positive acts of blessings and macarisms provide a counterpart for the negative acts of curses and woe statements. Similarly to a blessing, a curse is considered to operate by means of an inherent power and to derive its effectiveness from the deity invoked in the utterance. While a blessing grants vital power for living beings, curses use language to cause evil or bring misfortune on a person or a community.[24] Moreover, in the same way that macarisms are related but not identical to blessings, woe statements can be associated with curses as their "weakened" form. In terms of function, both curses and woe statements seem to be primarily about the self-control and identity construction for their users rather than for those who are being cursed or lamented upon. The acts appear in religious texts that seek to shape the self-image of their ingroup audiences; however, the content of curses and woe statements are typically directed at outgroups and even remain unknown to their targets (see more below).

Blessings and curses in particular, but also macarisms and woe statements, are sometimes presented as antithetical pairs in biblical texts.[25] Binary structures consisting of blessings and curses are also occasionally employed in complete texts or text collections.[26] How do such antithetical pairs operate in terms of their social reality, specifically in the case of 4Q525?

22 P. Assavavirulhakarn, "Blessing", in L. Jones (ed.), *Encyclopedia of Religion* (15 vol.; 2nd ed.; Detroit: Macmillan, 2005) 2.979–85, on pp. 2.979–80.

23 W. Janzen, "'AŠRÊ in the Old Testament", *HTR* 58 (1965) 215–26, on pp. 222–3.

24 K. van der Toorn, "Curse", in K. van der Toorn/B. Becking/P.W. van der Horst (ed.), *Dictionary of Deities and Demons in the Bible* (Leiden: Brill, 1995) 398–406, on pp. 400–1.

25 In the Hebrew Bible, macarisms and woe statements are placed antithetically only in two emended readings (Isa 3:10–11; Qoh 10:16–17), while counterpoised blessings and curses occur in Leviticus 26 and Deuteronomy 27–28 (see also Joshua 24). In the New Testament, antithetical macarisms and woe statements appear in Luke 6.

26 For example, the Pentateuch begins with the blessings of the creation account, while the curses in Deuteronomy (chs. 27–28) are located at its end. In the Gospel of Matthew, the list of macarisms occurs in chapter 5, whereas the last judgement and end-time curses are depicted towards the end of the work in chapter 25. The woes in Matthew 23 can also be seen as providing a counterpart for the macarisms in Matthew 5; see R. Hakola, "Social Identity and a Stereotype in the Making: Pharisees as Hypocrites in Matt 23", in B. Holmberg/M. Winninge (ed.), *Identity Formation in the New Testament* (WUNT 227; Tübingen: Mohr Siebeck, 2008) 123–39, on p. 134.

The Performative Role of Words in 4Q525

Since texts are rooted in real-life situations and, as acts, answer questions posed by them, every word should be interpreted with sensitivity to its placement and related performative force.[27] The performative role of words has been addressed by speech act theory, which was first introduced by J.L. Austin and further developed by J.R. Searle. The theory posits that speaking language means performing acts, and utterances enact something rather than merely describe.[28]

With regard to 4Q525, two features of speech acts discussed by Searle are particularly helpful: the *illocutionary* aspect emphasises the intention of delivering speech, while the *perlocutionary* aspect refers to the effects of illocutionary acts upon the hearers.[29] As I hope to show next, these two elements – the intentions and effects of speech acts – shed light on the identity formation process documented in 4Q525. Even though this text was probably not employed in any particular ritual, it contains performative elements and creates a certain state of affairs – or endorses an already existing one – in the context of wisdom teaching.

In 4Q525, the series of macarisms and the cursing account do more than describe. They are not abstract statements, but an attempt to do something by uttering and performing words in an educational context of some sort. First, both are *illocutionary* and intentional acts. In other words, these utterances have social and spiritual aims embedded in them. They imply a type of dualism and thus provide a framework for the text. Second, the macarisms and the description of curses have *perlocutionary* aspects insofar as they affect the recipients that recite the text. Since the dichotomy, expressed by the macarisms and the cursing account, mirrors the division of people into two groups, they serve as speech acts that set up two contrasted categories and mark social boundaries by disclosing who is in and who is out.

More specifically, the macarisms invite the intended audience to take part in the promised blessings. Their location in the second column of the scroll implies that they are used to enrol the audience in the text's agenda already at the outset, and the self-image of the group is formed when the listeners first identify themselves with the "fortunate ones". The macarisms create a sense of belonging among the wise ingroup, which then enables the audience to accept the binary view of the world that is reinforced later in the instruction.

27 A.C. Thiselton, "The Supposed Power of Words in the Biblical Writings", *JTS* 25 (1974) 283–99, on p. 293.

28 J.L. Austin, *How to Do Things with Words: The William James Lectures Delivered at Harvard University in 1955* (ed. J.O. Urmsson/M. Sbisà; 2nd ed.; Oxford: Clarendon, 1975); J.R. Searle, *Speech Acts: An Essay in the Philosophy of Language* (Cambridge: Cambridge University Press, 1969).

29 Searle, *Speech Acts*, 23–5.

The macarisms mirror the core values of 4Q525's background community: wisdom, prudence, Torah piety, and endurance. Janzen's notion that macarisms do not have a causative effect in the same sense as blessings should be borne in mind,[30] but even though they may not create a new state of "being fortunate", they can support the emerging or already existing state of happiness and related blessedness. The macarisms clearly congratulate the audience, create and construct its ingroup identity, and reinforce this self-image by inviting the audience to remain with the fortunate. The real effects of such verbal acts typically involve social cohesion and a sense of security.[31] In the case of 4Q525, this confirmation of positive group identity is more about the sense of affinity to others in the audience than creating strictly defined social boundaries.

In terms of location, the description of eternal curses appears much later in the scroll. The poem in fragment 15 declares the fate of the outgroup, which is excluded from receiving "eternal blessings" (cf. frags. 11–12). The curses pertain to future horrors that the "others" will encounter: judgement, divine wrath, and punishment. They also will not achieve "the paths of life". The portrayal of curses through events set in the dark and fiery underworld establishes and maintains boundaries between in- and outgroups, while (the fear of) being cursed heightens tensions between groups. The use of Deuteronomy 32 further "lends authority" to the text, and perhaps it attempts to justify the cursing, along with the invocation of scriptural imagery.

The use of cursing imagery instead of woe statements, which would form a natural counterpart for the macarisms, may suggest that the performative force of fragment 15 is particularly strong. At first glance, the element of cursing indeed seems to highlight the division between the fortunate and the cursed as imagined by the author. Even so, there is evidence to suggest that the cursing theme perhaps did not belong to the author's primary agenda.

The placement of fragment 15 in the ninth column is notable because, contrary to the macarisms that connect the audience to the promises instantly at the outset, the position of the description of curses points to its having a secondary significance. The curses serve as a warning and a means of group control, but they apparently are not directed at the intended audience, at least as long as those people remain within the ingroup. Instead, eternal curses portray the promised destiny of "others". Self-image of the audience is defined through a negative use of language and an external threat, but the attempt to form identity is indirect in comparison with the direct, positive effect of the macarisms; the same can be suggested by the lack of explicit cursing formulae in the poetic account.

In conclusion, the use of the macarism series and the description of curses

30 Janzen, "'AŠRÊ in the Old Testament", 222–3.

31 R.C.D. Arnold, *The Social Role of Liturgy in the Religion of the Qumran Community* (STDJ 60; Leiden: Brill, 2006), 17.

in 4Q525 mirrors the social functions of this wisdom teaching. The author first promotes the positive self-image of the ingroup, as well as its sense of belonging to the blessed. The separation of the audience from an abstract set of "others" is then endorsed and social boundaries maintained with the help of the cursing account. The text is preserved in fragments, but the extant evidence suggests that the border between "we" and "they" follows the person's relation to Torah. The blessed ones comprise those who lead a wise and Torah-oriented life, fear God, and behave cautiously (cf. frags. 2 ii and 5). They achieve wisdom, which is equated with walking in the path of the Torah of the Most High (2 ii 3–4), while the cursed ones are evil-doers that lack a devout life (frags. 16–23).

The influence of scripture on 4Q525 further enhances the role of Torah piety as a constituent of self. The macarisms include the intended audience among the blessed, whereas the impact of Psalm 119 leads those being addressed to resort to Torah; furthermore, the influence of Psalms 15 and 24 indicates that the addressees are familiar with liturgical poetry. The dichotomy between in- and outgroups is developed in the cursing account of fragment 15, which intersects with the traditions of Proverbs and Deuteronomy 32. 4Q525 promotes, therefore, a view of the world that protects the wise, defined as Torah-dedicated people, and exposes the foolish who lack such an orientation. The audience is made aware of the prospect of future horrors, but also – or even primarily – of the blessings that come along with Torah obedience.

The author's aim of promoting Torah devotion in the context of a wisdom teaching seems to have been valid in late Second Temple circles where Jewish groups expressed various notions of revealed wisdom. Most wisdom teachings from that era emphasise divine sources of wisdom in one way or another, but authors invoked revelation as a source for wisdom in different ways. In particular, this is indicated by texts such as *1/4QInstruction* and *1/4QMysteries*, of which several copies were found in the Qumran caves, as they stress the significance of revealed wisdom beyond Torah. They exhort the audience to pursue רז נהיה, which is often translated as "the mystery to come" or "the mystery of being", but whose exact meaning and significance continues to be debated.[32]

32 For this enigmatic source of revelation, see, for example, A. Lange, *Weisheit und Prädestination: Weisheitliche Urordnung und Prädestination in den Textfunden von Qumran* (STDJ 18; Leiden: Brill, 1995); M.J. Goff, *The Worldly and Heavenly Wisdom of 4QInstruction* (STDJ 50; Leiden: Brill, 2003). For the theme of divine wisdom more broadly, see G. Macaskill, *Revealed Wisdom and Inaugurated Eschatology in Ancient Judaism and Early Christianity* (JSJSup 115; Leiden: Brill, 2007).

Language and Creation of Social Reality in 4Q525

The language used to create and promote social identity by describing in- and outgroups is rather abstract in 4Q525, but this does not necessarily make it any less powerful in terms of identity formation. On the contrary, studies on linguistic intergroup bias have shown that the use of generalising language is not uncommon in attempts to induce social stereotypes, as vague statements are beyond verification and falsification.[33] In 4Q525, the author aims at constructing the positive identity of wisdom students and creating emerging social boundaries among them. This is carried out by inviting the addressees, who seem to form an "open" group, to identify themselves with those who search for understanding in Torah (perhaps instead of other revealed sources of wisdom).

Such an interpretation of the text does not mean, however, that it could not function efficiently in other kinds of communities. On the contrary, it is even likely that 4Q525, found at Qumran, was later used in the sectarian movement associated with some of the other Qumran finds, in order to confirm group identity among people who already had a fairly solid sense of belonging to an ingroup. In such a context, the text apparently reinforced the polarisation between the "wise" and "foolish" understood by the sectarian movement.[34]

This analysis of 4Q525 favours the observation, made previously by scholars of social identity, that the expressions and constructions of identity are not only "perceptions of collective self". They do not merely reveal the social situation in question, including existent social categories and fully developed group identities. Rather, such constructions offer a "project for the collective self"; that is, they actively *create* a future social reality, along with offering visions about what that social reality should be like.[35]

Furthermore, it is remarkable that group leaders typically needed to use common cultural knowledge and "received wisdom" as resources in order to be successful and effective in the construction and definition of new group

33 K. Fiedler/J. Schmid, "How Language Contributes to Persistence of Stereotypes as well as other, more general, Intergroup Issues", in R. Brown/S. Gaertner (ed.), *Blackwell Handbook of Social Psychology: Intergroup Processes* (Oxford: Blackwell, 2001) 261–80, on pp. 267, 272. With regard to biblical literature, this observation has been made by R. Hakola, "The Reception and Development of the Johannine Tradition in 1, 2 and 3 John", in T. Rasimus (ed.), *The Legacy of John: Second-Century Reception of the Fourth Gospel* (Leiden: Brill, 2010) 17–47, on p. 43.

34 Many ancient Jewish texts served various purposes. For example, Psalm 37 is antithetical but not regarded as sectarian, while the Qumran pešer on this psalm is often automatically read against the sectarian context (in which the antithetical form is considered to reinforce sectarian ingroup identity); see, for example, J. Jokiranta, *Social Identity and Sectarianism in the Qumran Movement* (STDJ 105; Leiden: Brill, 2012), 4.

35 S.A. Haslam/S.D. Reicher/M.J. Platlow, *The New Psychology of Leadership: Identity, Influence and Power* (Hove and New York: Psychology Press, 2011), 65, 72, 188.

identities.[36] The author of 4Q525 also absorbed much of the earlier Proverbs tradition, as well as the concept of Torah (generally regarded as highly important in Second Temple Judaism), before expressing his own views on the ideal social reality that should prevail in wisdom circles. The integration of the macarisms and the description of curses in his teaching offered powerful tools for defining what he wanted to create out of the wisdom tradition in the contemporary setting.

Conclusions

In this article, the question of intergroup identity as reflected in the wisdom text 4Q525 was approached by an analysis of 4Q525's language, which creates and conveys a sense of group membership. It was argued that the series of macarisms (frag. 2 ii) and the description of curses (frag. 15) operate as speech acts that do something to the community being addressed. In particular, they support a process of self-categorisation by marking social boundaries between in- and outgroups: the macarisms build up positive group identity by inviting the audience to take part in promised blessings and by reinforcing a perception of being fortunate, whereas threats of future judgement and punishment are projected onto cursed people lacking wisdom and Torah piety.

The emphasis in the text is on the positive consequence of belonging to the group of fortunate ones, while the description of curses serves as a warning and defines the audience's self-image only indirectly. Passages from Proverbs, Psalms, and Deuteronomy are employed to further underline the points being made. In particular, while the curses depicted in Deuteronomy are this-worldly, the cursing account of 4Q525 directs the reader's attention to the future horrors of the Sheol. Although 4Q525 does not promote a particularly sectarian identity – the happy ones are the wise and God-fearing Jews who do not reject their inheritance (frag. 5:7–8) – its theme is such that the text could be used to promote ingroup identity in various contexts, including the sectarian movement associated with some of the texts from Qumran.

36 Haslam, Reicher & Platlow, *The New Psychology of Leadership*, 177–8.

Rikard Roitto

Forgiveness, Rituals, and Social Identity in Matthew: Obliging Forgiveness

Introduction

Forgiveness permeates the Gospel of Matthew in several intermingling ways: The meaning of the Christ-event is interpreted as effecting divine forgiveness of sins more clearly than in any other Gospel (1:21; 20:28; 26:28). The ethics of interpersonal forgiveness is emphasized more strongly than in any other New Testament text (6:12, 14–15; 18:15–35; cf. 5:23–25, 38–39, 43–44). The integration between divine and interpersonal forgiveness is developed in several passages, in a way unique to Matthew (6: 12, 14–15; 9:8; 18:18–19, 23–35). Several ritual practices reflected in the text deal with forgiveness, one way or another (daily prayer, 6:9–15; intercessory prayer, 18:18–20; the Eucharist, 26:26–28). We may therefore assume that forgiveness was a central aspect of how the Matthean community[1] was perceived to be meaningful for its members. The question of this chapter is therefore not if but how forgiveness is integral to how Matthew depicts the social identity of the community of Jesus-followers.

Although Matthew's geographical location, social position, and exact relation to other forms of Judaism is important to our understanding of the identity of the Matthean community, it suffices for the purpose of this chapter to briefly state the basic assumptions I make on these issues. On geographic location, my argument is not dependent on whether the Matthean community was situated somewhere in Syria, for instance Antioch,[2] or Galilee, for instance Sepphoris,[3] or elsewhere. In any case, the Gospel was most probably produced

1 I agree with Robert K. McIver that even if Richard Bauckham is right that the Gospel of Matthew was written for an audience beyond the Matthean community, it does not follow that the social situation of the Matthean community, that is, the community to which the authors of he Gospel of Matthew belonged, has not formed the interests and worries of the Matthean redaction. Richard Bauckham, "For Whom Were the Gospels Written?" in Richard Bauckham (ed.), *The Gospels for All Christians: Rethinking the Gospel Audiences* (Grand Rapids, Mich.: Eerdmans, 1998) 9–48; R.K. McIver, *Mainstream or Marginal? The Matthean Community in Early Christianity* (Frankfurt: Peter Lang, 2012), 41–50.

2 E.g. D.C. Sim, *The Gospel of Matthew and Christian Judaism: The History and Social Setting of the Matthean Community* (Edinburgh: T. & T. Clark, 1998), 53–62.

3 E.g. A.M. Gale, *Redefining Ancient Borders: the Jewish Scribal Framework of Matthew's Gospel* (New York: T&T Clark, 2005), 41–63.

in an urban area.[4] Regarding social position, I agree with those who suggest that at least the scribes who wrote Matthew were educated scribes and belonged to the retainer class, while the majority of the members of the Matthean community were probably non-elite.[5] The delicate debate about what would be the most proper way to describe Matthew's relation to Judaism cannot be rehearsed here. For our purposes it is enough to agree with the broad consensus that Matthew is written by a group that considers itself Jewish and writes in debate with another form of Judaism which Matthew names "Pharisees" (e.g. 3:7; 5:17–20; 10:43; 23:14–15). Whether we should describe Matthew as in a process of breaking with Judaism,[6] polemizing within Judaism,[7] or even polemizing within Pharisaic Judaism,[8] is of less importance for our problem. The important point for our purposes is that Matthew defines the Matthean identity by contrasting it with another form of Judaism. In social identity theory, this is called "the meta-contrast principle", a well-tested hypothesis suggesting that groups tend to maximize the experience that their group is meaningful by defining their identity in a way that maximizes the perceived contrast with relevant outgroups.[9]

To understand how Matthew sees the role of forgiveness in the identity of the Matthean community, we will use the methodology that I developed in my dissertation on Ephesians, where I interacted with different strands of social psychology, particularly the social identity perspective.[10] There I suggested that a group's (more or less) shared cognition about their social identity typically has the following components:

1. an identity narrative, containing the narrative rationale of the group,
2. an understanding of the group's relations to relevant outgroups, and
3. an identity prototype, consisting of

4 Gale, *Redefining*, 41–6; R.K. McIver, *Mainstream or Marginal?*, 33–5.

5 E.g. E.J. Vledder/A. Van Aarde, "The Social Stratification of the Matthean Community", *Neot* 28 (1994) 511–22.

6 G.N. Stanton, *A Gospel for a New People: Studies in Matthew* (Edinburgh: T & T Clark, 1992), 124–31.

7 A.J. Saldarini, *Matthew's Christian-Jewish Community* (Chicago: Univ. of Chicago Press, 1994).

8 A. Runesson, "Behind the Gospel of Matthew: Radical Pharisees in Post-War Galilee?", *Currents in Theology and Mission* 37 (2010) 460–71.

9 E.g. P.J. Oakes, "The Categorization Process: Cognition of the Group in the Social Psychology of Stereotyping", in D. Abrams/M.A. Hogg (ed.), *Social Identity Theory: Constructive and Critical Advances* (London: Harvester Wheatsheaf, 1990) 28–47; S.A. Haslam/J.C. Turner/P.J. Oakes/C. McGarty/K.J. Reynolds, "The Group as a Basis for Emergent Stereotype Consensus", *European Review of Social Psychology* 8 (1998) 203–39.

10 R. Roitto, *Behaving as a Christ-Believer: A Cognitive Perspective on Identity and Behavior Norms in Ephesians* (ConNTS; Grand Rapids, Michigan, 2011). I have also applied this model to 1 John in R. Roitto, "Sinless Sinners who Remain in Him: Social Identity in 1 John", in B. Tucker/C. Baker (ed.), *The T&T Clark Handbook to Social Identity and the New Testament* (London: T&T Clark, 2013) 493–510.

a. attributes, that is the character traits of the ideal group member, which cause, or should cause,
b. behaviours, that is, the practical, visible, manifestation of the group's identity.

To my previous model, I would like to add one more component:

4. a set of rituals that function to manifest the just mentioned aspects of social identity.

That is, I consider rituals an integral and indispensable part of Matthew's social identity.

Forgiveness and the Narrative Rationale of the Group

For a group to experience itself as meaningful, it needs to have an identity narrative, that is, a narrative rationale describing its origin and goal, its relation to other groups, its purpose, et cetera, in a way that motivates why the group is important and why it has its characteristics.[11]

One possible approach to determining the identity narrative of the Matthean community is to analyse the narrative plot of the Gospel. Mark Powell, for example, concludes from his narrative analysis of Matthew that the overarching plot of Matthew is God's conflict with Satan in his attempt to save his people from their sin, and that within that plot the opposition from the elite and the development of the disciples' relation to Jesus are subplots.[12] Powell's analysis is agreeable, but we should not confuse the plot of the Gospel text with the narrative identity of the Matthean community. The two do of course overlap, since – as Ulrich Luz rightly argues – the drama of Matthew is not only history-writing but also symbolically reflects the self-understanding of the Matthean community.[13] Nevertheless, the Matthean community is not a character in the plot of the Gospel.

Petri Luomanen uses a combination of insights from narratology, redaction criticism, and social sciences in his study on Matthew's understanding of salvation.[14] His method, I think, has proved to be an excellent way to grasp the

11 D. Bar-Tal, *Group Beliefs: A Conception for Analyzing Group Structure, Processes, and Behavior* (Springer Series in Social Psychology; Berlin: Springer, 1990); D. Bar-Tal, "Group Beliefs as an Expression of Social Identity", in S. Worchel et al. (ed.), *Social Identity: International Perspectives* (London: SAGE, 1998) 93–113.

12 M.A. Powell, "The Plot and Subplots of Matthew's Gospel", *NTS* 38 (1992) 187–204.

13 U. Luz, "The Disciples in the Gospel According to Matthew", in G. Stanton (ed.), *The Interpretation of Matthew* (London: SPCK, 1983) 98–128.

14 P. Luomanen, *Entering the Kingdom of Heaven: A Study on the Structure of Matthew's View of Salvation* (WUNT R. 2; Tübingen: Mohr Siebeck, 1998).

narrative identity of the Matthean community. After a thorough analysis of Matthew's redactional activity and the narrative plot of Matthew, he is able to summarize what he calls "Matthew's basic convictions regarding salvation", which we may call the narrative rationale of the Matthean community:

> The implied starting point is (1) God's election, which grants Israel its favoured position among the nations. Although (2) Israel has fallen, God keeps to his covenantal mercy and (3) calls his people through John the Baptist, Jesus (and even through the disciples) just as he has called them through his prophets in the OT. The people, however, (4) reject Jesus, which results in their (5) replacement by a new people of God. This new people of God can be entered (6) through baptism, which is understood mainly as an act of repentance and as a total commitment to God's will, as it is set forth in Jesus' teaching. (7) For those who enter this new 'covenantal' community, salvation is present reality which can be (8) maintained by wholehearted commitment to God's will and by repentance in the case of transgression. Only those who remain faithful in their righteousness until the end will pass the final judgement and enter the kingdom of the Father.[15]

That is, the narrative rationale of the Matthean community is that they are the community of those who a) are saved in the present, b) do God's will, c) stand a chance to be saved in the final judgment. This salvation is programmatically stated as salvation from sin in the introduction to the Gospel. "You are to name him Jesus, for he will save his people from their sins" (1:21).

I agree with Luomanen's overall narrative. We should note, however, that some of his formulations touch on much debated issues in research on Matthew. Some scholars would not agree with Luomanen that grace and work stand side by side in the process of remaining in the covenant. Charles Talbert, for instance, argues that the indicative of grace governs the imperative of works in Matthew.[16] Willi Marxsen, on the other hand, argues that Matthew is a legalist who gives priority to works over grace.[17] Further, Luomanen's formulation that Matthew has a "new" covenant in mind is based on his conviction that the Matthean community has begun to separate itself from other forms of Judaism.[18] As noted above, scholars disagree on how intra-Jewish Matthew should be considered.

For our analysis of how Matthew understands forgiveness as a part of the Matthean identity, Luomanen's analysis has an important implication: according to Luomanen, Matthew's imagination has a covenantal structure. That is, it is structurally similar to what E.P. Sanders' calls "covenantal

15 Luomanen, *Entering*, 281.

16 C.H. Talbert, *Matthew* (Paideia; Grand Rapids: Baker, 2010), 9–27.

17 W. Marxsen, *New Testament Foundations for Christian Ethics* (Minneapolis: Fortress Press, 1993), 231–48.

18 Luomanen, *Entering*, 265–66.

nomism",[19] where forgiveness ("grace", in Sanders' terminology) is obtained continuously by staying in the covenant community. Therefore, divine forgiveness is not primarily given at the moment of entrance into the community but by continuously being in the community, according to Matthew's covenantal narrative.

Matthew does not interpret the baptism commanded by Jesus as a ritual that effects forgiveness. Rather, the meaning of baptism is an initiation into discipleship. "Make all nations disciples, by baptizing them ... and teaching them ..." (μαθητεύσατε πάντα τὰ ἔθνη, βαπτίζοντες αὐτοὺς ... διδάσκοντες αὐτοὺς ..., Matt 28:19–20). In Luke-Acts, repentance (Luke 3:3; Acts 2:38; 3:19; 5:13; 8:22; 26:18), faith in Christ (Luke 7:36–50; Acts 2:38; 10:43; 13:38; 26:18) and baptism (Acts 2:38; 22:16) are repeatedly said to effect the forgiveness of sins. Similarly, Paul argues that faith (e.g. Rom 4:23–25; 10:9–10) and baptism (e.g. Rom 6:1–10) are the human responses which allow the believer to partake in the redemption from the power of sin that Christ has achieved through his death and resurrection. As opposed to Paul and Luke, for whom the decisive moment of forgiveness is the entrance into the community of faith, Matthew does not associate entrance itself with forgiveness at all. Indeed, Matthew even cuts out Mark's claim that John's baptism was "for the forgiveness of sins" (Matt 3:2 // Mark 1:4–5). Matthew's redactional activity could be seen as an attempt to take away the authority to forgive sins from John the Baptist.[20] A better interpretation, however, is that Matthew simply does not think that baptism, neither John's nor Christ's, effects forgiveness.[21] If so, Matthew would agree with the majority of Jews in the first century, who assumed that immersion rites could not effect forgiveness of sins, but only ritual purification.[22] However, Matthew does not associate baptism with ritual purity either. The only meanings attached to baptism are repentance (3:6) and discipleship (28:19–20).

Rather, forgiveness is an aspect of the continuous life of the Matthean community. Forgiveness is part of the Lord's Prayer (6:9–13), which the *Didache* (8:2–3) gives us reason to think was a daily prayer. Mediation of divine forgiveness through intercession is part of the authority granted to the community (9:8; 18:18–20). Finally, Jesus' covenant "for the forgiveness" of sin was manifested regularly in the Matthean Eucharist (26:28). When Sanders contrasts Pauline theology with the "covenantal nomism" typical of Second Temple Judaism, he argues that it is precisely on the issue of when grace is

19 E.P. Sanders, *Paul and Palestinian Judaism: A Comparison of Patterns of Religion* (Philadelphia: Fortress, 1977). See p. 422 for a summary.

20 W.D. Davies/D.C. Allison, *A Critical and Exegetical Commentary on the Gospel According to Saint Matthew: Vol. 1, Introduction and Commentary on Matthew 1–VII* (ICC; Edinburgh: T&T Clark, 1988), 292.

21 Luomanen, *Entering*, 204–9.

22 T. Kazen, *Jesus and Purity Halakhah: Was Jesus Indifferent to Impurity?* (Rev. ed.; ConNTS; Winona Lake, Ind.: Eisenbrauns, 2010), 232–43.

granted that Paul differs from most forms of Judaism. For Paul, justification (he does not use the word "forgiveness") is granted at the moment of entrance into Christ, but in covenantal nomism, grace is continuously granted for those who repent and atone for their sins.[23] As Luomanen points out, Matthew is here typical for second temple Judaism when he narrates the place of forgiveness in the continuous life of the community rather than at the entrance into the community.[24]

Forgiveness and Contrast to Outgroups

Social identity theory argues that social groups tend to define their own identity as maximally distinct from relevant outgroups.[25] This tendency is called "the meta-contrast principle". Therefore, if divine forgiveness is central to the Matthean self-conception, we might suspect that Matthew contrasts the Matthean community with "the Pharisees" on this issue. This is for instance the case in Ephesians, where it is a central aspect of the community's self-understanding that they, who used to be sinful gentiles, have received atonement and thus salvation, as opposed to those who do not believe (Eph 1:7; 2:1–19). However, Matthew does not contrast the forgiveness available in community with lack of divine forgiveness for the Pharisees. Rather, Matthew almost seems to contradict the forgiving function of Jesus' death in some of the warnings about what will happen at the final judgment. "Not everyone who says to me, 'Lord, Lord,' will enter the kingdom of heaven, but only the one who does the will of my Father in heaven" (Matt 7:21, cf. 25:31–46). As David Seeley argues, salvation by works and Jesus as the salvation from sin stand side by side in Matthew, but at points seem poorly integrated.[26] The judgment scene in Matthew 25:31–46 depicts the judgment of all humanity, and being a member of Jesus' covenant for the forgiveness of sins does not merit special favour.

If there is anything that the Gospel of Matthew contrasts with the competing outgroup, the Pharisees, it is not superior forgiveness, but superior righteousness. "For I tell you, unless your righteousness exceeds that of the scribes and Pharisees, you will never enter the kingdom of heaven" (Matt 5:20). Superior ability to interpret the Torah and do God's will is the landmark of the (ideal) Matthean community, which distinguishes it from "the Pharisees" (e.g. 5:17–48; 12:1–14; 15:1–20; 16:5–12; 19:3–9; 23:1–39). An emphasis on superior access to forgiveness, which implies sinful community members in

23 Sanders, *Paul*, e.g. 543–9.
24 Luomanen, *Entering*, 278–81.
25 References in note 9.
26 D. Seeley, *Deconstructing the New Testament* (Leiden: Brill, 1994), 21–52.

need of forgiveness, was perhaps felt to undermine the self-perception of the Matthean community as more righteous than other forms of Judaism. Perhaps the oft-noted oscillation between grace and perfectionism in Matthew can be understood as the tension between two socio-cognitive needs in the Matthean community, a) a meaningful identity narrative, and b) a sharp meta-contrast between the community and competing outgroups.

If superior commitment to God's will is Matthew's foremost source of collective self-esteem,[27] then we can understand why the ethics of forgiveness is emphasized in longer and more elaborate passages than the promise of divine forgiveness is, in spite of divine forgiveness being central to Matthew's Christology. Although the very meaning of Jesus' birth and death is to inaugurate a covenant that saves from sin (1:21; 20:28; 26:28), this is not what comes into the forefront in passages that accentuate the identity of the community in contrast to other groups. Rather, when the Lord's prayer is introduced as an instruction on how to pray differently from "the hypocrites" (6:5), the prayer about forgiveness (6:12) is clarified with a threat that puts the moral obligation in the forefront: "If you do not forgive others, neither will your Father forgive your trespasses" (6:15). Divine forgiveness is by all means a central aspect of the Kingdom of Heaven in Matthew's theological narrative, but it comes attached with the demand to exercise superior morality.

In a preceding section of the Sermon on the Mount, 5:38–48, Jesus demands a moral practice of radical non-retaliation. (Although, the word "forgive" is not used in these verses, interpersonal non-retaliation and interpersonal forgiveness arguably overlap considerably.) This morality, too, is motivated with identity arguments. Non-retaliation and love of enemies are motivated with the argument that this is characteristic of those who belong to the community. It makes them "children of your Father in heaven" (5:45) and "perfect, as your heavenly Father is perfect" (5:48), in contrast to "tax collectors" (5:46) and "gentiles" (5:47). Later in the Gospel, the parable about the unforgiving servant provides an antitype for the behaviour expected of a prototypical group member (18:23–35).

In short, divine forgiveness is foundational to the Matthean identity narrative, but when the identity of the community is contrasted with other groups it is superior morality, including the practice of interpersonal forgiveness, that makes the community distinct. This is understandable if we assume that Matthew was written in a situation where the Matthean community competed with other forms of Judaism about who has the most valid interpretation of Jewish piety.

27 According to the self-esteem hypothesis in social identity theory, groups are motivated to interpret their social reality so that it allows them to feel self-esteem, see H. Tajfel/J.C. Turner, "An Integrative Theory of Intergroup Conflict", in W.G. Austin/S. Worchel (ed.), *The Social Psychology of Intergroup Conflict* (Monterey, Calif.: Brooks/Cole, 1979) 33–47.

The Imagination of Sin in Matthew

In order to grasp of how practices of forgiveness formed the identity of the Matthean community, we need to ask what Matthew means by sin. Gary Anderson has argued with the help of conceptual metaphor theory that in pre-exilic Jewish texts sin is mainly conceptualized as a substance, either a burden or a stain, which is removed through forgiveness, but in post-exilic texts this imagination is replaced by the imagination that sin is like a monetary debt and forgiveness remission of debt.[28] His analysis is an important methodological advance in our understanding of Ancient Jewish and Christian conceptions of sin. However, I have argued that a more proper understanding of early Christian forgiveness is that the debt-metaphor did not outcompete the substance-metaphor; sin was sometimes conceptualized as substance and sometimes as debt.[29]

Matthew imagines sin both as morally defiling substance and as monetary debt: in the Lord's prayer, the petition for forgiveness is unmistakably based on sin as debt. "And forgive us our debts, as we also have forgiven our debtors" (6:12). Nathan Eubank has thoroughly investigated how monetary metaphors permeate Matthew and shown that several passages presuppose an imagination of sin as debt and moral deeds as treasure.[30] Good deeds are "treasures" (6:19–21; 19:21; cf. 13:44; 13:52) and will give a "wage" (5:12, 46; 6:1–18; 10:41–42; 16:27; 21:41). Jesus death is a "ransom" (20:28). God's judgment will measure moral debt (5:25–26; 18:23–35; 25:13–30).

However, sin is also like a substance that causes moral impurity[31] in Matthew. "What comes out of the mouth proceeds from the heart, and this is what defiles" (15:18). As Anders Runesson demonstrates, Matthew is deeply concerned with moral purity.[32] The Pharisees are accused of being clean on the outside but morally unclean on the inside (23:25–28). Immoral speech defiles (15:11, 18–20). The need to reconcile with a brother before sacrificing in the temple (5:23–24) implies purity logic; someone who is morally impure is not fit to participate in the cult. I have argued elsewhere that the story of the

28 G. Anderson, *Sin: A History* (New Haven: Yale UP, 2009).

29 R. Roitto, "The Polyvalence of ἀφίημι and the Two Cognitive Frames of Forgiveness in the Synoptic Gospels", *NovT* 57 (2015) 136–58.

30 N. Eubank, *Wages of Cross-bearing and Debt of Sin: The Economy of Heaven in Matthew's Gospel* (Berlin: De Greyter, 2013).

31 The exact nature of moral impurity in second temple Judaism is debated. For a recent review of the scholarly debate, see T. Kazen, "The Role of Disgust in Priestly Purity Law: Insights from Conceptual Metaphor and Blending Theories", *Journal of Law, Religion, and the State* 3 (2014) 62–92. Many scholars would argue that moral "impurity" was not experienced as a mere metaphor for moral guilt, but as something quite real.

32 A. Runesson, "Purity, Holiness, and the Kingdom of Heaven in Matthew's Narrative World", in C. Ehrlich/A. Runesson/E. Schuller (ed.), *Purity and Holiness in Judaism and Christianity: Essays in Memory of Susan Haber* (WUNT; Tübingen: Mohr Siebeck, 2013) 144–80.

forgiven and healed paralytic makes the most sense if sin is seen as a substance that can cause sickness, and we will return briefly to that story below.[33]

Both these imaginations of sin do in different ways evoke an imagination of sin as something negative and dangerous. Thomas Kazen has demonstrated how fruitful it can be to use contemporary research on emotions to reflect upon how the Torah evokes moral emotions,[34] and I will follow his lead and reflect briefly on what moral emotions the two different imaginations of sin might stimulate.

The imagination of sin as a debt evokes the imagination of moral imbalance. We humans have a deep-seated tendency to become angry when we perceive something as unfair, and as soon as anger is triggered, we feel that we have the moral mandate to act for justice.[35] Most probably, therefore, the imagination of being in moral debt to God evoked an anthropomorphic fear of God's anger.[36] In the parable about the ungrateful servant (18:23–35), sin is likened to a monetary debt. God is portrayed as a king who is first forgiving, but when the servant fails to forgive his servant, God's previous forgiving attitude is turned into anger (18:34), and in anger he punishes the debtor. Similarly, God is said to be angry when he executes judgment in other passages, too (3:7; 22:7). Yet other passages do not specifically mention the emotion of anger, but portray God as someone punishes in what seems to be state of anger (7:23; 24:50–51; 25:26–28). In several passages that threaten with punishment monetary language is used (5:25–26; 18:34–35; 25:26–28). In short, when sin is a debt, it can easily evoke the imagination of God's just anger over this imbalance.

The imagination of sin as a defiling substance evokes intuitions about disgusting substances that we wish to avoid. The emotion of disgust originally evolved as an emotional response that helped us avoid bad food and sickness, but was gradually extended to also function as a moral emotion.[37] We can feel disgust for certain types of immorality, especially immoral actions that are perceived as violation of the sacred.[38] As Kazen shows, God is frequently portrayed as someone who is disgusted by human immorality in the Torah,

33 Roitto, "Polyvalence".

34 T. Kazen, *Emotions in Biblical Law: A Cognitive Science Approach* (Sheffield, U.K.: Sheffield Phoenix, 2011); Kazen, "Role of Disgust".

35 E. Mullen/L.J. Skitka, "Exploring the Psychological Underpinnings of the Moral Mandate Effect: Motivated Reasoning, Group Differentiation, or Anger?" *Journal of Personality and Social Psychology* 90 (2006) 629–43; D.T. Miller, "Disrespect and the Experience of Injustice", *Annual Review of Psychology* 52 (2001) 527–53.

36 Cf. Kazen, *Emotions*, 115–40.

37 P. Rozin/J. Haidt/C.R. McCauley, "Disgust", in M. Lewis/J.M. Haviland-Jones/L.F. Barrett (ed.), *Handbook of Emotions* (3rd ed.; New York: Guildford, 2000) 737–53; V. Curtis, *Don't Look, Don't Touch: The Science Behind Revulsion* (Oxford: Oxford University Press, 2013).

38 P. Rozin/L. Lowery/S. Imada/J. Haidt, "The CAD Triad Hypothesis: A Mapping Between Three Moral Emotions (Contempt, Anger, Disgust) and Three Moral Codes (Community, Autonomy, Divinity)", *Journal of Personality & Social Psychology* 76 (1999) 574–86.

and God's reaction to ritual impurity and immorality overlap considerably, as do the rituals to remedy sin and impurity.[39] Although God is never explicitly portrayed as disgusted by human immorality in Matthew, much of Matthew's language (discussed in the previous paragraph) is based on this imagination. Perhaps divine disgust is implied when "the king" (God) is provoked by a badly dressed wedding guest (22:11–12), in the expression "desolating sacrilege" (24:15), and in the assessment of a bad servant as "worthless" (25:30). If sin is perceived as a substance that makes us disgusting, this also makes it easy for us to imagine that there is a connection between sin and sickness, since we intuitively feel that disgusting things might make us sick.[40] This would then at least partially explain the widespread belief that there was a connection between sin and sickness, which seems to be taken for granted in the story about the forgiven paralytic (9:1–8).[41]

In short, sin as a moral debt is perceived as dangerous in Matthew because it evokes the imagination of God's righteous anger that might lead to punishment, and sin as a substance is perceived as dangerous because it evokes the imagination of God's moral disgust that might lead to rejection. These insights help us understand that the identity narrative that Jesus has come with "salvation from sin" (1:21) and instituted a "covenant … for the forgiveness of sins" (26:28) was probably perceived as emotionally engaging and motivating by the Matthean community. It also helps us appreciate why liberation from sin is such a central aspect of the ritual life of the Matthean community.

Formation of Social Identity through Rituals of Divine Forgiveness

Divine forgiveness is important in three rituals depicted by Matthew, the Lord's prayer (6:9–13) intercessory prayers for sinners (18:18–20) and the Eucharist (26:26–28). How did these rituals contribute to the social identity of the Matthean community?

The Lord's Prayer

The Sermon on the Mount is organized so that the Lord's Prayer is placed right at the centre of it.[42] The prayer is formulated so that the petitioners ask God to act in relation to "us" rather than "me" and was therefore probably jointly recited in the communal gatherings. In the Didache (8:2–3), the community is exhorted to pray the Lord's prayer three times a day, so we may suspect that it

39 Kazen, *Emotions*, 71–94; Kazen, "Role of Disgust".
40 P. Rozin/J. Haidt/C.R. McCauley, "Disgust".
41 Cf. Roitto, "Polyvalence".
42 U. Luz, *Matthew 1–7: A Commentary* (Hermeneia; Edinburgh: T&T Clark, 1990), 172–4.

was a daily prayer in the Matthean community, too. Thus, the Lord's Prayer (6:12) was most likely a central part of the communal life of the Matthean community.

The first three petitions in the prayer ask for the realization of Kingdom of Heaven, or the "rule" (βασιλεία) of Heaven, in different ways, and the last three ask for the concrete practical aspects of the realizations of that rule.[43] The Kingdom is realized when they have enough food, when they forgive and are forgiven, and when they are not led into trials.

Our focus here is the prayer for forgiveness in 6:12. With the words "debts" and "debtors", sin is cognitively modelled on monetary debt, and forgiveness is like remission of monetary debt. God is like an exceedingly generous debtor, a thought that is further developed in 18:23–35.

Our first observation must be that since the community asked for divine forgiveness on a daily basis, divine forgiveness was continuous in Matthean community. (That is, it was not something that happened at the entrance into the community as discussed above.) Being forgiven on a daily basis was a central aspect of being part of the Kingdom of Heaven, the covenant in which there is forgiveness of sins (26:28; cf. the discussion on the Eucharist below).

More difficult to interpret is the inclusion of "as we forgive our debtors" after the petition for forgiveness. The clause stands out, since none of the other petitions in the prayer contain formulations where the petitioners are agents. One popular interpretation of the phrase is that the petitioners acknowledge their duty to forgive in order to receive forgiveness.[44] Matthew's clarifying note right after the prayer that "if you do not forgive others, neither will your Father forgive your trespasses" (6:15; cf. 18:23–35) seemingly supports this interpretation.

This judicial, or legalistic, interpretation of how forgiveness works in Matthew has rightly been criticized for being potentially oppressive for those who might have good reason not to forgive powerful oppressors. If, for instance, battered wives are pressed to forgive their abusive husbands, it might lead to continued suffering.[45] The problem becomes even more accentuated in the light of all the threats of condemnation and judgment scenes in the Gospel of Matthew, where everyone who is anything less than morally perfect is judged (e.g. 5:20; 7:15–32, 25:31–46). A judicial or dogmatic interpretation of these passages would probably exclude all of humanity, including the Matthean community, from heaven. It is not very plausible that that the Matthean community entertained an interpretation of these passages that condemned more or less every community member. Rather, as several

43 Cf. J.D. Crossan, *The Greatest Prayer: Rediscovering the Revolutionary Message of the Lord's Prayer* (New York: HarperCollins, 2010).

44 G. Strecker, *The Sermon on the Mount: An Exegetical Commentary* (Edinburgh: T & T Clark, 1988), 121; Davies/Allison, *Matthew: Vol. 1*, 611.

45 E.J. Ramshaw, "Power and Forgiveness in Matthew 18", *Word & World* 18 (1998) 397–404.

scholars have pointed out, it is important to understand that although these passages seemingly just inform about the future judgment, the pragmatic function of these passages is to exhort.[46] In terms of social identity theory, threats and judgment scenes is a way to express the identity prototype of the community and urge its members to strive for it. In the light of this reasoning, the pragmatic force of the claim that God only forgives those who forgive (6:14–15; 18:23–35) should be seen a) as a moral exhortation to forgive, and b) as a way to express that the ideal community member is someone who forgives. There is indeed a threat that those who do not forgive will not be forgiven in 6:14–15 (and 18:23–35), but this threat is meant as a warning and probably not as a rigid mechanistic rule for God's forgiving action.

Consequently, it is not very meaningful to interpret "as we forgive our debtors" in the Lord's prayer as a recognition of the conditions of divine forgiveness. Rather, I agree with Arland Hultgren that the pragmatic function of "as we forgive our debtors" is performative.[47] He suggests that the liturgical function of the phrase is "as we *hereby* forgive our debtors". That is, every time the prayer is performed, those who pray forgive those who have wronged them. Hultgren does not discuss the grammatical justification for this interpretation in his article, but we can add to his argument that "we forgive" is in the aorist tense (ἀφήκαμεν) and that the aorist can function to express "a state of mind just reached, or … an act expressive of it" (so called "dramatic aorist").[48]

A performative understanding of "as we forgive our debtors" would certainly have an important function within the ritual and social life of the Matthean community. As ritual theorist Roy Rappaport argues, what you do in a ritual sticks to you and becomes a social obligation, since you have performed it in the midst of your community.[49] Consequently, there would be social pressure to actually forgive others in a community that on a daily basis ritually performs interpersonal forgiveness in a shared prayer, especially if interpersonal forgiveness is seen as a prototypical action.

Intercessory Prayers for Sinners

Matthew 18, where the Matthean Jesus gives instructions for "the assembly/congregation" (ἡ ἐκκλησία, 18:17), is probably one of our most transparent windows into the Matthean community. A central portion of this community

46 E.g. Luomanen, *Entering*, 190–93; S. Grindheim, "Ignorance Is Bliss: Attitudinal Aspects of the Judgment according to Works in Matthew 25:31–46", *NovT* 50 (2008) 313–31.

47 A. Hultgren, "Forgive Us, as We Forgive (Matt 6:12)", *Word & World* 16 (1996) 284–90.

48 E. DeWitt Burton, *Syntax of the Moods and Tenses in New Testament Greek* (3rd ed.; Whitefish: Kessinger, 2008[1892]), §45.

49 R.A. Rappaport, *Ritual and Religion in the Making of Humanity* (Cambridge: Cambridge UP, 1999), 119–25.

instruction deals with how to reintegrate erring community members (18:12–35). I have argued elsewhere that this passage reflects a practice for reintegrating wrongdoers in the community.[50] The practice consists of a) a reproof procedure (18:15–17) and b) a prayer ritual that "looses" the sinning "brother"[51] from sin (18:18–20). The procedure is preceded by a narrative about God's joy when a strayed sheep returns (18:12–14) and followed by a command to forgive sinning community members relentlessly, so that God will not stop forgiving (18:21–35). This framing of the practice clarifies that the goal of the community should always be to reintegrate the offender, and only marginalize him or her as a very last resort.

For this chapter, I focus on the ritual practice reflected in 18:18–20, where it is promised that whatever community members "bind" or "loose" (v. 18), whatever they pray for (v. 19), God will make it happen. The guarantee for this is the presence of Jesus when the community members gather in his name (v. 20). The presence of Jesus frames the whole Gospel (1:23; 28:20), and here his presence is the reason for why binding and loosing through prayer works. One might perhaps doubt the interpretation that 18:18–20 reflects a ritual practice in the Matthean community, since the verses are formulated as promises, not as ritual instructions. Admittedly, before the sayings in vv. 18–20 were put in their current literary context by the Matthean redactor, the promises may very well have been transmitted as disparate generally assuring sayings,[52] but when Matthew puts them in the context of Matthew 18 and binds vv. 15–20 together with repeated catchwords,[53] the sayings function as instructions. The greater part of the speech in chapter 18 (vv. 12–35) motivates and instructs on communal practices of reintegration and forgiveness. The verses preceding vv. 18–20 (vv. 15–17) contain instructions for reproof and the following verses (vv. 21–22) consist of instructions for forgiveness. That is, the literary context of vv. 18–20 is communal instruction, which makes it reasonable to assume that Matthew uses existing saying traditions to give instructions on how to bind and loose through prayer in these verses.

There is no scholarly consensus about what it means to bind and loose.[54] Many commentators argue that binding and loosing in 18:18 is a judicial

50 R. Roitto, "Reintegrative Shaming and a Prayer Ritual of Reintegration in Matthew 18:15–20", *Svensk exegetisk årsbok* 79 (2014) 95–123.

51 The designation of a community members as a "brother" (ἀδελφός) is probably gender inclusive, see P. Trebilco, *Self-designations and Group Identity in the New Testament* (Cambridge: Cambridge University Press, 2012), 16–67.

52 Cf. U. Luz, *Matthew 8–20: A Commentary* (Hermeneia; Minneapolis: Fortress, 2001), 448–9; W.D. Davies/D.C. Allison, *A Critical and Exegetical Commentary on the Gospel According to Saint Matthew: Vol. 2, Commentary on Matthew VIII–XVIII* (ICC; Edinburgh: T&T Clark, 1991), 752, 781.

53 Cf. W.G. Thompson, *Matthew's Advice to a Divided Community: Mt. 17,22–18,35* (Rome: Biblical Institute Press, 1970), 175–202.

54 For an overview of scholarly suggestions, see R.H. Hiers, "'Binding' and 'Loosing': The Matthean Authorizations", *JBL* 104 (1985) 233–50.

ruling of specific cases.[55] Other commentators argue, in my opinion rightly so, that loosing is not just a judicial decision, but an act of mediating divine forgiveness.[56] Given the multitude of possible interpretations of "bind" and "loose",[57] I am of the opinion that the meaning of the terms in this particular verse is best understood in the light of the preceding and following verses.[58] Both the preceding and the following verses deal with the reintegration (vv. 12–17) and forgiveness (vv. 21–35) of people *who are guilty*. An interpretation of "loose" as declaration of innocence does therefore not fit the literary context. The interpretation that "loose" means liberation from sin, on the other hand, fits the context perfectly. This interpretation also fits Matthew's theology in the story about the forgiven and healed paralytic (9:1–8). In that passage, Matthew's special theological interest comes through in his redaction of Mark's story, where Matthew ends the story with the comment that "when the crowds saw it, they were filled with awe, and they glorified God, who had given such authority [to forgive sins] *to human beings*" (9:8; cf. Mark 2:12). This comment can reasonably be considered an expression of the self-perception of the Matthean community as authorized to mediate the forgiveness of sins.[59]

Matthew's intercessory ritual is well integrated with the social identity of the group. First, it is well integrated on the narrative level. According to Matthew's identity narrative, Jesus a) came to save from sin (1:21; 20:28; 26: 28), b) is present in the community with heavenly authority (18:19; 28:18–20) and, c) has given his own authority to the community (9:8; 10:1; 18:18–20). As George Lakoff and Mark Johnson point out, we humans tend to think that presence and proximity means influence.[60] An identity narrative about Jesus' presence does therefore induce the intuition of divine influence over the community. Second, it is well integrated with the identity prototype of the group. A prototypical group member a) is righteous, which includes being forgiven and a willingness to forgive (see discussion above and below), and b) has been given heavenly authority to mediate forgiveness (9:8; 18:18–20; cf. 10:1). The presence of Jesus and the gift of authority does not relate primarily to individuals but to the community. Therefore, an intercessory prayer for a sinning group member should be performed in the presence of at least "two or three" community members (18:18–20). Thus performed, it was

55 E.g. Davies/Allison, *Matthew: Vol 2*, 787; C.S. Keener, *A Commentary on the Gospel of Matthew* (Grand Rapids: Eerdmans, 1999), 454–55; R.T. France, *The Gospel of Matthew* (NICNT; Grand Rapids: Eerdmans, 2007), 695.

56 E.g. Luz, *Matthew 8–20*, 454; R.H. Gundry, *Matthew: A Commentary on His Handbook for a Mixed Church Under Persecution* (2. ed; Grand Rapids: Eerdmans, 1994), 369.

57 For an overview of possible interpretations, see R.H. Hiers, "'Binding' and 'Loosing'", 233–50.

58 I have given a more full argument for this interpretation in Roitto, "Reintegrative Shaming".

59 Cf. Davies/Allison, *Matthew: Vol 1*, 98.

60 G. Lakoff/M. Johnson, *Metaphors We Live By* (Chicago: University of Chicago Press, 1980), 128.

most probably experienced as both effective and important for the identity of the community.

The practice of binding or loosing also fits well into Matthew's perception of sin as a dangerous substance (discussed above). Loosing a brother is a crisis ritual, which transforms the sinner from a negative state of being morally defiled by sin into a normalized state where s/he is no longer in danger.[61] Since the intercessory ritual was performed before at least a small portion of the community ("two or three", 18:19–20), perhaps even the whole community, the act informs the community that the transgressor is now to be treated as a fully acceptable member of the community.[62] A binding ritual, on the other hand, communicates to the community that the sinner has not listened to the reproof of the community (18:15–17), and should not be considered a good (prototypical) community member, but rather "a Gentile and a tax collector" (18:17).

If the intercessory ritual had the power to transform the sinner's status in the community, the ritual had several important group dynamic functions. First, it helped the community to be able to think of itself as freed from sin. We can reasonably imagine that in spite of all emphasis on righteousness in the Gospel of Matthew, the social life of the Matthean community was hardly free from moral transgression. These transgressions would then have created a cognitive dissonance between ideal self-perception and lived reality that had to be resolved in order to maintain a positive experience of the identity of the community.[63] "Loosing" the substance of sin from repentant community members fulfilled that function. Anders Runesson even suggests that the community felt the need to maintain the *collective* purity of the community in order to function as God's people.[64] I am a bit hesitant to go that far, though, because the idea that we find in for instance Leviticus 18:24–28 that God will collectively reject his people if they defile the land is not there in Matthew. Rather, God's rejection is always directed at the individual in the judgment scenes of Matthew (Matt 7:15–32, 25:31–46) and threats of collective rejection of the Matthean community are nowhere to be found. Nevertheless, if righteousness was an important aspect of the social identity prototype of the group, a ritual that could restore a sinning community member's status was of paramount importance to the collective self-perception of the group. Likewise, a binding ritual signalling that a group member should no longer be considered as prototypical probably also had a function for the identity of the group as a last resort. As José Marques shows, groups can strengthen their

61 On crisis rituals, see J.P. Schjødt, "Initiation and the Classification of Rituals", *Temenos* 22 (1986) 93–108.

62 Rappaport, *Ritual*, 52–4. Rappaport argues that rituals function to signal information in the community about the status of its participants.

63 Cf. Roitto, *Behaving*, 118–20.

64 Runesson, "Purity", 169–71.

social identity by labelling deviant group members as "black sheep", since labelling of deviants clarifies the borders and the prototype of the group.[65]

Second, as Roy Rappaport points out, many rituals reinforce "canonical information", that is, information about the world view of the group.[66] A ritual of intercession would not only reflect but also reinforce the identity narrative (discussed above) that the assembly is in Jesus' salvatory presence and thus given authority to mediate divine forgiveness.

The Eucharist

Although Matthew never explicitly writes "Do this in remembrance of me" (Luke 22:19; 1 Cor 11:24), his account of Jesus' last supper with his disciples most probably reflects a communal practice. Matthew's additions "Eat!" and "Drink from it, all of you!" to Mark's account of the last supper (Matt 26:26–28; Mark 14:22–24), are most probably liturgically motivated. For our discussion, we are interested in Matthew's addition of the words "for the forgiveness of sins" (v. 28) to Mark's account in order to clarify what the Eucharist is meant to celebrate.

From the perspective of ritual theory, a central analytical question is "What is the ritual believed to effect?" As we saw above in the analysis of Matt 18:18–20, for instance, intercessory prayers effect binding or loosing of sin. But does the Matthean account of the Eucharist really promise to effect anything? In later Christian texts, the ritual efficacy of the Eucharist is frequently described as transforming the participants and/or securing eternal life for the participants (e. g. John 6:51; Ignatius, *Ign. Eph.* 20.2; Justin Martyr, *1. Apol.* 66; Irenaeus, *Adv. Haer.* 5.2.2–3; Origen, *Cels.* 8.33). Matthew, however, does not really promise any direct ritual efficacy for the participants. (This goes for Mark 14:22–24; Luke 22:17–20; 1 Cor 11:23–25; *Did.* 9–10, too.) Although the words "for the forgiveness of sins" in Matthew's account of the Eucharist are interpreted in many church traditions as promising forgiveness of sins to those who participate in the ritual, Matthew does not actually say that. Rather, the claim is that "this is my blood of the covenant, which is poured out for many for the forgiveness of sins" (26:28). That is, the Eucharist somehow relates to a covenant in which there is forgiveness of sins. Forgiveness is thus said to come from participation in the covenant, and not directly from partaking in the Eucharist.

65 J.M. Marques, "The Black-Sheep Effect: Outgroup Homogeneity in Social Comparison Settings", in D. Abrams/M.A. Hogg (ed.), *Social Identity Theory: Constructive and Critical Advances* (London: Harvester Wheatsheaf, 1990) 131–51; J.M. Marques et al., "Social Categorization, Social Identification, and Rejection of Deviant Group Members", in M.A. Hogg/S. Tindale (ed.), *Blackwell Handbook of Social Psychology: Group Processes* (Malden: Blackwell, 2001) 400–424.

66 Rappaport, *Ritual*, 52–4.

Exegetical commentaries on Matthew are usually careful to avoid claiming that the phrase "for the forgiveness of sins" refers to the direct efficacy on the individual participating in the Eucharist. However, the exact relation between the Eucharist and forgiveness is often quite vaguely stated. I exemplify with three standard commentaries. Donald Hagner elusively suggests that "the celebration of the sacrament brings a fresh experience of the grace of God through the forgiveness of sins, a renewed participation in salvation already enjoined".[67] Hagner could just mean that the Eucharist creates a subjective experience of forgiveness already given, but the phrase "through the forgiveness of sins" could also be interpreted as meaning that it is through the forgiveness administered in the Eucharist that the participant can experience God's grace. Nothing he writes in his previous analysis helps us understand what he means. William Davies and Dale Allison state that the participant in the Matthean Eucharist takes part "in the effects of Jesus' self-sacrifice".[68] They avoid saying whether the ritual is participation in the covenant or, more directly, in the forgiveness of sins that Jesus effects. However, based on their exegesis of v. 28 a few pages earlier I conjecture that they mean to say that the Eucharist is a participation in the covenant, which is an interpretation I agree on.[69] Ulrich Luz, in his analysis of Matthew's account of the last supper, concludes that

> [the participants] share in the saving power of Jesus's death. That becomes most clear for the Matthean church in the experience and in the practice of the forgiveness of sins through which the saving power of Jesus becomes available to the church and in which it actively participates in that power.[70]

Luz's latter sentence is not easily exegeted, but I take him to mean that the Eucharist makes the community participate in the general domain of Jesus' salvation, but does not directly effect forgiveness to sinning individuals. If so, I would agree.

The believed efficacy of participating in the Eucharist according to Matthew is not directly forgiveness of sins, but participation in the covenant established by Jesus' death, in which there is forgiveness of sins. That is, the Eucharist was not experienced as a crisis ritual that saved from an acute state of sin but as a calendric ritual that maintained the community's covenant with God who could forgive sins.[71] There are other rituals in Matthew that effect forgiveness for transgressors: daily and intercessory prayers for forgiveness (6:12; 18:18–20, discussed above), so yet another ritual to effect forgiveness for

67 D.A. Hagner, *Matthew 14–28* (WBC, vol. 33B; Waco: Word books, 1995), 774.

68 W.D. Davies/D.C. Allison, *A Critical and Exegetical Commentary on the Gospel According to Saint Matthew: Vol. 3, Commentary on Matthew XIX–XXVIII* (ICC; Edinburgh: T.& T. Clark, 1997), 447.

69 Davies and Allison, *Matthew: Vol. 3*, 474–5.

70 U. Luz, *Matthew 21–28: A Commentary* (Hermeneia; Minneapolis: Fortress, 2005), 384.

71 On crisis rituals versus calendric rituals, see Schjødt, "Initiation".

individual sins seems redundant.[72] The wording of Matt 26:28 is not that the cup effects forgiveness, but that the cup "is the blood of the covenant ... for the forgiveness of sins". Among both Jews and Greeks, ritualized dining before a god typically functioned to maintain good relations with the god.[73] The ritual elements of the dinner were meant to honour the god, not to effect specified favours from the god. It is therefore reasonable that the Matthean community imagined that there was a need for a communal meal that upheld a good relation between God and the community – a "covenant". If Luomanen is right that Matthew's idea of salvation fits structurally into Sanders' covenantal nomism – and I think he is – it would be appropriate for the Matthean community to have a ritual to celebrate and uphold that covenant.

The Eucharist thus interpreted would have manifested the identity of Matthean community in several ways. First, the meal would have communicated "canonical information"[74] about the identity of the group. The meal expresses the narrative rationale of the community in a condensed manner: It is the community of those saved from sin in the presence of Jesus – those who belong to the covenant inaugurated by Jesus' death in which there is forgiveness of sins. (The community's identity as righteous would not be manifest in the Eucharist, though.) Second, on a practical level, celebrating a ritualized meal together would have strengthened the social bonds within the community. Third, each participant would signal "self-referential information",[75] that is, information to the community about his/her commitment to the group, just by regular participation in the meal.

Interpersonal Forgiveness and Identity Formation

Matthew emphasizes interpersonal forgiveness more than any other Gospel. One cluster of forgiveness-related ethics appears in the Sermon on the Mount. There, forgiveness (6:12, 14–15), non-retaliation (5:38–48) and reconciliation (5:23–24) are absolute demands and no exceptions to the rule are mentioned. The ethics there is not intra-group ethics but universal ethics that should be exercised towards anyone, even "your enemy" (5:44). Another cluster of forgiveness-ethics appears in Matt 18, which deals with intra-communal norms. The most famous saying about forgiveness in this passage, "not seven

72 In the Didache, which probably stems from a version of Jewish-Christian faith similar to Matthew's, confessing sins and reconciling with brothers should be done before celebration of the Eucharist, in order to avoid profaning the meal (14:1–3). That is, being forgiven is a prerequisite for the meal, not an effect.

73 E.g. D.E. Smith, *From Symposium to Eucharist: The Banquet in the Early Christian World* (Fortress: Minneapolis, 2003).

74 See discussion at n. 66.

75 Rappaport, *Ritual*, 52–4.

times, but, I tell you, seventy-seven times" (18:22), is by itself unconditional, but is placed in a context of conditional forgiveness. In the preceding verses (18:15–20), we learn that every effort should be made to reintegrate a sinning brother, but if the offender "refuses to listen even to the church, let such a one be to you as a Gentile and a tax collector" (18:17). It seems, then, that the saying about relentless forgiveness in 18:21–22 applies to those who have listened to the reproof (18:15–17) and been loosed through intercessory prayer (18:18–20) and not to unrepentant community members (cf. Luke 17:3–4).

In the light of research on how humans tend to forgive, it is quite surprising that Matthew's ethics of forgiveness is more restrictive towards group members than towards outsiders. Cognitive research on forgiveness shows that most people are more willing to forgive those who are close to them and game-theoretical simulations of forgiveness demonstrate that it is rational to be much more forgiving to established cooperation-partners than to strangers.[76] With only a few exceptions, most people in antiquity shared these ideals.[77] Being forgiving towards outsiders could make you look like a fool that could not defend your honour.[78] Forgiveness and lenience within the family, on the other hand, was considered good.[79] In short, Matthew's ethics of forgiveness appears to be counterintuitive, irrational, and countercultural. However, we may ask whether the ethics of forgiveness in Matthew contributed to the identity of the community.

Forgiveness and Non-Retaliation Towards Outsiders

As irrational as unconditional forgiveness and non-revenge towards outsiders may appear, it still seems to have been an important part of the social identity of the Matthean community. This is especially patent in Matt 5:38–48, where non-revenge and love of enemies are motivated with the argument that it is their identity. The motivation given is simply: "… so that you may be children of your Father in heaven; for he makes his sun rise on the evil and on the good, and sends rain on the righteous and on the unrighteous" (5:45) and "be perfect, therefore, as your heavenly Father is perfect" (5:48). This kind of

76 E.g. É. Mullet/G. Michèle, "Developmental and Cognitive Points of View on Forgiveness", in M.E. McCullough/K.I. Pargament/C.E. Thoresen (ed.), *Forgiveness: Theory, Research and Practice* (New York: Guilford Press, 1999) 111–32; M. Hartshorn/A. Kaznatcheev/T. Shultz, "The Evolutionary Dominance of Ethnocentric Cooperation", *Journal of Artificial Societies and Social Simulation* 16 (2013) 7.

77 M. Reiser, "Love of Enemies in the Context of Antiquity", *NTS* 47 (2001) 411–27.

78 J.H. Neyrey, *Honor and Shame in the Gospel of Matthew* (Louisville: Westminster John Knox Press, 1998), 190–211.

79 D. DeSilva, *Honor, Patronage, Kinship & Purity: Unlocking New Testament Culture* (Downers Growe: Inter-Varsity, 2001), 171–3.

thinking, where we assign certain actions as the logical consequence or duty of someone's social identity is quite typical for human psychology,[80] and I have given examples elsewhere that this was no less common in the first century Mediterranean than it is today.[81]

Quite naturally, an attitude of forgiving, non-retaliation, and love of enemies, would have prevented the Matthean community to become an "introversionist" community, like for instance the Qumranites, but inspired the community to remain in interaction with the rest of society as a "conversionist" community.[82] Matthew's Jesus even states that one reason for doing good deeds is to advertise the movement: "Let your light shine before others, so that they may see your good works and give glory to your Father in heaven" (5:16). But if outsiders would have found the ethics of forgiveness and love of enemies in Matthew foolish, as Jerome Neyrey argues,[83] one could argue that the strategy would have been bad advertisement for the community.

Here, sociologist Wolfgang Lipp's theory about self-stigmatizing leadership is illuminating.[84] According to Lipp, groups or individuals who wilfully and strategically act contrary to prevailing societal norms can sometimes challenge cultural beliefs about what should be considered normal societal order and even win people over to their side. Helmut Mödritzer employs Lipp's theory in New Testament studies; he gives several examples of this self-stigmatizing strategy in the first century and then applies it to John the Baptist, Jesus, and Paul.[85]

We can apply the idea of self-stigmatizing leadership to Matthew's interpretation of Jesus' ethics of relentless forgiveness and non-retaliation, too. Self-stigmatizing behaviour would probably have been one of the few viable strategies left for the Matthean community, if it was in the process of being marginalized by other Jews. Leviticus instructs that "You shall not hate in your heart anyone of your kin … You shall not take vengeance or bear a grudge against any of your people, but you shall love your neighbour as yourself" (19:17–18). The ethics of non-retaliation and love of enemy in Matt 5:38–48 could be said to take this covenantal ethics to a shocking, self-stigmatizing, extreme, that could perhaps subvert existing social orders. We should be under no illusion that the whole Matthean community practised this

80 M. Hewstone, *Causal Attribution: From Cognitive Processes to Collective Beliefs* (Oxford: Basil Blackwell, 1989); M. Augoustinos/M.I. Walker/N. Donaghue, *Social Cognition: An Integrated Introduction* (2. ed.; Thousand Oaks, CA: Sage Publications, 2006), 69–71, 225–70.

81 Roitto, *Behaving*, 74–106.

82 The terms "introversionist sect" and "conversionist sect" are suggested by R.B. Wilson, *Religious Sects: A Sociological Study* (New York: McGraw-Hill, 1970). I prefer the word "community" over "sect" here, to avoid confusion about the many different definitions of "sect" among scholars.

83 Neyrey, *Honor*, 190–211.

84 W. Lipp, *Stigma und Charisma: über soziales Grenzverhalten* (Berlin: Reimer, 1985).

85 H. Mödritzer, *Stigma und Charisma im Neuen Testament und seiner Umwelt: zur Soziologie des Urchristentums* (Freiburg: Univ.-Verl., 1994).

ethics unanimously, but to the extent they did, perhaps the Matthean community had some success in redefining the situation through self-stigmatizing behaviour, and thus in convincing at least some other Jews about the superiority of their ways.

Intra-group Forgiveness

The ethics of forgiveness in Matthew 18 is quite reasonable compared to its counterpart in the Sermon on the Mount. As discussed above, it is usually strategic to be very forgiving towards members of your ingroup and only stop forgiving in really hopeless cases. In Matthew 18, the community is urged to forgive relentlessly (18:21–22) with the sole exception of those who refuse to change their way even after a thorough process of reproof (18:15–17). The possibility of exclusion or marginalization of community members (18:17) is carefully embedded in a literary context of God's care for the sinner (18:12–14), a soft reintegrative reproof practice (18:15–17) and forceful exhortation to never grow tired of forgiving brothers (18:20–35). Compared to many other early Christian texts (Rom 16:17; 1 Cor 5:9–11; Eph 5:7; 2 Thess 3:6, 14; Tit 3:6; Did 15:3), Matthew's advice to the community appears quite lenient. Matthew's Jesus commands that the community should go to extraordinary length in its reproof before it marginalizes transgressors. We may therefore suspect that Matthew 18 was formulated as a reaction against a tendency to exclude people from the community too eagerly.[86] If the Matthean community was under social pressure from the surrounding society, we may suspect that the community felt a particularly strong need to maintain a self-perception as morally superior (cf. 5:20). In such situations, groups tend to be more eager than otherwise to exclude the "black sheep" from the community to reduce the discrepancy between ideal and reality.[87] If the eagerness to exclude went too far, this might have impaired the social climate in the community. Such a situation could explain the composition of Matt 18.

Integration of Divine and Interpersonal Forgiveness

Matthew integrates the ethics of interpersonal forgiveness with God's forgiveness in several ways, all of which contribute to the identity of the Matthean community. Interpersonal forgiveness is described as analogous to God's forgiveness in the Lord's prayers. "Forgive us … as (ὡς) we forgive" (6:12). Elsewhere Matthew expresses the idea that being a child of God (that is, an ideal community member) means to act in a non-retaliatory manner

86 For my full argument, see Roitto, "Reintegrative Shaming".
87 See discussion at n. 65.

inspired by God's benevolence (5:45). A forgiving prototypical group member is thus inspired by God's forgiving behaviour.

Divine forgiveness is also said to be causally dependent on interpersonal forgiveness (5:13–14; 18:34–35). However, the threat that one might not be forgiven if one does not forgive is mainly meant to function as an exhortation to forgive, as I argued in the discussion on the Lord's prayer. Nevertheless, by associating interpersonal forgiveness with the last judgment, it becomes integrated with the larger identity narrative: The hope of the community is, to quote Luomanen, that "those who remain faithful in their righteousness until the end will pass the final judgement".[88]

Interpersonal forgiveness is also presented as the proper response to divine forgiveness in the covenant inaugurated by Jesus. The Lord's prayer (5:9–13) is a prayer for the realization of the Kingdom of Heaven. By including a ritualized performance of interpersonal forgiveness as a response to God's forgiveness in the Lord's prayer (6:12b), interpersonal forgiveness becomes an essential part of the Kingdom of Heaven. In the parable of the ungrateful servant, the ungrateful servant does not understand that the proper response to God's great gift of forgiveness is interpersonal forgiveness (18:23–35). That is, the servant is a community member who does not understand the obligations that fall on those who wish to be part of the covenant "for the forgiveness of sins" (26:28). Just like the Sinai Covenant contained both divine and human obligations, so does the covenant inaugurated by Jesus. Interpersonal forgiveness is therefore not only a general ethical principle, but an expression of the identity narrative that the community partakes in the covenant for the forgiveness of sins.

In short, interpersonal forgiveness 1) is analogous to God's forgiveness, 2) is a condition for divine forgiveness in the final judgment (though we must remember the hortatory function of this conditionality), and 3) is a covenantal duty in the covenant "for the [divine] forgiveness of sins". All these ways of integrating divine and human forgiveness contribute in different ways to the experience that interpersonal forgiveness is central to the identity of the Matthean community.

Summary

In Matthew, divine and interpersonal forgiveness are well integrated aspects of the social identity of the Matthean community. According to the identity narrative of the Matthean community, they are those who belong to the covenant for the forgiveness of sins and who should respond to God's forgiveness by righteous exercise of interpersonal forgiveness in order to remain in the covenant. Forgiveness should be practiced in their everyday

88 Luomanen, *Entering*, 281.

interaction with outsiders and each other. That is, it was considered prototypical for a community member to be excessively forgiving. Ritually, there were several ways to express this identity as forgiven and forgiving. On a daily basis, the Lord's Prayer expressed a petition for forgiveness and simultaneously performed forgiveness towards others; the Eucharist functioned as a calendric ritual to maintain the covenant of forgiveness; and intercessory prayers functioned as a crisis ritual to loose sinning community members from the danger of sin.

Raimo Hakola

The Johannine Community as a Constructed, Imagined Community

It has long been usual among New Testament scholars to think that different New Testament writings give voice to a wide variety of distinct early Christian groups by expressing their collective convictions and shared view of the world. Scholars have not refrained from presenting far-reaching histories of different early Christian communities even though there is rarely any external historical evidence for these detailed reconstructions. In the field of Johannine studies, the Gospel of John has been read as a two-level drama that tells not only of Jesus' life but also of the contemporary situation of the Johannine community. According to this reading, John reflects a bitter and violent conflict between the Johannine group and its opponents in the synagogue, identified as representatives of the post-70 emergent rabbinic Judaism.[1] However, it has become increasingly clear that external evidence for this kind of conflict is meager.[2]

The above mentioned developments have led some scholars to propose that it is irrelevant to speak about specific early Christian communities. Richard Bauckham has summarized this critical perspective in his bold manifesto that "the Matthean, Markan, Lukan and Johannine communities should disappear from the terminology of Gospels scholarship".[3] I agree with these criticisms in that many earlier studies have gone quite too far in their detailed

1 A classic presentation of this theory is J.L. Martyn, *History and Theology in the Fourth Gospel* (3rd Edition; Louisville: Westminster John Knox, 2003 [originally 1968]).

2 Cf. R. Hakola *Identity Matters: John, the Jews and Jewishness* (Leiden: Brill, 2005) 41–86. For an update of my criticism of Martyn's theory, see R. Hakola, *Reconsidering Johannine Christianity: A Social Identity Approach* (New York and London: Routledge, 2015) 1–5. In the same vein, A. Reinhartz, *Befriending the Beloved Disciple: A Jewish Reading of the Gospel of John* (New York and London: Continuum, 2001) 37–53; T. Hägerland, "John's Gospel: A Two-Level Drama?", *JSNT* 25 (2003), 309–22; W. Carter, *John and the Empire: Initial Explorations* (New York and London: T&T Clark, 2008) 19–51, 68–72; J.S. Kloppenborg, "Disaffliation in Associations and the ἀποσυναγωγός of John", *HTS Teologiese Studies/Theological Studies* 67 (2011) 1–16.

3 R. Bauckham, "Introduction", in R. Bauckham (ed.), *The Gospels for All Christians: Rethinking the Gospel Audiences* (Grand Rapids: Eerdmans, 1998), 4. Thus also E.W. Klink III, *The Sheep of the Fold: The Audience and Origin of the Gospel of John* (SNTSMS 141; Cambridge: University Press, 2007), 251. Since Bauckham originally formulated this provocative assertion, there has appeared a lively debate about it. For example, see the articles in E.W. Klink III (ed.), *The Audience of the Gospels: The Origins and Function of the Gospels in Early Christianity* (LNTS 353; London & New York: T&T Clark, 2010). I have reviewed this debate critically in Hakola, *Reconsidering*, 5–21. In the following pages, I summarize some main points of my criticism.

reconstructions of the history of various early Christian communities. However, I still think that it is useful to postulate particular and distinct early Christian communities to account for various differences and even contradictions between early Christian sources. As Adele Reinhartz has said, Bauckham's denial of the community hypothesis "implies a homogenization of that [the early Christian] movement into a unified entity and therefore requires us to ignore the substantial evidence for difference and diversity within that movement".[4]

I propose in this article that while our possibilities to make exact conclusions about the actual social and historical context of early Christian writings are limited, it is still advisable to analyse how these sources construct and imagine portraits of ideal communities. As Joseph Verheyden and Mark Grundeken have recently remarked, early Christian sources may give us only "some reliable information on daily-life concerns and on concrete situations", but they inform us more directly about the aspirations of local early Christian communities and about their "dreams and ideals".[5] I suggest here that some theoretical concepts related to the symbolic construction of communities and imagined communities could be relevant in the study of early Christian portraits of ideal communities.[6]

No Johannine Community at all?

It is has long been common to think that various differences and even tensions between the New Testament gospels suggest that these writings were addressed to particular early Christian communities. In his criticism of this view, Richard Bauckham tries to refute "a view of an early Christian community as a self-contained, self-sufficient, introverted group, having little contact with other Christian communities and little sense of participation in a worldwide

4 A. Reinhartz, "Gospel Audiences: Variations on a Theme", in E.W. Klink III (ed.), *The Audience of the Gospels: The Origin and Function of the Gospels in Early Christianity* (LNTS 353, London & New York: T&T Clark, 2010) 134–52, on p. 143. For the diversity of early Christianity, see H. Räisänen, *The Rise of Christian Beliefs: The Thought World of Early Christians* (Minneapolis: Fortress Press, 2010), 5–6, 315–19.

5 J. Verheyden/M. Grundeken, "Introduction", in M. Grundeken/J. Verheyden (ed.), *Early Christian Communities between Ideal and Reality* (WUNT 342; Mohr Siebeck, 2015) XII–XIII.

6 See A.B. Cohen, *Symbolic Construction of Community* (London & New York; Routledge, 1985); B. Anderson, *Imagined Communities: Reflections on the Origin and Spread of Nationalism* (Revised Edition; London & New York: Verso, 2006 [originally 1983]). For earlier applications of these perspectives to the study of early Christianity, see J. Lieu, *Christian Identity in the Jewish and Graeco-Roman World* (Oxford: Oxford University Press, 2004), 12–13; T.-S.B. Liew, "Ambiguous Admittance: Consent and Descent in John's Community of 'Upward' Mobility", in M.W. Dube/J.L. Staley (ed.), *John and Postcolonialism: Travel, Space and Power* (London & New York: Sheffield Academic Press, 2002), 193–224.

Christian movement".[7] However, this view presents a caricature of the scholarship dealing with early Christian communities. Raymond Brown, one of the best-known advocates of the community hypothesis in the field of Johannine studies, has explicitly stated that "the Johannine attitude is just the opposite of the outlook of a sect" because Johannine Christians "had not followed their exclusivistic tendencies to the point of breaking communion (*koinōnia*) with these [Apostolic] Christians whose characteristics are found in many NT works of the late first century".[8] Brown's conclusion shows that it is quite possible to support the idea that there was a distinct Johannine community that could have been in contact with other Christian movements in a variety of ways.

Bauckham frames the community hypothesis as a question of the alleged audiences of each of the gospels, when he claims that the New Testament gospels were not addressed to specific early Christian communities but to all Christians at the end of the first century. However, it is quite plausible that the evangelists may have had their initial communities and a larger audience in mind at the same time when they produced their gospels. The question of John's original audience has not been a central concern in the community-hypothesis community but this theory has become widely applied in the Johannine studies because it has been regarded as a valid explanation for the distinctiveness of the Johannine writings in comparison to other early Christian sources on the one hand and the similarities and differences between the Gospel of John and the three Johannine Epistles on the other.[9]

The close comparison between the Gospel of John and the three Johannine Epistles reveals that the similarities and differences between these writings are best understood if we take the Gospel and the Epistles as independent witnesses of the shared tradition that is developed in different ways in different

7 R. Bauckham, "For Whom Were Gospels Written", in R. Bauckham (ed.), *The Gospels for All Christians: Rethinking the Gospel Audiences* (Grand Rapids: Eerdmans 1998) 9–48, on p. 31.

8 R.E. Brown, *The Community of the Beloved Disciple: The Life, Loves, and Hates of an Individual Church in New Testament Times* (New York: Paulist Press, 1979), 90. Jonathan Bernier ignores Brown's conclusion when he describes Brown's study as the "best known articulation" of the isolation of the Johannine community. Cf. J. Bernier, *Aposynagōgos and the Historical Jesus in John: Rethinking the Historicity of the Johannine Expulsion Passages* (BibInt Series 122; Leiden: Brill, 2013), 20 n. 72. Jürgen Becker, one of the most prominent German advocates of the Johannine community hypothesis, says that the Johannine community can be described as a sect in relation to Judaism but not in relation to other forms of early Christianity. J. Becker, *Das Evangelium nach Johannes* (3rd edn; Ökumenischer Taschenbuchkommentar zum Neuen Testament 4. Gütersloh: Gütersloher Verlagshaus Gerd Mohn, 1991), 61–2.

9 C.L. Blomberg, "The Gospels for Specific Communities and All Christians", in E.W. Klink III (ed.), *The Audience of the Gospels: The Origin and Function of the Gospels in Early Christianity* (LNTS 353, London & New York: T&T Clark, 2010) 111–33, on p. 117: "The clearest case for a specific initial community for a Gospel can be made with John, for the simple reason that the author or editors of the Fourth Gospel also produced the Johannine Epistles, clearly directed at a cluster of churches with an identifiable set of locally generated problems."

contexts.[10] The Gospel and the Epistles use a similar kind of language and share a common dualistic worldview that is distinctive among early Christian writings. Despite these similarities in the style and in theology, there are also subtle but significant variations that speak against the view that the Johannine writings were written by a single hand. Those who want to defend the common authorship of the Johannine writings often resort to idea that the writer behind these writings was a creative theologian who was capable of modifying his teaching in varying situations.[11] However, it could be asked whether theological reasons only explain satisfactorily the emergence of idiosyncratic Johannine view of the world and the tradition distinctive to the Fourth Gospel and the Johannine Epistles.[12] For the majority of New Testament scholars, the variations within the unity of the Johannine language and thought demonstrate that the Johannine writings were written in different sociohistorical contexts by at least two different hands using the common language belonging to a distinct early Christian circle or community.[13]

When it comes to the differences between the Gospel of John and the synoptic gospels, Bauckham has tried to explain these differences as a part of his claim that the gospels should be taken as based on eyewitness

10 For detailed analysis, see Hakola, *Reconsidering*, 67–95. My conclusion concurs with W.E. Sproston North, *The Lazarus Story within the Johannine Tradition* (JSNTSup 212; Sheffield: Sheffield Academic Press, 2001), 17–40; J. Lieu, *I, II and III John: A Commentary* (The New Testament Library; Louisville and London: Westminster John Knox Press, 2008), 17–18. For a review of recent studies on the topic, see R.A. Culpepper, "The Relationship between the Gospel of John and 1 John", in R.A. Culpepper/P.N. Anderson (ed.), *Communities in Dispute: Current Scholarship on the Johannine Epistles* (SBLECL 13; Atlanta, Georgia: Society of Biblical Literature, 2014) 95–122.

11 M. Hengel, *The Johannine Question* (London: SCM Press, 1989), 65–6. Cf. Bauckham's comments on the possibility of different redactional layers in John in R. Bauckham, *The Testimony of the Beloved Disciple: Narrative, History, and Theology in the Gospel of John* (Grand Rapids: Baker, 2007), 118: "Perhaps we are dealing, not with the product of an idiosyncratic community and its history, but with the work of a creative theologian who, in his long experience of teaching and on the basis of his rather special access to traditions about Jesus, developed a distinctive interpretation of the history of Jesus." For criticism of these views, see Hakola, *Reconsidering*, 77–8.

12 Cf. M. de Jonge, "The Gospel and the Epistles of John Read Against the Background of the History of the Johannine Communities", in T. Thatcher (ed.), *What We Have Heard from the Beginning: The Past, Present, and Future of Johannine Studies* (Waco, Texas: Baylor University Press, 2007) 127–44, on p. 143. De Jonge remarks that, although there is a certain uniformity in Johannine vocabulary and style, "one of the typical elements of Johannine style is repetition with variation and amplification." In light of this, the hypothesis of a Johannine school has much to recommend it: "I remain hesitant with regard to the tendency to assign (again) a decisive role to a theologically gifted person of great authority, supposedly active during a long period of the Johannine community's history and responsible for the Gospel in its final form. Even if such a person existed, he did not operate in a vacuum but had to respond to changes in the situation of the believers."

13 For scholars supporting two or more Johannine authors, see Hakola, *Reconsidering*, 92. nn. 8 and 9.

testimonies.[14] It seems that the only alternative to the community hypothesis for Bauckham and his supporters is a return – in some form or in another – to the traditional understanding of the gospels as eyewitness testimonies.[15] However, Bauckham has been criticized for ignoring the advances that have been made in the understanding of the gospels as theological and literary interpretations of Jesus' life.[16] Bauckham has argued that one of the faults of many gospel-community theories has been "a misplaced desire for historical specificity". But it is easy to recognize the same mistake in his attempt to anchor divergent gospel traditions to eyewitness testimonies.[17]

In his study Bauckham joins scholars who have referred to memory studies to support their claim that the gospels are ultimately based on eyewitness memories. However, there is now a growing awareness among New Testament scholars that various psychological, cognitive and anthropological studies dealing with the transmission of memories have repeatedly exposed the fallibility and constructive nature of memory.[18] As a matter of fact, the appeal

14 R. Bauckham, *Jesus and the Eyewitnesses: The Gospels as Eyewitness Testimony* (Grand Rapids, Michigan/Cambridge, U.K.: Eerdmans, 2006).

15 Cf. W. Cirafesi, "The Johannine Community Hypothesis (1968–Present): Past and Present Approaches and a New Way Forward", *Currents in Biblical Research* 12 (2014) 173–93, on p. 188. Cirafesi suggests that the paradigm shift proposed by Bauckham "is in essence a shift back to a scholarly setting that allows for the reconsideration of traditional perspectives on issues such as the authorship, audience and historical value of John's Gospel." See also Klink (*Sheep*, 151), who advocates a return to pre-critical, literal readings of the gospel narratives instead of what he regards as modern and anachronistic critical readings. These efforts are a part of a growing scholarly tendency to defend the historical reliability of the Gospel of John. For a critical review of these efforts, see I. Dunderberg, *Gnostic Morality Revisited* (WUNT 247; Tübingen: Mohr Siebeck, 2015), 191–208. Dunderberg justly remarks that some representatives of "the neo-historicizing approach" to John "have great difficulties in keeping themselves within the confines of academic historiography" (p. 208).

16 For a perceptive and detailed criticism of Bauckham's theory, see J. Schröter, "The Gospels as Eyewitness Testimony? A Critical Examination of Richard Bauckham's Jesus and the Eyewitnesses", *JSNT* 31 (2008) 195–209. Bauckham's claim (*Jesus and the Eyewitnesses*, 8–11) that eyewitness testimony played a key role in the formation of the gospels, is based to a great extent on Samuel Byrskog's work on ancient history writing, see S. Byrskog, *Story as History – History as Story: The Gospel Tradition in the Context of Ancient Oral History* (WUNT 123; Tübingen: Mohr Siebeck, 2000). However, Byrskog has later criticized Bauckham for assuming that "there was a rather straight road from the trusted testimony to history." See S. Byrskog, "The Eyewitnesses as Interpreters of the Past: Reflections on Richard Bauckham's *Jesus and the Eyewitnesses*", *JSNT* 6 (2008) 157–68, on p. 161.

17 Bauckham, "For Whom", 48. Cf. Byrskog, "The Eyewitnesses", 161: "Bauckham, while often perceptively critical of form criticism, reveals a similar and yet different tendency in that the Gospels—at least Mark and John—are seen as more or less immediately transparent of the history behind them."

18 See J.C.S. Redman, "How Accurate Are Eyewitnesses: Bauckham and the Eyewitnesses in the Light of Psychological Research", *JBL* 129 (2010) 177–97; D.C. Allison, *Constructing Jesus: Memory, Imagination, and History* (London: SPCK, 2010), 1–30; "Response to Rafael Rodriguez, 'Jesus as His Friends Remembered Him, A Review of Dale Allison's Constructing Jesus'", *Journal for the Study of the Historical Jesus* 12 (2014), 245–54; J.S. Kloppenborg, "Me-

to memory does not negate but rather reinforces the possibility that differences among various early Christian writings were at least partly due to different sociohistorical and cultural settings where memories of Jesus were transmitted and reinterpreted. Paul Foster has aptly remarked that psychological memory studies have something in common with an older quest for the Sitz im Leben of various gospel traditions because "both approaches agree that the remembered event functions within communities to promote group values and that the connection between past events and the social remembrance is often quite slight".[19] This makes it plausible that attempts to actualize early Christian traditions in new historical and cultural contexts resulted in variations and tensions reflected in diverse gospel traditions. Therefore, the concepts of eyewitness testimony and memory cannot cancel the relevance of later contexts for the development of gospel traditions, as Dale Allison has convincingly argued.[20]

The above discussion suggests that it is too early to throw away the hypothesis that takes some early Christian texts as representing distinct early Christian communities. I propose that we still can and should speak of different branches of early Christianity, not as localized and closed communities but as collective movements that developed and transmitted their own peculiar theological dialects and expressions to communicate their versions of the Christian faith. It may be impossible to reconstruct detailed histories of each early Christian community but I suggest that we can detect in the early Christian sources portraits of symbolic, imagined communities that construct social reality rather than reflect it.

mory, Performance and the Sayings of Jesus," *Journal for the Study of the Historical Jesus* 10 (2012) 97–132; P. Foster, "Memory, Orality, and the Fourth Gospel: Three Dead-Ends in Historical Jesus Research," *Journal for the Study of the Historical Jesus* 10 (2012) 191–227; Zeba A. Crook, "Collective Memory Distortion and the Quest for the Historical Jesus," *Journal for the Study of the Historical Jesus* 11 (2013) 53–76. P. Luomanen, "How Religions Remember: Memory Theories In Biblical Studies and in the Study of Cognitive Study of Religion," in I. Czashesz/R. Uro (ed.), *Mind, Morality and Magic: Cognitive Science Approaches in Biblical Studies* (Durham: Acumen, 2013) 24–42.

19 Foster, "Memory", 202.

20 Cf. Allison, *Constructing Jesus*, 30: "Even if one grants, for the sake of discussion, that eyewitnesses initiated the tradition and repeated parts of it again and again to multiple audiences, their initial and later tellings cannot have been unsullied by selective recall and distortion. This is because nobody's retrieval is immune to such. Retellings of the past are habitually shaped by (1) the mere prospect that there will be listeners; (2) a speaker's aim; (3) expectations about the interests and attitudes of auditors; and (4) the behavior and reactions of the latter. Context affects what one deems possible, appropriate, or desirable to discuss, and speakers will add, subtract, and distort in order to please and entertain, as well as to forestall negative reactions."

From Sociohistorical Relations to Communities as Imagined Constructions

The New Testament scholarship dealing with early Christian communities has focused almost completely on attempts to reconstruct the sociohistorical relations behind surviving written material. This is an understandable objective because any information related to the historical contexts of ancient literary works would be most valuable in their interpretation. An obvious problem in this line of enquiry is that we seldom have any firsthand evidence of the context of these sources, and, consequently, our historical conclusions are one-sidedly based only on the sources themselves.

Quite many of the surviving early Christian sources deal with various kinds of conflicts and we simply do not know how those who are the target of polemic perceived the alleged schism.[21] In spite of these problems, I think that the quest for a plausible social and historical background of early Christian sources should remain a legitimate and relevant field of the study in its own right. However, I suggest here that the study of early Christian communities could benefit from some recent developments in the study of various kinds of communities.

In the field of anthropological and sociological studies, the conceptualizations of community have gone through a change from approaching communities as forms of actual social interaction to regarding them as expressions of ideal collective identities.[22] Vered Amit has stated that, as a result of this development, community came to be seen as "much more than locality, for now it could be extended to virtually any form of collective cultural consciousness".[23] An important impetus for this understanding was given by Fredrik Barth's reformulation of ethnic groups. In many earlier studies, ethnicity and culture were seen as more or less the same thing and as relatively static categories, and ethnic groups were identified on the basis of shared cultural characteristics. Barth, however, emphasized the on-going negotiations of boundaries between different ethnic groups.[24] This perspective has

21 Cf. R. Hakola/N. Nikki/U. Tervahauta, "Introduction", in R. Hakola/N. Nikki/U. Tervahauta (ed.), *Others and the Construction of Early Christian Identities* (PFES 106; Helsinki: Finnish Exegetical Society, 2013) 9–30.

22 Cf. V. Amit, "Reconceptualizing Community", in V. Amit (ed.), *Realizing Community: Concepts, Social Relationships and Sentiments* (London and New York: Routledge, 2002) 1–20; R. Jenkins, *Social Identity* (4th Edition; London and New York: Routledge, 2014) 134–50.

23 Amit, "Reconceptualizing", 6. Amit's review of scholarship is a part of the introduction to a collection that tries to put the study of social relations and interaction back to the agenda of community studies. While this kind of emphasis is plausible in the study of various modern communities, it is often more difficult in case of ancient communities because of the lack of relevant source material.

24 F. Barth, "Introduction", in F. Barth (ed.), *Ethnic Groups and Boundaries: The Social Organi-*

opened a way to analyze ethnic identities as social constructions whose boundaries are "generated in transaction and interaction and are, at least potentially, *flexible*, *situational* and *negotiable*".[25]

A similar perspective appears in Anthony Cohen's book *The Symbolic Construction of Community*. According to Cohen,

> the community as experienced by its members does not consist in social structure or in "the doing" of social behaviour. It inheres, rather, in "the thinking" about it. It is in this sense that we can speak of the community as a symbolic, rather than a structural, construct.[26]

Rather than speaking of communities as well-defined collectivities with inherent and stable attributes, this approach maintains that portraits of communities are ideological because they express not only how things are but how they should be.[27]

In the field of the study of nationalism, Benedict Anderson has coined the term "imagined community". According to Anderson, "all communities larger than primordial villages of face-to-face contacts (and perhaps even these) are imagined. Communities are to be distinguished, not by their falsity/genuineness, but by the style in which they are imagined".[28] The discussion about Anderson's notion has quite often led to confusion between imagined and imaginary communities, and for this reason some scholars prefer to speak about communities in anonymity, a term used also by Anderson himself.[29] Anderson already made clear that the concept of imagined community does

zation of Culture Difference (Bergen: Universitetsforlaget, 1969) 9–37; idem, "Enduring and Emerging Issues in the Analysis of Ethnicity", in H. Vermeulen/C. Govers (ed.), *The Anthropology of Ethnicity: Beyond Ethnic Grups and Boundaries* (Amsterdam: Spinhuis, 1994) 11–32.

25 Jenkins, *Social Identity*, 133 (italics original).

26 Cohen, *Symbolic Construction*, 98. Cohen later expressed some self-criticism of his original thesis and dissociated himself from some of its applications, see A. Cohen, "Epilogue", in V. Amit (ed.), *Realizing Community: Concepts, Social Relationships and Sentiments* (London and New York: Routledge, 2002) 165–70. For a critical review of Cohen's proposition and subsequent scholarly discussion, including Cohen's self-criticism, see Jenkins, *Social Identity*, 136–43. Jenkins refers to some problems in Cohen's proposal but insists that it has been a useful advance on Barth's views. This has permitted the application of Cohen's model to a wide variety of communities, including religious ones.

27 Cf. Jenkins, *Social Identity*, 138.

28 Anderson, *Imagined Communities*, 6. For the impact of Anderson's thesis on the study of nationalism, see J. Pakkasvirta, "Notes on the Theory of Nationalism", in H. Haggrén/J. Rainio-Niemi/J. Vauhkonen (ed.), *Multi-Layered Historicity of the Present Approaches to Social Science History* (Publications of the Department of Political and Economic Studies 8; Helsinki; University of Helsinki, 2013) 75–91. Pakkasvirta says that "Anderson's work may not perfectly explain the nature of nationalism, but he is able to excellently describe the prerequisites of nationalism and nation state" which makes his work "a hotbed of ideas" and rewarding as "a methodological tool".

29 Cf. Pakkasvirta, "Notes", 86. Anderson, *Imagined Communities*, 36.

not in any way mean that national or other communities are described as untrue or fictional. As Richard Jenkins has remarked, a community can never be imaginary "even though it can never be anything other than imagined".[30]

Meredith McGuire has applied the notion of imagined community to various religious communities and she also notes that the use of this term does not suggest that such communities are "fake or pure fantasy"; rather, the term "highlights the ongoing conceptual work required to create an image of community, absent face-to-face experiences of group identity".[31] McGuire connects the idea of imagined community with her emphasis on lived religion, a theoretical perspective in the field of sociology of religion that challenges the image of religion as unitary and "relatively stable set of collective beliefs and practices" and that considers the boundaries of religions and religious identity "as contested, shifting and malleable".[32] This means that while various imagined religious communities struggle to present their group and its traditions as natural and authentic, "ongoing contestations over boundaries and meanings ... mean that people's group identity and traditions are neither fixed nor unproblematic".[33]

The above mentioned theoretical perspectives have many points in common with social psychological social identity approach.[34] This approach has recently been increasingly applied to early Jewish and Christian sources.[35] According to the social identity approach, social categorization is a fundamental aspect of group behavior. The process of categorization helps groups and their members orientate themselves in variable social environments by making those environments more predictable and meaningful.

30 Jenkins, *Social Identity*, 141.

31 M. McGuire, *Lived Religion: Faith and Practice in Everyday Life* (Oxford: Oxford University Press, 2008), 205.

32 McGuire, *Lived Religion*, 186–7.

33 McGuire, *Lived Religion*, 208. The concept of lived religion has mostly been applied to various modern forms of religious commitment and identity. However, McGuire aptly refers to recent scholarly trends that have tried to do justice to the diversity of early Christianity. In light of this diversity, many Christian communities, from their inception, "adaptively responded to the cultural meanings and practices of the diverse peoples who had become Christians"; furthermore, ancient Christian and Jewish "identities were threatened by extensive overlapping and religious blending" (p. 191). It can be argued that the tension between lived religion and attempts to authenticate a particular form of Christianity as the only true one has belonged to the construction of Christian identity from the beginning. Cf. J. Lieu, "From Us but Not of Us? Moving the Boundaries of the Community", in M. Grundeken/J. Verheyden (ed.), *Early Christian Communities between Ideal and Reality* (WUNT 342; Mohr Siebeck, 2015) 161–75, on p. 175: "The obsessive concern with determining who 'is not of us', which characterizes Christianity throughout its history, is there from the start."

34 For these connections, see Jenkins, *Social Identity*, 143–4.

35 For an introduction to social identity approach with relevant references, see Hakola, *Reconsidering*, 24–6. For various applications of the approach to early Christian literature, see J.B. Tucker/C.A. Baker, *T&T Clark Handbook to Social Identity in the New Testament* (London: Bloomsbury, 2014).

Social categories are not seen as inflexible and stable but always dependent on the specific social environment and those comparative relations that are present in that environment. It can be claimed that "people who are categorized and perceived as different in one context ... can be recategorized and perceived as similar in another context".[36] Social categorization, however, quite often results in exaggeration and a polarization of perception because individuals belonging to different groups are viewed as being more different from each other than they really are, while individuals belonging to the same group are perceived as more similar.[37] Therefore, categorization has been described as "a cognitive grouping process that transforms differences into similarities, and vice versa".[38] This point appears frequently in Cohen's understanding of communities as symbolic constructions.[39]

The idea that social categories can be seen as imagined constructions is inherent in the social identity approach. It is claimed that social categories "do not just reflect the existing organization of social reality" but are used "to invoke a vision of how social reality should be organized, and to mobilize people to realize that vision".[40] In this sense, social categories not only imitate but, first and foremost, create social reality. In other words, social categories can be seen as projections of future social realities when they express what a group wants to become in the future.[41]

The above-mentioned theoretical perspectives regard various communities and their boundaries as social constructs rather than as well-defined and objective entities. It should be noted that this kind of approach has become all the more common in the study of early Christianity.[42] Especially when it comes to such value-laden concepts as "heresy" or "orthodoxy", scholars have abandoned the use of these terms as neutral descriptive categories and understood them as prescriptive instruments in the process of self-definition that is always achieved in relation to those experienced and excluded as

36 P.J. Oakes/S.A. Haslam/J.C. Turner, *Stereotyping and Social Reality* (Oxford: Blackwell, 1994), 98.

37 Oakes/Haslam/Turner, *Stereotyping*, 95–6; P.J. Oakes/S.A. Haslam/K.J. Reynolds, "Social Categorization and Social Context: Is Stereotype Change a Matter of Information or of Meaning?" in D.M. Abrams and M.A. Hogg (ed.), *Social Identity and Social Cognition* (Oxford: Blackwell, 1999), 55–79, on pp. 57–61.

38 Oakes/Haslam/Reynolds, "Social Categorization", 62.

39 Cohen, *Symbolic Construction*, 21: "This relative similarity or difference [of a community] is not a matter for 'objective' assessment: it is a matter of feeling, a matter which resides in the minds of the members themselves. Thus, although they recognize important differences among themselves, they also suppose themselves to be more like each other than like the members of other communities."

40 S.A. Haslam/S.D. Reicher/M.J. Platlow, *The New Psychology of Leadership: Identity, Influence and Power* (Hove and New York: Psychology Press, 2011), 65.

41 Haslam/Reicher/Platlow, *The New Psychology*, 72, 162, 188.

42 Cf. J. Lieu, *Christian* Identity, 11–17; M. Kahlos, "Introduction", in M. Kahlos (ed.), *Faces of the Other: Religious Rivalry and Ethnic Encounters in the Later Roman* (Cursor Mundi 10; Turnhout, Belgium: Brepols, 2011) 1–15, on pp. 5–7; Hakola, *Reconsidering*, 21–4.

others.[43] As Ismo Dunderberg has recently remarked, boundaries between groups of people, for example those between various early Christian groups, "do not simply exist, those boundaries are always drawn by someone". Dunderberg continues that it has been all too usual, not only among various historical Christian groups but also in scholarly usage, to take such historically contingent and socially constructed categories as "heresy", "orthodoxy", or "gnosticism" as "naturalized".[44]

A theologian who played a pivotal role in "naturalizing" the portrait of a unified, distinctive and orthodox early Christian community as opposed to diverse heterodox groups is Ireneaus in his *Adversus Haereses.* However, Judith Lieu has recently traced various elements in earlier writings (the Epistles of Paul, John, and Ignatius) that already anticipated Irenaeus' maneuver. Therefore, "Irenaeus is not to be held responsible for inventing 'the idea of heresy', with all its destructive after-effects".[45] For example, the Johannine Epistles presuppose "a non-negotiable control of permitted membership".[46] In another connection, Lieu has concluded that the First Epistle of John projects a community even though it does not use any distinctive vocabulary for this community. The community constructed in the Epistle appears "as a cohesive, undifferentiated body, which possesses no distinguishing characteristics of status, of ethnicity, of religious background, or of historically shaped self-consciousness that might connect its members with any other sets of structures in society".[47] Earlier writers may not use later terminology related to orthodoxy and heresies but they already clearly try to set up strict boundaries and construct portraits of ideal followers of Jesus.

In the following, I examine how the portrait of an imagined community is constructed in the Gospel of John. Because I am interested in the portrait of the community envisioned in the Gospel, my analysis is not dependent on any detailed historical reconstruction of the Johannine community. I focus on how the following features of a symbolic, imagined community are constructed in the Gospel: (1) The origins of the community, (2), The boundaries of the community, (3) The symbols of belonging and the unity of the community, and (4) The community and the world.

43 K.L. King, *What is Gnosticism* (Cambridge, Massachusetts: Belknapp, 2003), 20–54; D. Boyarin, Border *Lines: The Partition of Judaeo-Christianity* (Philadelphia: University of Pennsylvania Press, 2004), 22–7; Räisänen, *The Rise*, 4.

44 Dunderberg, *Gnostic Morality*, 3.

45 J. Lieu, "From Us'", 175.

46 Lieu, "From Us'", 171.

47 J. Lieu, "The Audience of the Johannine Epistles", in R.A. Culpepper/P.N. Anderson (ed.), *Communities in Dispute: Current Scholarship on the Johannine Epistles* (SBLECL 13; Atlanta, Georgia: Society of Biblical Literature, 2014) 123–40, on pp. 139–40.

The Origins of the Community

All the varieties of early Christianity tried to relate themselves to Jesus' teachings and activity in one way or another. Among the four canonical gospels, John is the most explicit in its claim that the writing is based on the testimony of an eyewitness (John 19:35; 21:24).[48] In recent scholarship, there has appeared a renewed interest in defending the reliability of these mentions and reading the Gospel as an eyewitness account. However, scholars have surprisingly seldom analyzed the Gospel's references to Jesus' Beloved Disciple in detail and they quite often simply ignore the basic observation that the figure of the Beloved Disciple is absent from the synoptic parallels.[49] In light of this observation, the references to the Beloved Disciple "seem to be a secondary addition to earlier tradition. … They tell us a great deal about the Johannine community's regard for the witness who stood behind their traditions, but they tell us little about events at the death and resurrection of Jesus".[50]

The figure of the Beloved Disciple is exceptional among canonical writings, but Ismo Dunderberg has shown on the basis of the evidence from non-canonical early Christian texts how this figure is a part of a growing tendency to provide detailed accounts of how early Christian texts were produced.[51] Dunderberg concludes that "the more aware early Christian writers became of the diversity within early Christian traditions, the more important it became to convince their audiences that the specific branch of tradition they were

48 A reference to eyewitnesses of Jesus' life appears most probably already in John 1:14 ("And the Word became flesh and lived among us, and we have seen his glory), but it is not certain whether the opening of 1 John 1:1 ("We declare to you what was from the beginning, what we have heard, what we have seen with our eyes") refers to eyewitnesses; cf. Lieu, *I, II and III John*, 37–41.

49 Cf. Dunderberg *Gnostic Morality*, 204–5. Dunderberg has looked through how scholars claiming that the Beloved Disciple is an eyewitness have dealt with the problem that this disciple is not mentioned in the synoptic parallels. Dunderberg concludes that for scholars such as Martin Hengel, Richard Bauckham, Ben Witherington, Craig Bloomberg, or Craig Keener, this problem "simply does not exist … or they deliberately ignore it". Dunderberg also shows how many arguments that have lately been presented to support John's historical reliability were already articulated by Brooke Foss Westcott at the end of the nineteenth century (pp. 199–201).

50 R.A. Culpepper, *John, the Son of Zebedee: The Life of a Legend* (Columbia, South Carolina: University of South Carolina Press, 1994), 72. Cf. also A.T. Lincoln, *The Gospel According to Saint John* (BNTC 4; London/Peabody, MA: Continuum/Hendrickson, 2005): "There is no corroborative evidence from the Synoptics for a disciple doing any of these things and indeed these incidents appear to have been added to the substratum for the evangelist's narrative found in the Synoptic tradition."

51 I. Dunderberg, *The Beloved Disciple in Conflict? Revisiting the Gospels of John and Thomas* (Oxford: Oxford University Press, 2006), 165–98. See also M. Meyer, "Whom Did Jesus Love Most? Beloved Disciples in John and Other Gospels", in T. Rasimus (ed.), *The Legacy of John: Second Century Reception of the Fourth Gospel* (NovTSup 132; Leiden: Brill, 2010) 73–91. Cf. also Kari Syreeni's article in this collection.

representing was the most reliable".[52] The Beloved Disciple can be taken as part of the production of a distinct early Christian social identity rather than as a mirror image of some historical person – no matter whether we speculate that there is an actual, otherwise unknown and anonymous early Christian teacher behind this figure[53] or whether we are content to conclude that this figure is a literary device.[54]

In a sense, the Gospel of John projects the origins of the community of believers further back in time. It is stated several times that the Scriptures, Moses and other foundational figures in Israel's past have testified on Jesus' behalf even though his opponents' do not accept this testimony (John 5:39, 45–46; 8:56). However, I have argued elsewhere that it is not only continuity but also contrast that characterizes Jesus' relationship to Moses and Abraham.[55] Moses and Abraham have positive functions in John as Jesus' witnesses, but Jesus' superiority over them is made clear and there is no room for any continuing independent role of these figures from the past.[56] John's ambiguous references to representative scriptural figures can be taken as an example of the unresolved tension that characterizes his relationship to Jewishness.[57] On the ideological level, John emphasizes continuity with the

52 Dunderberg, *The Beloved Disciple*, 203.

53 Thus Culpepper, *John*, 84–5; Lincoln, *John*, 25.

54 J. Kügler, *Der Jünger den Jesus liebte. Literarische, theologische und historische Untersuchungen zu einer Schlüsselgestalt johanneischer Theologie und Geschichte. Mit einem Exkurs über die Brotrede in Joh 6* (SBB 16; Stuttgart: Verlag Katholisches Bibelwerk, 1988); Dunderberg, *The Beloved Disciple*, 147–8.

55 John's ambiguous references to Moses and his law may reflect a situation where the majority of John's community no longer observed such basics of Jewish identity as the Sabbath or circumcision, see Hakola, *Identity Matters*, 215–21; idem, "The Johannine Community as Jewish Christians? Some Problems in Current Scholarly Consensus", in M. Jackson-McCabe, *Reconsidering Jewish Christianity: Rethinking Ancient Groups and Texts* (Minneapolis: Fortress Press, 2007) 181–201. The question of John's relationship to the law remains debated. For recent contributions to this discussion, see W.R.G. Loader, "The Law and Ethics in John", in J.G. van der Watt/R. Zimmermann (ed.), *Rethinking the Ethics of John: "Implicit Ethics" in the Johannine Writings* (WUNT 291; Tübingen: Mohr Siebeck, 2012) 144–58, on p. 144 n. 1. I concur with Loader, who concludes that "John no longer assumes Torah observance".

56 Cf. M. Theobald, *Studien zum Corpus Johanneum* (WUNT 267; Tübingen: Mohr Siebeck, 2010), 282–348. See also F. Moloney, *Signs and Shadows: Reading John 5–12* (Minneapolis: Fortress Press, 1996), 113: "Abraham, for all his greatness, belongs to the sequence of events that mark time. There was a time when he belonged to a narrative. His story is finished; he has come and gone. 'The Jews' are only able to call upon the memory of his story." In a similar vein already N.A. Dahl, "The Johannine Church and History", in J. Ashton (ed.), *The Interpretation of John* (Philadelphia: Fortress Press/London: SPCK, 1986, 122–40) on p. 137: "The question may remain as to whether the OT is not, factually, deprived of a historical meaning of its own when Moses and the prophets are simply made supporters of John's own testimony to Christ." (Originally in W. Klassen/G.F. Snyder (ed.), *Current Issues in New Testament Interpretation* [New York: Harper & Row/London: SCM Press, 1962], 124–42.)

57 Cf. Loader, "The Law and Ethics", 155 n. 62: "The claim to continuity to Torah faithfulness clearly matters for the author, but it is substantiated by what in effect is in part a radical discontinuity: Torah's cultic and related provisions which served to foreshadow Christ can now

past but many features in his narrative suggest a growing social discontinuity between the followers of Jesus and their Jewish contemporaries.

John was, of course, not the only early Christian writer who struggled to emphasize continuity with the past in a situation where novel beliefs and practices moved many Christian communities away from other Jews. Heikki Räisänen has shown how "ambiguous continuity" characterizes what is said of Jews and Jewishness in various early Christian writings.[58] The claims for continuity with scriptural tradition in various early Cristian writings are in agreement with how various kinds of communities claim to preserve genuine cultural, social, or religious heritage while they, at the same time, introduce new and innovative ways to express their distinctive identity. When the issues of leadership have been examined from a social identity perspective, it has become clear that, in periods of social change, successful group leaders are able to root their account of who they and their group are in common cultural and historical traditions. They know how to select and reshape collective symbols and use them in new combinations and in this way establish "a continuity over time within the context of the salient group membership" so that "the speaker's version is no longer one version amongst many but rather the only valid version of identity".[59]

Abraham and other representative figures of the scriptural past are particularly convenient symbols who guaranteed the authenticity of the newly introduced faith in Jesus. In antiquity the old age of an ethnic group was held in high esteem, and many non-Jewish and Jewish writers frequently refer to Abraham, Moses or other patriarchs with admiration for their nobility and age-old wisdom.[60] Such symbolic figures are valuable in the construction of a community because – to use Anthony Cohen's words – "symbolism ... does not carry meaning inherently" and is thus "highly responsive to change". According to Cohen, communities often use various symbols to express their identity because "symbolic form has only a loose relation to its content" and, therefore, it "can persist while the content undergoes significant trans-

cease to be observed because what they promised has come." According to Loader, this means that "the law on the Johannine reading predicts its own eclipse by Jesus." Cf. also Lieu, *Christian Identity*, 41: "Even within the Jewishness of John, which is exemplified by its scriptural shaping, there is an unresolved ambivalence as to whether Scripture does still remain foundational for the readers' (or for the 'community's') identity, particularly in the face of the deliberate embrace of an otherness, a new identity, 'born from above' and 'not of this world' (3. 3; 17. 16)."

58 Räisänen, *The Rise*, 256–76.

59 Haslam/Reicher/Platlow, *The New Psychology*, 178. Cf. also McGuire, *Lived Religion*, 206: "Various (religious, ethnic, and national) imagined communities claim their cultural and historical tradition to be the uniquely authentic story out of which their people collectively live." Lieu, *Christian Identity*, 15: "Claims about past history and continuity are constitutive of nearly all articulations of identity."

60 For relevant ancient sources, see L. Feldman, *Jew and Gentile in the Ancient World: Attitudes and Interactions from Alexander to Justinian* (Princeton, New Jersey: Princeton University Press, 1993), 177–285.

formation. Frequently, the appearance of continuity is so compelling that it obscures people's recognition that the form itself has changed".[61] It is clear that John was convinced that there was only continuity in his portrait of Jesus as the fulfilment of the Scriptures but it is equally understandable that other Jews would have recognized a significant break in his fusion of past and present. Colleen Conway has argued that John's "supplanting of Moses and of the ancestors" should be recognized as a "counterhistory in the making" that reads "against the grains of the adversaries' trusted sources" and in this way deprives them of their positive identity and replaces it with "a pejorative counter image".[62] John's seizure of Israel's scriptural history anticipates later apologetic writers who tried to counter the claims that the faith in Jesus is a recent innovation by asserting the antiquity of Christian wisdom and by inventing a worthy past for Jesus' followers.[63] The inventors of Christian identity – including John – did what successful group leaders have always done; these pioneers "don't just repeat traditional stories of identity ... [but] weave familiar strands into novel patterns. They are careful not to violate what we know of ourselves. Their genius is to make the new out of elements of the old and thereby to present revolution as tradition."[64]

John not only appropriates Israel's history but anchors his story of Jesus to mythical beginnings. It is generally accepted that the opening of the Gospel (John 1:1–4) with its reference to "the beginning" is a rereading of the creation myth in the book of Genesis (Gen 1–2).[65] John reclaims various Jewish wisdom traditions and describes Jesus as the eternal Word (λόγος) who was with God already before the creation of the world. The myth of the eternal Word effectively moves John's story of Jesus above the contingencies of time and contributes to the construction of a vision of the world that supplants all competing visions.[66] In the framework of a myth, constructed identities that

61 Cohen, *Symbolic Construction*, 91 (italics original). Cf. also p. 104: "It is the very imprecision of these references to the past – timelessness masquerading as history – which makes them so apt a device for symbolism and, in particular, for expressing symbolically the continuity of past and present, and for re-asserting the cultural integrity of the community in the face of its apparent subversion by the forces of change."

62 C. Conway, "New Historicism and the Historical Jesus in John: Friends or Foes?" in P.N. Anderson/F. Just/T. Thatcher (ed.), *John Jesus and History, Volume 1: Critical Appraisals of Critical Views* (SBLSymS 44; Atlanta: Society of Biblical Literature, 2007) 199–215, on p. 212. Conway cites here A. Funkenstein, "History, Counterhistory, and Narrative," in S. Freidlander (ed.), *Probing the Limits of Representation: Nazism and the "Final Solution"* (Cambridge, Massachusetts: Harvard University Press, 1992) 66–81, on pp. 79–80.

63 For various appeals to the past as a part of early Christian self-definition, see Lieu, *Christian Identity*, 62–97; D.K. Buell, *Why This New Race: Ethnic Reasoning in Early Christianity* (New York: Columbia University Press, 2005), 63–93.

64 Haslam/Reicher/Platlow, *The New Psychology*, 149.

65 Cf. J. Painter, "Earth Made Whole: John's Rereading of Genesis", in J. Painter/R.A. Culpepper/F.F. Segovia (ed.), *Word, Theology and Community in John* (St. Louis, Missouri: Chalice Press, 2002) 65–84.

66 Cf. F.F. Segovia, "John 1.1–18 as Entrée into Johannine Reality: Representation and Ramifica-

are subject to historical change and renegotiation appear as stable and beyond contestation.[67]

The Boundaries of the Community

It is one of the basic observation in recent scholarship that the boundaries of various national, ethnic or religious communities are not naturally given with fixed and allegedly objective criteria but socially constructed.[68] This notion has important ramifications in Johannine studies because scholars have more often than not taken the boundaries set up in the Johannine writings as reflecting the actual boundaries between the Johannine community and its surroundings. In the Gospel a clear demarcation between Jesus' followers and the rest of world is accentuated with the use of such dualistic polarities as be from above vs. be from below, be from God vs. be from the devil, light vs. darkness. In earlier scholarship, the strict dualism has quite often been taken as evidence of the isolation of the Johannine Christians from their surrounding society and the sectarian nature of their community.[69]

I have recently argued that John's dualistic worldview cannot be used as evidence for factual separation but is rather an attempt to turn a diverse social reality into controllable categories.[70] The boundaries between emerging early Christian communities and Jewish synagogue communities seem to have remained fluid and permeable for a long time.[71] For example, there is evidence beginning from some New Testament writings for Christians who were

tions", in J. Painter/R.A. Culpepper/F.F. Segovia (ed.), *Word, Theology and Community in John* (St. Louis, Missouri: Chalice Press, 2002) 33–64, on p. 59: "John's vision of reality ... seeks to supplant all other visions at work with its own set of conceptions about the other-world, the this-world, and their correspondence."

67 Cf. Cohen, *Symbolic Construction*, 99: "Myth confers 'rightness' on a course of action by extending to it the sanctity which enshrouds tradition and lore. Mythological distance lends enchantment to an otherwise murky contemporary view. One reason which accounts for the particular efficacy of myth in this regard is its ahistorical character. ... It 'blocks off' the past, making it impervious to the rationalistic scrutiny." McGuire, *Lived Religion*, 207: "The myth legitimates group identity and solidarity, affirming: This is who we naturally – in our essence– are and always have been. And the myth legitimates oppositional boundaries toward the Other, whose identity is likewise constructed as historically fixed and essential."

68 Cf. Lieu, *Christian Identity*, 98: "It is part of the seduction of identity that the encircling boundary appears both given and immutable, when it is neither."

69 For a critical review of sectarian understandings of the Johannine community, see D.A. Lamb, *Text, Context and the Johannine Community: A Sociolinguistic Analysis of the Johannine Writings* (LNTS 477; London and New York: Bloomsbury T & T Clark, 2013), 103–44.

70 Hakola, *Reconsidering*, 1–5, 118–31.

71 Cf. J.M.G. Barclay, *Pauline Churches and Diaspora Jews* (WUNT 275; Tübingen: Mohr Siebeck, 2010), 22: "Although the boundaries of the Jewish community did not coincide with those of the believer-assemblies, Jewish believers [in Jesus] could generally participate in both 'synagogue' and 'church' communities at the same time."

Gentiles and "combined a commitment to Christianity with adherence in varying degrees to Jewish practices without viewing such behavior as contradictory".[72] As Michele Murray has shown, from the perspective of certain Christian leaders, these community members dangerously blurred boundaries between Christian and Jewish communities which aroused their fierce denunciation in some sources. The same kind of boundary-crossing continued to haunt various Christian theologians as various sources stemming from the second to the early fifth century demonstrate.[73]

The evidence for blurred boundaries between Christian and Jewish communities seems to be at odds with John's references to the exclusion from the synagogue (John 9:22; 12:42; 16:2). These references have long been taken as a reflection of the measures that the rabbinic establishment took against the Johannine community but this kind of policy is unattested in other sources.[74] John's passages mentioning the exclusion may not provide evidence for the formal and definite policy of the alleged opponents of his community but reflect a more prolonged and gradual process of separation among some Johannine Christians. As a result of this process, some members of the community may have become gradually alienated from their fellow Jews to the extent that they felt that they were excluded from synagogue gatherings. In this sense, the exclusion passages give a retrospective rationale for the separation and, at the same time, create a definite boundary between Jesus' followers and local synagogue communities.[75]

72 M. Murray, *Playing a Jewish Game: Gentile Christian Judaizing in the First and Second Century CE* (SCJ 13; Waterloo, Ontario: Wilfrid Laurier University Press, 2004), 2. Murray finds evidence for this phenomenon, for example, in Paul's Epistle to the Galatians, the Epistles of Ignatius, *Epistle of Barnabas*, The *Didache*, Pseudo-Clementine Literature and Revelation.

73 For relevant evidence, see R. Hakola, "Galilean Jews and Christians in Context: Spaces Shared and Contested in the Eastern Galilee in Late Antiquity", in J. Day/R. Hakola/M. Kahlos/U. Tervahauta (ed.), *Spaces in Late Antiquity: Cultural, Theological and Archaeological Perspectives* (New York & London: Routledge, 2016) 141–165.

74 Scholars have repeatedly tried to connect the Jewish prayer against heretics, *Birkat Ha-Minim*, with the Johannine situation, but this view is problematic. See Hakola, *Identity Matters*, 45–55; Kloppenborg, "Disaffliation", 1–5; R. Langer, *Cursing the Christians? A History of the Birkat haMinim* (Oxford: Oxford University Press, 2012), 26–9.

75 Hakola, *Reconsidering*, 56–62. See also A. Reinhartz, *Befriending*, 50: "The exclusion passages may have provided the Johannine community not with a direct reflection of their historical experience but rather with a divinely ordained etiology *in the time of Jesus* for a situation of separation which was part of their own experience." W. Carter, *John and the Empire*, 26: "[The expulsion passages] function as part of the Gospel's rhetoric of distance to indicate that some conflict and division between the Jesus believers and the rest of the synagogue *ought* to exist as a consequence of allegiance to Jesus." Kloppenborg, "Disaffliation", 13: "There is little doubt that the *result* of expulsion was the Fourth Gospel's articulation of a complex retrospective rationale, based on the group's claim to have seen in Jesus what their fellow synagogue members refused to see or were unable. But this interpretation, along with the corresponding demonizing of the *Ioudaioi* and *Pharisaioi*, should be seen as retrospective rather than a contemporary account of expulsion. Before they undertook to rationalise their expulsion in dogmatic terms, these par-

Despite John's inclination to set up dualistic polarities, there is evidence in the Gospel for a more diverse social reality. In John 8:31, there appear Jews who are said to believe in Jesus. These textual figures can be taken as a symbolic representation of those in John's environment who believed in Jesus as the Messiah but still continued to interact with local Jewish synagogue communities.[76] In the course of the dialogue in John 8:31–59, John connects Jews who had believed in Jesus with the devil (8:44), but the mere presence of these believing Jews in John's narrative suggests that the categories John wants to keep intact and separated were, as a matter of fact, overlapping and flexible. In a similar way, many scholars have recently observed how some Johannine characters, most notably Nicodemus, remain ambiguous in the narrative.[77] For example, Nicodemus has been taken as a narrative symbol of "Judaism ... in sympathetic dialogue with Johannine teaching" and of "the Jew who chooses to engage Jesus open-mindedly and ... does not fully believe in the Fourth Gospel's teachings".[78] Craig Koester has concluded that even if "dualistic statements create clear categories like light and darkness, the Gospel's approach to character portrayal recognizes that life is more complex".[79] I take this to mean that, even though John regularly portrays the world in black-and-white terms, diverse and unpredictable social reality has made its way into his narrative, especially through various loose ends in how its characters are presented.

I suggest that it is precisely the instability of the boundaries between the Johannine community and its environment that is a major motivational reason in the emergence of Johannine dualism. John's one-dimensional and polarized view of the world anticipates how various later Christian theologians tried to keep the symbolic boundaries of their communities intact even though there is ample evidence that the boundaries on the ground were unsettled and mutable.[80] These attempts can be seen as examples of the tension between

tisans of the Jesus movement began to assume behavioural practices which precipitated their exclusion and eventual expulsion."

76 Hakola, *Reconsidering*, 118–29.

77 C.M. Conway, "Speaking through Ambiguity: Minor Characters in the Fourth Gospel", *BibInt* 10 (2002) 324–41; S.E. Hylen, *Imperfect Believers: Ambiguous Characters in the Gospel of John* (Louisville, Kentucky: Westminster John Knox, 2009); C.R. Koester, "Theological Complexity and the Characterization of Nicodemus in John's Gospel", in C.W. Skinner (ed.), *Characters and Characterization in the Gospel of John* (LNTS 461; London and New York: Bloomsbury T & T Clark, 2013) 165–81; Hakola, *Reconsidering*, 132–46.

78 M. Kraus, "New Jewish Directions in the Study of the Fourth Gospel", in F. Lozada Jr./T. Thatcher (ed.), *New Currents through John: A Global Perspective* (SBLRBS 54; Atlanta, Georgia: Society of Biblical Literature, 2006) 141–66, on p. 165.

79 Koester, "Theological Complexity", 168.

80 Cf. Hakola, "Galilean Jews", 143–44. The use of various dualistic expressions was not, of course, a Christian innovation. It is commonly accepted that quite many of the dualistic images used in John have close parallels in some Qumran scrolls and other Second Temple Jewish sources. See Hakola, *Identity Matters*, 197–210. Not unlike in John, one may find a discrepancy between

religion-as-lived and the need to stabilize a particular form of religious identity as the only accepted alternative, a tendency that Meredith McGuire has seen to be a characteristic of various imagined communities. According to McGuire, the members of an imagined community customarily represent the boundaries between their community and others as natural rather than actively think their group as a social construction.[81] However, if we demystify the in-house rhetoric used in various sources and approach their ideal portraits of communities as symbolic constructions, we realize that group boundaries are not "objectively apparent" and that "boundaries perceived by some may be utterly imperceptible to others".[82] For this reason, it is problematic to take theological myth-making as equivalent to social reality.[83]

The Symbols of Belonging and the Unity of the Community

Boundaries contribute to the construction of communities as identifiable and distinct entities, but they also enhance the sense of unity and belonging among those who position themselves within the boundaries. The sense of belonging to a group of people is not necessarily based on the actual similarity of its members but it may be achieved through the "participation in a common symbolic domain" that allows individual group members to imagine themselves as a unified whole despite all their mutual differences.[84]According to the social identity approach, when persons recognize themselves as a member of a distinct group, they go through the process of self-stereotyping. As a result of this process they experience themselves and other members in the group not as differentiated individuals but as approximating common

overtly dualistic categories and a more diverse social reality in some of these sources. Cf. L.T. Stuckenbruck, "The Interiorization of Dualism within the Human Being in Second Temple Judaism: The Treatise of the Two Spirits (1QS III:13–IV:26) in its Tradition-Historical Context", in A. Lange/E.M. Meyers/B.H. Reynolds III/R. Styers (ed.), *Light Against Darkness: Dualism in Ancient Mediterranean Religion and the Contemporary World* (JAJSup 2; Göttingen: Vandenhoeck & Ruprecht, 2011) 145–68, on p. 168: "The Treatise [of the Two Spirits] provided its original community, and subsequently the Qumran community, with a theological framework that enabled these groups to come to terms with discrepancies between the ideology and identity they claimed for themselves on the one hand and realities of what they experienced on the other."

81 McGuire, *Lived Religion*, 207. Cf. Haslam/Reicher/Platlow, *The New Psychology*, 179: "Those who have the imagination and skill to justify whichever claims they are making about identity through links to the natural order will be in a better position to authenticate their version of who we are."

82 Cohen, *Symbolic Construction*, 13.

83 Cf. J.M. Lieu, *Neither Jew Nor Christian: Constructing Early Christianity* (London & New York: T & T Clark, 2002), 19. "Theological boundaries and social boundaries are not necessarily coterminous."

84 Cf. Jenkins, *Social Identity*, 138.

characteristics of their group.[85] This depersonalization does not mean that individuals lose their selves but rather that they redefine themselves and "all self-related terms, so that these relate to 'we' not 'I'".[86] Various empirical studies support the conclusion that depersonalization lays the foundation not only for the sense of sameness among group members but also enables an otherwise disparate collective of people to agree on their common goals and strive for these goals as a cohesive social force. According to this perspective, attraction to fellow group members and social cohesion are not so much a prerequisite for a shared social identity but rather its outcome.[87]

In the Gospel of John, the unity of Jesus' followers is a major theme, even though it was earlier claimed that John's focus is completely on the fate of an individual and he does not show any interest in the construction of a community of believers.[88] The unity of John's imagined community is addressed metaphorically in Jesus' image of the sheep who will listen to only one shepherd and who will become one flock (John 10:16) or in the image of the true vine with many branches (John 15:1–5). Jesus' reference to "other sheep that do not belong to this fold" is most often taken to mean that "Jesus, the one shepherd, will bring about the one flock of Jews and Gentiles".[89] In a similar way, the words "Jesus was about to die for the nation, and not for the nation only, but to gather into one the dispersed children of God," (John 11:51–52), most probably mean that John understood the inclusion of non-Jews in his community to fulfill the scriptural promises of the eschatological gathering of Jews and Gentiles on Mt. Zion.[90] Because John reinforces the unity of God's people mostly through various symbolic expressions, we may never be able to determine the ethnic components in his community in any more detail.

Before the story of his passion starts, Jesus asks his Father to protect his disciples so that they may be one as he and the Father are one (John 17:11, 23). It is clear from these formulations that the unity between God, the Father, and

85 See S.A. Haslam, *Psychology in Organizations: The Social Identity Approach* (London: Sage Publications, 2001), 29–30; Haslam/Reicher/Platlow, *The New Psychology*, 52–4.

86 Haslam/Reicher/Platlow, *The New Psychology*, 54.

87 Haslam/Reicher/Platlow, *The New Psychology*, 58–9.

88 Cf. R.E. Brown, *An Introduction to the Gospel of John* (ed. F.J. Moloney; ABRL; New York, Doubleday, 2003), 221–9. Scholars such as R. Bultmann, E. Schweizer, or E. Käsemann have claimed that there was no concept of church in John. However, Brown shows that, even though many ecclesial terms used elsewhere in early Christian literature do not appear in John, there is "no sharp distinction between community and personal union with Jesus. The foundation of community is the response of individuals to Jesus as the revealer of God and the unique way to God, but those individuals form a unity."

89 Lincoln, *John*, 298.

90 Hakola, *Reconsidering*, 111. A scriptural passage is revised in John 6:45 with the inclusion of the Gentiles in mind. While Isa 54:13 reads, "All your children shall be taught by the Lord", meaning the children of Israel, John has, "they shall all be taught by God". This change is quite commonly understood to suggest that, for John, salvation exceeds the borders of Israel. See Hakola, *Identity Matters*, 234.

Jesus, the Son, is a model for the interdependence of Jesus' followers. In the Johannine parlance, the close relationship between God, his Son and the believers is expressed in terms of mutual indwelling (μένω), even though there is a notable difference in how this language is developed in the Gospel and in the Epistles. In the Gospel, it is exclusively Jesus who abides in the believers or the believers in Jesus (John 6:56; 15:4–7),[91] while 1 John speaks of the direct mutual abiding between God and those who believe (1 John 3:24; 4:15). Furthermore, the Epistles lack the idea of the mutual indwelling of the Father and the Son that forms the foundation for the indwelling of the believers in God in the Gospel (John 14:10–11, 20; 17:21).[92] In the Gospel, social relations among Jesus' followers are seen to mirror very closely what Jesus has revealed of his relationship with God. This corresponds to how the knowledge of God is transmitted exclusively through Jesus (John 14:7) whereas 1 John 4:6–8 allows that everyone who loves God knows God.

The knowledge of God communicated only by Jesus constructs a close-knit community between those who receive this revelation. As Jesus declares to his disciples: "I have called you friends, because I have made known to you everything that I have heard from my Father" (John 15:15). The revealed knowledge not only creates a close bond among the disciples but also an imagined boundary between them and those who have not received Jesus' revelation. As Jesus explicitly says, the disciples do not belong to the world that does not know Jesus or God who has sent Jesus (John 15:18–21). The notion that only Jesus has revealed God effectively rules out other ways of receiving information of the divine world, which means that the Johannine author establishes a "strict control over access to and knowledge of the other-world".[93]

It has been a traditional crux of interpretation among Johannine scholars that regardless of the importance of Jesus' revelation of God, it is never told very clearly what Jesus actually reveals of God.[94] Since the appearance of Wayne Meeks' classic article drawing on the sociology of knowledge, Johannine scholars have become accustomed to thinking that there is a

91 However, cf. John 14:23: "Those who love me will keep my word, and my Father will love them, and we will come to them and make our home (μονὴν ποιησόμεθα) with them." This verse probably presents a Johannine reinterpretation (cf. 14:2) of traditional apocalyptic imagery. See Lincoln, *John*, 389 and 396.

92 Cf. Lieu, *I, II and III John*, 73; Hakola, *Reconsidering*, 74–5.

93 Segovia, "John 1.1–18", 52.

94 Cf. C. Koester, *Symbolism in the Fourth Gospel: Meaning, Mystery, Community* (2nd Edition; Minneapolis; Fortress Press, 2003), 289: "What does Jesus reveal about God? In its statements about God, the Fourth Gospel is remarkably sparing … and never spells out just what the Son has seen and heard. … What is distinctive about the Fourth Gospel's presentation of God concerns the relationship of the Father to the Son." Lieu, *Christian Identity*, 139–40: "The characteristic emphasis on 'knowing' in the Johannine tradition correlates with its lack of explicit concern about distinctive behavioural or structural patterns (John 8:31–2; 17:3, 6–8; 14:5–9)."

close relationship between knowledge, language and the construction of the community in John.[95] The point is not so much what Jesus reveals of God but how John's portrait of Jesus and the Gospel as a whole provides "a reinforcement for the community's social identity". The portrait of Jesus who comes down from heaven and makes God known only to a few chosen ones "defines and vindicates the existence of the community" that has "totalistic and exclusivistic claims" and that "evidently sees itself as unique, alien from its world, under attack, misunderstood, but living in unity with Christ and through him with God".[96] Judith Lieu has remarked how claims to revelation or exclusive knowledge are "solipcist" because they "by definition conjure a self-legitimating enclave". Lieu continues that the knowledge revealed as mystery is naturally "intangible" for outsiders and "hence its rhetorical evocation works rather for those inside, for whom it might also substitute for more tangible barriers".[97] The emphasis on knowing thus generates the sense of unity among the members of John's imagined community but also sets them apart from the surrounding world.

The emphasis on exclusive knowing shapes what John says about the relations among those who have received Jesus' revelation of God. In his farewell speech, Jesus says to his disciples: "I give you a new commandment, that you love one another. Just as I have loved you, you also should love one another. By this everyone will know that you are my disciples, if you have love for one another." (John 13:34–35). A well-known characteristic of John's love commandment is that the Johannine Jesus commands the disciples to love one another whereas Jesus' commandment to love one's neighbor (Mark 12:29–31 par.) or the commandment to love one's enemies (Matt 5:43–44; Luke 6:27–28) do not appear in the Johannine writings. There has emerged a significant discussion about the limits and possibilities of John's concept of love and the ethics in the Johannine writings. This discussion has shown that some attempts to deny that there are ethical principles in these writings are one-sided.[98] However, the basic thrust in John's love language is undoubtedly directed to mutual relations among Jesus' disciples. John's formulation of the

95 Liew has seen how the interrelatedness of knowledge, language and community in John is in line with how these concepts are bound together in Cohen's notion of symbolic construction of communities and in Anderson's imagined communities, see Liew, "Ambiguous Admittance", 200.

96 W.A Meeks, "The Man from Heaven in Johannine Sectarianism." *JBL* 91 (1972) 44–72, on pp. 71–2. I think that Meeks has understood well how John's portrait of Jesus may have reinforced a particular early Christian social identity even though I do not follow Meeks in describing the Johannine community as a sect.

97 Lieu, *Christian Identity*, 139.

98 Cf. M. Labahn, "'It's Only Love' – Is That All? Limits and Potentials of Johannine 'Ethic' – a Critical Evaluation of Research", 3–43; R: Zimmerman, "Is There Ethics in the Gospel of John? Challenging an Outdated Consensus", 44–80. Both articles in J.G. van der Watt/R. Zimmermann (ed.), *Rethinking the Ethics of John: "Implicit Ethics" in the Johannine Writings* (WUNT 291; Tübingen: Mohr Siebeck, 2012).

love commandment in terms of mutual love between Jesus' disciples is closely connected with the Gospel's dualism. For this reason, John's love commandment has been described as "particularistic in its formulation" and "sectarian".[99] Some scholars have seen this interpretation as too narrow but it is still difficult to avoid the conclusion that John's main aim is to "show that the only true love, the love of God, was focused in only one place: the family of God as it becomes evident in loving the followers of Jesus."[100] In John's formulation, love becomes a symbolic bond that helps to present the community of believers in Jesus as united and clearly separated from the world. The command of mutual love can thus be seen as an important instrument in the process of constructing an integrated social identity.[101]

The same identity building function can be seen in how John uses the image of friendship to express the intimate tie between Jesus and his followers (John 15:13–15). It has become increasingly evident that the theme of friendship in John is closely related to how various Greek and Roman philosophers or storytellers used friendship as a symbol of an ideal community or society. Jesus' words, "no one has greater love than this, to lay down one's life for one's friends" (John 15:13) fit to this recognizable pattern where noble death was seen as an ultimate act of friendship.[102] Michael Labahn has noted how "the power of love and friendship was usually related to a certain ingroup in the ancient world".[103] In light of this, it is not surprising how John uses the

99 Cf. R. F. Collins, "'A New Commandment I Give To You, That You Love One Another' (John 13:34", in R.F. Collins, *These Things Have Been Written: Studies on the Fourth Gospel* (Louvain/Grand Rapids, Michigan: Peeters/Eerdmans, 1990) 217–56, on p. 253.

100 J.G. van der Watt, "Ethics and Ethos in the Gospel according to John", *ZNW* 97 (2006) 147–76, on p. 176. Van der Watt echoes the consensus among Johannine scholars when he situates John's redefinition of the love commandment in "a context of hatred and opposition." As I have argued here and elsewhere, however, the incomplete external evidence for the conflict between the Johannine community and rabbinic Judaism should pave the way for understanding what John says about the world, not as a direct reflection of an actual, but otherwise unattested conflict, but as an attempt to construct and solidify the distinct social identity of a group of Jesus' early followers.

101 Cf. Labahn, "It's Only Love", 34: "The command of mutual love is part of the identity-formation of a certain group in a certain historical and sociological situation."

102 For relevant Greek and Roman material on friendship, see G. O'Day, "Jesus as Friend in the Gospel of John", *Int* 58 (2004) 144–57; R: Zimmerman, "Is There", 74–9.

103 Labahn, "It's Only Love", 35. Cf. also O'Day, "Jesus as Friend", 147: "The language of friendship provided language for talking about the construction of a community of like-minded people informed by a particular set of teachings." Zimmerman ("Is There", 78) agrees that the ancient ethics of friendship quite often may be "a partisan ethics." In the case of John, however, he argues that "Jesus' relentless openness to the world" (cf. John 18:20–21) shows that "John expands the ideal of friendship to take on a universal meaning." I doubt whether Jesus' words, "I have spoken openly to the world" really speak for "relentless openness to the world" and cancel out the force of dualism that determines the formulation of the love commandment in John. While the love commandment as it is presented in the Johannine writings is clearly related to the mutual love of Jesus' followers, I do not doubt that many past or contemporary real readers of these writings have been able to expand the scope of its application.

terminology related to love and friendship to promote the cohesive identity of his own group. If we approach the Johannine community as an imagined community, it is irrelevant to speculate how well individual members of the community were able to live according to the ideals established in the narrative but the point is how love and friendship function for the members as symbols of belonging.

While the Johannine Jesus describes the commandment of mutual love as a "new commandment", scholars have quite generally realized that "in a real sense, the love commandment is not a new commandment at all" because it is deeply rooted in the commandments of the Torah (Lev 19:18) and has parallels in contemporary Jewish traditions (*m. Abot.* 1:12).[104] The emphasis on the newness of the love commandment should most likely be seen in light of the new revelation brought by Jesus; the love commandment is new because it is given by Jesus and is based on his example.[105] I have earlier discussed how various groups quite often have an ambivalent relationship to the past in that they rely on a common stock of cultural symbols but give conventional symbols new meanings. In the case of the love commandment and the theme of friendship, I suggest that John has used common and widely valued cultural symbols but presented the love and friendship among Jesus' followers as an innovative and unique attribute that makes them distinguishable in the eyes of the rest of the world. In social identity terms, this could be seen as an attempt to accentuate the distinctiveness of John's imagined community.

The preceding discussion has made evident that John's love commandment is tightly connected with knowing what Jesus has revealed of God. This means that in John's vision of reality there is no room for those who do not accept Jesus but still show love or share mutual friendship because love is exclusively used as a visible distinguishing mark of Jesus' followers.[106] In the same way as mutual love symbolizes the community of Jesus' followers, hatred is seen as a characteristic of the world outside (John 15:18–19). The contrast between love and hatred is but one example of various polarities used in the Gospel, and these kinds of general terms are quite common in the context of intergroup tensions.[107] The so-called linguistic intergroup bias means that behavioral patterns among the members of the ingroup tend to be described in quite abstract, morally uplifting terms (love, good, true) whereas the behavior of outgroup members is often summarized in quite general morally defamed

104 Collins, "A New Commandment", 238. Thus also R.E. Brown, *The Gospel According to John* (2 Vols; AB 29; Garden City, New York: Doubleday, 1966 and 1970), 613.

105 Brown, *John*, 614; Collins, "A New Commandment", 239–42; Lincoln, *John*, 388.

106 Cf. van der Watt, "Ethics of/and the Opponents", 187: "At this point soteriology and ethics overlap. The only way the opponents [of Jesus] can hope to become positively moral is to receive life and become children of God." Van der Watt also sees how, according to the Gospel, hatred typifies those who do not accept Jesus (p. 190).

107 Cf. Hakola, *Reconsidering*, 89–90.

terms (hatred, evil, untrue).[108] When groups are described using this kind of general language, actions of individual group members are detached from specific situations. The characterizations of these actions as good vs. evil, true vs. untrue, or hate vs. love are too vague to be tested and, therefore, impossible to verify. The portrait of an imagined community whose members continue to embrace mutual love in the face of the world's hatred is thus particularly attractive as a way of strengthening a distinct social identity. Recent studies on various real-life intergroup conflicts can further clarify the relationship between John's imagined community and the world.

The Community and the World

One of the most distinctive features in John's story of Jesus is how the world (κόσμος) is presented as a cohesive and hostile force that opposes Jesus and his followers from the beginning. Already in the prologue of the Gospel, the world is described as the darkness that does not understand that Jesus is the true light (John 1:5, 9–10). In the course of the narrative, it is "the Jews" (Ἰουδαῖοι) who most closely represent the hostile world. I have argued elsewhere that the attempts at defining the meaning of the term Ἰουδαῖοι in John as referring only to some particular Jewish group, be it Judeans or the Jewish authorities are not totally satisfying in light of John's internal evidence.[109] As a matter of fact, John's tendency to present the Jews as a unified representative of the hostile world can be explained from a social identity perspective. One of the basic claims of Henri Tajfel, the originator of the social identity theory, was that human behavior varies along the "interpersonal and intergroup continuum".[110] Tajfel explains that the nearer a social situation is to the intergroup extreme, "the stronger the tendency will there be for members of the ingroup to treat members of the outgroup as undifferentiated items in a unified category, i. e. independently of the individual differences between them". Furthermore, ingroup members attribute to outgroup members "traits

108 A. Maass/D. Salvi/L. Arcuri/G. Semin, "Language Use in Intergroup Contexts: The Linguistic Intergroup Bias", *JPSP* 57 (1989) 981–93; K. Fiedler/J. Schmid, "How Language Contributes to Persistence of Stereotypes As Well As Other, More General, Intergroup Issues", in R. Brown/S. Gaertner (ed.), *Blackwell Handbook of Social Psychology: Intergroup Processes* (Oxford: Blackwell, 2001) 261–80, on p. 272; B.E. Whitley/M. E. Kite, *The Psychology of Prejudice and Discrimination* (2nd Edition; Belmont, California: Wadsworth/Cengage Learning, 2010), 109–10.

109 Hakola, *Identity Matters*, 10–16, 225–31; idem, *Reconsidering*, 26–9. In a similar vein, R. Sheridan, "Issues in the Translation of οἱ Ἰουδαῖοι in the Fourth Gospel." *JBL* 132 (2013) 671–95, on pp. 688–92.

110 H. Tajfel, *Human Groups and Social Categories: Studies in Social Psychology* (Cambridge: Cambridge University Press, 1981), 228–53.

assumed to be common to the groups as a whole".[111] In subsequent scholarship, this phenomenon has been called the outgroup homogeneity effect, which refers to the inclination of various communities to regard outsiders as homogenous.[112] I suggest that John contributed greatly to the invention of distinct early Christian identity by constructing the portrait of the Jews as united in their opposition to Jesus and his followers.[113]

According to John, there is a strong continuity between the fate of Jesus and that of his followers. Jesus' opponents hated him without a cause (John 15:25) and just as they persecuted Jesus, they will persecute his disciples (John 15:22). It is indisputable that, after Jesus' death, some early Christians were persecuted and even killed by some Jewish authorities even though it is difficult to estimate the scale and the exact motivation behind these early incidents.[114] However, given the lack of evidence for a synagogue-organized

111 Tajfel, *Human Groups*, 243.

112 It has been emphasized that the outgroup homogeneity effect is not always automatic but such variables as group size, group status, ingroup identification and the context of intergroup relations quite often moderate this effect. See S.A. Haslam/P.J. Oakes/J.C. Turner/C. McGarty, "Social Identity, Self-Categorization, and the Perceived Homogeneity of Ingroups and Outgroups: The Interaction between Social Motivation and Cognition", in R. Sorrentino and E. Higgins (ed.), *Handbook of Motivation and Cognition, Volume Three: The Interpersonal Context* (New York: Guilford Press, 1996) 182–222; M. Rubin/C. Badea, "Why Do People Perceive Ingroup Homogeneity on Ingroup Traits and Outgroup Homogeneity on Outgroup Traits?" *PSPB* 33 (2007) 31–42.

113 The tendency to present such groups as the Pharisees, Herodians, chief priests, scribes, elders, and Sadducees as consistent in their opposition to Jesus is already visible in the Gospel of Mark. Cf. E.S. Malbon, "The Jewish Leaders in the Gospel of Mark: A Literary Study of Marcan Characterization", *JBL* 108 (1989) 259–81, on pp. 270–72; D. Rhoads/J. Dewey/D. Michie *Mark as Story: Introduction to the Narrative of a Gospel* (3rd Edition; Minneapolis: Fortress Press, 2012), 117–18.

114 According to Acts 6:8–12, some Jews from the Diaspora started the events that led to Stephen's martyrdom, but it is difficult to say what exactly happened because Luke has modelled the story of Stephen's death on Jesus' trial. The lynch mob aspect is more likely to be original in the story, while Luke has emphasized the parallels between this first Christian martyr and Jesus. See C. Setzer, *Jewish Responses to Early Christians: History and Polemics, 30–150 CE* (Minneapolis: Fortress Press, 1994), 171–3. As Luke describes the persecution that followed Stephen's death (Acts 8:1–3), he admits that the apostles stayed in Jerusalem although others left the city as a result of the persecution (Acts 8:1). It is probable that this early persecution concerned only a more specific group that had presented far-reaching views related to the temple or circumcision but not all who believed in Jesus. Cf. Räisänen, *The Rise*, 59–60. Some early Christians later faced death at the hands of their Jewish opponents; Josephus states that James, the brother of Jesus, was executed by the high priest Ananus II (Ant. 20.199–203), and Luke relates how Herod Agrippa I killed James, the brother of John (Acts 12:1–3). However, each of these cases has its own distinctive features, and the reasons behind them may have varied. As E.P. Sanders has remarked, early Christian authors quite commonly saw every single martyrdom as a sign of general persecution and thought that Jesus' followers were persecuted "for the sake of Christ" or "for his name's sake". The historical problem in these accounts, however, is "that we cannot be sure what it was that the *other* side, those inflicting the punishment, found offensive". See E.P. Sanders, *Jesus and Judaism* (London: SCM Press, 1985), 284.

persecution of early Christians, especially in the years after the destruction of the temple, we should be cautious about overestimating the scale of Christian persecutions by other Jews. It is clear that the collective sense of being a martyr or victim quite soon became an inseparable part of early Christian self-understanding.[115] In the following, I do not deny that some Christians understood they were persecuted because of their faith in Jesus. However, I suggest that some recent studies dealing with collective victimhood, recollections of historical victimization and experiences of collective guilt or blame can be helpful in explaining why the majority of early Christians saw not only Jesus but also themselves as hated without a cause even though only a few among them may have had any firsthand evidence of actual persecutions.

Daniel Bar-Tal and his colleagues have examined the sense of victimhood from a social identity perspective and introduced the concept of self-perceived collective victimhood. They define collective victimhood "as a group mindset resulting from the perceived intent of another group to inflict harm on the collective".[116] In the context of actual intergroup conflicts, many communities or societies "believe that their goals in conflict are well-justified, perceive their own group in a very positive light, and delegitimize the rival". Therefore, collective victimhood often "constitutes an inseparable part of the shared narrative among society members as constructed in their collective memory of the conflict and ethos of conflict, and denotes that the rival group continuously inflicted unjust and immoral harm upon them throughout the conflict".[117] The sense of being a victim is appealing because a victim's position is viewed as "morally superior, entitled to sympathy and consideration and protected from criticism. As a result, a collective may cultivate the image of being a victim and embed it in their culture".[118]

115 Cf. E. Castelli, *Martyrdom and Memory: Early Christian Culture Making* (New York: Columbia University Press, 2004), 34–5. Castelli examines "the cultural production of a narrative of martyrdom among early Christians" and concludes that "meaningful suffering is always already present in the Christian worldview as a fundamental interpretative category, and Christian theorists repeatedly connect it to earlier textual remnants of such suffering". C. Moss, *The Myth of Persecution: How Early Christians Invented a Story of Martyrdom* (New York: HarperOne, 2013). Moss speaks about the emergence of "the myth of persecution" and "the invention of persecuted church" among Christian theologians in the first centuries. According to Moss, the formation of this myth was strategic, and persecution and martyrdom became "polarizing rhetorical tools" because they were "used in order to exclude and suppress other groups, to identify them with demonic forces, and to legitimize rhetorical and perhaps also literal violence against them" (p. 246).

116 D. Bar-Tal/ S. Cehajic-Clancy, "From Collective Victimhood to Social Reconciliation: Outlining a Conceptual Framework", In D. Spini/G. Elcheroth/D. Corkalo Biruski (ed.), *War, Community, and Social Change: Collective Experiences in the Former Yugoslavia* (New York: Springer, 2014) 125–36, on p. 127.

117 D. Bar-Tal/L Chernyak-hai/N. Shori/A. Gundar, "A Sense of Self-Perceived Collective Victimhood in Intractable Conflicts", *International Review of the Red Cross* 91 (2009) 229–58, on p. 230.

118 Bar-Tal *et al.*, "A Sense", 237.

The results and examples presented by Bar-Tal and his colleagues are consistent with a number of studies dealing with recollections of historical victimization and experiences of collective guilt or blame.[119] These studies have provided empirical proof that groups often ascribe guilt by association to contemporary members of an outgroup on the basis of events that have taken place in the distant past. Various communities may "encode important experiences, especially extensive suffering, in their collective memory, which can maintain a sense of woundedness and past injustice through generations".[120] Accordingly, members of a collective may have a shared sense of victimhood that has resulted from events that only some – past and contemporary – members have themselves experienced.[121]

The previously mentioned studies cannot explain the details of an alleged conflict between Johannine Christians and their Jewish neighbors. However, these studies explain how the remembrance of Jesus as an innocent victim became an important building block in the innovation of collective Christian identity. The collective sense of victimhood contributed especially to the construction of symbolic boundaries between emerging early Christian communities and other Jews, which is already seen in the passion narratives of the gospels. Scholars have long been aware that there is a clear tendency in

119 B. Doosje/N.R. Branscombe, "Attributions for the Negative Historical Actions of a Group" *EJSP* 33 (2003) 235–48; M.J.A. Wohl/N.R. Branscombe, "Forgiveness and Collective Guilt Assignment to Historical Perpetrator Groups Depend on Level of Social Category Inclusiveness", *JPSP* 88 (2005) 288–303; M.J.A. Wohl/N.R. Branscombe/Y. Klar, "Collective Guilt: Emotional Reactions When One's Group Has Done Wrong or Been Wronged", *ERSP* 17 (2006) 1–37; B. Lickel/N. Miller/D.M. Sternstrom/T.A. Denson/T. Schmader, "Vicarious Retribution: The Role of Collective Blame in Intergroup Aggression", *Personality and Social Psychology Review* 10 (2006) 372–90.

120 Bar-Tal *et al.*, "A Sense", 236. Cf. Wohl *et al.*, "Collective Guilt", 24: "Group members frequently discuss historical harms as if they had occurred only yesterday. As a result, contemporary members of the perpetrator group may be linked to their ancestors who committed the wrongs through shared category membership." Wohl/Branscombe, "Forgiveness," 288: "Transgressions committed against members of the ingroup in the past can evoke emotional responses that are as intense as those for harmdoing committed more recently. … people speak of atrocities committed against their group without necessarily differentiating between events that occurred yesterday, a decade ago, or hundreds of years ago. Emotional responses based on category membership can traverse generations, with the ancestors who committed the wrong and contemporary members of the perpetrator group being linked by a common category membership."

121 Bar-Tal *et al.*, "A Sense", 234: "Just as individuals experience a sense of victimhood because of personal experiences, collectives such as ethnic groups may also experience this sense. It may result from events that harm the members of the collective because of their membership, even if not all the group members experience the harm directly. Groups can suffer from collective victimization which, similarly to individual victimization, is not based only on an objective experience but also on the social construction of it." Lickel *et al.*, "Vicarious Retribution", 380: "Perceptions of 'bad character' … influence how people assign blame. We hypothesize that if one outgroup member attacks an ingroup member, people may perceive that other outgroup members share the same blameworthy qualities that define the provocateur."

passion narratives to accentuate the involvement and responsibility of Jewish leaders or sometimes even Jews in general for Jesus' crucifixion, even though it is historically more probable that the Roman governor, Pontius Pilate, jointly with the Jewish priestly establishment close to him, played a major part in the events leading to Jesus' death.[122] For the members of John's imagined community too, the sense of collective victimhood provided a rationale for their perceived marginalization from the world represented in the Gospel by the Jews.

Conclusion

In this article, I have examined how an ideal portrait of the community of Jesus' followers is created in the Gospel of John. I have approached this portrait as a symbolic, imagined construction and left aside the question how closely – or if at all – this portrait reflects any real-life concerns in the community where the Gospel and the three Johannine Epistles emerged. As a matter of fact, John's vision of imagined community is intangible and unspecific, which frustrates our attempts to reconstruct the sociohistorical situation of the Johannine community in any more detail. John's portrait of the community is embedded in a mythical framework and language since he presents this community as founded by the eternal Word who brought the light into the darkness of the world, where his followers are known for holding fast to his commandment of mutual love in the face of the hostility of the surrounding world. However, it can be argued that it is precisely the elusiveness of John's symbolic community that has enabled its later applications to various new and unpredictable contexts. The capacity of symbols is exactly that they "encompass and condense a range of … meanings" and in this way are

> always multi-faceted and frequently implicit or taken for granted in their definition. As a consequence, people can to some degree bestow their own meanings on and in symbols: they can say and do the "same" things without saying or doing the same things at all.[123]

The main features in John's symbolic and imagined community have become so self-evidently implanted in Christian self-understanding that it is probably impossible for many Christians to challenge them in any way. This can also be seen as a special accomplishment of the Johannine author, who has been able to essentialize a group identity that was actually blurred and in the making. For those of us who struggle with applying John's portrait of imagined

122 See R. Hakola, "Anti-Judaism, Anti-Semitism in the New Testament and Its Interpretation", in Steven L. McKenzie (ed.), *The Oxford Encyclopedia of Biblical Interpretation* (Oxford: Oxford University Press, 2013) 27–35.

123 Jenkins, *Social Identity*, 139.

community in our pluralistic and multicultural societies, John's achievement may appear as too exclusive and one-dimensional.[124] But the first step in the construction of new, and perhaps more open, Christian imagined communities, is to decode what John presents as fixed and timeless and understand it as socially constructed.

124 Cf. Segovia, "John 1.1–18", 59. "[John's vision], therefore, is a vision of oppression for humanity, a classic example of 'othering,' whereby all those who disagree with the vision and opt for a different path are regarded as misguided and antagonistic." D.M. Smith, "The Epistles of John: What's New Since Brooke's ICC in 1912?" *ExpTim* 120 (2009) 373–83, on p. 381: "In our age of the conflict of competing claims within and among religions, the Johannine posture appears to be less than helpful. Ironically, the Gospel that compresses Jesus' teaching into the command to love one another (13:34) and the Epistle that characterizes God himself as love (1 John 4:8, 16) seem to approve the most extreme dismissal of those who are deemed to reject the right confession or doctrine. The sympathetic commentator, whether or not Christian, tends to side with the ancient author. But should the modern commentator, least of all a Christian commentator, do so without reservation?"

Nina Nikki

Contesting the Past, Competing over the Future: Why is Paul Past-Oriented in Galatians and Romans, but Future-Oriented in Philippians?

Introduction

Paul's letters to the Galatians, Romans and Philippians are generally considered to be the central texts where Paul argues against circumcision and Law observance for Gentile Christ-believers. These letters show Paul in the process of defining and strengthening the identity of a Gentile Christ-believing ingroup against a competing vision of a Jewish Christ-believing outgroup. While the letters differ somewhat in intensity – Romans is more conciliatory than Galatians and Philippians – the line of Paul's argumentation is generally considered to be fairly similar. It has, however, gone with little notice that there is a significant difference between the letters in the temporal orientation of Paul's argumentation. In Galatians and Romans Paul is strongly invested in the past. He devotes considerable space to arguing for Abrahamic ancestry for Gentile Christ-believers (Gal 3–4, Rom 4). The role of the Mosaic Law in salvation history is also discussed and reinterpreted elaborately (Gal 3–4, Rom 7). The letter to the Philippians, on the other hand, is significantly less interested in the past and much more oriented to the future. The letter bears no mention of Abraham and makes no attempt to provide a fictive Jewish ancestry for the Gentile believers. In fact, references to the Philippian addressees' past before their conversion are missing completely. Unlike Galatians in particular, Philippians contains several references to the future and depicts the apocalyptic victory of the ingroup over the outgroup at Christ's *parousia.*

This article describes how Paul in Galatians, Romans and Philippians strengthens the social identity of the addressees by actively shaping their past and future. An explanation is also offered as to why these letters reflect very different temporal approaches. The social psychological *social identity approach* will be used as a general theoretical backdrop, as it works well in detecting elements of identity construction and maintenance in intergroup conflict situations. Special emphasis will also be given to the concept of *social time* and, as far as the group past is concerned, to *social memory.* Furthermore, the concept of *possible social identities*, as presented by Marco Cinnirella, is applied as a helpful link in combining the notion of social identity with temporal aspects. Inasmuch as Paul acts as an entrepreneur of the addressees' possible past and future identities, the question of Paul's *leadership* will also be of interest.

The article argues that Paul integrates Gentile Christ-believers into the historical narrative of Israel in a positive way only when the situation demands it. The matter is similar and related to the question of Paul's teaching on righteousness, which is often viewed as a reactive, polemical doctrine and not something idiosyncratic to Paul's message for the Gentiles. When unchallenged by Jewish reconstructions of the past, Paul seems to have described Gentile history negatively as suspicious idol worship, from which Christ has provided salvation. The focus of the story seems to have been on an apocalyptic depiction of a glorious future. This article argues that this is also the narrative reflected in Paul's letter to the Philippians. The Gentile audience is not offered a role in Israelite history, since it was not yet acquainted with the opponents and their rival reconstruction of history.

Social memory, possible social identities and leadership in inter-group conflict

"A subjective sense of endurance over time and space" is generally regarded a central feature of personal identity.[1] In terms of group-based social identities, however, research on the aspect of time has thus far been somewhat neglected. This is perhaps surprising, since it is the social identity – and not the personal identity – which actually has the capacity to extend in time beyond the individual's birth and death.[2] Susan Condor, for example, criticizes the way social categories are often viewed and investigated as overly context-contingent, static and reified entities.[3] She claims that a unilateral emphasis on "flexibility in microtime" to the effect of exclusion of large scale continuity was not the original intention of even Henri Tajfel, who was interested in "theorizing social relations in macrotime" while remaining aware of their contextual variability.[4] Condor urges instead to consider groups as ongoing

1 See examples in S. Condor, "Social Identity and Time", in P. Robinson (ed.), *Social Groups and Identities: Developing the Legacy of Henri Tajfel* (Oxford: Butterworth Heinemann, 1996) 285–315, quote on p. 303. For recent emphasis on *narrative identity* in personality psychology see D.P. McAdams, "Personal Narratives and the Life Story", in O.P. John/R.W. Robins/L.A. Pervin (ed.), *Handbook of Personality: Theory and Research* (3rd ed.; New York: Guilford Press, 2008) 242–62.

2 Condor, "Social Identity and Time", 306.

3 Condor, "Social Identity and Time", 302. Condor claims that the temporal, continuous aspect has been neglected by social identity theorists partly because laboratory experiments are necessarily synchronic in nature ("Social Identity and Time", 292–3).

4 Condor, "Social Identity and Time", 290. Accordingly, she suggests "social identity theorists should not focus on the question of psychological plasticity in microtime at the expense of appreciating trajectories of human activity over macrotime." ("Social Identity and Time", 302).

processes, where "the social world is constructed through the serial linking of events and the serial transmission of action and information between social actors and local domains."[5]

Condor takes up two ways in which time is relevant to the subjective experience of participation in a group. The first one concerns the management of time and space in a group, and especially the sense of temporal co-ordination and synchronicity between members.[6] A diachronic aspect, on the other hand, is perceived through the idea of participation in successive generations of the group, which extend to the past as well as the future.[7] This means that social categories can indeed be experienced and viewed as durable "historical processes".[8] Condor also stresses that when commitment to the group is emphasized, membership can be understood as involuntary and "ontological" (reflected in e.g. kinship language) as opposed to being voluntary and transient.[9]

Theories of social memory (or collective memory) provide a suitable framework for investigating the formation and function of a group's views of its past. The theories argue that memory is essentially social in nature,[10] and that recollections of the past are formulated mainly in order to serve present needs. Accordingly, history is essentially viewed as "a symbolic reserve",[11] and current interpretations of the past are understood as constructions, even to the point that a narrative concerning the past should be seen as "not so much a window onto the cognitive workings of [the person's] memory but rather as a description or performance designed for specific pragmatic and rhetorical purposes".[12] While there is wide agreement about a social and constructed element in memory, differences still remain between those, who view the past from a decidedly "presentist" point of view and those who insist that

5 Condor, "Social Identity and Time", 291.

6 Condor, "Social Identity and Time", 300–302, 306.

7 In the words of the historian of philosophy, David Carr, in his *Time, Narrative, and History* (Bloomington: Indiana University Press, 1991), 133–4: "the *we* with whose experience the individual identifies can both pre-date and survive the individuals that make it." (quoted at length also by Condor, "Social Identity and Time", 306).

8 Condor, "Social Identity and Time", 305.

9 Condor, "Social Identity and Time", 306–7.

10 M. Halbwachs, *On Collective Memory. Edited, Translated, and with an Introduction by Lewis A. Coser* (Chicago & London: University of Chicago Press, 1992), 38 deplores that in the psychology of his day memory was investigated by viewing individuals as "isolated beings", ignoring "all the bonds which attach individuals to the society of their fellows". Conversely, Halbwachs claims that "it is in society that people normally acquire their memories. It is also in society that they recall, recognize, and localize their memories."

11 A. Haslam et al., *The New Psychology of Leadership: Identity, Influence and Power* (Hove: Psychology Press, 2011), 178 quoting A. Reszler, "L'Europe à la recherche de ses symboles", *Les Temps Modernes* 550 (1992).

12 P. Esler, *Identity and Conflict in Romans: The Social Setting of Paul's Letter* (Minneapolis: Fortress Press, 2003), 175.

narratives of the past always require an interplay between memory retrieval and creativity and, thus, represent a mix of continuity and change.[13]

That expectations concerning the future are also constructed is perhaps easier to grasp. Just like stories concerning the past, beliefs about the future are also used in the formation and maintenance of present identity. Condor, however, underlines that groups are not always simply reactive but can also be genuinely anticipatory in their beliefs. Thus, while future expectations often serve to promote positive distinctiveness in the now, they can also aim to ensure the reproduction of the group across time and encourage change in group behaviour and status.[14]

Marco Cinnirella has developed a helpful tool for discussing social identity in temporal terms. He builds on the theory of *possible selves* by Hazel Markus and Paula Nurius (1986), where possible selves represent "individuals' beliefs about what the self was in the past and might become in the future, together with some estimate of the probability that different possible selves will be realized."[15] While Markus and Nurius concentrate on individual self-conception, Cinnirella extends the concept to social identities, with an aim to clarifying and extending the discussion in SIA about "cognitive alternatives" to identity.[16] Cinnirella suggests that "one particular kind of possible self is a *possible social identity*", meaning "perceptions of current and possible group memberships".[17] This entails the tendency to "fantasize ... about what might happen to current groups in the future", but also about "what it might have been like to have been a member of a particular group in the past."[18] The importance of group prototypes in this process has been emphasized lately.[19]

13 In his introduction to a translation of Maurice Halbwachs' work, Lewis A. Coser (*On Collective Memory*, 25–6) takes up the difference between Halbwachs and Barry Schwartz in this area. While Halbwachs was more "presentist", Schwartz in turn stressed that the past is formed of both memory retrieval and creativity. Coleman Baker also stresses the limits of reinterpretation. See, C. Baker, "A Narrative Model for Biblical Interpretation: The Role of Memory and Narrative in Social Identity Formation", in J.B. Tucker/C.A. Baker (ed.), *T & T Clark Handbook to Social Identity in the New Testament* (London, New York: T & T Clark & Bloomsbury, 2014) 105–18, on p. 111.

14 Condor, "Social Identity and Time", 305. Consult Esler, *Identity and Conflict*, 259 for newer perspectives which stress that myths about the future do not only justify the foundations of social order but can also stress its goal and promote change.

15 Summary by M. Cinnirella, "Exploring Temporal Aspects of Social Identity: The Concept of Possible Social Identities", *European Journal of Social Psychology* 28 (1998) 227–48, on p. 229. See e.g. H. Markus & P. Nurius, "Possible Selves", *American Psychologist* 41 (1986) 954–69.

16 Cinnirella, "Temporal Aspects", 228, 241–2. In SIA the question of cognitive alternatives to identity is generally discussed in terms of an individual's beliefs concerning his/her possibility to change groups or the possibility that a group can improve its status.

17 Cinnirella, "Temporal Aspects", 230.

18 Cinnirella, "Temporal Aspects", 231.

19 Emphasized in NT research by Esler, *Conflict and Identity*, 172 and Baker "A Narrative Model", 110–11. A prototype is "a summary representation that is considered to capture the central tendency of the category", "a person thought to typify the group" and "the image of an ideal person who embodies its character" (Esler, *Conflict and Identity*, 172).

Cinnirella argues that groups, like individuals, will be motivated to "re-interpret and re-construct the past, present and future" in order to achieve a sense of temporal continuity.[20] Even more importantly, various "desired" and "feared" possible selves have the potential to add to a group's positive distinctiveness or to diminish it.[21] In fact, Cinnirella claims that the drive to attain desired identities and to avoid feared ones directly impacts behaviour and motivation related to social identity maintenance.[22]

The role of the past and the future in identity maintenance means that they have a significant role in intergroup relations. Both the past and the future function as domains of social contest: groups compete over the ownership and interpretation of collective memory as well as over the future possibilities.[23] One group can challenge "the legitimacy of [another group's] past-oriented and desired possible social identity".[24] Naturally, the same happens in relation to the future desired/feared identities as well, for example, when an outgroup is cursed to future damnation in religious discourse.

Leaders are ideally active entrepreneurs of group identity.[25] Consequently, they also play a significant role in reconstructing the past and the future in a way that helps to form and maintain positive group distinctiveness. Alexander Haslam, Stephen D. Reicher and Michael J. Platow insist that one aspect of a leader's skill as "an artist of identity" is his/her ability to "root their proposals for the group in the sayings of cultural icons, in the received wisdom surrounding formative historical events, in the characterization of kings, liberators, and other group heroes".[26] A good leader is also able to present his/her interpretation of the past as "immutable" and as "the only valid version of identity" – indeed to transform a construction into a "fact".[27] Cinnirella also takes up the question of *source credibility* in relation to leadership. According to him, a possible social identity has a source, which can be the self, other ingroup members, an outgroup or, for example, opinion leaders. The credibility of this source influences the "acceptance of possible social identities and the choice made from competing alternatives".[28] In order to be believable and efficient, a leader then needs to represent prototypicality (to be "one of us"), which, in turn makes it possible for him/her to display creativity (to be an ingroup champion and entrepreneur).[29]

20 Cinnirella, "Temporal Aspects", 235–6.
21 Cinnirella, "Temporal Aspects", 229, 237–42.
22 Cinnirella, "Temporal Aspects", 243.
23 See Esler, *Conflict and Identity*, 175 on contesting the past. In Cinnirella's words: "some intergroup conflicts may be partly caused by struggles between in- and outgroups over the definition of possible social identities" ("Temporal Aspects", 243).
24 Cinnirella, "Temporal Aspects", 242.
25 Haslam et al., *New Psychology*, xxii, 137.
26 Haslam et al., *New Psychology*, 177.
27 Haslam et al., *New Psychology*, 178.
28 Cinnirella, "Temporal Aspects", 231.
29 Haslam et al., *New Psychology*, 107.

Contesting the past in Galatians

It has been noted that present day North Atlantic societies are much more oriented to the future than preindustrial, agrarian cultures, where expressions and expectations concerning the future were generally more attenuated.[30] Furthermore, it has been argued that ethnic and national identities are typically past-oriented.[31] In this light, it is not surprising that the Jewish identity at the turn of the Common Era was particularly anchored in history. The very central tenets included a belief that God played an active role in the history of Israel: he had chosen this particular people, liberated it from slavery in Egypt and, at a specific time in history, given it a Law to follow and obey. This interest in the past manifested itself in a deep sense of ethnic continuity and a special emphasis on common ancestry.

In Galatia, the outgroup Paul opposes had made an appeal to this Jewish past and suggested that the Galatian Gentile Christ-believers could and should join this historical lineage through circumcision and observance of the Mosaic Law. The Galatian Christ-believers were thus presented with a desired possible past social identity. Instead of remembering their past as one of Gentile idol worship (Gal 4:8), they were invited to rewrite their collective history. They could tap into an honourable Jewish history and view themselves as heirs of Abraham. The extreme flexibility of social memory and social identity is apparent in that the outgroup is able to offer a very "genetic" and "involuntary" ethnic ancestry through a choice that was, in reality, very voluntary, contingent and, as is evident from Paul's response, quite contestable.

While the outgroup seems to follow a fairly standard Jewish view of proselytism, Paul contests it with a more unusual interpretation of the Jewish past. It is noteworthy that Paul does not completely negate the opponents' interpretation, but seeks to incorporate the most desirable parts of their story into his own. Paul's tactic is to rewrite the more traditional view of Jewish history in order to wrest it away from the opponents and to claim it for the Gentile believers *without the demand of circumcision and Law observance.* It is important to notice that Paul's reinterpretation of Scriptural history does not take place in a vacuum, but amid a fierce competitive social situation.[32]

Philip Esler suggests convincingly that the opponents in Galatia did not mention Abraham only because circumcision and Abraham were so closely linked in Gen 17, as if circumcision was the primary interest of the

30 Esler, *Conflict and Identity*, 257.

31 Cinnirella, "Temporal Aspects", 236.

32 Esler, *Conflict and Identity*, 176–7 rightly notes the one-sidedness of Richard Hays' literary approach to Paul's reinterpretation of Scripture in *Echoes of Scripture in the Letters of Paul* (New Haven: Yale University Press, 1989). Instead, Esler calls for a deeper understanding of the "social processes", especially group competition, behind the reinterpretations.

opponents.[33] Rather, Abraham was valuable in himself as a prototype and as an ancestor to be gained by joining the Jewish people.[34] Paul does not rule out or deny this valuable prototype, but manipulates it heavily. In Paul's version the Gentile Christ-believers already belong to the Abrahamic lineage through belief in Christ. This means there is no need for circumcision. Paul insists on the fictive kinship of Gentile believers with Abraham, but through a rationalisation which differs significantly from the opponents' version (Gal 3:7).[35] As for the Mosaic Law, the opponents rely on it strongly and most likely assume that it is eternally valid. Paul again does not deny the historical event of the giving of the Law per se, but casts a suspicious shadow over the incident: the Law was perhaps not even given by God but merely by angels (Gal 3:19–20).[36] In Paul's interpretation the Law was only valid for an intermediate period, but no longer has a function after Christ (Gal 3:24–25). Thus, Paul does give the Law a role in the past, but only a negative one. It was a past prison (maybe even a mistake or deception of some kind?) from which the ingroup has been "saved" (Gal 4:5). The fact that Abraham is retained for the ingroup, whereas the Law is not, testifies to the importance of prototypes for the construction of social identities and collective memories.

Paul's reinterpretation of Scriptural history in Galatians is very exclusive in nature. In Romans he can at least once portray the Gentiles as being grafted into an olive tree of Israel and granted only a secondary status in the narrative of Israel (Rom 11:17–24). But in Galatians he does not settle for this. According to Paul, those who rely on faith in Christ, in fact, have the only legitimate claim to Abrahamic ancestry, as they descend from Abraham through Christ ("the seed", Gal 3:15–18) in a higher, spiritual manner. They are children of the promise, who receive the promised spirit (Gal 3:14). The opponents, on the other hand, can only claim a fleshly connection to Abraham (Gal 4:23), which makes them nothing but sons of Hagar and slaves. Thus, the narrative is also constructed with a view to attacking and denigrating the opponents and towards generating a maximal positive distinctiveness for the ingroup at the expense of the opponents.[37]

33 Esler, *Galatians* (London: Routledge, 1998), 73–4 argues that commensality was, in fact, the main exigency, to which the opponents suggested circumcision as a solution.

34 Esler, *Conflict and Identity*, 181–2 ("Get circumcised ... and you will gain Abraham ... as your glorious ancestor.")

35 See Esler, *Conflict and Identity*, 180–94 for both the differences and similarities in the treatment of Abraham in Galatians and Romans: in both Abraham constitutes a prototype, but in Rom Abraham legitimates both ethnic groups (which are not erased) in the Roman church and helps recategorise them.

36 H. Räisänen, *Paul and the Law* (WUNT 29; Tübingen: J.C.B. Mohr [Paul Siebeck], 1983), 128–33, esp. p. 130.

37 Esler, *Conflict and Identity*, 182–3 (also p. 31) discusses the dividing line between insiders and outsiders in the text. J.L. Martyn, *Theological Issues in the Letters of Paul* (Edinburgh: T & T Clark, 1997) and Esler agree that in Gal Paul seems to suggest that only the non-Jewish Christ-followers were children of Abraham and Sarah. This interpretation of Gal is possible and would,

The role of future expectation in Galatians is conspicuously scarce.[38] Altogether three very concise and conventional references to the future appear in Gal 5:5, 21b; 6:7–9. The first one presents a desired future identity, connects it with righteousness, and juxtaposes it with a feared identity outside Christ for those who let themselves be circumcised (Gal 5:4). The other two references are farther removed from the question of circumcision and represent quite conventional ethical exhortation. The second one (5:21b) visualises a feared future identity outside the kingdom of God as punishment for ethical misbehaviour (represented by a conventional list of vices).[39] The third one (6:7–9) expresses both the feared and desired future scenarios that follow from chosen ethical conduct; destruction and eternal life respectively. Although the future is thus clearly referred to, it is significant that the letter lacks any fuller apocalyptic speculation and does not, for example, mention Christ's *parousia* at all.

A simple explanation for the scarcity of future-oriented material in Galatians is that Paul is mainly following the agenda set by the opponents.[40] It has often been argued that Paul's teaching concerning righteousness is a "secondary crater" and "polemical doctrine", which he formulates only in the context of conflict with Jewish Christian opponents.[41] The same seems to be

of course, be viewed negatively by Jews. But it can hardly be what Paul has in mind. After all, he himself (as a Christ-believer of Jewish birth, 2:15) is clearly among the descendants of Abraham. I believe the dividing line exists between those who agree and disagree with Paul and his view of the past.

38 J.C. Beker, *Paul the Apostle. The Triumph of God in Life and Thought* (Philadelphia: Fortress Press, 1980), 58 states that in Gal "the eschatological present dominates the letter" and that "if we ignore the future apocalyptic hints in Galatians, the letter can easily be interpreted as a document of realised eschatology by a Paul who is 'the greatest of all Gnostics'". According to Y. Kwon, *Eschatology in Galatians* (WUNT 2. Reihe 183; Tübingen: Mohr Siebeck, 2004), 1–2 the traditional view of Galatians is one where Paul exhibits a form of realised eschatology (in a loose sense), that is, he stresses the realised aspect of salvation without being non-eschatological. Kwon himself argues that Gal is a future oriented letter, in which Paul counters the apostatising behaviour of the Galatians by warning them about future repercussions of backsliding. Kwon interprets the themes of justification, inheritance and kingdom of God in Gal as referring to future realities (see e.g. *Eschatology*, 213–14). In fact, Kwon argues (not convincingly to my mind) that "the future eschatological outlook of Galatians ... is similar to that in 1 Thessalonians" (*Eschatology*, 220).

39 In fact, the two lists of opposing behaviour may relate, respectively, to the two sons of Abraham mentioned in Gal 4 (Esler, *Galatians*, 227).

40 Beker, *Paul the Apostle*, 57–8: "The situation also dictates the virtual absence of an otherwise central feature in Paul's letters – the future apocalyptic dimension." He notes also that the theme of Christ's resurrection, the basis for future apocalyptic, is nearly missing.

41 According to W. Wrede, teaching related to righteousness is "the *polemical doctrine* of Paul" and "only made intelligible by the struggle of his life, his controversy with Judaism and Jewish Christianity, and is only intended for this." W. Wrede, *Paul* (trans. by E.W. Lummis; London: Philip Green, 1907), 122. A. Schweitzer famously depicts the doctrine of righteousness from faith as a "subsidiary crater" to the "mystical doctrine of redemption through the being-in-Christ".

the case with regard to the Jewish past: the Gentile believers are fitted into the story of Israel only when the opponents have already introduced the possibility. Consequently, the question arises as to how Paul had presented the Galatian Gentile believers' past *before* this conflict. I believe it is likely that he did not offer any positive history for them. Rather, the past was explained in very grim terms: the Gentile believers were nothing but idol worshippers doomed to destruction before Christ saved them. That this was probably Paul's reconstruction of the Galatian Gentile believers' past is reflected in Gal 4:8, where he claims that the Galatians "formerly ... did not know God" and "were slaves to those who by nature are not gods". The same idea appears in other letters addressed to similar audiences. The Thessalonian believers, for example, are commended for having "turned to God from idols" (1 Thess 1:9). The inability to provide a positive history in a cultural context that strongly valued the past may have been a serious disadvantage for Paul, and it could easily explain the willingness of the Galatians to lend an eager ear to the opponents.

Unlike the Thessalonian church, the Galatian ones consisted of both Jewish and Gentile members, whom Paul attempts to portray as a new entity of equals, "a new creation" where "neither circumcision counts for anything, nor uncircumcision" (Gal 6:15). The inability, however, to provide a positive history for Gentile members may have presented a source of serious inequality and envy inside the churches. Accordingly, it could be argued that Paul, in Galatians, does wisely when he does not try to completely deny the opponents' offer of a positive and legitimate past for the Gentiles, but recognises the value of the project and attempts to build on it.[42]

Despite this it is often argued that the letter to the Galatians ultimately turned out to be unsuccessful.[43] One reason for this could be the exclusive nature of Paul's reconstruction, which leaves no room for traditional Jewish ethnic identity.[44] The question of *source credibility* in proposing possible

A. Schweitzer, *The Mysticism of Paul the Apostle* (trans. by William Montgomery; Baltimore: Johns Hopkins University Press, 1998 [orig. 1931]), 225.

42 Esler (*Galatians*, 88–9) suggests that the way Paul constantly emphasizes the separate identity of the Galatian believers' group actually reveals that they had not been completely successful in forming them into a united "third group", either among themselves or in relation to the surrounding society. What I suggest here is that a lack of common history was another factor which added to the instability by 1) creating inequality among the Christ-believing members and 2) by inviting a solution to the problem by Jewish Christian outsiders.

43 Martyn, *Theological Issues*, 37–45; Esler, *Conflict and Identity*, 31.

44 Esler, *Conflict and Identity*, 31 believes this is what Paul in Rom tries to correct with his more inclusive stance. I think it is also doubtful whether Paul's story had the resources to challenge the opponents' offer on a concrete social level. Identification with Jews and their ancestral past was probably attractive for the Galatian Gentile Christ-believers not only for theological but also for political reasons. The Roman society held a deep-seated respect for ancestral tradition, and the fact Jews had a long and solid history seems to have been a major reason behind Roman leniency towards them. Paul's solution to provide the Gentiles with fictive Jewish ancestry would, ho-

social identities may be another one. If, as I believe, the opponents appealed to the Jerusalem leadership to back up their message,[45] Paul would have appeared less credible in comparison. Furthermore, in Galatians Paul fails to present a sufficient level of prototypicality in leadership. He not only stresses his own superior background (Gal 2:15), but frequently comes off as arrogant (Gal 1:6; 2:6; 3:1, 3), egotistical (Gal 1:12) and domineering (Gal 6:17).

Unity through a shared past in Romans

In Romans Paul repeats much of the same narrative as in Galatians. The situation, however, is not one of response to an outside threat. The emphasis has changed from the sharp discontinuity[46] and polarization of Galatians to an attempt to mediate between Jewish and non-Jewish believers in the Roman church.[47] As Philip Esler has pointed out, in Romans Paul is mediating between two parties by recategorising them into a new, common identity. This requires that the existing ethnic identities are maintained.[48]

In Romans Paul is chiefly interested in proving – not only that Gentiles receive righteousness through faith – but that God is the God of many people and that Abraham is the father of both Jews and Gentiles (4:16).[49] While in Galatians Abraham's circumcision is not mentioned at all, here it is taken up in a somewhat positive sense, and defined as the seal of that righteousness, which Abraham had *before* being circumcised (Rom 4:11). However, the distance to

wever, have had the potential to convince only those who were drawn to circumcision for *theological* reasons. It would not have been helpful in dealings with the outside Gentile society inasmuch as the non-Christian Jews would not have recognised these Gentiles as part of the group without physical circumcision. The opponents, on the other hand, could offer concrete, tangible relief for the Gentile Christ-believers.

45 Esler, *Galatians*, 74, too, allows the "involvement" of Jerusalem representatives. In my dissertation (Opponents and Identity in the Letter to the Philippians, Diss.; University of Helsinki, 2015) I argue that the Galatian crisis was a natural corollary to the Jerusalem meeting and the Antioch incident, and most likely involved the same players. The South-Galatian hypothesis explains why actions were quite naturally taken in Galatia of all places, as the church was an affiliate of the Antioch church and founded during Paul and Barnabas' first missionary journey. I also suggest that the vague "third party", often assumed to be the source of disagreement, is a Lukan creation designed to salvage his image of a harmonious relationship between Paul and Jerusalem.

46 Beker, *Paul the Apostle*, 100: "a sharp Christocentric discontinuity in salvation-history".

47 Esler, *Conflict and Identity*, 31 believes that when Paul wrote to the Roman congregations he needed to "build up the Judean side", and that the effort is visible in the different Abraham of Rom 4 and the pro-Judean sentiments in various part of Rom 9–11.

48 Esler, *Conflict and Identity*, 177–8. Recategorisation means "redefining a situation of conflict so that members of rival groups (or subgroups antagonistic to one another) are subsumed into a larger single, superordinate category" (Esler, *Conflict and Identity*, 29).

49 Beker, *Paul the Apostle*, 100.

the traditional Jewish view of the past is highlighted in that righteousness preceding the circumcision actually replaces the traditional Jewish view of the covenant made in and at circumcision.[50] Paul's reinterpretation of the past is really not so conciliatory: even those of Jewish background are required to trace their connection to Abraham from the righteousness preceding circumcision (Rom 4:12). The "true Jew" mirrors the believing Abraham. This means that agreement with Paul's reconstruction of the past is, again, necessary for being in the right.[51]

In Romans there is more interest in the future than in Galatians. First of all, the division between Gentiles and Jews is blurred by insisting that both are faced with the same desired and feared future identities regardless of their background (2:6–11, 3:5). Paul also frequently refers to the common fate and future of the addressees (e.g. 5:9, 21; 6:23; 8:18). This aligns well with his overall effort to recategorise the addressees into one group – not only by reminding them of what they already share (the past), but also by introducing new common factors (the future).[52]

The future is vividly present in Rom 8:19–39, where Paul depicts a forthcoming transformation of cosmic proportions. The passage does not, however, offer a full apocalyptic myth or any description of the coming kingdom and thus remains markedly different from the apocalyptic sections of, say, 1 Thess 2:19, 3:13, 4:15, 5:23 and 1 Cor 16:17.[53] The text has been deemed non-apocalyptic, and even "anti-apocalyptic", and it has been suggested that Paul there deliberately discourages detailed visualisations of eschatological events and instead ties the future closely with the present.[54] As for the functions of this eschatological passage, Esler suggests, feasibly, that the way the ingroup (which actually represented a "tiny minority") is given a universally significant role in history is designed to strengthen the cognitive, emotional and evaluative aspects of belonging to the group.[55] Furthermore, I consider it possible that the idea of a shared anticipation between the whole creation and the believers further serves to broaden and stress the general theme of unity so important in the letter.

In summary of the findings in Galatians and Romans, it may be noted that in both letters Paul is mainly occupied with reconstructing the past. In both he is faced with a challenge posed by Christ-believers of Jewish background,

50 Esler, *Conflict and Identity*, 189.

51 Beker, *Paul the Apostle*, 100: "The polemic in the dialogue is, to be sure, present: the blindness of the Jew who rejects his forefather Abraham as the one who lives by faith and not by Torah and circumcision ... "

52 Esler, *Conflict and Identity*, 30.

53 Esler, *Conflict and Identity*, 260.

54 Esler, *Conflict and Identity*, 263–4, takes that Paul here deliberately discourages anti-apocalyptic speculation with the view of stressing the present. J.D.G. Dunn, *Romans 9–16* (WBC 38B; Dallas:Word, 1988) 476 claims Paul is here only "non-apocalyptic".

55 Esler, *Conflict and Identity*, 262.

which demands him to rewrite the traditional Jewish history in order to make room for Gentile Christ-believers (as Gentiles). While Romans is clearly more conciliatory, both letters still end up in very radical reinterpretations of the Jewish past. As for the future, neither of the letters engages in elaborate apocalyptic myth: no visualisations of the *parousia* or resurrection are offered.

Forgetting the past and embracing the future in Philippians

In the letter to the Philippians Paul launches into vitriolic attack against the same (or similar) circumcision promoting group as in Galatians. In Phil 3 he begins by calling them "dogs" and "evil workers" (3:2), and ends up equating their observance of food laws with "belly-worship" (3:19).[56] However, whereas Gal and Rom concentrate on countering the same challenge by contesting the traditional view of the Jewish past, Phil on the whole shows significantly less interest in history and invests much more in the future.

The Philippian church is generally considered to consist exclusively of Gentile Christ-believers.[57] While it is reasonable to assume that Paul had originally explained the Philippians' past in the manner of 1 Thess 1:9 and Gal 4:8, it is interesting that there is no mention of the Gentile past of the audience in the letter. Recollections of the Philippians' history reach back only as far as their conversion, from where on Paul rehearses only positive memories: the Philippians have shared in the gospel "from the first day until now" (ἀπὸ τῆς πρώτης ἡμέρας ἄχρι τοῦ νῦν, Phil 1:5) and repeatedly offered Paul financial support (Phil 4:10, 15–16). Even if there was a feared possible identity as Gentile idol worshippers looming in the Philippians' past, Paul chooses not to mention it here. By focusing on the positive memories shared by the

56 There has been disagreement as to whether the accusations of libertinism in Phil 3:18–19 can also be meant to describe the Law-promoting opponents mentioned in Phil 3:2. I believe Paul is here engaging in gross polemical exaggeration and that the same group is most likely in view. For discussion, see N. Nikki, "The Flexible Apostle: Paul's Varied Social Identifications in 1 Corinthians 9 and Philippians 3", in R. Hakola/N. Nikki/U. Tervahauta (ed.), *Others and the Construction of Early Christian Identities* (PFES 106; Helsinki: The Finnish Exegetical Society), 75–101, on p. 91 n. 61, and Nikki, *Opponents*, 207–21.

57 M. Bockmuehl, *The Epistle to the Philippians* (BNTC; London: A & C Black, 1998), 17; M. Tellbe, *Paul between Synagogue and State: Christians, Jews, and Civic Authorities in 1 Thessalonians, Romans and Philippians* (ConBNT 34; Stockholm, Sweden: Almqvist & Wiksell International, 2001), 223. This is supported e.g. by the fact that all the names mentioned in Phil are Latin or Greek (Epaphroditos, Euodia, Syntykhe, Clement). Furthermore, Paul makes in the letter exceptionally little reference to the Hebrew Bible, as noted by e.g. B. Witherington, *Paul's Letter to the Philippians: A Socio-Rhetorical Commentary* (Grand Rapids, Michigan: William B. Eerdmans Publishing Company, 2011), 11–12. In my dissertation I also argue that the way Paul describes Jewish identity markers in Phil suggest a real distance from which the Gentile addressees view Judaism, see N. Nikki, *Opponents*, 159–60.

Philippians and himself, he thus avoids taking the risky step of depicting the letter recipients' past in negative terms.

Not only is the negative Gentile past of the Philippians muted, but – despite the tangible presence of a Jewish Christian challenge in the letter – no real effort is made at reconstructing for the Philippians a Jewish past either. In Phil 3:3 the Gentile believers are called the "true" Circumcision,[58] which could imply that they are the actual heirs of that very history and lineage the Jews entered through circumcision. Nonetheless, this idea is not elaborated in so many words. Interestingly, the concept of *circumcision* is never applied to Gentile believers in Gal and Rom, where it is starkly denied and replaced by belief in Christ as a covenantal entry requirement (e.g. Gal 5:2). This clearly suggests that the Philippians do not have recourse to a previously known story, which is similar to the one in Galatians. Overall, I find it interesting that Paul in Phil does not enter into speculation about Abrahamic descent in the manner of Gal and Rom. In fact, Abraham receives no mention whatsoever. The Philippian Gentile believers are simply not provided with a fictive Jewish ancestry. In fact, the conversion of the Philippians is recalled as "the first day" (1:5), which gives the impression that time itself began at that moment! It is as if life before the conversion does not even exist for the Philippians.

The question of Jewish lineage and past does, however, make an appearance in Paul's rehearsal of his own personal history as a Jew (3:4–6). Paul recounts his ethnic background, circumcision and Law obedience in standard Jewish manner. He follows the traditional Jewish categories even to the point of retaining the concept of righteousness in connection to the Law (emphatically denied for the Jews in Gal!), and suggests that a form of "righteousness according to the Law" is achievable (3:9). But this standard point of view is adopted only in order that Paul may immediately discard his past as "loss" and "garbage" (3:7–8). Thus, the traditional view of the Jewish past is *negated* but not really *reinterpreted.*

There has been reluctance in scholarship to read Paul's denigration of his Jewish past in Phil in all its brutality.[59] However, I have elsewhere argued that the passage should not be harmonised with Paul's other, more lenient

58 The definite article in ἡ περιτομή (viz. e.g. a participial "we are circumcised") justifies the meaning "true". "The Circumcision" was at the time a common shorthand for the Jewish people as an ethnic entity (Gal 2:7–9, Rom 15:8, Eph 2:11). Paul now assumes the term for the ingroup and reversely calls the opponents "The Mutilation" (ἡ κατατομή).

59 G.D. Fee, *Paul's Letter to the Philippians* (NICNT; Grand Rapids: Eerdmans, 1995), 316, for example, uses texts from Romans in order to argue that in Phil Paul does not "wish to renounce what was given to him in birth." J. Reumann, *Philippians. A New Translation with Introduction and Commentary* (New Haven: The Anchor Yale Bible Commentaries, 2008), 473 claims that Paul's invective κατατομή is "not intended against Judaism itself or what Jews do in their community." Bockmuehl, *Philippians*, 204 explains Phil 3:7–8a in relative commercial terms and claims (with Rom 3, 9 and 11 as evidence) that Paul continued to "value" "Israelite inheritance … in its own right" here as well. However, he sees in the reference to σκύβαλα in 3:8 a progress "beyond mere calculation of relative worth to one of emphatic rejection" (p. 207).

statements concerning Judaism (e.g. Rom 9:4–5, 11:1–2, Gal 2:15). Rather, it should be understood as a manifestation of Paul's flexible social identifications.[60] In fact, in 1 Cor 9:20–21 Paul himself testifies that he can be a Jew to the Jews and "one outside the Law" to "those outside the Law". I believe Paul's renouncement of his Jewish past should here be understood as an attempt to identify with the Gentile Philippian believers and to represent *prototypical leadership* in this particular community.[61]

It would be tempting to say that Paul in Philippians attempts to become "a Gentile to Gentiles".[62] In some ways this is indeed the case: Paul, for example, utilises typical Gentile stereotypes of Jews in a way that makes him anti-Jewish (as opposed to merely a representative of "prophetic" insider criticism).[63] The case is, however, not so simple. The suggestion that Paul adopts a Gentile identity, needs to be specified in the light that the Gentile past of the Philippian addressees is erased in the letter. In fact, the similarity between Paul and the Philippians does not only consist of Paul's step to become like the Philippians, but of the fact that *both have rejected their past*, although admittedly quite different ones: the Philippians have become non-Gentiles and Paul has become a non-Jew. In this light it is probably more correct to suggest that Paul in Phil attempts to reinforce a sense of a "Christ identity" pure and simple, with previous identities – his own as well as the addressees' – done away with completely.[64]

60 Nikki, "Flexible Apostle", 97–8. From the view point of personality psychology, it can also be said that Paul exhibits the very typical phenomenon of unstable autobiographical memory. The unstability is not understood simply to result simply from temporal distance and forgetting, but also from new interpretations of the past in the light of the present (McDonald, "Personal Narratives", 246).

61 Nikki, "Flexible Apostle", 94–6. That this was by no means easily done becomes evident from Paul's engagement in *approval-seeking outgroup violation.* Studies have shown that leaders who were unsure of their position are prone to engage in this kind of denigrating categorization between in- and outgroups. See J.M. Rabbie/F. Bekkers, "Threatened Leadership and Intergroup Competition", *European Journal of Social Psychology* 8 (1978) 9–20.

62 Nikki, "Flexible Apostle", 95.

63 D.R.A. Hare, "The Rejection of the Jews in the Synoptic Gospels and Acts", in A.T. Davies (ed.), *Antisemitism and the Foundations of Christianity* (New York and Toronto: Paulist Press, 1979) 27–47, on pp. 28–32 has made a helpful division of types of anti-Judaism, differentiating between prophetic intra-Jewish "anti-Judaism", sectarian Jewish-Christian anti-Judaism and Gentilising anti-Judaism. In Phil 3 Paul can be seen to represent the last type.

64 Recently, J.B. Tucker, *You Belong to Christ: Paul and the Formation of Social Identity in 1 Corinthians 1–4* (Eugene, OR: Pickwick Publications, 2010) has argued that in 1 Cor Paul seeks to clarify "the continuing role of gentile social identity" in the Corinthian church (p. 62) and that Paul's missionary strategy rested on the idea that "Jews remain Jews 'in Christ' while gentiles remain gentiles" (on p. 66). Tucker continues and builds upon the views of W. Campbell, who stresses that Paul did not seek to eradicate ethnic diversity in the churches especially in the sense of forcing Gentiles to become Jews (for a summary of Campbell's "particularistic" view, see Tucker, *You Belong to Christ*, 62–6). I find that Paul presents a very different stance in Philippians. Overall, I believe that Paul's identity discourse should be studied from a contextual point of view which does not require that he adopts a similar outlook in all his churches.

Since the opponents most probably were not present in Philippi, Paul is not tied to their agenda, which concentrated on arguments from the past. Thus he is free to choose the temporal arena for fighting the opponents, and it seems he is more comfortable in doing this through future-related apocalyptic imagery. Why unduly confuse the Gentile Philippians by creating an elaborate, fictive Jewish history for them? Phil 3, in particular, abounds with future-related material: in 3:11 Paul takes up his wish to be resurrected, and the next section 3:12–16 applies athletic imagery of *striving forward* towards the prize of the heavenly call. Paul's disinterest in rewriting the past may well be reflected in his own words about "forgetting what lies behind and straining forward to what lies ahead" (3:13). To top things off, the chapter ends with an explicit treatment of the opponents in the context of apocalyptic imagery. The opponents are depicted as worshippers of the belly and thinkers of earthly things, and contrasted with the glorious future state of the ingroup, who await Lord Jesus Christ as a Savior from heaven. The apocalyptic imagery is a little less detailed than that in 1 Thess 4:16–17 and 1 Cor 15:51–53, but clearly draws on the same tradition.

There has been lively discussion in scholarship about the centre of Paul's thought from a temporal perspective. Some have considered Paul an apocalyptic first and foremost.[65] Others have claimed that "the centre of gravity in Paul's theology lies in the past and not the future".[66] Inasmuch as the "past" in this discussion generally denotes the Christ-event (cross, death, resurrection) there is no reason to argue against it. However, I believe narratives or speculations concerning the pre-conversion past of the members of Paul's Gentile churches were probably of secondary importance. When Gentile converts were in question, Paul would probably concentrate on vivid imagery of future happenings as a means to bring hope and unity to the church. But, as Gal and Rom testify, he could also create an honourable Jewish past for the Gentile believers if the situation and welfare of the community demanded it.

Conclusions

Marco Cinnirella argues that the temporal orientation of a group "will fluctuate depending on contextual factors."[67] It was argued above that Paul engages in reinterpreting the Jewish historical narrative for his ingroup only

65 A strand of interpretation most prominently represented by A. Schweitzer (*Mysticism*, esp. p. 52ff).

66 H. Marshall, "A New Understanding of the Present and the Future: Paul and Eschatology", in R.N. Longenecker (ed.), *The Road from Damascus: The Impact of Paul's Conversion on his Life, Thought and Ministry* (Cambridge: Eerdmans, 1997) 43–61, p. 49. See Kwon, *Eschatology*, 216 n. 1 for more proponents.

67 Cinnirella, "Temporal Aspects", 236–7.

when the context somehow demands it. In Galatians he seeks to counter the historical narrative offered by the Jewish Christian circumcision promoting opponents. In Rome, a Jewish narrative of the past was already in use, because there were Jewish members in the church, and Paul's task is to rewrite the story in a way that creates a shared history and a sense of unity between the Jewish and Gentile members of the church.

In Philippians, however, the social context did not demand a reinterpretation of the Jewish history from the view point of Gentile members. Although Jewish Christian opponents are warned against, they do not seem to have had meaningful contact with the church. The Philippians are not yet familiar with the Jewish Christian reconstruction of the past, so there is no story to be contested or modified. In this context, Philippians follows what I believe to be Paul's usual temporal orientation in fully Gentile churches, and focuses on apocalyptic imagery of the future.

Instead of reminding the Philippians of their suspicious Gentile past, Paul chooses complete reticence over the matter and only recounts the positive past experiences he shares with the Philippians after their conversion. Furthermore, Paul gives an arresting account of a renunciation of his Jewish past in an effort to portray himself as a prototypical leader for the Philippians. It can be argued that, in terms of leadership, Paul displays a much more moderate and skilful approach in Philippians than he had previously done in Galatians.

Martin Wessbrandt

Covenant, Conflict and Collective Identity: The Relationship between Hebrews and *1 Clement*

The close relationship between the canonical letter to the Hebrews and the writing known as *1 Clement* (*circa* 90–120 CE) was recognised early in the church's history, and throughout the centuries many different proposals have been given to how one should understand it. In this essay I will make a contribution to that discussion by investigating some aspects of the construction of collective identity in the letters. They were both written at a time before a concretely "Christian" identity had been formed and they have in common a strong bond to Jewish traditions and concepts. This bond seems, however, to be construed in very different ways in the two letters. By looking at the concept of "covenant" – how it relates to the collective identity construction in the letters – and by comparing them in this regard, I hope to show that the relationship between them involves a certain tension that has often gone unnoticed.

Earlier Discussions of the Relationship

That *1 Clement* was authored by a certain "Clement", who wrote on behalf of the ἐκκλησία of Christ-believers in Rome, is based on an early tradition that many scholars accept still today.[1] Although it is uncertain who this Clement was, there is a consensus among scholars that he wrote the letter in Rome around the turn of the first century CE. The question of who wrote Hebrews is, as is well-known, a mystery, and one which goes back to the first centuries after it was written. It, however, soon became connected with *1 Clement*, since it was noted that the two letters had material in common. The church father Origen mentioned that some people even claimed that Clement was the author of Hebrews (*Hist. Eccl.* VI.25:14). And Eusebius, who maintained that Paul was the author of Hebrews, offered the explanation that Clement had translated the letter into Greek from an original Hebrew version. Clement had later, when he wrote his own letter, "used many thoughts from Hebrews" and even quoted some things literally (*Hist. Eccl.* III.38:1–3).

1 Cf. C. Jefford, *The Apostolic Fathers and the New Testament* (Peabody: Hendricksons, 2006), 17–19.

In modern times, while abandoning the solutions of these church fathers, scholars have still felt a need to explain the connection. In 1911, Edgar Goodspeed argued, in a short article entitled "First Clement Called Forth by Hebrews", that the letter to the Hebrews is to be understood as an exhortation to the Roman "church" to assume responsibility for the spiritual well-being of congregations around the empire. In response to this challenge the Roman congregation soon after receiving Hebrews wrote to Corinth (through the hand of Clement), making use of Hebrews in forty-seven places.[2] According to Goodspeed we cannot "refer this to mere chance coincidence".[3]

The mainstream opinion in modern scholarship about the relationship is, however, not quite as intriguing as that of Goodspeed. Instead, most scholars would probably agree with what William Lane writes in his commentary on Hebrews:

> Hebrews was first known and used in Rome. Clement of Rome, in his pastoral letter to the Corinthians, provides indisputable evidence of the circulation of Hebrews among the churches of Rome. Not only are there striking parallels to the form and statement of Hebrews throughout *1 Clement*, but Clement is literally dependent upon Hebrews in *1 Clem.* 36:1–6.[4]

The similarities between the letters, thus, prove that the author of *1 Clement*, who wrote his letter in the capital (*1 Clem.* pres.), had good knowledge of Hebrews at an early stage. As there is nothing to suggest that Hebrews was known elsewhere before the end of the second century, it is reasonable to suppose that the letter was originally addressed to a Roman gathering of believers. What this hypothesis does not take into account is the tension present in the content of the two letters.

A theory that does capture some of this tension was presented by Raymond Brown. Building on the notion that Roman Christianity derived from the Jerusalem church, Brown proposed that some "conservative Christians" in Rome, after the fall of the temple, "might logically have expected the Jerusalem Temple to be replaced by another earthly sanctuary of a peculiarly Christian character."[5] Through a mirror reading of Hebrews and taking aspects of the content of First Peter (which he also regarded as a Roman document) into account, Brown wondered if it is not plausible that some Roman believers would have thought that

> the Temple was to be replaced by a return to the levitical sacrificial cult of the desert – a cult no longer tied down to a fixed building in Jerusalem and for that reason

2 E.J. Goodspeed, "First Clement Called Forth by Hebrews", *JBL* 30 (1911) 157–60, on p. 158.

3 Goodspeed, "First Clement", 158.

4 W. Lane, *Hebrews 1–8* (WBC 47 A; Waco: Thomas Nelson, 1991), lviii.

5 R. Brown, "Part Two: Rome", in R. Brown/J.P. Meier (ed.), *Antioch & Rome: New Testament Cradles of Catholic Christianity* (Ramsey: Paulist, 1982) 87–216, on p. 153.

suitable to a spiritual Israel in the diaspora; a levitical cult not weighed down by the corruption of wealth and splendor and so more suitable to a pilgrim people?[6]

Brown suggested, well aware that some of these ideas were speculative, that Hebrews was written to correct such hopes. In his estimation, the author of Hebrews wanted the Romans to move in a more "spiritualising" direction in their worship, away from the old outdated orders of the Jewish cult. The author's efforts were, however, moderately successful, as Brown states that, "the Roman church 'domesticated' its [Hebrews'] challenge ... and the end product was a greater attachment at Rome to the levitical cult than Hebrews advocated".[7] The evidence for this Brown finds in *1 Clement*, which he claims is representative of a "revival of cultic terminology in a less spiritualized form".[8] Especially in *1 Clem.* 40:1–5 and 41:2, Brown found that the letter places an "admiring emphasis on the divinely assigned order in the Jerusalem cult and its personnel",[9] something which the author of Hebrews, in Browns estimation, would have been less than content with.

Although Brown's reading of these letters differs from mine in many respects (as will become apparent), and the categories that he used are different from the ones that I will use here, the observation that there is a tension in how these letters used and related to Jewish traditions and institutions raises questions of the type that I will deal with in this essay. Before turning to the investigation of Hebrews and *1 Clement* I shall first discuss the concept of "collective identity" that will be used.

Collective Identity

According to sociologist Richard Jenkins "identification can be defined minimally as the ways in which individuals and collectivities are distinguished in their social relations with other individuals and collectivities".[10] In his book *Social Identity*, Jenkins argues that "all human identities", individual as well as collective, "are by definition *social* identities".[11] By this he means that identification, being a matter of construction of meaning, necessarily involves human interaction and is thus a "social" activity. Identity is never "just there", he claims, but always has to be established through "agreement and disagreement, convention and innovation, communication and negotia-

6 Brown, "Rome", 154.
7 Brown, "Rome", 157.
8 Brown, "Rome", 169.
9 Brown, "Rome", 170.
10 R. Jenkins, *Social Identity* (2nd ed.; Key Ideas; London: Routledge, 2004), 5.
11 Jenkins, *Social Identity*, 4.

tion".[12] Never a finally settled matter, the word "identity" is only to be used, "as long as we remember that it always implies 'identification'. 'It' is *not* a 'thing'."[13]

In coming to the issue of collective identification, Jenkins begins with a discussion of *similarity* and *difference.* These two "criteria of comparison" are namely fundamental, he asserts, to every form of identification.[14] For it to be possible to speak of membership of a collectivity there must be some type of *similarity,* that is, "[p]eople must have something significant in common – no matter how vague, apparently unimportant or illusory".[15] But there has to be *differentiation* as well, as it is not enough to only have things in common. It must be possible to distinguish insiders from outsiders. Jenkins writes:

> Logically, *in*clusion entails *ex*clusion, if only by default. To define the criteria for membership of any set of objects is, at the same time, also to create a boundary, everything beyond which does not belong. It is no different in the human world: one of the things that *we* have in common is our difference from *others.* In the face of their difference our similarity often comes into focus. Defining "us" involves defining a range of "thems" also.[16]

"Boundary" becomes the key word here, as it is the drawing of such that makes identification possible. As he nicely puts it: "Similarity and difference reflect each other across a shared boundary. At the boundary, we discover what we are in what we are not."[17] Recognising these is then the first step in the process of collective identification.

In the next step Jenkins distinguishes conceptually between "two different types of collectivity, and hence two different modes of collective identification".[18] He calls these types "groups" and "categories", and they are said to represent different ways of looking at interaction between individuals. Succinctly described,

> In the first [i. e. groups], the members of a collectivity can identify themselves as such: they know who (and what) they are. In the second [i. e. categories], members may be ignorant of their membership or even of the collectivity's existence. The first exists inasmuch as it is recognised by its members; the second is constituted in its recognition by observers.[19]

12 Jenkins, *Social Identity,* 4.
13 Jenkins, *Social Identity,* 5.
14 Cf. Jenkins, *Social Identity,* 4.
15 Jenkins, *Social Identity,* 79.
16 Jenkins, *Social Identity,* 79. Italics original.
17 Jenkins, *Social Identity,* 79.
18 Jenkins, *Social Identity,* 81.
19 Jenkins, *Social Identity,* 81.

The reason for bringing this distinction up is that it "mirrors routine interactional processes".[20] Jenkins puts it in rather plain language when he writes: "Your external definition of me is an inexorable part of my internal definition of myself – even if I only reject or desist it – and *vice versa*."[21] This is true not only of individual identification but of collective identification also, so that "me" and "my" could just as well be changed into "us" and "our".

Thus far group *formation* has mainly been discussed, but what happens when major differences between members of the same group begin to surface? How can a group overcome the difficulties that arise when its members realise that they, in some matters, have more in common with people *outside* the group than inside? One answer is to "*symbolise belonging*". Theorist Anthony Cohen has written about this as "*the symbolic construction of community*". Jenkins explains this concept writing:

> Differences of opinion and more – of world view, cosmology and other fundamentals – among and between members of the same community are normal, even inevitable. They are masked by a semblance of agreement and convergence generated by shared communal symbols, and participation in a common symbolic discourse of community membership which constructs and emphasises the boundary between members and non-members. Thus members can present a consistent face to the outside world.[22]

Key to Cohen's argument is that the symbols are *ambiguous*, so that members can share them without necessarily meaning the same thing by them. A trivial example that Cohen gives is that of two lovers exchanging an expression of sentiment, telling each other "I love you". In doing so the couple does not feel "the need to engage in a lengthy and complicated disquisition on the meaning of the word 'love'. Yet it is, of course, a word which masks an extremely complex idea."[23] Actually, says Cohen, if they were to explain what they really mean, it is not unlikely that they would end up in a fight over this. The conclusion that Cohen draws is that "symbols are effective because they are imprecise".[24] In the following discussion we will find examples of how community was symbolically constructed in the early Jesus movement. We turn now to the letters of this investigation to see how collective identity is constructed in them.

20 Jenkins, *Social Identity*, 82.
21 Jenkins, *Social Identity*, 25.
22 Jenkins, *Social Identity*, 113.
23 A. Cohen, *The Symbolic Construction of Community* (Key Ideas; London: Routledge, 1985), 21.
24 Cohen, *Symbolic Construction*, 21.

The Letter to the Hebrews and Collective Identity

David deSilva, in his "socio-rhetorical" commentary on Hebrews, writes that: "[i]t is clear that the author of Hebrews envisions two opposing courses of action that lay before his hearers."[25] They can either hold on to the confession or they can turn away and leave the community. Therefore, "[m]uch of Hebrews is calculated to heighten the advantages that accompany, and the positive consequences that follow, the first course of action and the disastrous consequences that would follow the second course."[26] In this section, I will look at how the author uses the concept of "covenant" as a part of his collective identity construction in order to persuade his audience stay in the community. First, I will however discuss what the problem addressed by the author of Hebrews may have consisted in. As was discussed above, boundary drawing is crucial for identity formation, and thus it is important to determine against whom or what the boundaries are being drawn.

Benjamin Dunning, who in a book chapter discusses Hebrews from the perspective of identity formation with a specific interest in the concept of "marginality", understands the author as primarily drawing a boundary toward the surrounding Greco-Roman society. He asks, "How were Christians to mark their identity as *different* in a world in which so many of their values, norms, and ideals for living did not particularly stand out?"[27] Dunning responds to this question by turning to the "alien topos", particularly found in Hebrews 11, and claims that this topos in Hebrews "functions strategically to invent a specific communal identity for Christians (i. e., a community of aliens) while still allowing for a certain social integration in the larger Roman context".[28] A similar type of reading is provided by deSilva, who also places much weight on Hebrews 11 for understanding the social context of the letter, and thus also stresses the "foreigner" and "sojourner" aspect of the identity construction of the letter. According to deSilva, it appears that "some of the believers have begun to feel the weight of society's shaming techniques, the insults and abuse calculated to bring the Christian deviants back in line with society's values and worldview".[29] deSilva explains that "[t]he author of Hebrews meets this challenge first by presenting as praiseworthy models for imitation those figures that have chosen a lower status in this world for the sake of attaining greater and more lasting honor and advantages."[30] This is

25 D. deSilva, *Perseverance in Gratitude: A Socio-Rhetorical Commentary on the Epistle "to the Hebrews"* (Grand Rapids: Wm Eerdmans, 2000), 54.

26 deSilva, *Perseverance*, 56.

27 B. Dunning, *Aliens and Sojourners: Self as Other in Early Christianity* (Philadelphia: University of Pennsylvania Press, 2009), 46–7.

28 Dunning, *Aliens*, 47.

29 deSilva, *Perseverance*, 66.

30 deSilva, *Perseverance*, 66.

particularly done in chapter 11, with a list of examples from the Jewish Scriptures and tradition, and culminates in 12:2, where Jesus is said to have disregarded the shame of the cross "for the sake of the glory that was set before him". According to deSilva, the author of Hebrews "seeks to make the endurance of the unbelievers' hostility and reproach easier by reinterpreting that experience in a more honorable light".[31] For instance, by interpreting the shameful experiences that believers must endure in terms of loving divine discipline (12:5–11) these experiences are transformed into tokens of God's love and acceptance.

While many aspects of Dunning and deSilva's ideas just mentioned are helpful in understanding Hebrews from a social scientific perspective, they both seem to assume that the "parting of the ways" between "Christianity" and "Judaism" is already a done deal at the time of the writing of Hebrews. They therefore interpret Hebrews' discussion of things related to the Levitical covenant and the land of Israel in an analogous fashion, as in reality referring to things related to the community's relationship to the Roman society. Such a view can only be sustained on the assumption that the addressed community had long ago severed all bonds with the institutions of Judaism, something which must be deemed highly unlikely in the light of how scholars in general have re-evaluated the relations between "Christians" and "Jews" in the first couple of centuries CE (and even beyond that).[32]

According to the traditional view concerning Hebrews, the addressed community was tempted to *return* to Judaism from their newfound faith in "Christianity".[33] What I suggest is that the issue was not one of "return", but rather that it was not as clear to the members of the community as it was to the author that there was such a great difference between being part of this Jewish community of Jesus-believers and the neighbouring Jewish one where Jesus was not believed in.[34] Some members may have felt that there was no problem involved in moving between the communities and would have regarded them as complementary. We must remember that at this stage "Christianity" did not yet exist as a concept. I therefore agree with John Dunning's description of the addressed community as one which is "suffering from persecution from

31 deSilva, *Perseverance*, 67.

32 Cf. D. Boyarin, *Border Lines: The Partition of Judeo-Christianity* (Philadelphia: University of Pennsylvania Press, 2004); A. Becker/A.Y. Reed (ed.), *The Ways That Never Parted: Jews and Christians in Late Antiquity and the Early Middle Ages* (Minneapolis: Fortress, 2007).

33 E. g. F.F. Bruce, *The Epistle to the Hebrews* (NICNT; Grand Rapids: Eerdmans, 1990), 9; G.W. Buchanan, *To the Hebrews* (Anchor Bible; Garden City: Doubleday & Company, 1972), 266–267; B. Lindars, *The Theology of the Letter to the Hebrews* (NTT; Cambridge: Cambridge University Press, 1991), 4–15.

34 Cf. R. Hays' discussion in "'Here We Have No Lasting City': New Covenantalism in Hebrews", in R. Bauckham et al (ed.), *The Epistle to the Hebrews and Christian Theology* (Grand Rapids: Eerdmans, 2009) 151–73, on pp. 152–5.

outside and disillusionment and doubt within, and which is therefore tending to lose its hard edges and its firm centre".[35]

Hebrews 13 and the Drawing of Boundaries

Above, in the discussion of Jenkins, we saw the importance of *boundaries* for the construction of collective identity. Perhaps the clearest instance of boundary-making in the letter is found in chapter 13 – a chapter which has also been regarded as a key passage to understanding the letter.[36] In 13:9–14 the author urges the audience:

> Do not be carried away by all kinds of strange teachings; for it is well for the heart to be strengthened by grace, not by regulations about food, which have not benefited those who observe them. [10] We have an altar from which those who officiate in the tent have no right to eat. [11]For the bodies of those animals whose blood is brought into the sanctuary by the high priest as a sacrifice for sin are burned outside the camp. [12]Therefore Jesus also suffered outside the city gate in order to sanctify the people by his own blood. [13]Let us then go to him outside the camp and bear the abuse he endured. [14]For here we have no lasting city, but we are looking for the city that is to come.

I agree with Dunning when he calls these verses "the culmination of a project of identity construction".[37] In them the author engages in boundary drawing through the related themes of food, cult, and the holy city, and they are all clearly aimed at distinguishing the own group from other forms of Judaism.

If we are to take seriously the fact that Hebrews represents a type of *intra*-Jewish conflict then we may assume that the rejection of certain "regulations about food" in verse 9 is not intended as a complete dismissal of Mosaic dietary laws. Instead it probably concerns the *interpretation* of those laws, possibly something related to table fellowship with non-Jewish Christ-believers as in Gal 2:11–13 or other prescriptions concerning meals such as those in Matt 15:2. If Christ-believers were excluded from certain Jewish gatherings, or in any other way reproached by them based on some accusation of uncleanness, then the author is now responding by excluding those who "officiate in the tent" from the Christ-believers' "altar". Although it is difficult to determine exactly who the "officiators in the tent" are and what the "altar" of the Christ-believers denotes, the author is clearly here drawing a sharp line between the respective table fellowship of these communities.[38]

35 J. Dunnill, *Covenant and Sacrifice in the Letter to the Hebrews* (SNTSMS 75; Cambridge: Cambridge University Press, 1992), 37.

36 N. Young, "'Bearing His Reproach' (Heb 13.9–14)", *NTS* 48 (2002) 243–61, on p. 243.

37 Dunning, *Aliens*, 59.

38 Cf. H.W. Attridge, *A Commentary on the Epistle to the Hebrews* (Hermeneia; Minneapolis: Fortress, 1989), 396–7.

The boundary between them is further drawn in chapter 13 when the author speaks of the "camp" and the "city gate". Believers are called to go out to Jesus "outside the camp and bear the abuse he endured" (v. 13). The author continues, "[f]or here we have no lasting city, but we are looking for the city that is to come" (v. 13–14). While Dunning thinks that this serves to "reinforce the audience's radical sense of itself at the margins of society, while at the same time advocating a not particularly radical course of conduct",[39] I find such a general application to be anachronistic. It is highly unlikely that an audience around 100 CE would hear the words about the rejection of the "camp" of the Israelites and of the "city gate" of Jerusalem and interpret it as a general message about their place in margins of the Roman society. What the author is doing is rather to claim the Jewish heritage while rejecting some of the Jewish institutions connected to Jerusalem.

By way of comparison one can think of the Qumran community, which, at least during certain times of its existence, considered the Jerusalem priesthood to be corrupt and mistaken in matters concerning calendar and purity (among other things), and therefore viewed the rituals performed in the temple as illegitimate.[40] Among the strategies of the community to "cope" with the separation from the temple was the participation in the heavenly liturgy of angels, as evidenced in the *Songs of the Sabbath Sacrifice.*[41] According to Timothy Wardle, such experiences strengthened the community members' resolve to remain separate, "for if the God of Israel could be worshipped in the desert in the same manner in which he was acclaimed in heaven, what was the need for traveling to the polluted temple in Jerusalem?"[42] While critical of the Jerusalem establishment, the Qumran community certainly still defined itself as Jewish, and was in this way similar to how the author of Hebrews wanted his community to identify itself.

While the author of Hebrews (probably) did not want to encourage his audience to settle in the desert like the Qumran covenanters, the call to "go to him [Jesus] outside the camp" had a fairly concrete application in that they were to separate themselves from certain Jewish communities and institutions. They should not long for the day when Jewish believers in Jesus and other, "unbelieving", Jews would be reconciled and live together happily ever after in Jerusalem, as Jesus had revealed that the earthly institutions, in fact, have no lasting future.

39 Dunning, *Aliens*, 60.

40 T. Wardle, *The Jerusalem Temple and Early Christian Identity* (WUNT II/291; Tübingen: Mohr Siebeck, 2010), 139–40.

41 Wardle, *Jerusalem*, 153–5. Comparisons between Hebrews and the *Songs of the Sabbath Sacrifice* has been made recently in Jared Calaway's *The Sabbath and the Sanctuary* (WUNT II/349; Tübingen: Mohr Siebeck, 2013), e.g. on pp. 25–31.

42 Wardle, *Jerusalem*, 155.

Covenant and the Construction of Community in Hebrews

So far we have looked at the author's efforts to distinguish his addressed community from other Jewish communities, and thus we have dealt with the *difference*-side of Jenkins model of the process of identification. The other side of this model has to do with *similarity.* The author, thus, has to convincingly define what it is that binds the addressed group together, while also connecting this identity to the Jewish heritage. His task is to show what his own particular community has to offer that is lacking in "Jerusalem-loyal" Judaism. One of the ways that he does this is by introducing the concept of the "new covenant" – a concept found in Paul's letters (2 Cor 3:1–18; cf. Gal 4:21–31), but which is otherwise missing in Jewish sources.[43]

In Hebrews 8, the author quotes from the prophecy in Jer 31:31–34 which speaks of "a new covenant with the house of Israel and with the house of Judah" (Heb 8:8). This covenant is "not like the covenant that [God] made with their ancestors" (v. 9) at Sinai, since the Lord "says" concerning this covenant:

> I will put my laws in their minds, and write them on their hearts, and I will be their God, and they shall be my people. And they shall not teach one another or say to each other, "Know the Lord," for they shall all know me, from the least of them to the greatest. For I will be merciful toward their iniquities, and I will remember their sins no more. (vv. 10b–12)

The author then concludes that "in speaking of a new covenant, [God] has made the first one obsolete" (8:13), and thus according to his logic this "new covenant" cancels out the "old" one. Again, the author is drawing a line between his own community and the one committed to Jerusalem, but here he also underlines the necessity of being on the right side of that line, as the Jerusalem-loyal community belongs to the past while his own community represents the future. What Hebrews has to offer is thus membership in the "new covenant" community; a bold move which certainly promises great privilege for those who will join him. But what does it really imply?

If we look at this argument from the standpoint of identity formation we could say that the author is in this instance *symbolically constructing community.* The concept of the new covenant has the ability to evoke strong feelings with the audience as it connects the community to the special scriptural prophecy of Jeremiah. At the same time, however, the concept is vague and ambiguous enough to suit the letter's rhetorical purposes. Its strong value lies not in actual contents but in the symbolism.

If we look closer at the statements in Jeremiah's prophecy we notice that

43 C. Koester, *Hebrews: A New Translation with Introduction and Commentary* (AYB 36; New Haven: Yale University Press, 2001), 113. The new covenant mentioned in the Dead Sea Scrolls refers to a covenant renewal of the Mosaic covenant and contains no reference to Jer 31:31–34.

probably *any* pietistic Jewish group with enough self-confidence could have applied them to themselves, since basically they are saying that God will forgive the people their sins and make them obedient by putting his laws in their hearts. These are clearly things that belong to an invisible realm, beyond the possibility of empirical falsification. It contains no mention of the Messiah, the suffering servant, the Eucharist, baptism or anything of that kind. Another possible perspective on this prophecy's fulfilment is that of Mark Nanos, who asserts that "[t]he author and the addressees know that such a *new* covenant has not in fact been experienced".[44] According to Nanos the very fact that the author of Hebrews has to write to the addressed community to exhort them to remain obedient proves that the law has *not* been written on their hearts in the way that the prophecy teaches. Hence, Nanos concludes that the application of this prophecy in relation to the addressed community "seems to be quite discontinuous not only with the language of Jer. 31, but with the reality of their own experiences of covenantal life."[45] Such conclusions and possible perspectives strengthen the notion that the author is involved in *constructing* the social world of his audience and is, as it were, speaking things into existence. The aim of the author is doubtless to use this concept to give the community a strong sense of election and of having a special place in God's plan. They are not just any Jewish community, but the community of the "new covenant."

In sum, I understand the author of Hebrews to be involved in an intra-Jewish conflict, in which he finds it necessary to establish that his Christ-believing community represents something so radically different from other Jewish communities that one cannot participate in it and at the same time be a part of others. He does this by distancing his group from certain Jewish institutions related to Jerusalem, regarding them as obsolete, and instead, positively, establishes a new collective identity for his group around the concept of a new covenant.

We turn now to *1 Clement* to see how the concept of "covenant" works in relation to collective identification there.

1 Clement and Collective Identity

The question of the relationship between the author of *1 Clement* and the Jewish synagogues in Rome has provided something of a puzzle to scholars. The Jewish traits of the writing have frequently been recognised and the letter

44 M. Nanos, "*New* or *Re*newed Covenantalism? A Response to Richard Hays", in Richard Bauckham et al (ed.), *The Epistle to the Hebrews and Christian Theology* (Grand Rapids: Eerdmans, 2009) 183–8, on p. 186 (italics original).

45 Nanos, "*New* or *Re*newed Covenantalism?", 187.

has been characterised as a "storehouse of Jewish-Christian traditions".[46] Rudolf Bultmann, for instance, wrote that, "[i]t is quite a problem to say what it really is that makes I Clem. a Christian document" as Bultmann felt that it revealed a much stronger influence from "the Hellenistic synagogue" than from "genuine Paulinism".[47] Before Bultmann, William Wrede had commented that in contrast to the piety ("Frömmigkeit") of Paul, which was characterised by a full focus on the resurrected Lord and participation in him, one could remove the scattered christological statements from *1 Clement* and the piety presented there would still be essentially the same, centred as it was around faith in God's word and promise, and faithfulness in prayer.[48] Jean Daniélou likewise asserted that "Clement's theological setting is Jewish Christian", and noted that "[t]he work belongs to the class of edifying Jewish literature with a moral purpose, such as is to be found in Palestinian Judaism, and was continued in the *midrashim.*"[49] According to Daniélou, "Clement appears to be in touch with the archaic literature of Christianity [i. e. Jewish literature], though himself belonging to a later phase."[50] Why then the puzzlement? James Walters writes,

> Whereas the common approach to the Old Testament for early Christian writers was to claim the traditions while attacking the Jewish institutions, Clement used both and attacked neither. He seems completely unconcerned that his approach might blur the boundary between Christianity and Judaism and result in defections to the synagogues or open the door to Judaizers.[51]

In a similar vein Reidar Hvalvik writes that "we find no hint of a theological reflection about the relationship between 'Judaism' and 'Christianity.' Nor is there any polemic against Jews and Judaism."[52] This impression causes both Hvalvik and Walters to conclude that there was no direct communication between the "church" and the synagogues in Rome at this point. In Hvalvik's words, "The heritage from the synagogues had been 'domesticated' and taken for granted, but its source seems to have been forgotten."[53] This is a conclusion

46 J. Walters, "Romans, Jews, and Christians: The Impact of the Romans on Jewish/Christian Relations in First-Century Rome", in K. Donfried/P. Richardson, *Judaism and Christianity in First-Century Rome* (Grand Rapids: Eerdmans, 2005) 175–95, on p. 191.

47 R. Bultmann, *Theology of the New Testament* (trans. Kendrick Grobel; London: SCM, 1955), 2:187.

48 W. Wrede, *Untersuchungen zum Ersten Klemensbrief* (Göttingen: Vandenhoeck & Ruprecht, 1891), 103.

49 J. Daniélou, *The Theology of Jewish Christianity (A History of Early Christian Doctrine Before the Council of Nicaea* (vol. 1; trans. J. Baker; Philadelphia: Westminster Press, 1964), 44.

50 Daniélou, *Jewish Christianity*, 44.

51 Walters, "Romans", 193.

52 R. Hvalvik, "Jewish Believers and Jewish Influence in the Roman Church until the Early Second Century", in O. Skarsaune/R. Hvalvik (ed.), *Jewish Believers in Jesus* (Peabody: Hendrickson, 2007) 179–216, on p. 211.

53 Hvalvik, "Jewish Believers", 211; Cf. Walters "Romans", 194.

that not all have agreed with. Instead, some scholars have interpreted the lack of anti-Jewish polemics as implying either that "Clement" himself was a Jewish believer in Jesus,[54] or that he was at least "very much in direct linkage with a Jewish environment".[55] In the following I will make my contribution to this discussion by turning to the issue of how the collective identity of Christ-believers is constructed in relation to other "Judaisms" in *1 Clement*.

Covenant in *1 Clement*

It was noted that the concept of the new covenant is an important one for the author of Hebrews in constructing a collective identity for his addressed community. Even though the author of *1 Clement* knew Hebrews, this concept never occurs in *1 Clement*, and when the letter speaks of "covenant" (διαθήκη), which it does on two occasions (15:4; 35:7), it is both times in LXX quotations.

In the first of these, the author has exhorted his Corinthian audience to "unite with those who devoutly practice peace, and not with those who hypocritically wish for peace" (15:1).[56] To support this exhortation, he quotes from several LXX passages, one of them being Ps 78:36–37: "They loved him with their mouth, but with their tongue they lied to him; their heart was not right with him, nor were they faithful to his *covenant*" (15:4, italics mine). The fact that the term "covenant" is mentioned here seems purely accidental, since the thing that ties the five quoted passages in *1 Clement* 15 together is that they all speak of "mouths", "lips", and/or "tongues".[57]

In the other instance where "covenant" is used the sense is similar to the first one. The author is again exhorting his audience, this time to "make every effort to be found in the number of those who patiently wait for him [God], so that we may share in his promised gifts" (35:4). The way to be "found in this number" is then explained in terms of seeking out "those things which are well-pleasing and acceptable to him", "in harmony with his faultless will", and in "casting off from ourselves all unrighteousness and lawlessness, covetousness, strife, malice, deceit," and so on (35:5). The author then claims that "those who do these things are hateful to God; not only those who do them, but also those who approve of them" (35:6). He next quotes a rather long passage from Ps 50:16–23, which begins by speaking of the covenant:

> But to the sinner God said, "Why do you recite my statutes, and take my *covenant* upon your lips? You hated instruction and threw away my words behind you. If you

54 E. g. L. Barnard, "The Early Roman Church, Judaism, and Jewish Christianity", *AThR* 49 (1967) 371–84, on pp. 372–8.

55 Jefford, *Apostolic Fathers*, 166.

56 All quotes from the Apostolic Fathers are taken from M. Holmes, *The Apostolic Fathers: Greek Texts and English Translations* (Grand Rapids: Baker Books, 1999).

57 Isa 29:13; Ps 62:4; Ps 31:18; Ps 12:4–6.

saw a thief, you joined with him, and with adulterers you threw in your lot." (35:7–8, italics mine).

The use of the term "covenant" in this passage is clearly a way of speaking of the obligations that one has toward God, and as in *1 Clement* 15 the point is that one should be consistent in both words and actions. There appears then to be no special intention behind the usage of the word "covenant" neither in this verse.

It thus seems rather safe to conclude that the term does not in *1 Clement* point to an important theological concept but is used by the author, together with many other words and concepts, to speak of a favourite topic of his; the obedience to God that will be richly rewarded. The impression gained from looking at these two passages is that those who claim that the author "recognizes no discontinuity between a Jewish past and his own present"[58] are correct in this assertion. Judith Lieu has, in a discussion of Jewish and Christian identity, characterised such a perspective in relation to the view of the Jewish "scriptures":

> In both Hebrews and *I Clement* believers are drawn into a history which for the most part can only be described as "scriptural", and to that extent as "Jewish"; in what sense such a history constitutes for them a "Christian" identity – a term that neither text uses – is to introduce alien and inappropriate categories.[59]

While this may sound very well and is a statement that I would generally agree with, it still leaves the question unanswered whether the author of *1 Clement* was consistently "scriptural" also when it came to issues regarding typically Jewish (in the non-Christian sense) matters, such as circumcision, dietary laws, the land of Israel, and the Jerusalem temple cult. The way that some scholars speak of the author of *1 Clement's* "naïve" use of the Jewish scriptures we would expect him to consider complete observation of the Mosaic law as binding for all Christ-believers; if the author really saw *no* discontinuity between Israel and the ἐκκλησία that would presumably be the consequence.[60]

While *1 Clement* does not touch upon the issues of circumcision and dietary regulations, the letter refers on several occasions to things concerning the Jewish cult, as was noted in the beginning of this article in the discussion about Raymond Brown and the Roman church. We turn now to look at some of these passages, to see how the Jewish cult is related to the "scriptural" identity construction of Christ-believers in *1 Clement.*

58 J. Lieu, *Christian Identity in the Jewish and Greco-Roman World* (Oxford: Oxford University Press, 2004), 134.

59 Lieu, *Christian Identity*, 78–9.

60 Cf. Hvalvik who speaks of "Clement's naïve use of Old Testament texts: They are applied directly to the Christian church, which is seen as the immediate continuation of Israel in the Old Testament" ("Jewish Believers", 211).

The Jerusalem Cult in *1 Clement*

In *1 Clement* 31–32, the author is discussing the "blessings" and "gifts" that God has granted freely to his people throughout history, beginning with Abraham and Isaac (31:2–3). When he comes to Jacob he writes: "Jacob with humility departed from his land because of his brother and went to Laban and served him, *and the twelve tribes of Israel were given to him*" (31:4, italics mine). He then continues to speak of the "gifts" that God has given, writing: "If anyone will consider them sincerely one by one, he will understand the magnificence of the gifts that are given by him [God]" (32:1). These gifts are then discussed:

> For from Jacob come all the priests and Levites who minister at the altar of God; from him comes the Lord Jesus according to the flesh; from him come the kings and rulers and governors in the line of Judah; and his other tribes are held in no small honor, seeing that God promised that "your seed shall be as the stars of heaven." All, therefore, were glorified and magnified, not through themselves or their own works or the righteous actions which they did, but through his will. (32:2–3)

The priests and Levites are thus mentioned first in this list of gifts that God gave to Jacob in return for his humble departure from his land. There is clearly in this passage an historical awareness, as the author right afterward turns to speak of his own group as "we, having been called through his will in Christ Jesus" (32:4). It can therefore be ruled out that he is here speaking of "Christian" priests or Levites, or some "Christian" altar. Rather this refers to the ministry of the actual Jerusalem cult which *1 Clement* regards as a gift from God. A great contrast can thus be seen between *1 Clement's* words in this passage and what Hebrews says about the Levitical cult and ministry.

The same, very positive, perspective on the Jerusalem cult appears again in chapters 40–41 where the author uses the temple service as an example of order and reverence for God. In his usual manner, the author gives the Corinthians an exhortation – "we ought to do, in order, everything that the Master has commanded us to perform at the appointed times" (40:1) – and thereafter supports his appeal with an argument. He writes: "Now he [God] commanded the offerings and services to be performed diligently and not to be done carelessly or in disorder, but at designated times and seasons. Both where and by whom he wants them to be performed" he has determined (40:2–3). That the author is speaking specifically of the Jewish cult becomes apparent in verse 5 where he explains that "to the high priest the proper services have been given, and to the priests the proper office has been assigned, and upon the Levites the proper ministries have been imposed".

What is then the point in bringing this into the argument for the author of *1 Clement?* The lesson that he is teaching here is not that the Jewish cultic ministry is somehow spiritually fulfilled in the Christ-believing community.

The lesson is rather that there is an analogy between the divinely revealed order of the Jerusalem cult and the order that God demands from his communities. It is only in 42:4–5 that the author begins to speak of "bishops" and "deacons," and it is clear that though he sees parallels between these and the priestly services, there is no question of a mix-up or supersession here.[61] Nowhere does he argue for the validity of these offices from the Levitical cult, but instead he mentions a prophecy from the book of Isaiah (LXX version) to prove that they are divinely established (42:5).

After he has dealt with the question of *by whom* the offerings are to be performed, he turns to the issue of *where*, and writes:

> Not just anywhere, brothers, are the continual daily sacrifices offered, or the freewill offerings, or the offerings for sin and trespasses, but only in Jerusalem. And even there the offering is not made in every place, but in front of the sanctuary at the altar, the offerings having been inspected for blemishes by the high priest and the previously mentioned ministers. (41:2)

Again, the contrast here is very sharp to Hebrews' relativizing of the earthly cult. Even though *1 Clement*, in chapter 36, has a number of quotations from Hebrews, and in that context speaks of Christ as "the high priest of our offerings", the letter can go on to speak of the uniqueness of Jerusalem as the place that God has ordained for worship. It is interesting to note that the author can discuss the various sacrifices and offerings performed in the temple – even "the offerings for sins and trespasses" – without moving on to speak of Jesus' perfect sacrifice (cf. Heb 10:11–14).

Around the same time that this was written, the *Epistle of Barnabas* asserted that God "has made it clear to us through all the prophets that he needs neither sacrifices nor whole burnt offerings nor general offerings" (2:4). "Therefore," "Barnabas" says, God has "abolished these things, in order that the new law of our Lord Jesus Christ, which is free from the yoke of compulsion, might have its offering, one not made by man" (2:7). Similarly, the *Epistle to Diognetus* harshly criticised the Jews for their sacrificial cult, likening it to idolatry, when its anonymous author stated that those who try to honour God "by means of blood and fat and whole burnt offerings ... do not seem to me to be the least bit different from those who show the same respect to dead images" (3:5). While *1 Clement* too can state that God is in need of nothing, even in relation to sacrifices (52:1), the attitude to the cult in the letter is still to view it as revealed by God and therefore as a gift and a blessing, a perspective which comes across as remarkable when juxtaposed to the just mentioned examples. The "scriptural" perspective of *1 Clement* can thus be said to be surprisingly consistent and perhaps then not as naïve has some have thought.

61 The fact that he can speak in 44:4 of the bishops as "those who have offered the gifts blamelessly" does not go against this conclusion. If this is to be interpreted in a sacrificial sense, it was regarded by the author as a parallel "cult" to the one in Jerusalem.

Collective Identity in *1 Clement*

The investigation above, into the matters of covenant and cult in *1 Clement*, has revealed a very different perspective from that of Hebrews. The author of *1 Clement* has not adopted the concept of a "new covenant" and he refers to the Jerusalem cult in a way that it is clear that he does not regard it as a mere shadow of something else. Was this author then at all aware of any other collective identity for himself and his community than a Jewish one?

The answer to the question is yes! Even though he has no concept of "Christianity", the author clearly has certain ways of referring to the Christ-believing communities that mark them out from other groups connected to Judaism. First, he has the term ἐκκλησία. He addresses the letter from "the ἐκκλησία of God which sojourns in Rome" to the "ἐκκλησία of God which sojourns in Corinth" (prescript), and further describes his addressees as "those who are called and sanctified by the will of God through our Lord Jesus Christ" (prescript). While the origin and significance of the general use of the term ἐκκλησία as a designation for the earliest communities of Christ-believers are debated matters, it is evident that the author uses it here to address a specific body of believers in Corinth which shares his loyalty to Christ. 'Εκκλησία is used in two other places in *1 Clement* (44:3; 47:6), both times referring to local communities, and never carrying the sense of a universal "church", as it does in, for instance, Eph 1:22–23.

To speak of the supralocal community of Christ-believers, the author uses a second expression, namely "the flock of Christ" (τὸ ποίμνιον τοῦ Χριστοῦ; 44:3; 54:2; 57:2; cf. 16:1). While this expression certainly defines and delimits the collectivity, it carries none of the exclusiveness of concepts such as the "new covenant"-community or the "new Israel" (cf. Heb 8). Put in a different way, the collective identification that this expression offers does not appear to have its function in opposition to Israel. It would be quite possible to imagine a situation in which "the flock of Christ" and "Israel", in a non-metaphoric sense, existed side by side and served God in their own ways.

Before such a conclusion could be reached with any degree of certainty one would, however, have to look at a number of other aspects of the text. Oskar Skarsaune is right when he points out that in explaining the lack of "anti-Jewish polemics" one must not forget that *1 Clement* is mainly an "in-house" document; "The author was concerned with an intra-Christian conflict in Corinth and found no reason to expand on outer-limit problems for the Christian community."[62] Although Skarsaune does not completely rule out the possibility that the author had a positive attitude to the Jewish synagogues, he

62 O. Skarsaune, *In the Shadow of the Temple: Jewish Influences on Early Christianity* (Downers Grove: InterVarsity, 2002), 212.

writes that such a notion "may also be an overinterpretation of Clement's silence".[63]

Conclusion

The author of *1 Clement* was familiar enough with the letter to the Hebrews to quote from it and allude to it in dozens of places throughout his own letter. Despite this, he seems wholly unaffected both by Hebrews' notion of a new covenant, and of Hebrews' rejection of the Levitical cult and the special role of Jerusalem. In this essay I have looked at these aspects from an identity perspective and it has become plain that those things, which I have argued were central to Hebrews' collective identity construction, are the same things that the author of *1 Clement* has passed by in Hebrews. There is thus an interesting, and perhaps even unsettling, tension between the letters that raises a number of questions, such as: How were writings circulated in the early Jesus movement? How were they used? And, to what degree were they regarded as authoritative? Is it possible that the author of *1 Clement* only had access to some parts of Hebrews,[64] or that Hebrews is in fact literarily dependent upon *1 Clement*, so that *1 Clement* is the earlier writing?[65] While there seems to be much speaking in favour of the majority view concerning these issues, other opinions exist, and there are perhaps good reasons to go over the arguments again.

63 Skarsaune, *In the Shadow*, 212.

64 A. Lindemann, "The First Epistle of Clement", in W. Pratscher (ed.), *The Apostolic Fathers: An Introduction* (trans. E. Wolfe; Waco: Baylor University Press, 2010) 47–70, on p. 59.

65 Jefford, *Apostolic Fathers*, 132.

Bibliography

Adams, F./K. Aizawa, "Defending the Bounds of Cognition", in R. Menary (ed.), *The Extended Mind* (Cambridge, MA.: MIT Press, 2010) 67–81.

Alexander, L., *The Preface to Luke's Gospel: Literary Convention and Social Context in Luke 1.1–4 and Acts 1.1* (SNTSMS 78; Cambrigde: University Press, 1993).

— "Memory and Tradition in the Hellenistic Schools", in W.H. Kelber/S. Byrskog (ed.), *Jesus in Memory: Traditions in Oral and Scribal Perspectives* (Waco: Baylor University Press, 2009) 113–53.

Alexander, P.S./G. Vermes, *Qumran Cave 4 XIX: 4QSerekh Ha-Yahad* (DJD 26; Oxford: Clarendon Press, 1998).

Alkier, S., "Der 1. Thessalonicherbrief als kulturelles Gedächtnis", in G. Sellin/F. Vouga, *Logos und Buchstabe: Mündlichkeit und Schriftlichkeit im Judentum und Christentum der Antike* (TANZ 20; Tübingen: Francke 1997) 175–94.

— "Auferweckung denken. Oder: wie das Markusevangelium mit seinen Wundergeschichten seine Leser theologisch bildet", *BiLi* 84 (2011) 258–67.

Allison, D.C., "Response to Rafael Rodriguez, 'Jesus as His Friends Remembered Him, A Review of Dale Allison's Constructing Jesus'", *JSHJ* 12 (2014) 245–54.

— *Constructing Jesus: Memory, Imagination, and History* (London: SPCK, 2010).

Amit, V., "Reconceptualizing Community", in V. Amit (ed.), *Realizing Community: Concepts, Social Relationships and Sentiments* (London and New York: Routledge, 2002) 1–20.

Anderson, B., *Imagined Communities: Reflections on the Origin and Spread of Nationalism* (Revised Edition; London & New York: Verso, 2006 [originally 1983]).

Anderson, G., *Sin: A History* (New Haven: Yale UP, 2009).

Anderson, G.A., "Intentional and Unintentional Sin in the Dead Sea Scrolls", in D.P. Wright/D.N. Freedman/A. Hurvitz (ed.), *Pomegranates and Golden Bells: Studies in Biblical, Jewish, and Near Eastern Ritual, Law, and Literature in Honor of Jacob Milgrom* (Winona Lake, Ind.: Eisenbrauns, 1995) 49–64.

Anna, J., "Aristotle on Memory and the Self", in M.C. Nussbaum/A. Oksenberg Rorty (ed.), *Essays on Aristotle's* De Anima (Oxford: Clarendon Press, 1992) 297–311.

Arnold, R.C.D., *The Social Role of Liturgy in the Religion of the Qumran Community* (STDJ 60; Leiden: Brill, 2006).

Assavavirulhakarn, P., "Blessing", in L. Jones (ed.), *Encyclopedia of Religion* (15 vol.; 2nd ed.; Detroit: Macmillan, 2005) 2:979–85.

Assmann, A., *Einführung in die Kulturwissenschaft. Grundbegriffe, Themen, Fragestellungen* (GrAA 27; Berlin: Erich Schmidt, 2008).

Assmann, A./J. Assmann, "Das Gestern im Heute: Medien und soziales Gedächtnis", in K. Merton/S.J. Schmidt/S. Weischenberg (ed.), *Die Wirklichkeit der Medien: Eine Einführung in die Kommunikationswissenschaft* (Opladen: Westdeutscher Verlag, 1994) 114–40.

Assmann, J., *Das kulturelle Gedächtnis: Schrift, Erinnerung und politische Identität in frühen Hochkulturen* (München: C.H. Beck, 1992).

— "Halbwachs, Maurice", in N. Pethes/J. Ruchatz (ed.), *Gedächtnis und Erinnerung. Ein interdisziplinäres Lexikon* (Hamburg: Rowohlt, 2001) 247–9.

— "Form as Mnemonic Device: Cultural Texts and Cultural Memory", in R.A. Horsley/J.A. Draper/J.M. Foley (ed.), *Performing the Gospel: Orality, Memory, and Mark* (Minneapolis: Fortress, 2006) 67–82.

Attridge, H.W., *A Commentary on the Epistle to the Hebrews* (Hermeneia; Minneapolis: Fortress, 1989).

Augoustinos, M./M.I. Walker/N. Donaghue, *Social Cognition: An Integrated Introduction* (2nd ed.; Thousand Oaks, CA: Sage Publications, 2006).

Austin, J.L., *How to Do Things with Words: The William James Lectures Delivered at Harvard University in 1955* (ed. J.O. Urmsson/M. Sbisà; 2nd ed.; Oxford: Clarendon, 1975).

Baker, C.A., "A Narrative Model for Biblical Interpretation: The Role of Memory and Narrative in Social Identity Formation", in J. B. Tucker/C. A. Baker (ed.), *T & T Clark Handbook to Social Identity in the New Testament* (London, New York: Bloomsbury, 2014) 105–18.

Barclay, J.M.G., *Pauline Churches and Diaspora Jews* (WUNT 275; Tübingen: Mohr Siebeck, 2010).

Barnard, L., "The Early Roman Church, Judaism, and Jewish Christianity", *AThR* 49 (1967) 371–84.

Bar-Tal, D., *Group Beliefs: A Conception for Analyzing Group Structure, Processes, and Behavior* (SSSP; Berlin: Springer, 1990).

— "Group Beliefs as an Expression of Social Identity", in S. Worchel et al. (ed.), *Social Identity: International Perspectives* (London: SAGE, 1998) 93–113.

Bar-Tal, D./S. Cehajic-Clancy, "From Collective Victimhood to Social Reconciliation: Outlining a Conceptual Framework", in D. Spini/G. Elcheroth/D. Corkalo Biruski (ed.), *War, Community, and Social Change: Collective Experiences in the Former Yugoslavia* (New York: Springer, 2014) 125–36.

Bar-Tal, D./L Chernyak-hai/N. Shori/A. Gundar, "A Sense of Self-Perceived Collective Victimhood in Intractable Conflicts", *International Review of the Red Cross* 91 (2009) 229–58.

Barth, F., "Introduction", in F. Barth (ed.), *Ethnic Groups and Boundaries: The Social Organization of Culture Difference* (Bergen: Universitetsforlaget, 1969) 9–37.

— "Enduring and Emerging Issues in the Analysis of Ethnicity", in H. Vermeulen/C. Govers (ed.), *The Antropology of Ethnicity: Beyond Ethnic Groups and Boundaries* (Amsterdam: Spinhuis, 1994) 11–32.

Bartlett, F.C., *Remembering: A Study in Experimental and Social Psychology* (Cambridge: Cambridge University Press, 1995 [original 1932]).

Bauckham, R., "For Whom Were the Gospels Written?", in R. Bauckham (ed.), *The Gospels for All Christians: Rethinking the Gospel Audiences* (Grand Rapids, Mich.: Eerdmans, 1998) 9–48.

— "Introduction", in R. Bauckham (ed.), *The Gospels for All Christians: Rethinking the Gospel Audiences* (Grand Rapids: Eerdmans, 1998) 1–7.

— *Jesus and the Eyewitnesses: The Gospels as Eyewitness Testimony* (Grand Rapids, Michigan/Cambridge, U.K.: Eerdmans, 2006).

— *The Testimony of the Beloved Disciple: Narrative, History, and Theology in the Gospel of John* (Grand Rapids: Baker, 2007).

Baumgarten, J., "'Halakah' in Miqṣat Ma'aśê ha-Torah [MMT]", *JAOS* 116/3 (1996) 512–16.

— *The Damascus Document (4Q266–273): Qumran Cave 4, XIII* (DJD 18; Oxford: Clarendon Press, 1996).

Becker, A./A.Y. Reed (ed.), *The Ways That Never Parted: Jews and Christians in Late Antiquity and the Early Middle Ages* (Minneapolis: Fortress, 2007).

Becker, J., *Das Evangelium nach Johannes* (3rd edn; Ökumenischer Taschenbuch-kommentar zum Neuen Testament 4. Gütersloh: Gütersloher Verlagshaus Gerd Mohn, 1991).

Berger, P.L./T. Luckmann, *The Social Construction of Reality: A Treatise in the Socology of Knowledge* (Garden City, NY: Anchor Books, 1966).

Bergson, H., *Matière et mémoire. Essai sur la relation du corps à l'esprit* (Paris: F. Alcan, 1896).

— *Matter and Memory* (transl. N.M. Paul/W. Scott Palmer; London: George Allen and Unwin, 1911).

Bernier, J., *Aposynagōgos and the Historical Jesus in John: Rethinking the Historicity of the Johannine Expulsion Passages* (BibInt Series 122; Leiden: Brill, 2013).

Bernstein, M., "The Employment and Interpretation of Scripture: Preliminary Observations", in J. Kampen/M. Bernstein, *Reading 4QMMT: New Perspectives on Qumran Law and History* (SBL Symposium Series 2; Atlanta, GA: Scholars Press) 29–51.

Berntsen, D./D.C. Rubin, "Cultural Life Scripts Structure Recall from Autobiographical Memory", *M&C* 32 (2004) 427–42.

Bertram, G., "μακάριος in the LXX and Judaism", in G. Kittel (ed.), *Theological Dictionary of the New Testament* (10 vol.; Grand Rapids: Eerdmans, 1967) 4:364–7.

Birt, T., *Die Buchrolle in der Kunst: Archäologisch-antiquarische Untersuchungen zum antiken Buchwesen* (Leipzig: B.G. Teubner, 1907).

Black, M., "The Tradition of Hasidean-Essene Asceticism: Its Origin and Influence", in *Aspects du Judéo-Christianisme: Collogue de Strasbourg 23–25 avril 1964* (Paris: Presses Universitaires de France, 1965) 19–33.

Blanck, H., *Das Buch in der Antike* (München: C.H. Beck, 1992).

Blasi, A.J./J. Duhaime/P.-A. Turcotte (ed.), *Handbook of Early Christianity: Social Science Approaches* (Walnut Creek, California, AltaMira Press, 2002).

Bloch, D., *Aristotle on Memory and Recollection: Text, Translation, Interpretation, and Reception in Western Scholasticism* (PA 110; Leiden: Brill, 2007).
Bloch, M. E.F., *How We Think They Think: Anthropological Approaches to Cognition, Memory, and Literacy* (Boulder, CO: Westview Press, 1998).
Blomberg, C.L., "The Gospels for Specific Communities and All Christians", in E.W. Klink III (ed.), *The Audience of the Gospels: The Origin and Function of the Gospels in Early Christianity* (LNTS 353, London & New York: T&T Clark, 2010) 111–33.
Bockmuehl, M., *The Epistle to the Philippians* (BNTC; London: A & C Black, 1998).
Bonner, S.F., *Education in Ancient Rome: From the Elder Cato to the Younger Pliny* (Berkeley: University of California Press, 1977).
Bornkamm, G., "In Memoriam Rudolf Bultmann. * 20. 8. 1884 † 30.7 1976", *NTS* 23 (1977) 235–42.
Borsò, V., "Gedächtnis und Medialität: Die Herausforderung der Alterität. Eine medienphilosophische und medienhistorische Perspektivierung des Gedächtnis-Begriffs," in V. Borsò/G. Krumeich/B. Witte (ed.), *Medialität und Gedächtnis: interdisziplinäre Beiträge zur kulturellen Verarbeitung europäischer Krisen* (Weimar: Metzler, 2001) 23–54.
Botha, P.J.J., "'Publishing' a Gospel: Notes on the Historical Constraints to Gospel Criticism", in A. Weissenrieder/R.B. Coote (ed.), *The Interface of Orality and Writing: Speaking, Seeing, Writing in the Shaping of New Genres* (Tübingen: Mohr Siebeck, 2010) 335–52.
— *Orality and Literacy in Early Christianity* (Eugene: Cascade Books, 2012).
Boyarin, D., *Border Lines: The Partition of Judeo-Christianity* (Philadelphia: University of Pennsylvania Press, 2004).
Brooke, G.J., "The Wisdom of Matthew's Beatitudes", *ScrB* 19 (1989) 35–41.
— "The 'Apocalyptic' Community, the Matrix of the Teacher and Rewriting Scripture", in M. Popović (ed.), *Authoritative Scriptures in Ancient Judaism* (JSJSup 141; Leiden: Brill, 2010) 37–53.
Brown, P., *Augustine of Hippo: A Biography: A New Edition with an Epilogue* (Berkeley and Los Angeles: University of California Press, 2000).
Brown, R.E., "The Paraclete in the Fourth Gospel", *NTS* 13 (1966–67) 113–32.
— *The Gospel According to John* (2 Vols; AB 29; Garden City, New York: Doubleday, 1966 and 1970).
— *The Community of the Beloved Disciple: The Life, Loves, and Hates of an Individual Church in New Testament Times* (New York: Paulist Press, 1979).
— "Part Two: Rome", in R. Brown/J.P. Meier (ed.), *Antioch & Rome: New Testament Cradles of Catholic Christianity* (Ramsey: Paulist, 1982) 87–216.
— *An Introduction to the Gospel of John* (ed. F.J. Moloney; ABRL; New York, Doubleday, 2003)
Bruce, F.F., *The Epistle to the Hebrews* (NICNT; Grand Rapids: Eerdmans, 1990).
Bruner, J./C. Fleisher Feldman, "Group Narrative as a Cultural Context of Autobiography", in D.C. Rubin (ed.), *Remembering Our Past: Studies in Autobiographical Memory* (Cambridge: Cambridge University Press, 1996) 291–317.

Buchanan, G.W., *To the Hebrews* (Anchor; Garden City: Doubleday & Company, 1972).

Buell, D.K., *Why This New Race: Ethnic Reasoning in Early Christianity* (New York: Columbia University Press, 2005).

Bultmann, R., *Die Geschichte der synoptischen Tradition* (FRLANT 29; Göttingen: Vandenhoeck & Ruprecht, 1921).

— *Jesus* (Tübingen: Mohr [Siebeck], 1926).

— *History and Eschatology: The Gifford Lectures 1955* (Edinburgh: The University Press, 1957). Also published as *The Presence of Eternity: History and Eschatology. The Gifford Lectures 1955* (New York: Harper & Brothers, 1957).

— *Theology of the New Testament* (trans. Kendrick Grobel; London: SCM, 1955).

Burke, P., "Geschichte als soziales Gedächtnis", in A. Assmann/D. Harth (ed.), *Mnemosyne. Formen und Funktionen kultureller Erinnerung* (Frankfurt: Fischer, 1991) 289–304.

Byrskog, S., *Story as History – History as Story: The Gospel Tradition in the Context of Ancient Oral History* (WUNT 123; Tübingen: Mohr Siebeck, 2002).

— "A New Quest for the *Sitz im Leben:* Social Memory, the Jesus Tradition and the Gospel of Matthew", *NTS* 52 (2006) 319–36.

— "The Eyewitnesses as Interpreters of the Past: Reflections on Richard Bauckham's *Jesus and the Eyewitnesses*", *JSNT* 6 (2008) 157–68.

— "From Memory to Memoirs: Tracing the Background of a Literary Genre", in M. Zetterholm/S. Byrskog (ed.), *The Making of Christianity: Conflicts, Contacts and Constructions* (FS Bengt Holmberg; CBNTS 47; Winona Lake: Eisenbrauns, 2012) 1–21.

— "Theissen, Form-Criticism, and Social Memory: Ways to Reconfigure Jesus the Galilean", in P. von Gemünden/D.G. Horrell/M. Küchler (ed.), *Jesus – Gestalt und Gestaltungen. Rezeptionen des Galiläers in Wissenschaft, Kirche und Gesellschaft. FS für Gerd Theißen zum 70. Geburtstag* (NTOA/StUNT 100; Göttingen: Vandenhoeck & Ruprecht, 2013) 499–513.

— "The Message of Jesus", in B.W. Longenecker/M.C. Parsons (ed.), *Beyond Bultmann: Reckoning a New Testament Theology* (Waco, TX: Baylor University Press, 2014) 3–22.

— "What is Historical about the Mission of the Historical Jesus? Rudolf Bultmann and the Hermeneutics of Memory", in S. Byrskog/T. Hägerland (ed.), *The Mission of Jesus: Second Nordic Symposium on the Historical Jesus, 7–10 October 2012* (WUNT II 391; Tübingen: Mohr Siebeck, 2015) 41–58.

Calaway, J., *The Sabbath and the Sanctuary* (WUNT II/349; Tübingen: Mohr Siebeck, 2013).

Carr, D.M., *Time, Narrative, and History* (Bloomington: Indiana University Press, 1991).

— *Writing on the Tablet of the Heart: Origins of Scripture and Literature* (Oxford: Oxford University Press, 2005).

Carter, W., *John and the Empire: Initial Explorations* (New York and London: T&T Clark, 2008).

Castelli, E., *Martyrdom and Memory: Early Christian Culture Making* (New York: Columbia University Press, 2004).

Cavallo, G., "Between Volumen and Codex: Reading in the Roman World", in G. Cavallo/R. Chartier (ed.), *A History of Reading in the West* (Oxford: Polity, 1999) 64–89.

Cavallo, G./R. Chartier, "Introduction", in G. Cavallo/R. Chartier (ed.), *A History of Reading in the West* (Oxford: Polity, 1999) 1–36.

Charlesworth, J.H., Introduction to E. Qimron/J.H. Charlesworth (ed.), *Rule of the Community and Related Documents* (The Dead Sea Scrolls: Hebrew, Aramaic, and Greek Texts with English Translations 1; Tübingen: Mohr Siebeck, 1994) 1–103.

Charlesworth, J.H., "The Qumran Beatitudes (4Q525) and the New Testament (Mt 5:3–11; Lk 6:20–26)", *RHPR* 80 (2000) 13–35.

Charlesworth, S.D., "Indicators of 'Catholicity' in Early Gospel Manuscripts", in C.E. Hill/M.J. Kruger (ed.), *The Early Text of the New Testament* (Oxford: Oxford University Press, 2012) 37–48.

Cinnirella, M., "Exploring Temporal Aspects of Social Identity: The Concept of Possible Social Identities", *EJSP* 28 (1998) 227–48.

Cirafesi, W., "The Johannine Community Hypothesis (1968–Present): Past and Present Approaches and a New Way Forward", *Currents in Biblical Research* 12 (2014) 173–93.

Clark, A., *Being There: Putting Brain, Body, and World Together Again* (Cambridge, MA: MIT Press, 1997).

— "Word, Niche, and Super-Niche: How Language Makes Minds Matter More", *Theoria* 54 (2005) 655–68.

— "Material Symbols", *Philosophical Psychology* 19 (2006) 291–307.

Clarke, M.L., *Higher Education in the Ancient World* (London: Routledge & K. Paul, 1971).

Cohen, A.B., *The Symbolic Construction of Community* (Key Ideas; London: Routledge, 1985).

— "Epilogue", in V. Amit (ed.), *Realizing Community: Concepts, Social Relationships and Sentiments* (London and New York: Routledge, 2002) 165–70.

Coleman, J., *Ancient and Medieval Memories: Studies in the Reconstruction of the Past* (Cambridge: Cambridge University Press, 1992).

Collins, J.J., "Wisdom Reconsidered, in Light of the Scrolls", *DSD* 4 (1997) 265–81.

— "The Yahad and the 'Qumran Community'", in C. Hempel/J.M. Lieu (ed.), *Biblical Traditions in Transmission: Essays in Honour of Michael A. Knibb* (JSJSup 111; Leiden: Brill, 2006) 81–96.

— *Beyond the Qumran Community: The Sectarian Movement of the Dead Sea Scrolls* (Grand Rapids, MI: Eerdmans, 2009).

Collins, R.F., "'A New Commandment I Give To You, That You Love One Another' (John 13:34)", in R.F. Collins, *These Things Have Been Written: Studies on the Fourth Gospel* (Louvain/Grand Rapids, Michigan: Peeters/Eerdmans, 1990) 217–56.

Condor, S., "Social Identity and Time", in P. Robinson (ed.), *Social Groups and Identities. Developing the Legacy of Henri Tajfel* (Oxford: Butterworth Heinemann, 1996) 285–315.

Conway, C., "New Historicism and the Historical Jesus in John: Friends or Foes?" in P.N. Anderson/F. Just/T. Thatcher (ed.), *John Jesus and History, Volume 1: Critical Appraisals of Critical Views* (SBLSymS 44; Atlanta: Society of Biblical Literature, 2007) 199–215.

Conway, C.M., "Speaking through Ambiguity: Minor Characters in the Fourth Gospel", *BibInt* 10 (2002) 324–41.

Conway, M.A., "Remembering: A Process and a State", in H.L. Roediger III/Y. Dudai/S.M. Fitzpatrick (ed.), *Science of Memory: Concepts* (Oxford/New York: Oxford University Press, 2007) 237–41.

Conzelmann, H., *Acts of the Apostles* (Hermeneia; Philadelphia: Fortress, 1987).

Coope, U., *Time for Aristotle: Physics IV. 10–14* (Oxford Aristotle Studies; Oxford: Oxford University Press, 2005).

Corkum, P., "*Et Mirum si Non Ipsius Animi:* On Augustine, *Confessions*, Book XI" (Master's thesis, Dalhousie University, Halifax, 1994).

Craik, F.I.M., "On the Making of Episodes", in H.L. Roediger III/F.I.M. Craik (ed.), *Varieties of Memory and Consciousness: Essays in Honour of Endel Tulving* (Hillsdale, NJ: Erlbaum, 1989) 43–57.

Crook, Z.A., "Collective Memory Distortion and the Quest for the Historical Jesus", *JSHJ* 11 (2013) 53–76.

Crossan, J.D., *The Birth of Christianity: Discovering What Happened in the Years Immediately After the Execution of Jesus* (New York: HarperCollins, 1998).

— *The Greatest Prayer: Rediscovering the Revolutionary Message of the Lord's Prayer* (New York: HarperCollins, 2010).

Culpepper, R.A., *John, the Son of Zebebee: The Life of a Legend* (Columbia, South Carolina: University of South Carolina Press, 1994).

— "The Relationship between the Gospel of John and 1 John", in R.A. Culpepper/P.N. Anderson (ed.), *Communities in Dispute: Current Scholarship on the Johannine Epistles* (SBLECL 13; Atlanta, GA: Society of Biblical Literature, 2014) 95–122.

Curtis, V., *Don't Look, Don't Touch: The Science behind Revulsion* (Oxford: Oxford University Press, 2013.

Czachesz, I./R. Uro (ed.), *Mind, Morality and Magic: Cognitive Science Approaches in Biblical Studies* (London: Routledge, 2014).

Dahl, N.A., "The Johannine Church and History", in J. Ashton (ed.), *The Interpretation of John* (Philadelphia: Fortress Press/London: SPCK (1986) 122–40. (Orig. in W. Klassen/ G.F. Snyder [ed.], *Current Issues in New Testament Interpretation* [New York: Harper & Row/London: SCM Press, 1962]) 124–42.

Daniélou, J., *The Theology of Jewish Christianity: A History of Early Christian Doctrine Before the Council of Nicaea*, vol. 1; trans. J. Baker; Philadelphia: Westminster Press, 1964.

Davies, G., "Togate Statues and Petrified Orators", in D.H. Berry/A. Erskine (ed.), *Form and Function in Roman Oratory* (Cambridge: Cambridge University Press, 2010) 51–72.

Davies, P., "The Ideology of the Temple in the Damascus Document", *JJS* 33 (1982) 287–301.

Davies, P.R., *Damascus Covenant: An Interpretation of the "Damascus Document"* (JSOTSup 25. Sheffield: JSOT Press, 1983).

Davies, W.D./D.C. Allison, *A Critical and Exegetical Commentary on the Gospel According to Saint Matthew: Vol. 1, Introduction and Commentary on Matthew 1-VII* (ICC; Edinburgh: T&T Clark, 1988).

— *A Critical and Exegetical Commentary on the Gospel According to Saint Matthew: Vol. 2, Commentary on Matthew VIII–XVIII* (ICC; Edinburgh: T&T Clark, 1991).

— *A Critical and Exegetical Commentary on the Gospel According to Saint Matthew: Vol. 3, Commentary on Matthew XIX–XXVIII* (ICC; Edinburgh : T.& T. Clark, 1997).

Deacon, T.W., *The Symbolic Species: The Co-Evolution of Language and the Brain* (New York/London: Norton, 1997).

DeSilva, D., *Perseverance in Gratitude: A Socio-Rhetorical Commentary on the Epistle "to the Hebrews"* (Grand Rapids: Wm Eerdmans, 2000).

— *Honor, Patronage, Kinship & Purity: Unlocking New Testament Culture* (Downers Growe: Inter-Varsity, 2001).

DeWitt Burton, E., *Syntax of the Moods and Tenses in New Testament Greek* (3rd ed.; Whitefish: Kessinger, 2008[1892]).

DiMaggio, "Culture and Cognition", *ARS* 23 (1997) 263–87.

Dimant, D., "The Composite Character of the Qumran Sectarian Literature as an Indication of Its Date and Provenance", *RevQ* 22 (2006) 615–30.

Doering, L., "New Aspects of Qumran Sabbath Law from Cave 4 Fragments", in M.J. Bernstein et al (ed.), *Legal Texts and Legal Issues: Proceedings of the Second Meeting of the International Organization for Qumran Studies, Cambridge, 1995. Published in Honour of Joseph M. Baumgarten* (Leiden: Brill, 1997) 251–74.

Donald, M., *Origins of the Modern Mind: Three Stages in the Evolution of Culture and Cognition* (Cambridge, MA: Harvard University Press, 1991).

— "Hominid Enculturation and Cognitive Evolution", in C. Renfrew/C. Scarre (ed.), *Cognition and Material Culture: The Archaeology of Symbolic Storage* (Cambridge: MacDonald Institute for Archaeological Research, 1998) 7–18.

Doosje, B./N.R. Branscombe, "Attributions for the Negative Historical Actions of a Group", *EJSP* 33 (2003) 235–48.

Dschulnigg, P., "Grenzüberschreitungen im Markusevangelium. Auf dem Weg zu einer neuen Identität", *MThZ* 52 (2001) 113–20.

Dunderberg, I., *The Beloved Disciple in Conflict? Revisiting the Gospels of John and Thomas* (New York: Oxford University Press, 2006).

— "Johannine Traditions and Apocryphal Gospels", in J. Schröter (ed.), *The Apocryphal Gospels within the Context of Early Christian Theology* (BETL CCLX; Leuven - Paris - Walpole: Peeters, 2013) 67–93.

— *Gnostic Morality Revisited* (WUNT 247; Tübingen: Mohr Siebeck, 2015).
Dunn, J.D.G., *Romans 9–16* (WBC 38B; Dallas: Word, 1988).
Dunnill, J., *Covenant and Sacrifice in the Letter to the Hebrews* (SNTSMS 75; Cambridge: Cambridge University Press, 1992).
Dunning, B., *Aliens and Sojourners: Self as Other in Early Christianity* (Philadelphia: University of Pennsylvania Press, 2009).
Durkheim, E., "Individual and Collective Representations", in É. Durkheim (ed.), *Sociology and Philosophy* (London: Cohen and West, 1953 [French original 1898]) 1–34.
Dusen van, D., *The Space of Time: A Sensualist Interpretation of Time in Augustine,* Confessiones *X to XII* (SST 6; Leiden: Brill, 2014).
Ebner, M., "Im Schatten der Großen. Kleine Erzählfiguren im Markusevangelium", *BZ* 44 (2000) 56–76.
Erll, A./K. Seibel, "Gattungen, Formtraditionen und kulturelles Gedächtnis", in V. Nünning/A. Nünning (ed.), *Erzähltextanalyse und Gender Studies* (Weimar: Metzler, 2004) 180–208.
Eshel, H., *The Dead Sea Scrolls and the Hasmonean State* (Grand Rapids, MI: Eerdmans, 2008) 45–53.
Eshel, H. et al., "New Data on the East of Khirbet Qumran", *DSD* 9/2 (2002) 135–65.
Esler, P., *Community and Gospel: The Social and Political Motivations of Lucan Theology* (SNTSMS 57; Cambridge University Press, 1987).
— (ed.), *Modelling Early Christianity: Social-Scientific Studies of the New Testament in Its Context* (London: Routledge, 1995).
— *Galatians* (London: Routledge, 1998).
— "Models in New Testament Interpretation: A Reply to David Horrell", *JSNT* 78 (2000) 107–13.
— *Identity and Conflict in Romans. The Social Setting of Paul's Letter* (Minneapolis: Fortress Press, 2003).
— "Abraham as Prototype of Group Identity", Ch. 8 in *Conflict and Identity in Romans* (Minneapolis, MN: Augsburg Fortress, 2003) 171–94.
— "An Outline of Social Identity Theory", in J.B. Tucker/C.A. Baker (ed.), *T & T Clark Handbook to Social Identity in the New Testament* (London: Bloomsbury, 2014) 13–39.
— "Group Norms and Prototypes in Matthew 5.3–12", in J.B. Tucker/C.A. Baker (ed.), *T & T Clark Handbook to Social Identity in the New Testament* (London: Bloomsbury, 2014) 147–71.
Eubank, N., *Wages of Cross-bearing and Debt of Sin: The Economy of Heaven in Matthew's Gospel* (Berlin: De Greyter, 2013).
Eve, E., *Behind the Gospels: Understanding the Oral Tradition* (London: SPCK, 2013).
Fabry, H.-J., "Der Makarismus – mehr als nur eine weisheitliche Lehrform: Gedanken zu dem neu-edierten Text 4Q525", in J. Hausmann/H.-J. Zobel (ed.), *Alttestamentlicher Glaube und Biblische Theologie: Festschrift für Horst Dietrich Preuß zum 65. Geburtstag* (Stuttgart: Kohlhammer, 1992) 362–71.

Fantham, E., "Orator and/et actor", in P. Easterling/E. Hall (ed.), *Greek and Roman Actors: Aspects of an Ancient Profession* (Cambridge: Cambridge University Press, 2002).

Fee, G.D., *Paul's Letter to the Philippians* (NICNT; Grand Rapids: Eerdmans, 1995).

Feldman, C. Fleisher, "Genres as Mental Models", in M. Ammaniti/D. Stern (ed.), *Psychoanalysis and Development: Representations and Narratives* (New York: New York University Press, 1994) 111–22.

Feldman, L., *Jew and Gentile in the Ancient World: Attitudes and Interactions from Alexander to Justinian* (Princeton, NJ: Princeton University Press, 1993).

Fentress, J./C. Wickham, *Social Memory* (Oxford: Blackwell, 1992).

Fiedler, K./J. Schmid, "How Language Contributes to Persistence of Stereotypes As Well As Other, More General, Intergroup Issues", in R. Brown/S. Gaertner (ed.), *Blackwell Handbook of Social Psychology: Intergroup Processes* (Oxford: Blackwell, 2001) 261–80.

Fiske, S.T., "Social Cognition and Social Perception", *ARP* 44 (1993) 155–94.

Fitzmyer, J.A., "A Palestinian Collection of Beatitudes", in F. van Segbroeck et al. (ed.), *The Four Gospels 1992: Festschrift Frans Neirynck* (3 vol.; BETL 100; Leuven: Leuven University Press, 1992) 1:509–15.

Fleteren Van, F. (ed.), *Martin Heidegger's Interpretations of Augustine: Sein und Zeit und Ewigkeit* (Collectanea Augustiniana 6; Lewiston: Edwin Mellen Press, 2005).

Foster, P., "Memory, Orality, and the Fourth Gospel: Three Dead-Ends in Historical Jesus Research", *JSHJ* 10 (2012) 191–227.

France, R.T., *The Gospel of Matthew* (NICNT; Grand Rapids: Eerdmans, 2007).

Frey, J., "Different Patterns of Dualistic Thought in the Qumran Library: Reflections on their Background and History", in M. Bernstein/F. García Martínez/J. Kampen (ed.), *Legal Texts and Legal Issues: Proceedings of the Second Meeting of the International Organization for Qumran Studies, Cambridge 1995* (STDJ 23; Leiden: Brill, 1997) 275–335.

Funkenstein, A., "History, Counterhistory, and Narrative", in S. Freidlander (ed.), *Probing the Limits of Representation: Nazism and the "Final Solution"* (Cambridge, Mass.: Harvard University Press, 1992) 66–81.

Gale, A.M., *Redefining Ancient Borders: the Jewish Scribal Framework of Matthew's Gospel* (New York: T&T Clark, 2005).

Gamble, H.Y., "Literacy, Liturgy, and the Shaping of the New Testament Canon", in C. Horton (ed.), *The Earliest Gospels: The Origins and Transmission of the Earliest Christian Gospels: the Contribution of the Chester Beatty Codex P45* (London: T&T Clark, 2004) 27–39.

García Martínez, F./A.S. van der Woude, "A 'Groningen' Hypothesis of Qumran Origins and Early History", *RevQ* 14 (1990) 521–41.

Gärtner, B., *Ett nytt evangelium: Thomasevangeliets hemliga Jesusord* (Stockholm: Diakonistyrelsens bokförlag, 1960).

Geertz, C., *The Interpretation of Cultures* (New York: Basic Books, 1973).

George, A., "La « forme » des béatitudes jusqu'à Jésus", in *Mélanges bibliques rédigés en l'honneur de André Robert* (TICP 4; Paris: Bloud & Gay, 1956) 398–403.

Gergen, K., "Erzählung, Moralische Identität und historisches Bewusstsein", in J. Straub (ed.), *Erzählung, Identität, Historisches Bewusstsein* (Frankfurt am Main: Suhrkamp, 1998) 170–202.

Gerhardsson, B., *Memory and Manuscript: Oral Tradition and Written Transmission in Rabbinic Judaism and Early Christianity* (ASNU 22; Lund: Gleerup, 1964).

— *Tradition and Transmission in Early Christianity* (CB 20; Lund: Gleerup, 1964).

— "Mark and the Female Witnesses", in H. Berens/ D. Loding/ M.T. Roth (ed.), *Dumu—E2-Dub-Ba-A* (FS Åke W. Sjöberg; OPSNKF 11; Philadelphia: The Samuel Noah Kramer Fund, 1969) 217–26.

— *The Reliability of the Gospel Tradition* (Grand Rapids: Baker Academic, 2010).

Giesen, B., *Kollektive Identität* (Die Intellektuellen und die Nation 2; Frankfurt am Main: Suhrkamp, 1999).

Gillihan, Y.M., *Civic Ideology, Organization, and Law in the Rule Scrolls: A Comparative Study of the Covenanters' Sect and Contemporary Voluntary Associations in Political Context* (SSTDJ 97; Leiden Brill, 2012).

Goff, M.J., *The Worldly and Heavenly Wisdom of 4QInstruction* (STDJ 50; Leiden: Brill, 2003).

— *Discerning Wisdom: The Sapiential Literature of the Dead Sea Scrolls* (VTSup 116; Leiden: Brill, 2007).

Gomila, A., "Mending or Abandoning Cognitivism?" in M. de Vega/A.M. Glenburg/ A.C. Graesser (ed.), *Meaning and Cognition* (Oxford: Oxford University Press, 2008) 357–74.

Goodspeed, E.J., "First Clement Called Forth by Hebrews", *JBL* 30 (1911) 157–60.

Grindheim, S., "Ignorance Is Bliss: Attitudinal Aspects of the Judgment according to Works in Matthew 25:31–46", *NovT* 50 (2008) 313–31.

Gundry, R.H., *Matthew: A Commentary on His Handbook for a Mixed Church under Persecution* (2. ed; Grand Rapids: Eerdmans, 1994).

Hachlili, R., "The Qumran Cemetery Reassessed", in T. Lim/J. Collins (ed.), *The Oxford Handbook of the Dead Sea Scrolls* (Oxford: Oxford University Press, 2000) 46–78.

Hägerland, T., "John's Gospel: A Two-Level Drama?" *JSNT* 25 (2003) 309–22.

Hagner, D.A., *Matthew 14–28* (WBC; vol. 33B; Waco: Word books, 1995).

Haines-Eitzen, K., "The Social History of Early Christian Scribes", in B.D. Ehrman/ M.W. Holmes (ed.), *The Text of the New Testament in Contemporary Research: Essays on the Status Quaestionis* (Leiden: Brill, 2013) 479–96.

Hakola, R., *Identity Matters: John, the Jews and Jewishness* (Leiden: Brill, 2005).

— "Social Identities and Group Phenomena in Second Temple Judaism", in P. Luomanen/I. Pyysiäinen/R. Uro (ed.), *Exploring Christian Origins and Early Judaism* (BibInt Series 89; Leiden: Brill, 2007) 259–76.

— "The Johannine Community as Jewish Christians? Some Problems in Current Scholarly Consensus", in M. Jackson-McCabe (ed.), *Reconsidering Jewish Christianity: Rethinking Ancient Groups and Texts* (Minneapolis: Fortress Press, 2007) 181–201.

— "Social Identity and a Stereotype in the Making: Pharisees as Hypocrites in Matt 23", in B. Holmberg/M. Winninge (ed.), *Identity Formation in the New Testament* (WUNT 227; Tübingen: Mohr Siebeck, 2008) 123–39.

— "The Burden of Ambiguity: Nicodemus and the Social Identity of the Johannine Christians", *NTS* 55 (2009) 438–55.

— "The Reception and Development of the Johannine Tradition in 1, 2 and 3 John", in T. Rasimus (ed.), *The Legacy of John: Second-Century Reception of the Fourth Gospel* (Leiden: Brill, 2010) 17–47.

— "Pharisees as Others in the New Testament", in R. Hakola/N. Nikki/U. Tervahauta (ed.), *Others and the Construction of Early Christian Identities* (PFES 106; Helsinki: The Finnish Exegetical Society, 2013) 13–65.

— "Anti-Judaism, Anti-Semitism in NT and Its Interpretation", in S.L. Mckenzie (ed.), *The Oxford Encyclopedia of Biblical Interpretation* (Oxford: Oxford University Press, 2013) 27–35.

— *Reconsidering Johannine Christianity: A Social Identity Approach* (New York and London: Routledge, 2015).

— "Galilean Jews and Christians in Context: Spaces Shared and Contested in the Eastern Galilee in Late Antiquity", in J. Day/R.Hakola/M. Kahlos/U. Tervahauta (ed.), *Spaces in Late Antiquity: Cultural, Theological and Archaeological Perspectives* (Replace with: New York and London: Routledge, 2016) 141–165.

Hakola, R./N. Nikki/U. Tervahauta, "Introduction", in R. Hakola/N. Nikki/U. Tervahauta (ed.), *Others and the Construction of Early Christian Identities*, Tervahauta (PFES 106; Helsinki: Finnish Exegetical Society, 2013) 9–30.

Halbwachs, M., *La Topographie lègendaire des Èvangiles en Terre Sainte* (Paris: Presses Universitaires de France, 1941).

— *La mémoire collective* (Bibliothèque de l'Évolution de l'Humanité 28; Paris: Presses Universitaires de France, 1949/1950).

— *Les cadres sociaux de la mémoire* (Paris: Presses Universitaires de France, new ed. 1952).

Halliday, M.A.K., *Explorations in the Functions of Language* (Explorations in Language Study; London: Arnold, 1973).

Hammann, K., *Rudolf Bultmann. Eine Biographie* (2nd ed.; Tübingen: Mohr Siebeck, 2009) 179–92.

Hanson, K.C. "How Honourable! How Shameful! A Cultural Analysis of Matthew's Makarisms and Reproaches", *Semeia* 68 (1994) 81–111.

Hare, D.R.A., "The Rejection of the Jews in the Synoptic Gospels and Acts", in A.T. Davies (ed.), *Antisemitism and the Foundations of Christianity* (New York and Toronto: Paulist Press, 1979) 27–47.

Harrington, H.K., *The Purity Texts* (Companion to the Qumran Scrolls 5; London: T&T Clark International, 2004).

Harris, C.B./H. M. Paterson/R.I. Kemp, "Collaborative Recall and Collective Memory: What Happens When We Remember Together", *Memory* 16 (2008) 213–30.

Hartshorn, M./A. Kaznatcheev/T. Shultz, "The Evolutionary Dominance of Ethnocentric Cooperation", *JASSS* 16 (2013); http://jasss.soc.surrey.ac.uk/16/3/7.html

Hasher, L., "Inhibition: Attentional Regulation of Cognition", in H.L. Roediger III/Y. Dudai/S.M. Fitzpatrick (ed.), *Science of Memory: Concepts* (Oxford/New York: Oxford University Press, 2007) 291–4.

Haslam, S.A., *Psychology in Organizations: The Social Identity Approach* (London: Sage Publications, 2001).

Haslam, S.A./S.D. Reicher/M.J. Platlow, *The New Psychology of Leadership: Identity, Influence and Power* (Hove and New York: Psychology Press, 2011).

Haslam, S.A./J.C. Turner/P.J. Oakes/C. McGarty/K.J. Reynolds, "The Group as a Basis for Emergent Stereotype Consensus", *ERSP* 8 (1998) 203–39.

Haslam, S.A./P.J. Oakes/J.C. Turner/C. McGarty, "Social Identity, Self-Categorization, and the Perceived Homogeneity of Ingroups and Outgroups: The Interaction between Social Motivation and Cognition", in R. Sorrentino/E. Higgins (ed.), *Handbook of Motivation and Cognition, Volume Three: The Interpersonal Context* (New York: Guilford Press, 1996) 182–222.

Haslam, S.A./S.D. Reicher/M.J. Platlow, *The New Psychology of Leadership: Identity, Influence and Power* (Hove and New York: Psychology Press, 2011)

Hawley, R., "On *Maskil* in the Judean Desert Texts", *Henoch* 28 no. 2 (2006) 43–77.

Hayes, C., *Gentile Impurites and Jewish Identities: Intermarriage and Conversion from the Bible to the Talmud* (Oxford: Oxford University Press, 2002).

Hays, R., *Echoes of Scripture in the Letters of Paul* (New Haven: Yale University Press, 1989).

— "'Here We Have No Lasting City': New Covenantalism in Hebrews", in R. Bauckham et al (ed.), *The Epistle to the Hebrews and Christian Theology* (Grand Rapids: Eerdmans, 2009) 151–73.

Hearon, H.E./P. Ruge-Jones/T.E. Boomershine, *The Bible in Ancient and Modern Media: Story and Performance* (Eugene: Cascade Books, 2009).

Heger, P., "Celibacy in Qumran – Hellenistic Fiction or Reality? Qumran's Attitude toward Sex", *RevQ* 26/101 (2013) 53–90.

Heidegger, M., *Sein und Zeit* (Halle: Niemeyer, 1927). Also published in *Jahrbuch für Philosophie und phänomenologische Forschung* 8 (1927) 1–438.

Hempel, C., "The Penal Code Reconsidered", in M. Bernstein/F. García Martínez/J. Kampen (ed.), *Legal Texts and Legal Issues: Proceedings of the Second Meeting of the International Organization for Qumran Studies, Cambridge 1995* (STDJ 23; Leiden: Brill, 1997) 337–48.

— *The Laws of the Damascus Document: Sources, Tradition, and Redaction* (STDJ 29; Leiden: Brill, 1998).

— "The Community and Its Rivals According to the Community Rule from Caves 1 and 4", *RevQ* 81 (2003) 47–81.

— "The Teaching on the Two Spirits and the Literary Development of the Rule of the Community", in G. Xeravits (ed.), *Dualism in Qumran* (LSTS 76; London: T&T Clark, 2010) 102–20.

— "Who is Making Dinner at Qumran?", *JTS* 63 no. 1 (2012) 49–65.

— *The Qumran Rule Texts in Context: Collected Studies* (TSAJ 154; Tübingen: Mohr Siebeck, 2013).

— "The Long Text of the Serekh as Crisis Literature", *RevQ* 27 (2015) 3–24.

Hengel, M., *The Johannine Question* (London: SCM Press, 1989).

Hewstone, M., *Causal Attribution: From Cognitive Processes to Collective Beliefs* (Oxford: Basil Blackwell, 1989).

Hiers, R.H., "'Binding' and 'Loosing': The Matthean Authorizations", *JBL* 104 (1985) 233–50.

Himmelfarb, M., "Impurity and Sin in 4QD, 1QS, and 4Q512", *DSD* 8 no. 1 (2001) 9–37.

Hinchman, L.P./S.K. Hinchman (ed.), *Memory, Identity, Community: The Idea of Narrative in the Human Sciences* (Albany, NY: State University of New York Press, 1997).

Hirst, W./D. Manier, "Remembering as Communication: A Family Recounts its Past", in D.C. Rubin (ed.), *Remembering Our Past: Studies in Autobiographical Memory* (Cambridge: Cambridge University Press, 1996) 271–90.

Hochschild, P.E., *Memory in Augustine's Theological Anthropology* (OECS; Oxford: Oxford University Press, 2012).

Holmes, M., *The Apostolic Fathers: Greek Texts and English Translations* (Grand Rapids: Baker Books, 1999).

Holtz, G., "Purity Conceptions in the Dead Sea Scrolls: 'Ritual-Physical' and 'Moral' Purity in a Diachronic Perspective", in C. Frevel/C. Nihan (ed.), *Purity and the Forming of Religious Traditions in the Ancient Mediterranean World and Ancient Judaism* (Dynamics in the History of Religion 3; Leiden Brill, 2013) 519–36.

Hopkins, N./S. Reicher, "Identity, Culture and Contestation: Social Identity as Cross-Cultural Theory", *Psychological Studies* 56 (2011) 36–43.

Hübenthal, S., "Social and Cultural Memory in Biblical Exegesis: The Quest for an Adequate Application", in P. Carstens et al. (ed.), *Cultural Memory in Biblical Exegesis* (PHSC 17; Piscataway: Gorgias, 2012) 191–216.

— *Das Markusevangelium als kollektives Gedächtnis* (FRLANT 253; Göttingen: Vandenhoeck & Ruprecht, 2014).

— "Social Memory", "Communicative Memory", "Collective Memory" and "Cultural Memory", in T. Thatcher/C. Keith/R.F. Jr. Person/E. Stern (ed.), *Dictionary of the Bible in Ancient Media* (London: T&T Clark, 2015).

Hübner, H., "Bultmanns 'existentiale Interpretation': Untersuchungen zu ihrer Herkunft", *ZTK* 100 (2003) 280–324.

Hultgren, A., "Forgive Us, as We Forgive (Matt 6:12)", *WW* 16 (1996) 284–90.

Hurtado, L.W., "Manuscripts and the Sociology of Early Christian Reading", in C.E. Hill/M.J. Kruger (ed.), *The Early Text of the New Testament* (Oxford: Oxford University Press, 2012) 49–62.

— "Oral Fixation and New Testament Studies? 'Orality', 'Performance' and Reading Texts in Early Christianity", *NTS* 60 (2014) 321–40.

Hutchins, E., "Material Anchors for Conceptual Blends", *JP* 37 (2005) 1555–77.

Hutchison P./D. Abrams/R. Gutierrez/G. Tendayi Viki, "Getting Rid of the Bad Ones: The Relationship Between Group Identification, Deviant Derogation, and Identity Maintenance", *JESP* 44 no. 3 (2008) 874–81.

Hvalvik, R., "Jewish Believers and Jewish Influence in the Roman Church until the Early Second Century", in O. Skarsaune/R. Hvalvik (ed.), *Jewish Believers in Jesus* (Peabody: Hendrickson, 2007) 179–216.

Hylen, S.E., *Imperfect Believers: Ambiguous Characters in the Gospel of John* (Louisville, KY: Westminster John Knox, 2009).

Ilan, T., *Jewish Women in Greco-Roman Palestine* (Peabody, MA: Hendrickson Publishers, 1995).

Janzen, W., "'AŠRÊ in the Old Testament", *HTR* 58 (1965) 215–26.

Jefford, C., *The Apostolic Fathers and the New Testament* (Peabody: Hendricksons, 2006).

Jenkins, R., *Social Identity* (2nd ed.; Key Ideas; London: Routledge, 2004).

— *Social Identity* (4th Edition; London and New York: Routledge, 2014).

Johnson, W.A., "Toward a Sociology of Reading in Classical Antiquity", *AJP* 121 (2000) 593–627.

Jokiranta, J., "Social Identity in the Qumran Movement: The Case of the Penal Code", in P. Luomanen/I. Pyysiäinen/R. Uro (ed.), *Explaining Christian Origins and Early Judaism: Contributions from Cognitive and Social Science* (BibInt 89; Leiden: Brill, 2007) 277–98.

— "An Experiment on *Idem* Identity in the Qumran Movement", *DSD* 16 no. 3 (2009) 309–29.

— *Social Identity and Sectarianism in the Qumran Movement* (STDJ 105; Leiden: Brill, 2013).

— "Conceptualizing *Ger* in the Dead Sea Scrolls", in K. De Troyer et al (ed.), *In the Footsteps of Sherlock Holmes: Studies in the Biblical Text in Honour of Anneli Aejmelaeus* (Contributions to Biblical Exegesis and Theology 72; Leuven: Peeters Publishers, 2014) 659–77.

— "What is 'Serekh ha-Yahad (S)'? Thinking About Ancient Manuscripts as Information Processing", in J. Baden/H. Najman/E. Tigchelaar, with the assistance of L. Carlson (ed.), *Festschrift in Honor of John J. Collins* (Leiden: Brill, forthcoming).

Jokiranta, J./H. Vanonen. "Multiple Copies of Rule Texts or Multiple Rule Texts? Boundaries of the S and M Documents", in M.S. Pajunen/H. Tervanotko (ed.), *Crossing Imaginary Boundaries: The Dead Sea Scrolls in the Context of Second Temple Judaism* (PFES 108; Helsinki: Finnish Exegetical Society, 2015) 11–60.

Jonge, M. de, "The Gospel and the Epistles of John Read Against the Background of the History of the Johannine Communities", in T. Thatcher (ed.), *What We Have Heard from the Beginning: The Past, Present, and Future of Johannine Studies* (Waco, Texas: Baylor University Press, 2007) 127–44.

Kahlos, M., "Introduction", in M. Kahlos (ed.), *Faces of the Other: Religious Rivalry and Ethnic Encounters in the Later Roman World* (Cursor Mundi 10; Turnhout, Belgium: Brepols, 2011) 1–15.

Kaiser, U.U., "Die Kinderheitserzählung des Thomas", in C. Markschies/J. Schröter (ed.), *Antike christliche Apokryphen in deutscher Übersetzung, Band 1/2* (Tübingen: Mohr Siebeck, 2012) 930–59.

Kampen, J., *Wisdom Literature* (Eerdmans Commentaries on the Dead Sea Scrolls; Grand Rapids: Eerdmans, 2011).

Käsemann, E., "Das Problem des historischen Jesus", *ZTK* 51 (1954) 125–53.

Käser, W., "Beobachtungen zum alttestamentlichen Makarismus", *ZAW* 82 (1970) 235–50.

Kazen, T., *Emotions in Biblical Law: A Cognitive Science Approach* (Sheffield, U.K.: Sheffield Phoenix, 2011).

— "The Role of Disgust in Priestly Purity Law: Insights from Conceptual Metaphor and Blending Theories", *JRLS* 3 (2014) 62–92.

Keener, C.S., *A Commentary on the Gospel of Matthew* (Grand Rapids: Eerdmans, 1999).

Kelber, W.H., *The Oral and the Written Gospel: The Hermeneutics of Speaking and Writing in the Synoptic Tradition, Mark, Paul, and Q* (Philadelphia: Fortress, 1983).

Keppler, A., *Tischgespräche. Über Formen kommunikativer Vergesellschaftung am Beispiel der Konversation in Familien* (Frankfurt am Main: Suhrkamp, 1995).

King, K.L., *What is Gnosticism* (Cambridge, Massachusetts: Belknapp, 2003).

King, R.A.H., *Aristotle and Plotinus on Memory* (QSP 94; Berlin: de Gruyter, 2009).

Kirk, A., "Memory", in W.H. Kelber/S. Byrskog (ed.), *Jesus in Memory: Traditions in Oral and Scribal Perspectives* (Waco, TX: Baylor University Press, 2009) 155–72.

— "The Memory-Tradition Nexus in the Synoptic Tradition: Memory, Media, and Symbolic Representation," in T. Thatcher (ed.), *Memory and Identity in Ancient Judaism and Early Christianity: A Conversation with Barry Schwartz* (Atlanta: SBL Press, 2014) 131–60.

Kirk, A./T. Thatcher (ed.), *Memory, Tradition, and Text* (Semeia Studies 52; Atlanta: Society of Biblical Literature, 2005).

Kirk, A./T. Thatcher, "Jesus Tradition as Social Memory", in A. Kirk/T. Thatcher (ed.), *Memory, Tradition, and Text: Uses of the Past in Early Christianity* (SBLSS 52; Atlanta: SBL, 2005) 25–42.

Klawans, J., *Impurity and Sin in Ancient Judaism* (Oxford: Oxford University Press, 2000).

Kleiner, D.E.E., *Roman Imperial Funerary Altars with Portraits* (Rome: Bretschneider, 1987).

Klink III, E.W., *The Sheep of the Fold: The Audience and Origin of the Gospel of John* (SNTSMS 141; Cambridge: University Press, 2007).

— (ed.), *The Audience of the Gospels: The Origins and Function of the Gospels in Early Christianity* (LNTS 353; London & New York: T&T Clark, 2010).

Kloppenborg, J.S., "Disaffiliation in Associations and the ἀποσυναγωγός of John", *HTS Teologiese Studies/Theological Studies* 67 (2011) 1–16.

— "Memory, Performance and the Sayings of Jesus", *JSHJ* 10 (2012) 97–132.

Klostergaard Petersen, A., "Wisdom as Cognition: Creating the Others in the Book of Mysteries and 1 Cor 1–2", in C. Hempel/A. Lange/H. Lichtenberger (ed.), *The Wisdom Texts from Qumran and the Development of Sapiential Thought* (BETL 159; Leuven: Leuven University Press, 2002) 405–32.

Knauer, R., "Roman Wall Paintings from Boscotrecase: Three Studies in the Relationship between Writing and Painting", *MMJ* 28 (1993) 13–46.

Koester, C., *Hebrews: A New Translation with Introduction and Commentary* (AYB 36; New Haven: Yale University Press, 2001).

— *Symbolism in the Fourth Gospel: Meaning, Mystery, Community* (2nd Edition; Minneapolis; Fortress Press, 2003).

— "Theological Complexity and the Characterization of Nicodemus in John's Gospel", in C.W. Skinner (ed.), *Characters and Characterization in the Gospel of John* (LNTS 461; London and New York: Bloomsbury T & T Clark, 2013).

Kooij, A. van der, "The Yaḥad – What is in a Name?", *DSD* 18 no. 2 (2011) 109–28.

Koriat, A./M. Goldsmith/A. Pansky, "Toward a Psychology of Memory Accuracy", *ARP* 51 (2000) 431–587.

Kosmala, H., "The Three Nets of Belial", *ASTI* 4 (1965) 91–113.

Kraus, M., "New Jewish Directions in the Study of the Fourth Gospel", in F. Lozada Jr./ T. Thatcher (ed.), *New Currents through John: A Global Perspective* (SBLRBS 54; Atlanta, GA: Society of Biblical Literature, 2006) 141–66.

Kügler, J., *Der Jünger den Jesus liebte. Literarische, theologische und historische Untersuchungen zu einer Schlüsselgestalt johanneischer Theologie und Geschichte. Mit einem Exkurs über die Brotrede in Joh 6* (SBB 16; Stuttgart: Verlag Katholisches Bibelwerk, 1988).

Kwon Y., *Eschatology in Galatians* (WUNT 2. Reihe 183; Tübingen: Mohr Siebeck, 2004).

Labahn, M., "'It's Only Love' – Is That All? Limits and Potentials of Johannine 'Ethic' – A Critical Evaluation of Research", in J.G. van der Watt/R. Zimmermann (ed.), *Rethinking the Ethics of John: "Implicit Ethics" in the Johannine Writings* (WUNT 291; Tübingen: Mohr Siebeck, 2012) 3–43.

Lakoff, G./M. Johnson, *Metaphors We Live By* (Chicago: University of Chicago Press, 1980).

Lamb, D.A., *Text, Context and the Johannine Community A Sociolinguistic Analysis of the Johannine Writings* (LNTS 477; London and New York: Bloomsbury T & T Clark, 2013).

Lane, W., *Hebrews 1–8* (WBC 47 A; Waco: Thomas Nelson, 1991).

Lang, H.S., "On Memory: Aristotle's Corrections of Plato", *JHP* 18 (1980) 379–93.

Lange, A., *Weisheit und Prädestination: Weisheitliche Urordnung und Prädestination in den Textfunden von Qumran* (STDJ 18; Leiden: Brill, 1995).

Langer, R., *Cursing the Christians? A History of the Birkat haMinim* (Oxford: Oxford University Press, 2012).

Lickel, B./N. Miller/D.M. Sternstrom/T.A. Denson/T. Schmader, "Vicarious Retribution: The Role of Collective Blame in Intergroup Aggression", *PSPR* 10 (2006) 372–90.

Lieu, J.M., *Neither Jew Nor Christian: Constructing Early Christianity* (London & New York: T & T Clark, 2002).

— *Christian Identity in the Jewish and Graeco-Roman World* (Oxford: Oxford University Press, 2004).

— *I, II and III John: A Commentary* (The New Testament Library; Louisville and London: Westminster John Knox Press, 2008).

— "The Audience of the Johannine Epistles", in R.A. Culpepper/P.N. Anderson (ed.), *Communities in Dispute: Current Scholarship on the Johannine Epistles* (SBLECL 13; Atlanta, GA: Sociaty of Biblical Literature, 2014) 123–40.

— "From Us but Not of Us? Moving the Boundaries of the Community", in M. Grundeken/J. Verheyden (ed.), *Early Christian Communities between Ideal and Reality* (WUNT 342; Mohr Siebeck, 2015) 161–75.

Liew, T.-S.B., "Ambiguous Admittance: Consent and Descent in John's Community of 'Upward' Mobility", in M.W. Dube/J.L. Staley (ed.), *John and Postcolonialism: Travel, Space and Power* (London & New York: Sheffield Academic Press, 2002) 193–224.

Lincoln, A.T., *The Gospel According to Saint John* (BNTC 4; London/Peabody, MA: Continuum/Hendrickson, 2005).

Lincoln, B., *Discourse and the Construction of Society: Comparative Studies of Myth, Ritual, and Classification* (New York: Oxford University Press, 1989).

Lindars, B., *The Theology of the Letter to the Hebrews* (NTT; Cambridge: Cambridge University Press, 1991).

Lindemann, A., "The First Epistle of Clement", in W. Pratscher (ed.), *The Apostolic Fathers: An Introduction* (trans. E. Wolfe; Waco: Baylor University Press, 2010) 47–70.

Lipp, W., *Stigma und Charisma: über soziales Grenzverhalten* (Berlin: Reimer, 1985).

Loader, W., *The Dead Sea Scrolls on Sexuality: Attitudes towards Sexuality in Sectarian and Related Literature at Qumran* (Grand Rapids, MI: Eerdmans, 2009).

— "The Law and Ethics in John", in J.G. van der Watt/R. Zimmermann (ed.), *Rethinking the Ethics of John: "Implicit Ethics" in the Johannine Writings* (WUNT 291; Tübingen: Mohr Siebeck, 2012) 144–58.

Lord, A.B., *The Singer of Tales* (Cambridge: Harvard University Press, 1960).

Lowe, E.J, "Personal Experience and Belief: The Significance of External Symbolic Storage for the Emergence of Modern Human Cognition", in C. Renfrew/C. Scarre (ed.), *Cognition and Material Culture: The Archaeology of Symbolic Storage* (Cambridge: MacDonald Institute for Archaeological Research, 1998) 89–96.

Luomanen, P., *Entering the Kingdom of Heaven: A Study on the Structure of Matthew's View of Salvation* (WUNT R. 2; Tübingen: Mohr Siebeck, 1998).

— "The Sociology of Knowledge, the Social Identity Approach and the Cognitive Science of Religion", in P. Luomanen/I. Pyysiäinen/R. Uro (ed.), *Explaining Christian Origins and Early Judaism: Contributions from Cognitive and Social Science* (BibInt Series 89; Leiden: Brill, 2007) 199–229.

— *Recovering Jewish-Christian Sects and Gospels* (VCSup; Leiden - Boston; Brill, 2012).

— "Social-Scientific Modeling in Biblical and Related Studies", *Perspectives on Science* 21 (2013) 202–220.

— "How Religions Remember: Memory Theories In Biblical Studies and in the Study of Cognitive Study of Religion", in I. Czashesz/R. Uro (ed.), *Mind, Morality and*

Magic: Cognitive Science Approaches in Biblical Studies (Durham: Acumen, 2013) 24–42.

Luomanen, P./I. Pyysiäinen/R. Uro, "Introduction: Social and Cognitive Perspectives in the Study of Christian Origins and Early Judaism", in P. Luomanen/I. Pyysiäinen/R. Uro (ed.), *Explaining Christian Origins and Early Judaism: Contributions from Cognitive and Social Science* (BibInt Series 89; Leiden: Brill, 2007) 1–33.

Luz, U., *Matthew 1–7: A Commentary* (Hermeneia; Edinburgh: T&T Clark, 1990).

— *Matthew 8-20: A Commentary* (Hermeneia; Minneapolis: Fortress, 2001).

— *Matthew 21-28: A Commentary* (Hermeneia; Minneapolis: Fortress, 2005).

Maass, A./D. Salvi/L. Arcuri/G. Semin, "Language Use in Intergroup Contexts: The Linguistic Intergroup Bias", *JPSP* 57 (1989) 981–93.

Macaskill, G., *Revealed Wisdom and Inaugurated Eschatology in Ancient Judaism and Early Christianity* (JSJSup 115; Leiden: Brill, 2007).

Macquarrie, J., *An Existentialist Theology: A Comparison of Heidegger and Bultmann* (London: SCM, 2012 [1955]).

Malafouris, L., "The Brain-Artefact Interface (BAI): a Challenge for Archaeology and Cultural Neuro-Science", *SCAN* 5 (2010) 264–73.

Malafouris, L./C. Renfrew, "The Cognitive Life of Things: Archaeology, Material Engagement, and the Extended Mind", in L. Malafouris/C. Renfrew (ed.), *The Cognitive Life of Things: Recasting the Boundaries of the Mind* (Cambridge: MacDonald Institute of Archaeology, 2010) 1–12.

Malbon, E.S., "Fallible Followers: Women and Men in the Gospel of Mark", *Semeia* 28 (1983) 29–48.

— "The Jewish Leaders in the Gospel of Mark: A Literary Study of Marcan Characterization", *JBL* 108 (1989) 259–81.

Malkki, L.H., *Purity and Exile: Violence, Memory, and National Cosmology among Hutu Refugees in Tanzania* (Chicago/London: University of Chicago Press, 1995).

Mandler, J.M., *Stories, Scripts, and Scenes: Aspects of Schema Theory* (Hillsdale, N.J./London: Erlbaum, 1984).

Mandler, J.M./N.S. Johnson, "Remembrance of Things Parsed: Story Structure and Recall", *Cognitive Psychology* 9 (1977) 111–51.

Markus, H./P. Nurius, "Possible Selves", *AP* 41 (1986) 954–69.

Marques, J.M., "The Black-Sheep Effect: Out-Group Homogeneity in Social Comparison Settings", in D. Abrams/M.A. Hogg (ed.), *Social Identity Theory: Constructive and Critical Advances* (London: Harvester Wheatsheaf, 1990) 131–51.

Marques, J.M./D. Abrams/D. Páez/M.A. Hogg, "Social Categorization, Social Identification, and Rejection of Deviant Group Members", in M.A. Hogg/S. Tindale (ed.), *Blackwell Handbook of Social Psychology: Group Processes* (First published 2001; Oxford: Blackwell, 2003) 400–24.

Marques, J.M./D. Páez/D. Abrams. "Social Identity and Intragroup Differentiation as Subjective Social Control", in S.Worchel/J. F. Morales/D. Páez/J.-C. Deschamps (ed.), *Social Identity: International Perspectives* (London: Sage Publications, 1998) 124–41.

Marques, J.M./V.Y. Yzerbyt/J.-P. Leyens, "The 'Black Sheep Effect': Extremity of Judgments towards Ingroup Members as a Function of Group Identification", *EJSP* 18 (1988) 1–16.

Marshall, H., "A New Understanding of the Present and the Future: Paul and Eschatology" in R.N. Longenecker (ed.), *The Road from Damascus: The Impact of Paul's Conversion on his Life, Thought and Ministry* (Cambridge: Eerdmans. 1997) 43–61.

Martyn, J.L., *Theological Issues in the Letters of Paul* (Edinburgh: T & T Clark, 1997).

— *History and Theology in the Fourth Gospel* (3rd Edition; Louisville: Westminster John Knox, 2003 [originally 1968]).

Marxsen, W., *New Testament Foundations for Christian Ethics* (Minneapolis: Fortress Press, 1993).

Mason, S., "Jews, Judeans, Judaizing, Judaism: Problems of Categorization in Ancient History", *JSJ* 38 (2007) 457–512.

McAdams, D.P., "Personal Narratives and the Life Story", in John/Robins/Pervin (ed.), *Handbook of Personality: Theory and Research.* 3rd ed. New York: Guilford Press, 2008.

McGuire, M., *Lived Religion: Faith and Practice in Everyday Life* (Oxford: Oxford University Press, 2008).

McIver, R.K., *Memory, Jesus, and the Synoptic Gospels* (SBLRBS 59; Atlanta, GA: Society of Biblical Literature, 2011).

— *Mainstream or Marginal?: The Matthean Community in Early Christianity* (Frankfurt: Peter Lang, 2012).

Meeks, W.A., "The Man from Heaven in Johannine Sectarianism", *JBL* 91 (1972) 44–72.

Meijering, E.P., *Augustin über Schöpfung, Ewigkeit und Zeit. Das elfte Buch der Bekenntnisse* (PP 14; Leiden: Brill, 1979).

Mendelson, M., "*venter animi/distentio animi:* Memory and Temporality in Augustine's *Confessions*", *Augustinian Studies* 31 (2000) 137–63.

Metso, S., *The Textual Development of the Qumran Community Rule* (STDJ 21; Leiden: Brill, 1997).

— *The Serekh Texts* (Companion to the Qumran Scrolls 9; London: T&T Clark, 2007).

Meyer, M., "Whom Did Jesus Love Most? Beloved Disciples in John and Other Gospels", in T. Rasimus (ed.), *The Legacy of John: Second Century Reception of the Fourth Gospel* (NovTSup 132; Leiden: Brill, 2010) 73–91.

Milgrom, J., *Leviticus 1–16: A New Translation with Introduction and Commentary* (The Anchor Bible 3; New York: Doubleday, 1991).

Miller, D.T., "Disrespect and the Experience of Injustice", *Annual Review of Psychology* 52 (2001) 527–53.

Miller, R.J., (ed.), *The Complete Gospels* (Sonoma: Polegridge, 1992).

Misztal, B.A., *Theories of Social Remembering* (Philadelphia: Open University Press, 2003).

Mödritzer, H., *Stigma und Charisma im Neuen Testament und seiner Umwelt: zur Soziologie des Urchristentums* (Freiburg: Univ.-Verl., 1994).

Moeser, M.C., *The Anedote in Mark, the Classical World and the Rabbis* (JSNTSup 227; Sheffield: Sheffield University Press, 2002).

Moloney, F., *Signs and Shadows: Reading John 5–12* (Minneapolis: Fortress Press, 1996).

Moore, A., "Enigmatic Endings and Delayed Signs: The Ending of Mark's Gospel", in J.H. Ellens (ed.), *Text and Community: Essays in Memory of Bruce M. Metzger, Vol. 1* (NTM 19; Sheffield: Sheffield Phoenix Press, 2007) 103–20.

Moss, C., *The Myth of Persecution: How Early Christians Invented a Story of Martyrdom* (New York: HarperOne, 2013).

Mullen, E./L.J. Skitka, "Exploring the Psychological Underpinnings of the Moral Mandate Effect: Motivated Reasoning, Group Differentiation, or Anger?", *JPSP* 90 (2006) 629–43.

Mullet, É./G. Michèle, "Developmental and Cognitive Points of View on Forgiveness", in M.E. McCullough/K.I. Pargament/C.E. Thoresen (ed.), *Forgiveness: Theory, Research and Practice* (New York: Guilford Press, 1999) 111–32.

Murphy-O'Connor, J., "An Essene Missionary Document? CD II, 14–VI, 1", *RB* 77 (1970) 201–29.

Murray, M., *Playing a Jewish Game: Gentile Christian Judaizing in the First and Second Century CE* (SCJ 13; Waterloo, Ont.: Wilfrid Laurier University Press, 2004).

Nanos, M., "*New* or *Re*newed Covenantalism? A Response to Richard Hays", in R. Bauckham et al (ed.), *The Epistle to the Hebrews and Christian Theology* (Grand Rapids: Eerdmans, 2009).

Nässelqvist, D., "Stylistic Levels in Hebrews 1.1–4 and John 1.1–18", *JSNT* 35 (2012) 31–53.

— *Public Reading in Early Christianity: Lectors, Manuscripts, and Sound in the Oral Delivery of John 1–4* (Novum Testamentum Supplements 163; Leiden: Brill, 2015).

Nässelqvist, D., "Contextualizing First-Century Education and Public Reading Practices: The Funerary Altar of Quintus Sulpicius Maximus", forthcoming.

Newsom, C.A., *The Self as Symbolic Space: Constructing Identity and Community at Qumran* (STDJ 52; Leiden: Brill, 2004).

— "Constructing 'We, You, and the Others' through Non-Polemical Discourse", in F. García Martínez/M. Popović (ed.), *Defining Identities: We, You, and the Other in the Dead Sea Scrolls. Proceedings of the Fifth Meeting of the IOQS in Groningen* (STDJ 70; Leiden: Brill, 2008) 13–21.

Neyrey, J.H., *Honor and Shame in the Gospel of Matthew* (Louisville: Westminster John Knox, 1998).

Nikki, N., "The Flexible Apostle: Paul's Varied Social Identifications in 1 Corinthians 9 and Philippians 3", in R. Hakola/N. Nikki/U. Tervahauta (ed.), *Others and the Construction of Early Christian Identities* (PFES 106; Helsinki: The Finnish Exegetical Society, 2013) 75–101.

— *Opponents and Identity in the Letter to the Philippians* (Doctoral dissertation; University of Helsinki, 2015).

Nineham, D.E., “Eyewitness Testimony and the Gospel Tradition”, *JTS* n.s. 9 (1958) 13–25, 243–52; *JTS* n.s. 11 (1960) 253–64.

Noam, V., “Divorce in Qumran in Light of Early Halakhah”, *JJS* 56/2 (2005) 206–23.

Nocita, M., “L’ara di Sulpicio Massimo: Nuove osservazioni in occasione del restauro”, *BCACR* 101 (2000) 81–100.

Norenzayan, A./I. Choi/K. Pen, “Perception and Cognition”, in S. Kitayama/D. Cohen (ed.), *Handbook of Cultural Psychology* (New York: Guilford, 2007) 569–644.

Nünning, A./V. Nünning, “Multiperspektivität aus narratologischer Sicht. Erzähltheoretische Grundlagen und Kategorien zur Analyse der Perspektivenstruktur narrativer Texte”, in A. Nünning/V. Nünning (ed.), *Multiperspektivisches Erzählen. Zur Theorie und Geschichte der Perspektivenstruktur im englischen Roman des 18.–20. Jahrhunderts* (Trier: Wissenschaftlicher Verlag 2000) 39–77.

O’Daly, G.J.P., “Time as *distentio* and St Augustine’s Exegesis of Philippians 3:12–14”, *REAug* 23 (1977) 265–71.

— “Augustine on the Measurement of Time: Some Comparisons with Aristotelian and Stoic Texts”, in H.J. Blumenthal/R.A. Markus (ed.), *Neoplatonism and Early Christian Thought: Essays in Honor of A.H. Armstrong* (London: Variorum, 1981) 171–9.

— *Augustine’s Philosophy of Mind* (Berkeley and Los Angeles: University of California Press, 1987).

O’Day, G., “Jesus as Friend in the Gospel of John”, *Int* 58 (2004) 144–57.

O’Donnel, J.J., *Augustine Confessions* (3 vols; Oxford: Clarendon Press, 1992).

Oakes, P.J., “The Categorization Process: Cognition of the Group in the Social Psychology of Stereotyping”, in D. Abrams/M.A. Hogg (ed.), *Social Identity Theory: Constructive and Critical Advances* (London: Harvester Wheatsheaf, 1990) 28–47.

Oakes, P.J./S.A. Haslam/K.J. Reynolds, “Social Categorization and Social Context: Is Stereotype Change a Matter of Information or of Meaning?” in D.M. Abrams/M.A. Hogg (ed.), *Social Identity and Social Cognition* (Oxford: Blackwell, 1999) 55–79.

Oakes, P.J./S.A. Haslam/J.C. Turner, *Stereotyping and Social Reality* (Oxford: Blackwell, 1994).

— “The Role of Prototypicality in Group Influence and Cohesion: Contextual Variation in the Graded Structure of Social Categories”, in S. Worchel et al. (ed.), *Social Identity: International Perspectives* (London: Sage, 1998) 75–92.

Olick, J.K./J. Robbins, “Social Memory Studies: From ‘Collective Memory’ to the Historical Sociology of Mnemonic Practices”, *Annual Review of Sociology* 24 (1998) 105–40.

Otten, S./E.H. Gordijn, “Was It One of Us? How People Cope with Misconduct by Fellow Ingroup Members”, *SPPC* 8 no. 4 (2014) 165–77.

Painter, J., “Earth Made Whole: John’s Rereading of Genesis”, in J. Painter/R.A. Culpepper/F.F. Segovia (ed.), *Word, Theology and Community in John* (St. Louis, Missouri: Chalice Press, 2002) 65–84.

Pakkasvirta, J., "Notes on the Theory of Nationalism", in H. Haggrén/J. Rainio-Niemi/J. Vauhkonen (ed.), *Multi-Layered Historicity of the Present Approaches to Social Science History* (Publications of the Department of Political and Economic Studies 8; Helsinki; University of Helsinki, 2013) 75–91.

Parry, D.W./E. Tov (ed.), The Dead Sea Scrolls Reader: Calendrical and Sapiential Texts (6 vol.; Leiden: Brill, 2004).

Paulo de, C.J.N. (ed.), *The Influence of Augustine on Heidegger: The Emergence of an Augustinian Phenomenology* (Lewiston: The Edwin Mellen Press, 2006).

Pellegrini, S., "Das Protoevangelium des Jakobus", in C. Markschies/J. Schröter (ed.), *Antike christiliche Apokryphen in deutscher Übersetzung, Band 1/2* (Tübingen: Mohr Siebeck, 2012) 903–29.

Petersen, N.S., "Die 'Perspektive' in der Erzählung im Markusevangelium", in F. Hahn (ed.), *Der Erzähler des Evangeliums: Methodische Neuansätze in der Markusforschung* (SBS 118/119; Stuttgart: Katholisches Bibelwerk, 1985) 67–91.

Pethes, N., "Gedächtnismetapher", in N. Pethes/J. Ruchatz (ed.), *Gedächtnis und Erinnerung. Ein interdisziplinäres Lexikon* (Hamburg: Rowohlt, 2001) 196–8.

— *Kulturwissenschaftliche Gedächtnistheorien. Zur Einführung* (Hamburg: Junius, 2008).

Powell, M.A., "The Plot and Subplots of Matthew's Gospel", *NTS* 38 (1992) 187–204.

Puech, É., "Un hymne essénien en partie retrouvé et les beatitudes", *RevQ* 13 (1988) 59–88.

— "4Q525 et les péricopes des beatitudes en Ben Sira et Matthieu", *RB* 98 (1991) 80–106.

— "The Collections of Beatitudes in Hebrew and in Greek (4Q525, 1–4 and Matt 5, 3–12)", in F. Manns and E. Alliata (ed.), *Early Christianity in Context: Monuments and Documents: Essays in Honour of Emmanuel Testa* (SBFCM 38; Jerusalem: Franciscan, 1993) 353–68.

—"4QBéatitudes", in É. Puech (ed.), *Qumrân Grotte 4 - XVIII: Textes Hébreux (4Q521–4Q528, 4Q576–4Q579)* (DJD 25; Oxford: Clarendon, 1998) 115–78.

Qimron, E., "Celibacy in the Dead Sea Scrolls and the Two Kinds of Sectarians", in J. Trebolle Barrera/L. Vegas Montaner (ed.), *The Madrid Qumran Congress: Proceedings of the International Congress on the Dead Sea Scrolls, Madrid 18–21 March 1991* (STDJ 11; Leiden: Brill, 1992) 1.286–94.

Qimron, E., et al., "Some Works of the Torah: 4Q394–4Q399 (=4QMMT^{a-f}) and 4Q313", in J. Charlesworth, *Damascus Document Fragments, Some Works of the Torah and Related Documents* (The Dead Sea Scrolls: Hebrew, Aramaic, and Greek Tests with English Translations 3; Tübingen: Mohr Siebeck, 2006) 187–251.

Qimron, E./J. Strugnell, *Qumran Cave 4. V. Miqsat Ma'ase ha-Torah* (DJD 10; Oxford: Clarendon Press, 1994).

Rabbie, J.M./F. Bekkers, "Threatened Leadership and Intergroup Competition", *EJSP* 8 (1978) 9–20.

Räisänen, H., *Paul and the Law.* 2nd edition. (WUNT 29; Tübingen: J.C.B. Mohr & Paul Siebeck, 1983).

— *The Rise of Christian Beliefs: The Thought World of Early Christians* (Minneapolis: Fortress Press, 2010).

Ramshaw, E.J., "Power and Forgiveness in Matthew 18," *WW* 18 (1998) 397–404.

Rappaport, R.A., *Ritual and Religion in the Making of Humanity* (Cambridge: Cambridge UP, 1999).

Redman, J.C.S., "How Accurate Are Eyewitnesses: Bauckham and the Eyewitnesses in the Light of Psychological Research", *JBL* 129 (2010) 177–97.

Reese, E/R. Fivush, "The Development of Collective Remembering", *Memory* 16 (2008) 201–12.

Reese, G./M.C. Steffens/K.J. Jonas, "When Black Sheep Make us Think: Information Processing and Devaluation of In- and Outgroup Norm Deviants", *Social Cognition* 31 no. 4 (2013) 482–503.

Reicher, S., "Making a Past Fit for the Future: The Political Dimensions of Historical Continuity", in F. Sani (ed.), *Self Continuity: Individual and Collective Perspectives* (New York: Psychology Press, 2008) 145–58.

Reicher, S./N. Hopkins, *Self and Nation: Categorization, Contestation and Moblization* (London: Sage Publications, 2001).

Reicher, S./R. Spears/ S. A. Haslam, "The Social Identity Approach in Social Psychology", in M. Wetherell/C. T. Mohanty (ed.), *The Sage Handbook of Identities* (London: Sage Publications, 2010) 45–62.

Reinhartz, A., *Befriending the Beloved Disciple: A Jewish Reading of the Gospel of John* (New York and London: Continuum, 2001).

— "Gospel Audiences: Variations on a Theme", in E.W. Klink III (ed.), *The Audience of the Gospels: The Origin and Function of the Gospels in Early Christianity* (LNTS 353, London & New York: T&T Clark, 2010) 134–52.

Reiser, M., "Love of Enemies in the Context of Antiquity", *NTS* 47 (2001) 411–27.

Reszler, A., "L'Europe à la recherche de ses symboles", *Les Temps Modernes* 550 (1992) 209–20.

Reumann, J., *Philippians: A New Translation with Introduction and Commentary* (New Haven: The Anchor Yale Bible Commentaries, 2008).

Rhoads, D., "Performance Criticism: An Emerging Methodology in Second Testament Studies: Part I", *BTB* 36 (2006) 118–33.

— "Performance Criticism: An Emerging Methodology in Second Testament Studies: Part II", *BTB* 36 (2006) 164–84.

Rhoads, D./J. Dewey/D. Michie, *Mark as Story: Introduction to the Narrative of a Gospel* (3rd Edition; Minneapolis: Fortress Press, 2012).

Ricoeur, P., "Narrative Time", *Critical Inquiry* 7 (1980) 169–90.

— *Temps et Récit* (Paris: Seuil, 1983–85). English translation *Time and Narrative* (transl. K. McLaughlin and D. Pellauer; 3 vols.; Chicago: University of Chicago Press, 1984–88).

— *La mémoire, l'histoire, l'oubli* (L'ordre philosophique; Paris: Seuil, 2000). English translation *Memory, History, Forgetting* (transl. K. Blamey/D. Pellauer; Chicago: The University of Chicago Press, 2004).

Roark, T., *Aristotle on Time: A Study of the Physics* (Cambridge: Cambridge University Press, 2013).

Robbins, V.K., "By Land and By Sea: The We-Passages and Ancient Sea Voyages", in C.H. Talbert (ed.), *Perspectives on Luke-Acts* (PRSMS 5; Macon, Ga: Mercer Univ. Press and Edinburgh: T.& T. Clark, 1978) 215–42.

Roitto, R., *Behaving as a Christ-Believer: A Cognitive Perspective on Identity and Behavior Norms in Ephesians* (CBNTS; Grand Rapids, Michigan, 2011).

— "Sinless Sinners who Remain in Him: Social Identity in 1 John", in B. Tucker/C. Baker (ed.), *The T&T Clark Handbook to Social Identity and the New Testament* (London: T&T Clark, 2013) 493–510.

— "Reintegrative Shaming and a Prayer Ritual of Reintegration in Matthew 18:15–20", *SEÅ* 79 (2014) 95–123.

— "The Polyvalence of ἀφίημι and the Two Cognitive Frames of Forgiveness in the Synoptic Gospels", NovT 57 (2015) 136–58.

Roo, J.C.R. de, "Is 4Q525 a Qumran Sectarian Document?", in S.E. Porter/C.A. Evans (ed.), *The Scrolls and the Scriptures: Qumran Fifty Years After* (JSPSup 26; Sheffield: Sheffield Academic Press, 1997) 338–67.

Rozin, P./J. Haidt/C.R. McCauley, "Disgust", in M. Lewis/J.M. Haviland-Jones/L.F. Barrett (ed.), *Handbook of Emotions* (3rd ed.; New York: Guildford, 2000) 737–53.

Rozin P./L. Lowery/S. Imada/J. Haidt, "The CAD Triad Hypothesis: A Mapping Between Three Moral Emotions (Contempt, Anger, Disgust) and Three Moral Codes (Community, Autonomy, Divinity)", *JPSP* 76 (1999) 574–86.

Rubin, D.C., *Autobiographical Memory* (Cambridge: Cambridge University Press, 1986).

— *Memory in Oral Traditions: The Cognitive Psychology of Epic, Ballads, and Counting-out Rhymes* (New York/Oxford: Oxford University Press, 1995).

Rubin, M./C. Badea, "Why Do People Perceive Ingroup Homogeneity on Ingroup Traits and Outgroup Homogeneity on Outgroup Traits?" *PSPB* 33 (2007) 31–42.

Rullo, M./F. Presaghi/S. Livi, "Reactions to Ingroup and Outgroup Deviants: An Experimental Group Paradigm for Black Sheep Effect", *PLoS ONE* 10 no. 5 (2015) 1–14.

Runesson, A., "Behind the Gospel of Matthew: Radical Pharisees in Post-War Galilee?" CurTM 37 (2010) 460–71.

— "Purity, Holiness, and the Kingdom of Heaven in Matthew's Narrative World", in C. Ehrlich/A. Runesson/E. Schuller (ed.), *Purity and Holiness in Judaism and Christianity: Essays in Memory of Susan Haber* (WUNT; Tübingen: Mohr Siebeck, 2013) 144–80.

Saldarini, A.J., *Matthew's Christian-Jewish Community* (Chicago: Univ. of Chicago Press, 1994).

Sanders, E.P., *Paul and Palestinian Judaism: A Comparison of Patterns of Religion* (Philadelphia: Fortress, 1977).

— *Jesus and Judaism* (London: SCM Press, 1985).

Sapir, E., *Selected Writings of Edward Sapir* (Berkeley/Los Angeles: University of California Press, 1949).

Schacter, D.L., *The Seven Sins of Memory: How the Mind Forgets and Remembers* (Boston/New York: Houghton Mifflin, 2001).

Schacter, D.L./K.A. Norman/W. Koutstaal, "The Cognitive Neuroscience of Constructive Memory", *ARP* 49 (1998) 289–318.

Schiffman, L., *The Halakhah at Qumran* (SJLA 16; Leiden: Brill, 1975).

— "Laws Pertaining to Women in the Temple Scroll", in D. Dimant/U. Rappaport (ed.), *The Dead Sea Scrolls: Forty Years of Research* (Leiden: Brill/Jerusalem: Magness Press, 1992) 210–28.

— *Reclaiming the Dead Sea Scrolls: The History of Judaism, the Background of Christianity, the Lost Library of Qumran* (Philadelphia: The Jewish Publication Society, 1994).

— "The Place of 4QMMT in the Corpus of Qumran Manuscripts", in J. Kampen/M. Bernstein, *Reading 4QMMT: New Perspectives on Qumran Law and History* (SBL Symposium Series 2; Atlanta, GA: Scholars Press, 1996) 81–98.

— "Non-Jews in the Dead Sea Scrolls", in *Qumran and Jerusalem: Studies in the Dead Sea Scrolls and the History of Judaism* (Grand Rapids, MI: Eerdmans, 2010) 365–80.

Schjødt, J.P., "Initiation and the Classification of Rituals", *Temenos* 22 (1986) 93–108.

Schmidt, K.M., *Wege des Heils. Erzählstrukturen und Rezeptionskontexte des Markusevangeliums* (NTOA 74; Göttingen: Vandenhoeck & Ruprecht, 2010).

Schmidt, S.J., *Kognitive Autonomie und soziale Orientierung: Konstruktivistische Bemerkungen zum Zusammenhang von Kognition, Kommunikation, Medien und Kultur* (3rd edn; Münster: Lit Verlag, 2003).

Schmidt, S.J./S. Weischenberg, "Mediengattungen, Berichterstattungsmuster, Darstellungsformen", in K. Merton/S.J. Schmidt/S. Weischenberg (ed.), *Die Wirklichkeit der Medien: Eine Einführung in die Kommunikationswissenschaft* (Opladen: Westdeutscher Verlag, 1994) 212–36.

Schniewind, J., "Zur Synoptiker-Exegese", *TRu* 2 (1930) 129–89.

Schofield, A., *From Qumran to the Yahad: A New Paradigm of Textual Development for the Community Rule* (STDJ 77; Leiden: Brill, 2009).

Schröter, J., "The Gospels as Eyewitness Testimony? A Critical Examination of Richard Bauckham's Jesus and the Eyewitnesses", *JSNT* 31 (2008) 195–209.

Schuller, E., "Women in the Dead Sea Scrolls", in M. Wise et al. (ed.), *Methods of Investigation of the Dead Sea Scrolls and the Khirbet Qumran Site: Present Realities and Future Prospects* (Annals of the New York Academy of Sciences 722; New York: New York Academy of Sciences, 1994) 115–31.

— "Women in the Dead Sea Scrolls", in P.W. Flint/J. VanderKam (ed.), *The Dead Sea Scrolls after Fifty Years: A Comprehensive Assessment* (Leiden: Brill, 1998) 2.117–44.

Schuller, E./C. Wassen, "Women: Daily Life", in L.H. Schiffman/J.C. VanderKam (ed.), *Encyclopedia of the Dead Sea Scrolls* (New York: Oxford University Press, 1999) 2.981–4.

Schwartz, B., "Christian Origins: Historical Truth and Social Memory", in A. Kirk/T. Thatcher (ed.), *Memory, Tradition, and Text: Uses of the Past in Early Christianity* (SBLSS 52; Atlanta: SBL, 2005) 43–56.

Schwartz, D.R., "Doing Like Jews or Becoming a Jew? Josephus on Women Converts to Judaism", in J. Frey et al (ed.), *Jewish Identity in the Greco-Roman World* (Ancient Judaism and Early Christianity 71; Leiden: Brill, 2007) 93–109.

Schweitzer, A., *The Mysticism of Paul the Apostle* (Transl. by W. Montgomery; Baltimore: Johns Hopkins University Press. [1st ed. 1931, 2nd ed. 1953], 1998).

Searle, J.R., *Speech Acts: An Essay in the Philosophy of Language* (Cambridge: Cambridge University Press, 1969).

Seeley, D., *Deconstructing the New Testament* (Leiden: Brill, 1994).

Setzer, C., *Jewish Responses to Early Christians: History and Polemics, 30–150 CE* (Minneapolis, MN: Fortress Press, 1994).

Sherif, M., *Group Conflict and Cooperation: Their Social Psychology* (London: Routledge, 1966).

Shiell, W.D., *Reading Acts: The Lector and the Early Christian Audience* (Boston: Brill, 2004).

— *Delivering from Memory: The Effect of Performance on the Early Christian Audience* (Eugene: Pickwick, 2011).

Shiner, W., *Proclaiming the Gospel: First-Century Performance of Mark* (Harrisburg: Trinity, 2003).

Sim, D.C., *The Gospel of Matthew and Christian Judaism: The History and Social Setting of the Matthean Community* (Edinburgh: T. & T. Clark, 1998).

Skarsaune, O., *In the Shadow of the Temple: Jewish Influences on Early Christianity* (Downers Grove: InterVarsity, 2002).

Smith, D.E., *From Symposium to Eucharist: The Banquet in the Early Christian World* (Fortress: Minneapolis, 2003).

Smith, D.M., "The Epistles of John: What's New since Brooke's ICC in 1912?" *ExpTim* 120 (2009) 373–83.

Smith, E.R./S. Queller, "Mental Representations", in M.B. Brewer/M. Hewstone (ed.), *Social Cognition* (Oxford: Blackwell, 2004) 5–27.

Sorabji, R., *Aristotle on Memory* (2nd ed.; London: Duckworth, 2004).

Spear, N.E., "Retrieval: Properties and Effects", in H.L. Roediger III/Y. Dudai/S.M. Fitzpatrick (ed.), *Science of Memory: Concepts* (Oxford/New York: Oxford University Press, 2007) 215–19.

Sperber, D., "Anthropology and Psychology: Towards an Epidemiology of Representations", *Man* 20 (1975) 73–89.

Sproston North, W.E., *The Lazarus Story within the Johannine Tradition* (JSNTSup 212; Sheffield: Sheffield Academic Press, 2001).

Squire, L.R./E.R. Kandel, *Memory: From Mind to Molecules* (New York: Scientific American Library, 1999).

Standhartinger, A., "Bultmann's *Theology of the New Testament* in Context", in B.W. Longenecker/M.C. Parsons (ed.), *Beyond Bultmann: Reckoning a New Testament Theology* (Waco, TX: Baylor University Press, 2014) 233–55.

— "Modernisierte Theologie. Zeitgeschichtliche Reflexionen in Rudolf Bultmanns Theologie des Neuen Testaments", *TRu* 29 (2014) 161–89.

Stanton, G.N., *A Gospel for a New People: Studies in Matthew* (Edinburgh: T & T Clark, 1992).

Stegemann, H., "The Qumran Essenes, Local Members of the Main Jewish Union in Late Second Temple Times", in J. Trebolle Barrera/L. Vegas Montaner (ed.), *The Madrid Qumran Congress: Proceedings of the International Congress on the Dead Sea Scrolls, Madrid 18–21 March 1991* (STDJ 11; Leiden: Brill, 1992) 2:83–166.

Stegemann, W./R. E. DeMaris (ed.), *Alte Texte in neuen Kontexten: Wo steht die sozialwissenschaftliche Bibelexegese?* (Stuttgart: Kohlhammer, 2015).

Steudel, A., "The Houses of Prostration in CD XI,21–XII,1 - Duplicates of the Temple", *RevQ* 16 (1993) 49–63.

Strauss, C./N. Quinn, *A Cognitive Theory of Cultural Meaning* (Cambridge: Cambridge University Press, 1997).

Strecker, G., *The Sermon on the Mount: An Exegetical Commentary* (Edinburgh: T & T Clark, 1988).

Strugnell, J., "Second Thoughts on a Forthcoming Edition", in E. Ulrich/J. VanderKam (ed.), *The Community of the Renewed Covenant: The Notre Dame Symposium on the Dead Sea Scrolls* (Christianity and Judaism in Antiquity Series 10; Notre Dame, IN: Notre Dame, 1995) 57–73.

Stuckenbruck, L.T., "The Interiorization of Dualism within the Human Being in Second Temple Judaism: The Treatise of the Two Spirits (1QS III:13–IV:26) in its Tradition Historical Context", in A. Lange/E.M. Meyers/B.H. Reynolds III/R. Styers (ed.), *Light Against Darkness: Dualism in Ancient Mediterranean Religion and the Contemporary World* (JAJSup 2; Göttingen: Vandenhoeck & Ruprecht, 2011) 145–68.

Surkamp, C., "Die Perspektivenstruktur narrativer Texte aus der Sicht der possible-worlds-theory. Zur literarischen Inszenierung der Pluralität subjektiver Wirklichkeitsmodelle", in A. Nünning/V. Nünning (ed.), *Multiperspektivisches Erzählen. Zur Theorie und Geschichte der Perspektivenstruktur im englischen Roman des 18.–20. Jahrhunderts* (Trier: Wissenschaftlicher Verlag 2000) 111–32.

Sutton, J., "Representation, Reduction, and Interdisciplinarity, in the Sciences of Memory", in H. Clapin/P. Staines/P. Slezak (ed.), *Representation in Mind: New Approaches to Mental Representation* (London: Elsevier, 2004) 187–216.

— "Material Agency, Skills, and History: Distributed Cognition and the Archeology of Memory", in C. Knappett/L. Malafouris (ed.), *Material Agency: Toward a Non-anthropocentric Approach* (New York: Springer, 2007) 37–55.

— "Remembering", in P. Robbins/M. Aydede (ed.), *The Cambridge Handbook of Situated Cognition* (Cambridge: Cambridge University Press, 2009) 217–35.

— "Exograms and Interdisciplinarity: History, the Extended Mind, and the Civilizing Process", in *The Extended Mind* (Cambridge, MA.: MIT Press, 2010) 189–225.

Sutton, J./C.B. Harris/P.G. Keil, "The Psychology of Memory, Extended Cognition, and Socially Distributed Remembering", *PCS* 9 (2010) 521–60.

Swol, L.M. van, "Performance and Process in Collective and Individual Memory: The Role of Social Decision Schemes and Memory Bias in Collective Memory", *Memory* 16 (2008) 274–87.

Syreeni, K., "Peter as Character and Symbol in the Gospel of Matthew", in K. Syreeni/ D. Rhoads (ed.), *Characterization in the Gospels: Reconceiving Narrative Criticism* (Sheffield: Sheffield Academic Press, 1999) 106–52.

— "The Witness of Blood: The Narrative and Ideological Function of the 'Beloved Disciple' in John 13–21", in A. Mustakallio (ed.), *Lux Humana, Lux Aeterna: Essays on Biblical and Related Themes in Honour of Lars Aejmelaeus* (PFES 89; Helsinki: Finnish Exegetical Society/Göttingen: Vandenhoeck & Ruprecht, 2005) 164–85.

— "Satanic Disciples: A Narrative and Cognitive Analysis of Two Gospel Scenes", in J.A. Ramos/P.R. Davies/M.A. Travassos Valdez (ed.), *From Antiquity to the Present: the 2008 European Association of Biblical Studies Lisbon Meeting* (Lisbon: Centro de História da Universidade de Lisboa, 2008) 69–80.

— "Testament and Consolation: Reflections on the Literary Form of the Johannine Farewell of Jesus", in J. Pakkala/M. Nissinen (ed.), *Houses Full of All Good Things: Essays in Memory of Timo Veijola* (PFES 95; Helsinki: Finnish Exegetical Society, 2008) 573–90.

— "Resurrection or Assumption? Matthew's View of the Post-Mortem Vindication of Jesus", in W. Weren/H. van de Sandt/J. Verheyden (ed.), *Life Beyond Death in Matthew's Gospel: Religious Metaphor or Bodily Reality?* (Biblical Tools and Studies 13; Leuven: Peeters, 2011) 57–77.

Tajfel, H., *Human Groups and Social Categories: Studies in Social Psychology*; Cambridge: Cambridge University Press, 1981).

Tajfel, H./J.C. Turner, "An Integrative Theory of Intergroup Conflict", in W.G. Austin/ S. Worchel (ed.), *The Social Psychology of Intergroup Conflict* (Monterey, Calif.: Brooks/Cole, 1979) 33–47.

Talbert, C.H., *Matthew* (Paideia; Grand Rapids: Baker, 2010).

Tellbe, M., *Paul between Synagogue and State. Christians, Jews, and Civic Authorities in 1 Thessalonians, Romans and Philippians* (ConBNT 34; Stockholm, Sweden: Almqvist & Wiksell International, 2001).

Thatcher, T., "Why John Wrote a Gospel: Memory and History in an Early Christian Community", in A. Kirk/T. Thatcher (ed.), *Memory, Tradition, and Text: Uses of the Past in Early Christianity* (Semeia Studies 52; Atlanta: SBL, 2005) 79–97.

Thatcher, T./A. Le Donne, "Introducing Media Culture to Johannine Studies: Orality, Performance and Memory", in T. Thatcher/A. Le Donne (ed.), *The Fourth Gospel in First-Century Media Culture* (London: T&T Clark, 2011) 1–8.

Theissen, G., *The Gospels in Context: Social and Political History in the Synoptic Tradition* (Minneapolis: Fortress, 1991).

Theobald, M., *Studien zum Corpus Johanneum* (WUNT 267; Tübingen: Mohr Siebeck, 2010).

Thiselton, A.C., "The Supposed Power of Words in the Biblical Writings", *JTS* 25 (1974) 283–99.

Thomas, R., *Oral Tradition and Written Record in Classical Athens* (Cambridge/New York: Cambridge University Press, 1989).

Thompson, P., *The Voice of the Past: Oral History* (3d ed.; Oxford: Oxford University Press, 2000).

Thompson, W.G., *Matthew's Advice to a Divided Community: Mt. 17,22–18,35* (Rome: Biblical Institute Press, 1970).

Tigchelaar, E.J.C., *To Increase Learning for the Understanding Ones: Reading and Reconstructing the Fragmentary Early Jewish Sapiential Text 4QInstruction* (STDJ 44; Leiden Brill, 2001).

Tonkin, E., *Narrating Our Pasts: The Social Construction of Oral History* (Cambridge: Cambridge University Press, 1992).

Toorn, K. van der, "Curse", in K. van der Toorn/B. Becking/P. W. van der Horst (ed.), *Dictionary of Deities and Demons in the Bible* (Leiden: Brill, 1995) 398–406.

Tov, E. (ed.), *The Dead Sea Scrolls Electronic Library: Texts and Images.* (Partially based on The Dead Sea Scrolls Reader, edited by D.W. Parry/E. Tov, morphological analysis by M. Abegg, Jr., produced by N.B. Reynolds, associate producer K. Heal; Leiden: Brill, 2006).

Travaglino, G.A./D. Abrams/G. Randsley de Moura/J.M. Marques/I.R. Pinto, "How Groups React to Disloyalty in the Context of Intergroup Competition: Evaluations of Group Deserters and Defectors", *JESP* 54 (2014) 178–87.

Trebilco, P., *Self-designations and Group Identity in the New Testament* (Cambridge: Cambridge University Press, 2012).

Tucker, J.B., *You Belong to Christ: Paul and the Formation of Social Identity in 1 Corinthians 1–4* (Eugene, OR: Pickwick Publications, 2010).

Tucker, J.B./C.A. Baker (ed.), *T&T Clark Handbook to Social Identity in the New Testament* (London: Bloomsbury, 2014).

Tuckett, C.M., *The Gospel of Mary* (Oxford Early Christian Gospel Texts; Oxford: Oxford University Press, 2007).

Tulving, E., "Episodic and Semantic Memory", in E. Tulving/W. Donaldson, *Organization of Memory* (New York: Academic Press, 1972) 381–403.

Turner, J.C., (with M.A. Hogg/P.J. Oakes/S.D. Reicher/M.S. Wetherell), *Rediscovering the Social Group: A Self-Categorization Theory* (Oxford: Basil Blackwell, 1987).

— "Henri Tajfel: An Introduction", in P. Robinson (ed.), *Social Groups and Identities: Developing the Legacy of Henri Tajfel* (Oxford: Butterworth-Heinemann, 1996) 1–23.

— "Some Current Issues in Research on Social Identity and Self-Categorization Theories", in N. Ellemers/R. Spears/B. Doosje (ed.), *Social Identity: Context, Commitment, Content*; Oxford: Blackwell, 1999) 6–34.

Uusimäki, E., "Use of Scripture in 4QBeatitudes: A Torah-Adjustment to Proverbs 1–9", *DSD* 20 (2013) 71–97.

— *Turning Proverbs towards Torah: An Analysis of 4Q525.* Studies on the Texts of the Desert of Judah 117. Leiden: Brill, 2016.

Vaage, L.E., "An Other Home: Discipleship in Mark as Domestic Ascetism", *CBQ 71* (2009) 741–61.

Vansina, J., *Oral Tradition as History* (Madison: University of Wisconsin Press, 1985).
Verheyden, J./M. Grundeken, "Introduction", in M. Grundeken/J. Verheyden (ed.), *Early Christian Communities between Ideal and Reality* (WUNT 342; Mohr Siebeck, 2015) VII–XIII.
Vermes, G., *The Complete Dead Sea Scrolls in English* (New York: Penguin Press, 1997).
Viviano, B.T., "Eight Beatitudes at Qumran and in Matthew?", *SEÅ* 58 (1993) 71–84.
Vledder, E.J./A. Van Aarde, "The Social Stratification of the Matthean Community", *Neot* 28 (1994) 511–22.
Walters, J., "Romans, Jews, and Christians: The Impact of the Romans on Jewish/Christian Relations in First-Century Rome", in K. Donfried/P. Richardson, *Judaism and Christianity in First-Century Rome* (Grand Rapids: Eerdmans, 2005) 175–95.
Wang, Q., "On the Cultural Constitution of Collective Memory", *Memory* 16 (2008) 305–17.
Wang, Q./J. Brockmeier, "Autobiographical Remembering as Cultural Practice: Understanding the Interplay Between Memory, Self, and Culture", *Culture and Psychology* 8 (2002) 45–64.
Wang, Q./M. Ross, "Culture and Memory", in S. Kitayama/D. Cohen (ed.), *Handbook of Cultural Psychology* (New York: Guilford, 2007) 645–67.
Ward, R.F., "Pauline Voice and Presence as Strategic Communication", in J. Dewey (ed.), *Orality and Textuality in Early Christian Literature* (Atlanta: Society of Biblical Literature, 1994) 95–107.
Ward, R.F./D.J. Trobisch, *Bringing the Word to Life: Engaging the New Testament through Performing It* (Grand Rapids: Eerdmans, 2013).
Wardle, T., *The Jerusalem Temple and Early Christian Identity* (WUNT II/291; Tübingen: Mohr Siebeck, 2010).
Wassén, C., *Women in the Damascus Document* (Academica Biblica 21; Atlanta: Society of Biblical Literature, 2005).
— "Common Meals in the Qumran Movement with Special Attention to Purity Regulations", in D. Hellholm/D. Sänger (ed.), *The Eucharist – Its Origins and Contexts: Sacred Meal, Communal Meal, Table Fellowship in Late Antiquity, Early Judaism, and Early Christianity. Vol. 1* (Tübingen: Mohr Siebeck, forthcoming 2015) 55–78.
— "Women, Worship, Wilderness, and War: Celibacy and the Construction of Identity in the Dead Sea Scrolls", in J. Baden/H. Najman/E. Tigchelaar (ed.), *A Festschrift for John J. Collins in Celebration of His 70th Birthday* (JSJSup; Leiden: Brill) forthcoming 2015.
Wassén, C./J. Jokiranta, "Groups in Tension: Sectarianism in the Damascus Document and the Community Rule", in D.J. Chalcraft (ed.), *Sectarianism in Early Judaism: Sociological Advances* (London: Equinox, 2007) 205–45.
Watson, F., *The Fourfold Gospel* (Grand Rapids: Baker Academic, 2016, forthcoming).
Watt, J.G. van der, "Ethics and Ethos in the Gospel according to John", *ZNW* 97 (2006) 147–76.

Weinfeld, M., *The Organizational Pattern and the Penal Code of the Qumran Sect: A Comparison with Guilds and Religious Associations of the Hellenistic-Roman Period* (NTOA 2; Fribourg: Éditions universitaires, 1986).

Weissenberg, H. von, “Miqṣat Maʿaśê ha-Torah (MMT)”, in J.J. Collins/D.C. Harlow (ed.), *The Eerdman Dictionary of Early Judaism* (Grand Rapids, MI: Eerdmans, 2010) 952–4.

Welzer, H., “Das gemeinsame Verfertigen von Vergangenheit im Gespräch”, in H. Welzer, *Das soziale Gedächtnis: Geschichte, Erinnerung, Tradierung* (Hamburg: Hamburger Edition, 2001) 160–78.

— “Das soziale Gedächtnis”, in H. Welzer, *Das soziale Gedächtnis: Geschichte, Erinnerung, Tradierung* (Hamburg: Hamburger Edition, 2001) 9–21.

— *Das kommunikative Gedächtnis: Eine Theorie der Erinnerung* (München: Beck, 2002).

Werrett, I., *Ritual Purity and the Dead Sea Scrolls* (STDJ 72; Leiden: Brill, 2007).

White Crawford, S., “Mothers, Sisters, and Elders: Titles for Women in Second Temple Jewish and Early Christian Communities”, in J. Davila (ed.), *The Dead Sea Scrolls as Background to Postbiblical Judaism and Early Christianity* (STDJ 46; Leiden: Brill, 2003) 177–91.

— “Not According to Rule: Women, the Dead Sea Scrolls and Qumran,” in S. Paul et al. (ed.), *Emanuel: Studies in Hebrew Bible, Septuagint, and Dead Sea Scrolls in Honor of Emanuel Tov* (VTSup 94; Leiden: Brill, 2003) 127–50.

Whitley, B.E./M.E. Kite, *The Psychology of Prejudice and Discrimination* (2nd Edition; Belmont, CA: Wadsworth/Cengage Learning, 2010).

Wilson, R.A./A. Clark, “How To Situate Cognition: Letting Nature Take Its Course”, P. Robbins/ M. Aydede (ed.), *Cambridge Handbook of Situated Cognition* (Cambridge: Cambridge University Press, 2009) 55–77.

Wilson, R.B., *Religious Sects: A Sociological Study* (New York: McGraw-Hill, 1970).

Witherington, B., *Paul’s Letter to the Philippians: A Socio-Rhetorical Commentary.* (Grand Rapids, Michigan: William B. Eerdmans Publishing Company, 2011).

Wohl, M.J.A./N.R. Branscombe, “Forgiveness and Collective Guilt Assignment to Historical Perpetrator Groups Depend on Level of Social Category Inclusiveness”, *JPSP* 88 (2005) 288–303.

— “Remembering Historical Victimization: Collective Guilt for Current Ingroup Transgressions”, *JPSP* 94 (2008) 988–1006.

Wohl, M.J.A/N.R. Branscombe/Y. Klar, “Collective Guilt: Emotional Reactions When One’s Group Has Done Wrong or Been Wronged”, *ERSP* 17 (2006) 1–37.

Wrede, W., *Untersuchungen zum Ersten Klemensbrief* (Göttingen: Vandenhoeck & Ruprecht, 1891).

— *Paul* (Transl. by E. W. Lummis; London: Philip Green, 1907).

Wright III, B.G., “Wisdom and Women at Qumran”, *DSD* 11/2 (2004) 240–61.

Young, N., “‘Bearing His Reproach’ (Heb 13.9–14)”, *NTS* 48 (2002) 243–61.

Zangenberg, J., “Bones of Contention: ‘New’ Bones from Qumran Help Settle Old Questions (and Raise New Ones): Remarks on Two Recent Conferences”, *The Qumran Chronicle* 9/1 (2000) 51–76.

Zerubavel, E., "Social Memories: Steps to a Sociology of the Past", *QS* 19 (1996) 283–99.

— *Time Maps: Collective Memory and the Social Shape of the Past* (Chicago: Chicago University Press, 2003).

Zias, J., "The Cemeteries of Qumran and Celibacy: Confusion Laid to Rest?" *DSD* 7/2 (2000) 220–53.

Zimmermann, R., "Formen und Gattungen als Medien der Jesus-Erinnerung: Zur Rückgewinnung der Diachronie in der Formgeschichte des Neuen Testament", in O. Fuchs/B. Janowski (ed.), *Die Macht der Erinnerung* (*JBTh* 22; Neukirche-Vluyn: Neukirchener Verlag, 2008) 131–67.

— "Gleichnisse als Medien der Jesuserinnerung: Die Historizität der Jesusparabeln im Horizont der Gedächtnisforschung", in R. Zimmerman (ed.), *Hermeneutik der Gleichnisse Jesu: Methodische Neuansätze zum Verstehen urchristlicher Parabeltexte* (WUNT 231;Tübingen: Mohr-Siebeck, 2008) 87–121.

— "Is There Ethics in the Gospel of John? Challenging an Outdated Consensus", in J.G. van der Watt/R. Zimmermann (ed.), *Rethinking the Ethics of John: "Implicit Ethics" in the Johannine Writings* (WUNT 291; Tübingen: Mohr Siebeck, 2012) 44–80.

Zwick, R., *Montage im Markusevangelium: Studien zur narrativen Organisation der ältesten Jesuserzählung* (SBB 18; Stuttgart: Katholisches Bibelwerk, 1989).

Abbreviations

ABRL	Anchor Bible Reference Library
AJP	American Journal of Philology
AP	American Psychologist
ARP	Annual Review of Psychology
ARS	Annual Review of Sociology
ASNU	Acta seminarii neotestamentici upsaliensis
ASTI	Annual of the Swedish Theological Institute
AThR	Anglican Theological Review
AYB	Anchor Yale Bible
BCACR	Bullettino della Commissione Archeologica Comunale di Roma
BETL	Bibliotheca ephemeridum theologicarum lovaniensium
BibInt	Biblical Interpretation
BiLi	Bibel und literatur
BNTC	Black's New Testament Commentaries
BTB	Biblical Theology Bulletin
BZ	Biblische Zeitschrift
CB	Cultura biblica
CBQ	Catholic Biblical Quarterly
ConBNT/CBNTS	Coniectanea biblica: New Testament Series
CurTM	Currents in Theology and Mission
DSD	Dead Sea Discoveries
DJD	Discoveries in the Judaean Desert
EJSP	European Journal of Social Psychology
ERSP	European Review of Social Psychology
ExpTim	Expository Times
FRLANT	Forschungen zur Religion und Literatur des Alten und Neuen Testaments
GrAA	Grundlagen der Anglistik und Amerikanistik
HTR	Harvard Theological Review
ICC	International Critical Commentary
Int	Interpretation
JAJSup	Journal of Ancient Judaism Supplements
JAOS	Journal of the American Oriental Society
JASSS	Journal of Artificial Societies and Social Simulation

JBL	Journal of Biblical Literature
JBTh	Journal of Biblical Theology
JESP	Journal of Experimental Social Psychology
JHP	Journal of the History of Philosophy
JJS	Journal of Jewish Studies
JLRS	Journal of Law, Religion, and the State
JP	Journal of Pragmatics
JPSP	Journal of Personality and Social Psychology
JSHJ	Journal for the Study of Historical Jesus
JSJSup	Journal for the Study of Judaism in the Persian, Hellenistic, and Roman Periods Supplements
JSNT	Journal for the Study of the New Testament
JSNTSup	Journal for the Study of the New Testament Supplement Series
JSPSSup	Journal for the Study of Pseudepigrapha, Supplement Series
JTS	Journal of Theological Studies
LNTS	Library of New Testament Studies
LSTS	Library of Second Temple Studies
M&C	Memory and Cognition
MMJ	Metropolitan Museum Journal
MThZ	Münchener Theologische Zeitschrift
Neot	Neotestamentica
NICNT	New International Commentary on the New Testament
NovT	Novum Testamentum
NTM	New Testament Monographs
NTOA	Novum Testamentum et Orbis Antiquus
NTS	New Testament Studies
NTT	New Testament Theology
OECS	Oxford Early Christian Studies
OPSNKF	Occasional Publications of the Samuel Noah Kramer Fund
PA	Philosophia Antiqua
PCS	Phenomenology and the Cognitive Sciences
PFES	Publications of the Finnish Exegetical Society
PHSC	Perspectives on Hebrew Scriptures and its Contexts
PP	Philosophia Patrum
PRSMS	Perspectives in Religious Studies Monograph Series
PSPB	Personality and Social Psychology Bulletin
PSPR	Personality and Social Psychology Review
QS	Qualitative Sociology
QSP	Quellen und Studien zur Philosophie
REAug	Revue des études augustiniennes
RevQ	Revue de Qumran
RHPR	Revue d'histoire et de philosophie religieuses
SBB	Stuttgarter biblische Beiträge

SBFCM	Studium Biblicum Franciscanum Collectio Maior
SBLECL	Society of Biblical Literature: Early Christianity and Its Literature
SBLRBS	Society of Biblical Literature Resources for Biblical Study
SBLSymS	Society of Biblical Literature Symposium Series
SBS	Stuttgarter Bibelstudien
SCAN	Social, Cognitive, and Affective Neuroscience
ScrB	Scripture Bulletin
SEÅ	Svensk exegetisk årsbok
SJLA	Studies in Judaism in Late Antiquity
SNTSMS	Society for New Testament Studies Monograph Series
SPPC	Social and Personality Psychology Compass
SSSP	Springer Series in Social Psychology
SST	Supplements to the Study of Time
STDJ	Studies on the Texts of the Desert of Judah
TANZ	Texte und Arbeiten zum neutestamentlichen Zeitalter
TSAJ	Texte und Studien zum antiken Judentum
VCSup	Vigilae Christianae Supplements
VTSup	Supplements to Vetus Testamentum
WBC	Word Biblical Commentary
WUNT	Wissenschaftliche Untersuchungen zum Neuen Testament
WW	Word and World
ZAW	Zeitschrift für die alttestamentliche Wissenschaft
ZNW	Zeitschrift für die neutestamentliche Wissenschaft und die Kunde der älteren Kirche
ZTK	Zeitschrift für Theologie und Kirche